701

WITHDRAWN

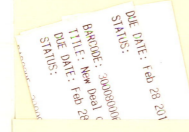

DUE DATE: Feb 28 201
STATUS:
BARCODE: 300080006
TITLE: New Deal
DUE DATE: Feb 28
STATUS:

And a Time for Hope

And a Time for Hope

Americans in the Great Depression

JAMES R. McGOVERN

PRAEGER

Westport, Connecticut
London

Library of Congress Cataloging-in-Publication Data

McGovern, James R.
    And a time for hope : Americans in the Great Depression / James
R. McGovern.
        p.   cm.
    Includes bibliographical references (p.   ) and index.
    ISBN 0–275–96786–7 (alk. paper)
    1. United States—History—1933–1945. 2. United States—Social
life and customs—1918–1945. 3. United States—Social
conditions—1933–1945. 4. National characteristics, American.
I. Title.
E806.M45   2000
973.917—dc21   99–41959

British Library Cataloguing in Publication Data is available.

Library of Congress Catalog Card Number: 99–41959
ISBN: 0–275–96786–7

First published in 2000

Praeger Publishers, 88 Post Road West, Westport, CT 06881
An imprint of Greenwood Publishing Group, Inc.
www.praeger.com

Printed in the United States of America

The paper used in this book complies with the
Permanent Paper Standard issued by the National
Information Standards Organization (Z39.48–1984).

10 9 8 7 6 5 4 3 2

Contents

Acknowledgments

For all the many helpful librarians at the Library of Congress, the Roosevelt Library, Hyde Park, the kind persons who found and dispatched materials via inter-library loan from libraries all over the country, and for the library staff at the University of West Florida, especially Debbie Marshall and Bob Perdue, and those in the public library at Rangeley, Maine, my everlasting gratitude.

Thanks are also in order for the support I received from the University of West Florida, in particular from Provost Douglas Friedrich, who provided encouragement and assistance for typing the manuscript, Vice President Parks Dimsdale and the University of West Florida Foundation for financial assistance, and for Evelyn Grosse who was both a careful typist and an attentive reader.

Special acknowledgment goes to Professor William E. Leuchtenburg for reading the manuscript and making useful suggestions.

My deepest appreciation goes to my wife, Joan, who believed in the project and in me.

Introduction

The years of the Great Depression (1929–1939) were one of the most critical decades in American history. Americans then sustained the most severe and most persistent economic setback of any major western nation, and yet they did so with relative poise and ease. Other western countries, though less affected by the Depression, felt its pressures much more. Germany and Spain experienced major changes in government and reverted to authoritarian systems, in part, to control its disordering and destabilizing effects on their societies. Other European countries experienced the Depression's tremors as class and ideological factionalism, at times, challenging to their democratic priorities.

How are we to explain the good fortunes of the American republic which achieved reform without revolution or significant class turmoil, while tenaciously preserving its cohesive morale as a nation? These successes may well have served America even beyond the 1930s; they may have provided underpinning for the impressive achievements of America's citizen-military in World War II and a basis for confidence and fortitude to engage victoriously in the later Cold War.

Those who have attempted to explain the special achievements of America in the 1930s have usually relied on a political analysis: the unusual leadership and communication skills of President Roosevelt and implementation through the New Deal of an unprecedented reform and regulatory program; these innovations diminished threats to democracy and capitalism and eliminated dangers of social upheavals, hence America's stability.

Franklin Roosevelt's innovative and protective leadership unquestionably made America a better place to live during a protracted Depression. His words as well as his deeds lifted public confidence, and for millions he made the difference between fear and, at least, assured survival. New Deal programs for relief and work relief, mandates permitting effective unions, protection for homeowners and bank depositors, and security for the elderly, among other measures provided major fiscal as well as symbolic protection for millions otherwise vulnerable to the vagaries of a very uncertain 1930s marketplace.

Although Roosevelt's caring leadership and New Deal programs were very helpful, they do not explain adequately the remarkable stability of American society or the confidence manifested by Americans in the 1930s. Regardless of the Depression and independence of Roosevelt and the New Deal, the American people retained positive and hopeful attitudes about themselves and their country, and these attitudes helped to lighten the heavy pressures of the times and were essential to produce a relatively tranquil decade in America. Furthermore, the New Deal was hardly a panacea. Severely depressed economic conditions, after all, persisted in the first two years of the Roosevelt presidency and unemployment levels hovered at 15–20% after 1933 and throughout the 1930s, except in 1937. New Deal relief and work relief programs were typically underfunded. They failed to benefit sizable percentages of the unemployed and usually offered paltry sums—well below minimum standards for living—for those who did receive benefits. President Roosevelt himself was over cautious about these programs, calling off fiscal support for his own better relief programs, expressing fear that relief would foster dependency and even waffling on labor legislation supporting collective bargaining. Most indicative of his concern over welfare extravagance, he never worked for changes in the tax system to sustain a comprehensive and adequately supportive welfare system. At the tail end of the Depression, millions of Americans still experienced the same difficult conditions that characterized the early years of Roosevelt's first term.

This study about the responses of Americans to the severe problems raised by the Great Depression is not intended to be another political history, slightly adding to or subtracting from a large number of excellent studies concerned primarily with the impact of politics on American society in the 1930s. Now, more than a half century after the Depression, we are encouraged to pursue a new route for understanding of that incredibly interesting period. As a social history, this study breaks ground by focusing on the American people in widely different dimensions of their experience in order to attempt a new and challenging interpretation of those times. Also, *And a Time for Hope* is not presented as a historical narrative, rather as thirteen connected essays. This focus and methodology yield the refreshing view that the strengths of the American people, too, played a decisive role, along with the New Deal, in explaining the country's smooth landing in the 1930s.

A great variety of subjects for this study, including government investigations, polls, statistics, photography, post office murals, radio and movies (after 1934), breathtaking technological achievements—herculean dams, giant bridges, the world's tallest building and the world's most efficient airplane—plus popular world's fairs, one described as "Building the World of Tomorrow," all signify that the American people were far from flattened by their economic problems. The same can be said for groups which made up the society. Rural Americans, nearly half of America's overall population, were sustained by the particular strengths of their way of life—family mutual help, church, community mindedness, patriotism, and a psychology of limited expectations. These influences worked in rural areas along with New Deal programs to promote hopeful attitudes. Urban Americans were also especially advantaged to ward off the Depression's most dire perils by virtue of their commitments to unions and to numerous ethnic support systems centering in family, clan, and related people of each ethnic group. This was a time when one-third of Americans were either born abroad or had one parent who had been born there. Again, most Americans living in the great metropolitan cities knew they enjoyed exceptional opportunities for living. They compensated for receiving fewer dollars during the Depression by attending first-class ballgames, shows, and museums, all at reduced Depression prices.

An exciting discovery of this approach to the 1930s through social history is the realization that even those groups written off as beaten and hollowed-out by sad historical experience—the Okies and African Americans in the Cotton South—were actually still confident and hopeful, believing in their opportunities, and were, in degree, succeeding within the system in the 1930s. Indeed the most sanguine revelation of a surprisingly sanguine decade concerns the remarkable gains of African Americans in places like Chicago and New York and their continuing confidence in a better future despite confronting major impediments.

This book shows that a single decade of adversity could not entirely erase Americans' sense of their country's overall historical successes, the equity of its democratic institutions, the power of its technology, or its promising future; "Tomorrow" a great summary line of a 1930s novel declared, "after all is another day." These strengths of the American people were keys to the country's remarkable achievements during the Great Depression.

This study is, of course, based on the research of numerous scholars in the social sciences. My own experience in the sources has included materials in the Franklin D. Roosevelt Library at Hyde Park, New York, the Library of Congress for the Life Histories and the Folklore Project of the Federal Writers' Project, and the photographs of the Resettlement and Farm Security Administrations. The latter, a very large collection exceeding 60,000 photos, though seldom used explicitly for social history, proved invaluable for the purpose. The Southern History Collection at Chapel Hill, North Carolina also provided materials from the Federal Writers' Project, for southern states. Another helpful source came from extensive reading in twelve newspapers from small towns and small cities across the country in the 1930s, along with radio scripts, voice recordings, and old movies from that decade. My research also includes source materials from the NAACP in the Library of Congress used in a previous study, *Anatomy of a Lynching: The Killing of Claude Neal* (Baton Rouge: Louisiana State University Press, 1983).

1

A Troubled Nation,
1929–1934

March 4, 1933, the inaugural date of Franklin D. Roosevelt, was a cloudy, blustery day with only occasional speckles of sunlight. That morning before the ceremonies the president-elect attended church services at St. John's Episcopal, Roosevelt's place of worship on his earlier tour of duty in Washington when Assistant Secretary of the Navy. Reverend Endicott Peabody, the headmaster of Groton where Roosevelt had gone to prep school, officiated at the services. All this was appropriate. As Frances Perkins observed, "If ever a man wanted to pray, that was the day." And for Franklin Roosevelt the presence of Peabody as minister was probably more than an acknowledgment of his indebtedness to his boyhood hero. Peabody had then emphasized for Roosevelt that religious devotion and prayer were essential for responsible leadership in government and life. It is likely that the incoming president sought Peabody's invocation and counsel as reassurance because, though usually a very confident person, he may have been beset by fears as he neared the moment when he would have ultimate responsibility for the nation he loved—a nation adrift in the throes of a relentless Depression.

For all previous presidents, even those who presided over earlier depressions, images of America still included prosperous farms or bustling river traffic or growing shops, factories, and use of engines—symbols of progress. However, in the early months of 1933 these images included deserted factories, unprecedented numbers of embittered men on city streets, and farmers frightened that they would soon lose their farms, defiantly withholding milk and grain because sale prices had fallen below costs of production. The New York Stock Exchange and the Chicago Commodity Exchange were closed and the country's banking system, including its state banks, was collapsing or closed. "What if there are to be no more normal times?" inquired a reporter for *The New Republic* just two months before Roosevelt assumed office.[1]

The president delivered his inaugural address to a shivering crowd, hatless and without an overcoat, with great clarity and verve. As reported later, he seemed to speak in a personal way to each of his listeners. This, as much as his confident delivery and abundant energy, made a deep impression. His most effective line, "The only thing to fear is fear itself," was a tour de force designed to restore confidence to a troubled nation, but his entire address stated similar themes. He reminded those attending, "We are stricken by no plague of locusts. . . . Plenty is at our doorstep . . . but America has failed to utilize it." "Primarily," he continued, "this is because rulers of the exchange of mankind's goods have failed through their own stubbornness and their own incompetence," and, raising his jaw as if in defiance, he declared, "The moneychangers have fled from their high seats in the temple of our civilization. We may now restore that temple to its ancient truths."[2]

Americans could meet the crisis, but they would now have to respond "as a trained and disciplined army." And he promised he would also take action. He would ask Congress to formulate a plan to meet the emergency and reserved the right, if Congress did not act, to ask that body "for the one remaining instrument to meet the crisis—broad executive power to wage a war against the emergency, as great as the power that would be given me if we were in fact invaded by a foreign foe."[3] Roosevelt reassured that there was nothing inherently wrong with America: "We do not distrust the future essential democracy. The people of the United States have not failed." But now they, too, like him, would have to pledge their best; live up to their heritage and remain steadfast in crisis.

Thoughtful people in attendance, perhaps sobered by the gravity of the times and the immediate moment, may have underestimated the crowd's enthusiasm. Only later when one heard a replay of the address on radio did that groundswell become obvious.[4] Edwin C. Hill, the popular radio commentator who described the scene on radio, recalled the vital quality of the president's address and its immediate impact on the audience. He asserted, "At the first tones of his calm and confident voice . . . you could see the new spirit, the new determination creeping into the faces of those people. . . . Never was there a more kindling response to the call of a leader."[5]

The fact that Franklin Roosevelt embodied hope and courage and was able to instill these qualities in those who watched and listened to him explained his immediate public appeal. That confidence was also a measure of the dispirit they felt with his predecessor. Herbert Hoover was actually the first modern president, neither inhuman nor insensitive to the government's responsibilities at a time of national economic crisis, but heavily burdened by preemptive economic theory that made it difficult to experiment with government assistance beyond providing credits to banks, industries, and farm mortgage associations. He also created the impression of being uncaring by his heavy-handed treatment of the Bonus Army in 1932. In the same year, a large and steadily growing number of needy people had overwhelmed the resources of private philanthropic agencies and local and county government, the latter undermined by tax delinquencies brought on by the Depression. The states, with economic problems of their own, offered little assistance, although Roosevelt did initiate a program of unemployment relief as governor of the state of New York.[6] President Hoover stood firm against federal distribution of relief until the summer of 1932, when social problems were reaching epidemic proportions. Under pressure from Democrats, Hoover then agreed to sign a bill to enlarge the lending powers of the Reconstruction Finance Corporation (RFC) by $300 million to assist states in local relief. Given the magnitude of the problem, the sum was negligible, but only $30 million of the $300 million had been expended for relief by the end of 1932.[7]

Hoover was also handicapped as president in such critical times because he was temperamentally incapable of inspiring others. All was rational to him, a matter of the certainties of facts and figures, the business cycle, and historical experience. Yet, no matter that for him these problems would work out in the long run, his theories did little to reassure hungry or frightened people who required food every day of the week. When his formulas became increasingly suspect in the last three years of his term, Hoover indulged in equally unrewarding explanations that malign forces in Europe (and Roosevelt after the 1932 campaign) were interfering with the return to prosperity he promised. Although 14 million voters chose Hoover in 1932, surely a sign of abiding confidence for some, Roosevelt's landslide victory declared that new approaches and policies were imperative. It was this sense that inspired Will Rogers to champion Roosevelt: "If he burned down the capitol, we would cheer and say, 'Well, we at least got a fire started, anyhow.'"[8] An upper-middle-class woman having witnessed the failure of major banks in Chicago and her husband's loss of employment suggests that this view was widespread:

If only nothing worse happens before President Roosevelt is actually in command! This was the thought expressed by everyone with whom we talked. I will not say that one heard it in the crowds, because in the days immediately following the panic, we saw no crowds. I do not know how it may have been in other places, but in Chicago, as we saw it, the city seemed to have died.

On inaugural day, she wrote:

We awoke with a feeling of relief, but we were filled with apprehension for the safety of our new President. Surely no President since Lincoln had faced such a crisis. If this man, in whom the people had placed such a mighty trust, should be assassinated by some fanatic or some hireling of his enemies, what would become of us all?[9]

The country Roosevelt inherited had been deeply chastened by three years of Depression; the effects on the American people were as clear as they were disturbing. Metaphorically, the Depression resembled a maelstrom, a downward spiral with the near-simultaneous failures of production, employment, and consumption. The great fear among consumers, induced by the failure of the stock market and over 5,000 commercial banks between 1929 and 1932, prompted cutbacks in their spending. This, in turn, led to contractions in capital goods industries (especially steel and their suppliers), in construction, mining, and transportation—hence, to broad layoffs of workers. The downward curve then accelerated, with unemployment leading to further cutbacks in consumption and consequently also production. Meanwhile, losses for banks that had originally loaned money to manufacturers who could not sell their goods prompted bank managers to withhold further loans, thereby producing business failures and intensifying declines in employment. When banks failed because they could not collect on their earlier loans, the entire economy went into a tailspin and confidence disappeared. American farmers also became captives of the process. Their problems began in the early 1920s when European farmers recovered their markets after the Great War and closed them to American farm surpluses. As a consequence, the nation's farmers experienced serious losses of income before the national Depression. Once that struck, miseries compounded, with farm incomes dropping to near or below a farmer's cost of production. This situation threatened the security of the farmer's land and house because farm mortgages taken out in more prosperous times remained fixed and relatively high compared to immediate income.

In 1932, Edmund Wilson observed a quirky scribble chalked up on a wall in a work area of Chicago. It read, "VOTE RED. THE PEOPLE ARE GOOFY," truly a statement of despair.[10] The most serious failure in terms of its human consequences was, of course, unemployment. According to official figures, this peaked in 1933 at 12.8 million or 25% of the workforce, figures that barely changed in 1934 after one year of the Roosevelt administration when 11.3 million were jobless, still nearly 22% of available workers.[11] Expert advisors to the government calculated even higher numbers for 1933, with monthly unemployment averaging 13.1 million. March 1933 was the nadir for the entire 1930s, with 15 million, nearly 30%, out of work.[12] Because unemployed workers usually had families exclusively dependent on them, between 40 and 50 million Americans were without regular job income during the most severe period of the Depression. Another large number of workers with dependents, larger even than the number unemployed, were forced to work with reduced income as part-time workers. Since part-time workers were considered "employed," the actual loss in income by workers was far more devastating than data on unemployment suggest. The records of U.S. Steel are often cited for illustrative purposes. The company employed nearly 225,000 full-time workers in its last good year, 1929, but by 1930 only 211,000 full-time workers survived, down to 54,000 in 1931, 19,000 in 1932, and zero full-time workers in early 1933. Those part-time workers who remained were only one-half the number that worked full-time in 1929.[13] Thus, when a social worker asked a friend, a manufacturer in Utica, New York, in 1932 how they were dealing with their unemployment problem, he was reassured that Utica had solved that problem. "We have taken the amount of work we have in the city and divided it among the workers. By this he meant everybody was working two days a week."[14]

Almost every American family lost savings, income, or a degree of confidence; many became financially marginal, even poor for the first time, and large numbers already poor became even more so. Any analysis of the social experience of Americans in the Depression decade needs, of course, to underscore the large number of Americans who were poor before 1929. According to economists at the Brookings Institution, nearly 60% of American families in 1929, the last golden year of a supposedly prosperous decade, were unable to buy basic necessities; hence they were not well off, if not marginally poor.[15] At the lower end of the scale were tenants and sharecroppers, the aged, sick, and disabled, children in female-headed families, members of disadvantaged groups, and unskilled laborers. Even though prices of goods fell nearly 20% by 1932, their incomes often declined more precipitously or ceased. President Roosevelt may have underestimated when he spoke of America's responsibility to that "one-third of the nation ill-housed, ill-clad, and ill-nourished."[16] In the early 1930s, probably closer to one-half of all Americans fit this description when one considers the number already poor in 1929 and adds the "new poor," formerly middle class and now suddenly impoverished. Occupationally, this latter group included farmers, white-collar employees, professionals (dentists were particularly hard hit), businessmen, and skilled laborers, especially auto and steelworkers.

To be poor, even to be ill housed and ill clad, does not presuppose that individuals were needy, (i.e., preoccupied with basic survival needs for housing and food), a more desperate condition that was virtually unquantifiable. Probably one-half of Americans could supply at least some of their own food given the available garden plots in the small towns in which most lived. Of these, at least 23% were considered farm families; most of them could provide or nearly supply their own food needs. Many others, particularly in the South, had been poor, even needy, for so long that these conditions were customary and hence less bothersome. Still others could and did deal with desperate needs by severe economies or doubling up with relatives. Russell Baker's very poor single-parent family with two children managed to move in with relatives, but when they arrived in Newark, New Jersey, from Virginia, his uncle expressed disappointment that Russell's mother had allowed her third child to be adopted by other relatives. He chided her with "Three can starve as cheap as two." Russell's indomitable mother, Lucy, his sister, and himself lived happily in his uncle's household without income from their

mother for over three years.[17] Yet, with allowance for such considerations, in September 1932, in the midst of these troubled times, *Fortune* magazine in a celebrated article, "No One Has Starved," estimated that 25 million Americans were actually needy.[18]

Poor urban families often adapted at first by using up savings and cashing in insurance policies. If they remained unemployed longer, they pawned goods, or attempted to borrow, or sought credit from grocers or landlords, then moved to older tenement areas and finally, if they were threatened with eviction, attempted to live with relatives or friends. One survey of 1,000 families on relief in Philadelphia in 1932 revealed that 20% had moved twice within six months and 40% twice or more within a year.[19] Evictions were often unpleasant scenes, but at least they demonstrated the solidarity of neighbors who registered angry protests on behalf of the evicted family. *The New York Times* described on February 2, 1932, the eviction of three families in the Bronx in early 1932:

Inspector Joseph Leonary deployed a force of fifty detectives and mounted and foot patrolmen through the street as Marshal Louis Novick led ten furniture movers into the building. Their appearance was the signal for a great clamor. Women shrieked from the windows, the different sections of the crowd hissed and booed and shouted invectives. Fighting began simultaneously in the house and in the street. The marshal's men were rushed on the stairs and only got to work after the policemen had driven the tenants back into their apartments.[20]

Dorothy Kahn, a relief worker in Philadelphia, described her private relief agency overwhelmed with requests for assistance by dispossessed families in late 1932. She reported daily encounters with persons "stretched . . . beyond the limits of human endurance." She observed:

Only the other day a case came to my attention where a family of ten had just moved in with a family of 5 in a 3-room apartment. . . . it is almost an everyday occurrence in our midst. Neighbors do take people in. They sleep on chairs. They sleep on the floor. These are conditions in Philadelphia that beggar description.[21]

Foreclosures on homes also often forced searches for cheaper quarters that sometimes led to shantytowns. Records on twenty-two cities as of January 11, 1934, showed at least one-fifth of owners defaulted on their loans in each city since 1929 with a rate of 40% on average in half the cities, 60% in Birmingham, Alabama, and 62% in Cleveland. Furthermore, farmhouses, also heavily mortgaged, were perhaps one-third of the houses foreclosed in the United States in 1932. In early 1933, over 45% of mortgaged farms were reported delinquent in mortgage payments. Here, too, the stage was set for mass suffering and mass protest.[22]

Vulnerable Americans were forced to be tough and adaptive in locating food just as they were in obtaining housing. Food became for many of them a desperate concern, the daily goal of their precarious existence. The traditional poor were better prepared to live this way than the "new poor" who, before the Depression, had been shielded from primitive dangers. But as an executive social worker in New York noted in 1931: "The situation which has now arisen is that the spectre of starvation faces millions of people who had never before known what it was to be out of a job for a considerable period and certainly had never known what it was to be absolutely up against it."[23]

Numerous frightened people lived in big cities. Lorena Hickok, who investigated relief conditions in New York in 1933 (after Roosevelt became president), reported 1,250,000 persons wholly dependent on public funds and many others—perhaps a million more—were on "thin ice, barely existing."[24] One survey earlier in Philadelphia by the Wharton School estimated 71,000 families (perhaps 300,000 people) in Philadelphia experienced inadequate food, clothing, or home fuel.[25] A relief worker described an unrelenting quest for food by that city's poor in early 1933:

The families rustled for themselves as much as they could. A common source of supply for one group was the docks where fruit and vegetables for market are sorted. Children and adults hung around the stalls and snatched at anything that was cast out. . . . There is little doubt, however, that gifts of food from groceries, reported by a considerable number of families, was usually obtained by a form of begging. Children, it seems, had the habit of going to a store and by pleading hunger inducing the grocer to give them a little food. . . . The myriad ways in which a family, its entire attention concentrated on food—just food—succeeded in obtaining it constitutes abundant evidence of the ingenuity and perseverance of these people.[26]

A boy from Nashville, Tennessee, remembered eating dog food in 1933. He told the following story to a government interviewer:

The first hard times I remember came in 1933, when I was in the eighth grade. . . . Then we were really up against it. For a whole week one time we didn't have anything to eat but potatoes. Another time my brother went around to grocery stores and got them to give him meat for his dog—only he didn't have any dog. We ate that dog meat with the potatoes. I went to school hungry and came home to a house where there wasn't any fire. . . . Every now and then my brother or Dad would find some sort of odd job to do, or the other brother in Chicago would send us a little something. Then we'd go wild. I mean we'd go wild over food. We'd eat until we were sick.[27]

Concerns over food needs sometimes ruled out observances of even the most basic kinds of family amenities. When the full fury of the Depression descended on a Polish-American family living on the south side of Milwaukee in 1930–1931, two married sisters, unable to make a go of it, returned to live with their parents, one with a husband and a baby. All together twelve people were living in a small house with two bedrooms. The father lost his job, so only Rose, a daughter, was employed. The fact that she had a job ruled out meager county relief, and unemployment relief from the federal government under RFC provisions in 1932 was considered unlikely. In that year the mother, fifty-six, died of a stroke, undoubtedly aggravated by the stresses of the family. Rose sacrificed to have food:

We were penniless. I was the only one working. But we belonged to the Polish Roman Catholic Union Fraternal Organization and we had insurance [on Mother] for $500. The undertaker told us the casket was $600. I told him he would have to make it cheaper for us. "Take one for $400, $300." I said, "No, we can't even take one for $300." And he stood just like a post. He said to me, in front of my father, "Wasn't she worth more than that?" I said, "This is not a time of how much she was worth. We had no money and we must have enough money [from the insurance] for our taxes because this is the third year we paid no property tax." He asked how much was needed for the tax and I wouldn't tell him. "For the whole funeral I can't spend more than $300 for everything." My father stood paralyzed; he wanted to spend whatever the undertaker felt necessary for a decent funeral. I told him that it wasn't mother's money. "It's you who paid that money. It's all going into the ground and we are starving."[28]

Things were no better in Arkansas, where a Red Cross official reported in 1931 that families existed on below-subsistence food supplies. In one home a widow living with her seven children had only a pint of flour and a few scraps of chicken bones. The mother was making clothing for the younger children out of ragged underwear. In another instance a widow with eight children had no food in the house.[29]

In Kentucky, mountain men "proud as Lucifer" were waiting in "corn-bread" lines as early as 1930.[30] In East Texas, where rabbits were hunted, wives cut the meat from the bones and mixed it with lard to produce "rabbit sausage."[31]

George Huddleston, a congressman from the 9th district of central Alabama, testified January 5, 1932, before a Senate committee that many of his constituents were close to perishing for want of food and other basic necessities:

Many of these people, especially the negro tenants, are now in the middle of a winter, practically without food and without clothes, and without anything else, and how are they going to live? Many of these local counties have no charitable organizations. . . . Many white people are in the same kind of a situation. They beg around among their neighbors. The neighbors are poor and they have no means of helping them. They stay here and there. Any thought that there has been no starvation, that no man has starved, and no man will starve, is the rankest nonsense. . . . I do not mean to say that they are sitting down and not getting a bite of food until they actually die, but they are living such a scrambling, precarious existence, with suffering from lack of clothing, fuel, and nourishment, until they are subject to be swept away at any time, and many are now being swept away.[32]

In Louisiana, a black plantation manager wrote in 1933 to his white employer that he was worried because his black tenants were asking for more oats for their livestock than usual. He proceeded to investigate and found they "had to eat all the time out of [the feed] themselves."[33]

Even as family cooperation buffered the stark imminence of homelessness and starvation, however precariously, there were millions of Americans who, by choice or circumstance, were forced to face the awful dilemmas of the Depression without family support. The men in breadlines and Hoovervilles were mostly single, or widowers, or husbands who could not then face the tasks of providing or parenting. When the working middle class first saw these groups they seemed shockingly incongruous with their understanding of America. All the more so if that confrontation first occurred at night on flashy Times Square near 45th Street. A young newspaperman described them in that setting in 1931:

Distribution began somewhere around 7:00 or 7:30 P.M., I believe, but the line would begin to take form as early as six o'clock. By 7:00, there were thousands of men, two abreast, in the line, which had doubled back and forth in long serpentine folds, each perhaps a block long. While the line waited for handouts to begin, it was of course stationary, and there was the spectacle: thousands of able-bodied Americans, young and old, waiting quietly for their handout. To see the line for the first time, as I happened to in a January blizzard, was to wonder what on earth it could be. The realization was slow, hardly credible, that this pattern of dark shapes was made up of men, ordinary men, who were hungry enough to stand there in the storm, in the glow of the marvelously irrelevant electric advertising displays, the finest of their kind in all the world.[34]

An actual participant in a breadline of 2,000 persons on a wet and cold day on Ritch Street in San Francisco in 1931, Hugo Jorgenson, recalled:

At last, after hours of nervous shuffling on the sidewalk, it was my turn to enter the kitchen. From the counter I grabbed a bowl of mush without milk or sugar and a tin cup of coffee likewise without any sweetening. . . . After a short time the concrete floor became mired with an inch-deep film of spilled mush and coffee. The air was indescribably foul—clammy with vapors from the huge steam cookers, plus the thousand and one stenches of unwashed bodies, dirty clothing, and wet brogans.

I always ended breakfast cursing under my breath, determined never to return, but when it was time for the afternoon handout this twentieth-century inferno found me waiting outside, tail wagging, heart aflutter, anxious to put up with anything, be it ever so filthy and meager.[35]

The Hoovervilles, like gigantic ash heaps, appeared on the outskirts of cities, often close to garbage dumps or relatively inaccessible land or swamps. Here people lived close to animal level in impoverished tarpaper shacks often not much bigger than large doghouses and spent their days in breadlines or foraging for scraps of food and junk. At night they lighted up the sky with their bonfires and cooked their cornmeal mulligan stew. Although their lives provided few comforts, they felt the strength of their numbers and found their "community" more satisfying than the lives of those who slept in doorways or subways.[36]

Many single women who lost their jobs and could not or did not wish to return to their family of origin lived in types of communes as well, but with more gentility than men in Hoovervilles. Women were conspicuously absent from breadlines; it seemed to involve their pride and sense of role, a humiliation not to have family or private resources. "Single women," a veteran social worker confided to a government observer, "I'll tell you how they live. Huddled together in small apartments, three or four of them living on the earnings of one, who may have a job. Half a dozen of them, sometimes, in one room, sharing with each other, just managing to keep alive. They've left the YWCAs and the settlement houses. They can't afford to live in those places anymore."[37] A journalist for *American Mercury* made similar observations based on her personal knowledge of five different women, all unemployed for at least two years, highly intelligent and college educated, and all also on the verge of being swept away. The life of one of them, Louise, undoubtedly illustrated the plight of many other women. She lived with three other women in a room in which there was no heat, light, or running water. It was so undesirable that they paid no rent. Their lives were described as follows:

The girls have to sleep in shifts because there are only two cots. Other furniture is at a minimum, but they do not mind that as much as they do the absence of cooking facilities. Because they can't cook they have to live on bananas: they read somewhere that bananas are more filling than anything else at the same price. Pooling their resources in the way of clothing, the girls have one costume fit to appear on the street. They try to keep it clean and in repair, and in rotation each of them wears it for a day and goes out job hunting. While she is gone the others sit around in their rags and talk about food. Sometimes they are so hungry that they visit the owner of the house around meal time, hoping she will offer them something to eat.[38]

Another group outside the family was the astonishing number of Americans, perhaps two million, on the road during the early years of the Depression, mostly young men and mostly in search of jobs. And so they climbed into the boxcars, hopped off where they pleased and looked for work, hitchhiked, and shared temporary campsites set up by fellow transients.[39] Sometimes they fared well and found temporary jobs. Sometimes they were overcome by hunger with unfortunate consequences for others. Two young men who had not eaten for some time finally decided to descend on a small restaurant in a Colorado town and ordered a sumptuous breakfast. They then divulged that they couldn't pay. The lady who owned the restaurant, also feeling the effects of the Depression, was almost in tears. She asked them why they had to order "her best breakfast."[40] Nevertheless, transients' travel was their ticket to opportunity. Among the transients who were underage another motive was to lighten the economic burden of their families. One remarked quite typically to sociologist Thomas Minehan who rode the rails with them, "Dad tried to keep home for the four of us kids. He was as good as any man can be, considering. But what could he do . . . I just sort of scrammed."[41] Although it is difficult to estimate the number of women and girls on the road, they were numerous, and perhaps one in ten among them was underage. They, too, were without jobs or prospects at home. For protection they traveled with another woman, with groups, or a lover, though it is clear that many bargained sex with a variety of men in return for food and favors.[42]

The least expendable persons whom the Depression forced to live outside the family were those children increasingly committed by financially distressed parents to "homes" or to orphanages for better care. Dr. Jacob Billikopf, a veteran social worker, estimated before a Senate committee that their number had gone from 284,000 on July 1, 1930, to 400,000 twenty-seven months later in October 1932. He explained: "It is the belief of those familiar with the facts that this increase in child dependence has been caused chiefly by the breaking up of family groups caught in the Depression and unable any longer to care for their children because of inadequate relief or other conditions precipitated by unemployment."[43]

Although the Depression experiences of African Americans are told in part in a general description of American life in the 1930s, their numbers and significant differences justify additional comment. It has often been said that black Americans have all the same problems of other Americans plus the fact that they are black. Because most of the 12 million blacks in America in the 1930s were poor even before the Depression, they, like poor whites, did not experience the same degree of loss or fear as middle-class whites. They also resembled poor whites in that they generally lacked job skills and so they would suffer great losses in numbers employed. But because they were black, they were distinguished from whites of similar class and education. They became convenient targets in a society that was bold about its racial preferences. Employers could easily justify discrimination against them and eliminate their jobs and so, in the end, they were doubly jeopardized.

Nearly four of five American blacks lived in the South during the 1930s and half of them (49%) lived in communities of less than 2,500 people— the rural South. Most obtained their living from cotton either as tenants or croppers, or in the cotton-servicing towns near the plantations. As such, they were prime exhibits of the South's chronic poverty even before the Depression that then worsened as cotton prices tumbled 70% from 1929 to 1933 when cotton was being sold for a ruinous six cents a pound. By October 1933, the cotton counties of the South sustained a large relief load.[44]

There are an unusual number of excellent sociological studies of southern communities in the early and mid-1930s.[45] These focus on dynamics of racial interaction and underscore the difficulties confronting blacks living in the rural South, especially their poverty. Their houses as sharecroppers were flimsy and small and lacking conveniences except for a wasteful woodstove and maybe a wash basin. Many lacked outside as well as inside toilets. Those houses, with cracks and leaks, were cold in the winter and, lacking screens, filled with gnats and mosquitoes in the summer. Houses for blacks in the cotton towns were only slightly better, again bare and without indoor bathrooms and on dirt streets.

If many African Americans in the South were pauperized because they were tied to the cotton crop depression, their race also cost them numerous chances for improvement. Southern whites exploited them economically and benefited from social sanctions that forced blacks into subservient roles. Blacks most often did the hard work in the economy and fawning manners and speech (yes sir, no sir, boss, captain, etc.) were expected from them by whites at all times. Whites enforced the system rigorously through solidarity and by terrorizing blacks with the specter of lynching.[46] Because black sharecroppers seldom voted and could not effectively contest decisions made by whites in authority, they were likely to be cheated at year's end when the final cash settlement was reached with white owners.[47] The poor quality of education for blacks closed the circle on their opportunities: schools for blacks in the rural South generally lacked equipment and new books, the school year was short (some blacks remembered going to school only when it was raining), and black teachers were notoriously underpaid.

The Depression accentuated the chronic poverty of southern agriculture for black and white sharecroppers, but they also fell victim to the remedial policies of the New Deal that attempted to reduce farm surpluses by paying owners for acreage reduction. Owners then benefited as the price of cotton rose modestly, but they regularly denied tenants and sharecroppers commensurate shares of government subsidies and even encouraged them to leave or possibly retained them as poorly paid farm laborers. As their income worsened, tenants and croppers, black and white, went on relief rolls in legions after stable income in the form of relief became available under the New Deal's Federal Emergency Relief Administration (FERA). Here too, however, blacks were discriminated against with lower relief rates than whites, and greater difficulties in securing relief.[48] In 1934, the New Deal also began an FERA rehabilitation program including the Rehabilitation Administration for poor farmers and sharecroppers designed to resettle them on land rented from owners, but by 1935 only a small number of families had received guidance or loans under its varied programs. Although federal guidelines prohibited discrimination against blacks in these programs, and they were recipients in large numbers in some areas, they were often treated as less than equal.[49]

African Americans in Harlem and other northern cities, like blacks in the South, lost jobs and income because they were unskilled and, also like them, lost heavily because of their race. Harlem was not a prosperous place for most blacks, even in the 1920s. Median income then was $1,300 for black Harlem families, while for white New Yorkers it was $1,750. This differential occurred despite many more black women working and contributing to family income than white women. Black males were heavily employed in poor-paying, unskilled labor and service jobs while nearly three-quarters of black women were in domestic work or other unrewarding personal-service areas.[50] Working-class blacks were also disadvantaged economically because their apartment rentals cost on average $160 a year more than for comparable white apartments in Manhattan; Harlem's tenants could not rent anywhere else and so were exploited by landlords.[51]

The Depression shattered Harlem's fragile economy just as it did for blacks in other urban ghettoes. A New York Welfare Council study in the early Depression reported that African Americans lost jobs three to four times as fast as whites and were only half as likely to be reemployed. Laborers and domestics were the first to lose their jobs, and this meant a collapse of the barely decent family income provided by both parents working in the 1920s. Blacks were also forced to compete with whites in the service/labor sector that blacks had monopolized in better times. Businesses run by blacks lost income because of a buying drop-off, but this area of decline should not be overstated because most businesses in Harlem were owned by whites. African-American professionals lost clients and income and were often forced to live on a level below that of a skilled worker in the white community. In 1932, a philanthropic fund estimated that Harlem's median household income had dropped 43% between 1929 and 1932.[52] In Cleveland, nearly 54% of black families surveyed in 1933 had incomes of less than $500, twice the percentage of whites. And consistently, in city after city, one and one-half times more black males were unemployed than whites. Without relief under federal auspices from FERA, it is difficult to see how African Americans in American cities could have avoided inhuman suffering on a mass scale. Indeed, Federal Writers' Project investigators expressed the opinion that "the majority of Harlem's population was 'on the verge of starvation' " when FERA relief programs first began in mid-1933 in New York City.[53]

There is a popular misconception that, once Herbert Hoover departed the presidency and Franklin Roosevelt succeeded, the nation began its steady recovery. This notion mistakes a great increase in public confidence for solid economic accomplishments. Roosevelt was able, however, to ease fears among the desperate by his caring manner and beginning the expenditure of federal relief funds in 1933 once it became clear that state and local governments did not have sufficient resources to relieve mass suffering. By 1934, federal relief programs such as FERA, and work-relief programs, the Civilian Conservation Corps (CCC) and the Civilian Works Administration (CWA), were providing assistance for approximately 8 million households— 28 million people or 22% of the population. Although the amount dispensed, especially that of FERA, for direct relief was small, usually $25 per household per month, "One rather important matter has been settled [in the public mind]" as an observer of the relief programs noted for Harry Hopkins in 1934. "People are going to be cared for."[54]

Encouraging signs in the economy were still slight, but things were not getting worse. Retail sales in new automobiles, department stores, furniture stores, and household appliances improved in 1933 and 1934. The 1933 improvements, however, were only marginal over anemic sales in 1932, and in 1934 they were still only half those of 1929 (with the exception of department store sales, which represented about two-thirds of 1929 sales).[55]

The depths of the Depression were still evident in the relative absence of new jobs in steel and construction, a continuing slump in mining, the growing numbers living on relief (some without hope of finding a job, now looking to relief work as their job), the deteriorating morale of the young who could not break into the job market, and the old—those men forty or forty-five or older who were now no longer considered for rehiring. A heavy atmosphere of poverty still hung over one community or another. And, to top it off, an ecological disaster—intensified drought in North Dakota, South Dakota, Kansas, Nebraska, Oklahoma, and Colorado—would prolong the ravages of the Depression.

The best assessment of the Depression in late 1933 and 1934 may be found in the dispatches of an able group of sixteen investigators appointed by Harry Hopkins (FERA director) to gauge the effectiveness of government relief programs. Their reports, mostly from July 1933 through December 1934—over 100 in total—constitute an incomparable source for understanding the unremitting severity of the Depression in those years.[56]

None of Hopkins's special appointees held out the promise of business expansion or new employment in late 1933 or 1934. Edward Webster, whose territory was the Southwest, decided about those on relief: "The statement that these people could get jobs if they wanted them is unconvincing."[57] From Scranton, Pennsylvania, a center for the nation's anthracite coal mining, where working miners in 1934 had declined from 18,000 to 10,000, Julian Claff reported, "Absolutely no signs of any broadening of operating base to pick up employment."[58] From Chicago another investigator wrote Hopkins in November 1934 that "the prospect for the future . . . is definitely unpromising."[59] "Is it going to be a harder winter?" Ernestine Ball asked "scores in all walks of life" in Troy, New York, a manufac-

turing center, "and always the answer was fatefully affirmative."[60] Henry
Francis informed Hopkins, also in November 1934, that in Fayette County,
Pennsylvania, where 70% of miners were out of work, there was a critical
need for clothing for schoolchildren.[61] Hazel Reavis wrote from the Pittsburgh area about U.S. Steel affiliates in late 1934. Only two of its sixteen
plants were functioning with more than 50% of their workers.[62] The Hopkins team also noticed by late 1934 that relief recipients were beginning to
look on their work-relief benefits as their real jobs, some even calling their
work "wage relief." For those on relief for some time there was no longer
any stigma attached and, in fact, some had come to believe that the government should supply them with jobs. One man on work relief who was
purchasing a secondhand truck justified his purchase with the observation,
"I figure this job will last at least two years anyhow."[63] The same durability
of work relief is strongly suggested in Edward Webster's disclosure about
St. Louis: "An increasing number of young persons, without what was once
deemed 'reasonable prospects,' are marrying and going almost directly from
the altar to the relief station, the apparent reason being to gain the status
of families on relief."[64]

Conditions in 1934 resembled the Hoover Depression in other ways. The
young and the old still found jobs eluding them. Wrote Martha Bruere from
western New York state:

One of the special problems—and perhaps the most serious—in relation to the relief
situation, is that of the young men and women who have finished their education
during the past five years and have never had jobs of any sort. . . . According to
temperament and surroundings they are becoming careless, listless, inert; or unruly,
violent and di[e]structive.[65]

Martha Gellhorn, writing from Rhode Island, highlighted the same problem, which was national in scope. She declared, "The greatest single tragedy
in this whole mess" was the plight of unemployed young people.[66]

And the old were squeezed out of the shrunken job market at the same
time the very young were denied access. The shocking aspect of their dismissal was the age at which they were judged old. Wayne Parrish alerted
Hopkins in a letter from New York City November 11, 1934, "Men of 40
and 50 years of age are realizing very definitely that they are out for good
and this results in a sense of futility."[67] Bruce McLure in the Pittsburgh area
also recognized that problem. He wrote Hopkins that "unemployed men
of 45 and over, including steel mill office workers, have given up all hope
of ever returning to their usual job."[68]

Many Americans were frightfully needy in the first year and a half of
Roosevelt's first term. Lorena Hickok, Hopkins's premier reporter, wrote
October 31, 1931, to her close friend Mrs. Roosevelt about North Dakota:
"But, oh, the terrible, crushing drabness of life here." She related to Mrs.

Roosevelt that when a social worker accompanying her asked one miserable looking woman whether her entire family slept on the house's solitary bed which was filthy, with rags for blankets, the woman replied, "We have to, to keep warm."[69]

Another observer relayed information to Hopkins about Duquesne, Pennsylvania, a community of 23,000 with a large Carnegie steel plant employing only part-time, with 70% of the mill employees on supplementary relief: "And still Duquesne looks like a town that is hungry in spite of stomachs shrunken by years of dieting, enforced. There is considerable begging. Clothing is ragged and inadequate, more conspicuously so than in the other mill towns visited. Haggard men and scrawny children have the listlessness of old people."[70] In Chicago, in the vicinity of the stockyards, Thomas Steep engaged a number of "intelligent-looking" relief recipients in conversation. He reported to Hopkins:

One lifted his foot to show me that the soles of his shoes were worn through. He unwrapped from a newspaper his wife's shoes which were certainly in tatters. He said both pairs of shoes had been repaired so much they were now beyond repair, and he asked whether I couldn't induce them to give him new shoes. "I had a part time job working in a ditch and the mud went right through these shoes," he said. Another man, an ex-truck driver about 30, said he had a wife and 2 children and had been out of a job 2 years. I asked him what his hope for the future was. "I don't know," he said. "I just don't know." The bewilderment of all of these men as to the future is apparent.[71]

Henry W. Francis alerted Hopkins to his discovery in headlines in a local newspaper in western Pennsylvania for November 10, 1934. It read:

Parents, Two Kiddies Live in Coke Oven
Have Struggle for Food and Clothing
Starvation is Feared; Need Help

Mr. and Mrs. Joseph Pasko
Forced into Dire
Circumstances

One Youth Shoeless[72]

If poverty was still visible and widespread through the last days of 1934, a solvent and sympathetic onlooker retained a reassuring semblance of rational control over circumstances; he or she could weigh the gravity of the misfortune, relative to the predicaments of others, and might assist personally or communicate with an official in government, seeking redress. The psychological or spiritual malaise experienced by countless suffering families or individuals, however, usually escaped notice except for an occasional off-guard revelation. When that disclosure came, it often revealed a state of anxiety and even terror for which there were no immediate remedies. Poor struggling people were most affected, but fear of failure, poverty, and even revolution affected the middle class as well. One woman in her late thirties in Bakersfield, California, opened one of those emotional seams for Lorena Hickok:

I can talk to you about this now, because we aren't on relief any more. . . . It's this thing of having babies. You've got no protection at all. You don't have any money, you see, to buy anything at the drugstore. . . . And there you are, surrounded by young ones you can't support. And always afraid. . . . I suppose you can say the easiest way would be not to do it. But it wouldn't be. You don't know what it's like when your husband is out of work. He's gloomy all the time and unhappy. You haven't any money for movies, or anything to take his mind off his troubles. You must try all the time to keep him from going crazy. And many times—well that is the only way.[73]

Some wives were painfully candid about problems that embarrassed them and which they felt they could not conceal. One declared:

My husband still loves me, I think, but you know it isn't just you that men like, but it's the way you look, as well. Now you take me. I've had these two teeth knocked out and I can't have them changed. I can't have them fixed, because we haven't the $40 that the dentist says it would cost to have them fixed. And then my clothes. Now just look at them! . . . I'm ashamed of my looks, but what can I do about it? . . . Now, you tell me how any man that has any red blood in him can think that I'm as attractive as I used to be. The worst of it is that I could be if I could just have that money to get those teeth and buy some new clothes.

Still another woman queried anxiously:

How can I keep looking nice so that my husband will like me when all that we have is macaroni and potatoes to eat? These foods don't cost much and they fill you up. . . . Then, to make matters worse, my husband says he guesses I don't worry much about his being out of work, because if I did I'd be getting thin. How can I get thin on the kind of food that we eat? It makes me furious when he says I don't take our troubles seriously because if I did I'd be getting thin.[74]

Based on her experiences in the early 1930s, Louise Armstrong provided palpable grounds for middle-class anxiety:

Our circles of friends, acquaintances and business associates in Chicago were just an average group of well-educated American citizens of moderate means, and none in the group had ever been the hysterical type; but this was our plight. There were two phrases we heard constantly: "In case of trouble" and "If anything happened." If you tried to pin anyone down as to just what they meant, the answer was usually

evasive. No one wanted to put the awful truth into cold, brutal words, but we all
knew that those phrases meant that we feared an uprising of the great masses.[75]

Fortune in its celebrated article, "No One Has Starved," addressed another type of middle-class fear in the Depression—embarrassment over failure. The article provided a helpful description of steps that an unemployed
person might take to deal with unemployment and hunger. The caption
read, "What Do You Do?" and described the hypothetical case: "You are a
carpenter. Your last cent is gone. They have cut off the gas. The [your] kid
is white and stupid looking." After providing suggestions in the form of
charitable agencies that would help, the editors of *Fortune* began another
brief paragraph, "You are a white collar man. You have a wife and two
children. What do you do?" The answer was, "You do as the carpenter
did."[76]

To these misfortunes, unruly nature beginning in the 1930s conspired
with depressed rural economies to produce severe hardships, especially for
the peoples of the Great Plains, North Dakota and South Dakota, the western areas of Nebraska, Kansas, and Oklahoma, and the eastern part of Colorado. Every year after 1930 was drier than the previous year, and 1934 was
one of the driest on record, so crops could not be produced easily and in
some areas there were "total failures." This was accompanied by a plague
of grasshoppers, in some instances laying in piles four inches deep. Dust
storms completed the devastation. It was estimated that 350 million tons of
topsoil from North and South Dakota swirled into the air, with some deposited as far east as the Atlantic Ocean. Farmers in these states were hungry,
deprived of basic necessities, and the townspeople who depended on their
trade were almost as badly devastated.[77]

Fortunately for them and for the large numbers still inflicted with the full
fury of a Depression now into its fifth winter, Franklin Roosevelt was regarded by most as a caring president who would eventually help them. Here
and there, Hopkins's observers noticed that he was no longer the idol of
the first days after the inaugural, but he still commanded allegiance, perhaps
even the devotion of most. Thus, Martha Gellhorn, recounting the troubles
of blacks and whites she had encountered in North and South Carolina in
the fall of 1934, noted one bright spot—"and though everything else fails,
he [President Roosevelt] is there, and will not let them down."[78] A more
graphic rendering of that faith was supplied by Hopkins's aide, Henry W.
Francis, the day after Democrats scored a sweeping victory in the congressional elections of 1934.

Meet Charles Zosky, coal miner, House 96, Alicia Patch, Monessen Coal & Coke
Company, somewhere near Brownsville, Pa. [Western Pennsylvania]. Sit down carefully, the chair is broken. Perhaps you had better take the box. It's clean. Everything
in the house is fairly so, except the bedding; that wouldn't survive any attempt to

wash it; it's in pieces now. The cleanest object in the house, however, is the lithograph of Franklin D. Roosevelt. Today it is wreathed with festoons of hand-cut colored paper. It's the day after election; a big day in Zosky's life, or at least he thinks so. "Yes, sir," he assures me, "we've got'em licked now."[79]

2

The President

On President Roosevelt's fifty-second birthday in 1934, the *New York Journal American* published a sketch congratulating him, entitled "The Champion." He is therein portrayed as an apparition, above and distantly behind the occupants of the room, with a thoughtful expression and quiet, reassuring smile. Actually, he is present only in the thoughts of the humble family that give thanks to him, seated around a modest table on which sits a birthday cake with a single candle. Family members look profoundly grateful, perhaps even prayerful.[1]

This drawing only nine months after he became president suggests that Roosevelt was beginning to assume legendary proportions. One can find nothing remotely resembling this depiction describing President Hoover who presided, as did Roosevelt, in a period of enveloping depression and who, like Roosevelt, also spoke confidently about America's economic recovery. Hoover, as far as the public was concerned, however, appeared flat, abstract, and friendless; Roosevelt was believable, comforting, and admirable.

This changeover in attitudes toward the new president was remarkable both for its rapidity and because it became for the public the basis for lasting convictions favorable to Roosevelt; the effects of the Depression would not get worse under Roosevelt, and there was a good chance, given his willingness to experiment and his humane vision, that conditions would improve, however gradually.

The press corps in Washington marveled at the swift transformation. A reporter for *The New York Times* observed a change even during the inaugural parade. He noted among those lining the streets, "Their spirits are lifted by his smile of confidence as they watch the parade," and a week later, a *Times* correspondent noted about the American people, "with what eagerness they have welcomed the coming of a new man to the presidency."[2] For Marquis Childs, recalling those days, "Mr. Roosevelt had provided a magic that has restored our society."[3] Walter Lippman went further: "In one week [after the inauguration] the nation which had lost confidence in everything and everybody, had regained confidence in government and itself."[4] A feature writer for *Current History* in April 1933 agreed, describing "the wave of hope which swept over much of the nation as Mr. Roosevelt assumed control in Washington."[5] And Will Rogers, noting that Roosevelt smiled often, declared "a smile in the White House again [after Hoover] seemed like a meal to us."[6]

That same renewal of faith and hope in the future of the country and the president's critical role in promoting it were strikingly evident in contemporary letters to the new president and in newspaper editorials. These were especially impressive because they appeared to transcend class and party lines. The president received nearly 500,000 letters in response to his inaugural address, and an average of 5,000 to 8,000 letters a week during his long term in office. Although a few clerks were sufficient to handle President Hoover's mail, twenty-three were regularly employed while Roosevelt was president and on occasion as many as seventy.[7]

Responses to FDR's first "Fireside Chat" on banking delivered March 12, just eight days after he became president, were typical of his early impact. A doctor from Chicago was so pleased with the address that he felt immediately obliged to express his gratitude: "Your radio talk unites our strength and courage and shows us the way to new hope."[8] From a wholesale distributor in Evansville, Indiana:

The American people, I am satisfied, have faith in you and in this address, honestly and conscientiously spoken . . . will be one never forgotten. You will appreciate this— coming from a Republican, whose father, before him, was a Republican. This, however, has nothing to do with it—you are our President and we are here for you.[9]

The owner of a million-dollar warehouse company in Milwaukee apologized to President Roosevelt for not having voted for him in the election of 1932 and then declared, "I sincerely hope that your acts will be successful in relieving our country of at least some of its present depressing influences so that I will feel even more ashamed of myself."[10] A letter summarizing the upbeat impact of Roosevelt's presence came at the end of March to Senator Robert Wagner of New York from a Brooklyn man: "We now feel that in truth Washington is the throbbing heart of U.S.A. Fear has gone. . . . Humbly, but with grateful hearts, we thank God for raising in our hour of need, a fearless leader and a courageous staff." He then asked "God's guidance and protection for Mr. Roosevelt, his Cabinet and Congress."[11]

Editorial comments on Roosevelt's inaugural address in the nation's press also praised the president for his courage and inspiration. From the tenaciously Republican *Chicago Tribune* came "President Roosevelt strikes the dominant note of courageous confidence." The *Philadelphia Inquirer*, also a Republican paper, stated that if "feelings" generated by the inaugural address effectively reached the people, "then the atmosphere of fearfulness will soon be changed to real hopefulness." The independent *St. Louis Globe-Democrat* commented, "The spirit of courage and confidence with which he addresses his prodigious tasks is itself impressive, and particularly so at a time when it is just that spirit which is most needed by the country." A Democratic paper, the *Cleveland Plain Dealer*, concluded unequivocally, "The people ask for leadership in a crisis and look to President Roosevelt. The president is ready to lead." A legion of small-town newspapers shared similar conclusions.[12]

Perhaps it is not surprising that the new president, who invariably embellished his public life with unusual drama and excitement, would have quickly caught the attention of the press and the public. What was more impressive is that many Americans began to see him in heroic, even reverential terms as if he were a charismatic leader. Charisma (literally, a gift from God in Greek), while an endowment of the raising and socializing of very exceptional individuals, is only effective when great numbers of people acknowledge its presence; strictly speaking, although charisma's potential is residual in a unique person, its award is always conferred by a grateful public. For many Americans, this strict sense of charisma defined Roosevelt's image in the public mind, and not mere popularity.[13]

The crowds during the president's first term were huge and profoundly respectful. Mrs. Roosevelt remembers a trip she took with her children to New England during the campaign of 1936:

I remember vividly the trip into Rhode Island, Massachusetts, and Connecticut, when we drove through miles of small towns where the streets were lined with people. Very little local preparation had been made, for the authorities did not believe there would be much of a crowd, but even on the country roads people had gathered to stand and watch the president go by. As we progressed the Secret Service men got more and more worried and finally, at their insistence, the states assigned troopers and National Guardsmen. Boston Common was a seething mass of people who had waited for a long time for Franklin's arrival.[14]

Mrs. Roosevelt later expressed concern in Stamford, Connecticut, that she might be "trampled to death as the crowd tried to get a glimpse of the president, who was already on the train."[15] When the president landed at Portland, Oregon, from Hawaii in 1934, on a leisurely trip across country, people at crossroads stayed up all night to watch his train speed by even though they had no hope of seeing him.[16] At Franklin Field in Philadelphia in 1936, when Roosevelt used the famous phrase "rendezvous with destiny," the audience "nearly went crazy." But even more telling was the reverential spirit of those who remained in the stadium after the president left the arena; "Most of the crowd remained as if in a trance," or perhaps because what had transpired was akin to a sacred moment that many did not wish to relinquish.[17]

Letters to the president most clearly express these devotional feelings. One man wrote shamelessly after Roosevelt's speech accepting the Democratic nomination in the summer of 1932, "I began to adore you."[18] Another frankly confessed in 1933, "While listening to you . . . our little house seemed a church, our radio the pulpit and you the preacher."[19] Still another reported overhearing a conversation between two old ladies that purportedly included the remarks, "President Roosevelt can have anything I have to assist him in his grand work. I willingly would lay down my life for him. He was sent by God to lead us out of the wilderness and God will preserve and direct him."[20]

During the 1936 election campaign, when his leadership was challenged, Roosevelt received numerous testimonials declaring varieties of religiously inspired devotion and hero worship. These statements came in letters in response to his Franklin Field address.

God in heaven and the American people cannot but be with him.[21]

May God's blessing give you all the strength to be Our Beloved Father of our Country, friend and president on March 4, 1937 [Inaugural date for president].[22]

If you are re-elected, it will not be by the people, but God through the people . . . I am going to pray for the people by praying for you.[23]

You are a second God to the people of the United States of America, the one and only man that helped and saved the people of the United States.[24]

Your God-inspired message last night . . . [25]

It [your speech] was ethically sound as the Sermon on the Mount and politically inspiring as the Declaration of Independence . . . a great mass of helpless people are praying for strength for you in carrying on this fight and to this I add my humble prayers.[26]

The president continued to captivate Americans in his second term and indeed throughout his years in office. One woman without the slightest equivocation wrote in 1938, "I salute your Divinity, for God sets HIMSELF up on high as Franklin Delano Roosevelt and knows his name as Franklin Delano Roosevelt, President of the United States of America."[27] And another felt emboldened to ask, "Why do religious leaders tell us that Jesus Christ died and lives no more and why do they, our religious leaders, not realize that Jesus Christ lives today with us in the form of Franklin Delano Roosevelt?"[28] It was this same mystique that prompted members of a professional football team touring the White House to ask a seamstress employed there, Lillian Rogers Park, whether she ever saw the president. She replied she did and had shook his hand the day before. Whereupon one member of the team asked whether he could touch her hand. When she replied yes, everyone on the team lined up and followed suit.[29] Martha Gellhorn witnessed a similar attitude of awe and reverence in mill towns in North and South Carolina in 1934: "The feeling of these people for the President is one of the most remarkable phenomena I have ever met. He is at once God and their intimate friend; he knows them all by name, knows their little town and mill, their little lives and problems. And though everything else fails, he is there, and will not let them down." She noted that his picture over the mantel in their houses occupied a position analogous to the Italian peasant's Madonna.[30]

Since no American president before or since has ever won this type of devotional admiration, it is important to inquire why he was so accomplished. The answers tell us as much about the personality of the president as the troublesome times over which he presided. Roosevelt possessed in extraordinary degree personal strengths that elicited profound respect among Americans suffering from the Depression. His personal confidence, courage, and caring, all central to his personality, explained why so many ardently admired him and some even regarded him as a God-sent man.[31]

Roosevelt's personal confidence, affected by an almost unlimited sense of self-importance, provided compensatory strength in a period of dislocation like the 1930s. How many other presidents have cherished the ambition to be president as a young man and, moreover, thought this a realizable goal? When he once announced in the presence of a Boston family, whose daughter he apparently considered marrying, that he thought he would be president some day, an older cousin of the young woman retorted, "Who *else* thinks so?" and everyone chuckled at the young man's brashness.[32] Who else ever decided he was virtually indispensable as president and won the public office four separate times? Who but Roosevelt, as president, warned that he might seek and assume dictatorial powers in peacetime, or felt the magisterial authority to lead a generation of Americans to their "rendezvous with destiny," or was so supremely self-possessed as to describe a national election [1936] as one that hinged on a single issue: "It's myself, and people must be either for me or against me."[33] His wife's judgments quietly underscore his pretensions to grandeur. She wrote: "I have never known anyone less really influenced by the opinions of others" and again declared, "He lived his life exactly as he wanted it."[34] And, of course, his famous accouterments—pince-nez glasses, the cigarette holder, slouch hat, and flowing loose black cape—suggest great flair, if not grandiosity as well.

The courage and caring that Roosevelt displayed so conspicuously in the

1930s and that were major sources of his public appeal and charismatic effect were fundamental to his personality. Each quality developed early in his childhood and persisted in his life. They were so unmistakable to most Americans of the Depression era that they explain his unique public appeal.

Franklin was a mother's boy, though the son of a very special mother to be sure. Sara Delano, daughter of a family enriched by the China trade in the nineteenth century, and herself a resident of Macao as a child, was also, before her marriage, a friend of socially prominent persons in several European countries. Described later, after she was married, by one of her perceptive French-speaking employees as *très formidable*, Sara was an attractive, strong-minded woman seldom in doubt about values or appropriate conduct.[35] She married in 1880 when twenty-six, a pleasant, kindly, religious widower, James Roosevelt, twice her age. Sara had an extremely difficult delivery with Franklin (b. January 30, 1882) and was told by her physician that she should not have other children. This intensified the bonding between the young wife and her only child. She breast-fed him for almost a year, and probably coddled him excessively. He did not begin to walk until he was almost sixteen months. She was usually present when the youngster bathed, governesses presumably otherwise, so that he was eight and one-half years old before he bathed alone, when his mother, off on a visit, temporarily left the family home. We do not know whether the ritual resumed after she returned. Although Sara's influence on her son was dominant, it was not exclusive. James Roosevelt provided companionship for Franklin, sharing with him his fondness for riding, sailing, sleigh riding, and conservation and undoubtedly exerted some masculine influence despite their age difference. And both he and his wife helped to shape a religiously based sense of noblesse oblige in Franklin. Both taught him that he was fortunate to live well and that he must therefore assume responsibility for the welfare of those less fortunate. That he followed through on this is evident from his joining, when at college, the Harvard Social Service Society, and the genuine shock he felt when he discovered the lives of poor people living in the area of the Rivington Settlement House where Eleanor volunteered while they were engaged. Eleanor Roosevelt later underscored this sense of altruism as her husband's prime motive for engaging in politics. "Throughout the whole of Franklin's career," she declared, "there never was any deviation from his original objective—to help make life better for the average man, woman and child."[36]

Even so, Franklin remained, as one careful historian observed, "pampered and overmothered, protected to an unusual degree."[37] Sara's prime techniques of child raising were to shower Franklin with warmth and almost smothering nurture when he did as she wished, and to withdraw her affection with hurt and disappointment when he failed to live up to her standards. When, for example, as a youngster of four, he was upset over losing games of steeplechase to his mother and insisted on changing horses with her for the next game and lost that as well, and then showed his temper, Sara gathered up the game and announced she would not play with him again until he showed better sportsmanship. As was typical of the boy who had become quite dependent on his mother, he changed so that she never saw this quality in him again.[38]

Sara spent countless hours with her son as a "sweet autocrat." Following her own childhood example, she directed his activities including stamp collecting, his most important lifelong hobby. And his youthful sailing, including a fifty-one-foot yacht at age nine, she represented as a hereditary trait derived from her family.[39] She read to him while he sailed and tended to his stamps, and would proudly proclaim that Franklin was "a Delano, not a Roosevelt at all."[40]

There was hardly a respite from her incessant mothering, although one time he did cry out for more freedom and was given a brief reprieve. His father's complaints about Sara's "nagging the boy" apparently proved unavailing, but James may have continued to object to her methods with a reference to Sara as "The Mother" in a later letter to Franklin.[41] As an only child, pressures on him to conform were exceptionally high, and although he had carefully selected childhood friends, he was not allowed to stay overnight at their houses. Similarly, he was unable to attend school outside his home on a regular basis until he began Groton at age fourteen.[42] Even later, when Franklin was an adult, Sara maintained an unusual degree of intimacy with him. On her son's twenty-first birthday, she presented him with a portrait of herself. She might indulge him, a friend of the family once noted, "but would not let her son call his soul his own."[43] Indeed, after he became president, she wrote him, "I do not want *ever* to leave you."[44]

In view of Franklin Roosevelt's mother dependency it may at first seem paradoxical that his mother was largely responsible for the remarkable courage and confidence that later served to inspire Americans of the Great Depression. Sara Delano Roosevelt was, in fact, a very brave woman, and she expected the same from her son. She faced death with her husband and son, then three, when a liner carrying them back to the United States from Europe appeared to be sinking. "I never get frightened," she explained later, and declared she was not frightened then either. She wrapped a coat around Franklin and said to her husband, "Poor little boy. If he must go down, he's going down warm."[45] Nor is there any indication of fear in her later life when, in her mid-sixties, she accompanied a lady friend pilot in a two-seater flying from London to Paris. She wrote in 1921, still a time of aviation's infancy, "M and I are over the Channel, a little foggy and pretty steady up here. Very interesting." Later she commented, "If I do it again I shall take an open plane as one sees more and it is more like flying." The following year, when speaking of a fall leading to the rupture of a vein while touring in Europe, she declared, "Of course, I hopped up and swore it was nothing."[46]

Although the abundant time mother and son spent together assured that
Franklin would have some feminine characteristics, Sara had no intention of
raising an effeminate boy. She wished, of course, to raise Franklin a gentle-
man, courteous and thoughtful of the rights of others, but she was pleased
he was not sentimental and that he would try daring enterprises even at an
early age. She read to him while he sailed a large boat through the rocky
and schoaled waters off Campobello Island. Later, when he went out for
intramural sports at Groton, she was proud of his accomplishments, if somewhat anxious about his playing against bigger boys in football.[47]

One incident in Franklin's childhood particularly stands out in illustrating
her expectations of him to perform bravely and his ready compliance. In the
summer of 1896 when Franklin, fourteen, and his friend were batting peb-
bles, he was struck in the mouth by a large stick from an errant swing by
his companion. It broke off one tooth and chipped another, thus exposing
its nerve. Although the pain was very severe, he refused to disclose the
incident or the nature of the injury to his mother who discovered his problem when she began to note its effects on his pale, drawn face. Franklin was
then removed from Campobello by ferry to Eastport, Maine, and taken to
a dentist where, after considerable time elapsed, the second tooth with its
dangling nerve was removed under gas. He remained stoical during the
entire incident, his mother proudly recording that Franklin had managed
the incident appropriately "without fuss." Her son's tour de force could
only have come from careful coaching with explicit or implied signals earlier
in his life. Sara was well known for not responding to unpleasantries or, as
Eleanor once described her, "She never heard anything she didn't want to
hear."[48]

The classic illustration of this pattern of mutual expectations occurred
after Roosevelt came down with polio in August 1921 and his 6'3" frame
was completely paralyzed below the waist. He suffered intensely; his bowels
and urination had been affected, requiring enemas and catheterization, and
his children were on the verge of tears as he attempted to talk with them
while lying on his back in bed. Sara Roosevelt, having been informed that
he was quite ill, had hastily returned from Europe to Campobello on September 1. She found him smiling and cheerful with his typical combination
of bravery and thoughtfulness toward her, "Well, I'm glad you are back,
Mummy, and I got up this party for you." Neither Sara nor Franklin could,
despite the extreme sadness of the situation, allow themselves to divulge
their true feelings. It was at once a statement of how much denial had
become a fixture in Franklin Delano's life as well as his ability and willingness
to inspire good cheer in others by almost superhuman acts of bravery. It is
perhaps superfluous to add that he apparently never discussed his illness in
other than scientific terms—never reflexively as to his personal feelings, nor
could he fully admit the grave consequences of his illness, even to declaring
that he could not walk again. Later, when he became president, his wife

perceptively recognized the political implications of his courageous attitude toward polio for Americans in the Depression. "He never talked about his doubts. . . . I never knew him to face life, or any problem that came up, with fear, and I have often wondered if that courageous attitude was not communicated to the people of the country." She then speculated, "It may well be what helped them to pull themselves out of the depression in the first years of his administration as president."[49]

Roosevelt's personality, so sharply drawn in childhood with, as one observant reporter noted, "an infinite capacity for remaining himself," would spread strength and hope contagiously among Americans.[50] His strong personal qualities first surfaced for public notice when he flew in heavy winds in a Ford tri-motor plane to Chicago to accept his party's nomination. Despite head winds that delayed the plane's arrival for several hours, Roosevelt described the trip as "fine" and smiled broadly for photographers. He had decided on the airplane for travel in part "to dispel any belief that the Governor was incapable, because of his physical condition [the effects of polio], to fulfill duties of the president."[51] In Miami, on February 15, 1933, the president demonstrated remarkable courage and experienced a near-miraculous escape from assassination when a deranged gunman fired point-blank at him and narrowly missed because Lillian Gross, wife of a local physician, courageously reached out and threw off his aim. The shots wounded six people, including Mayor Anton Cermak of Chicago in another car of the entourage. Cermak would succumb three weeks later. Roosevelt's stellar behavior in the crisis was public knowledge at least to the extent that he refused to speed off from the dangerous scene, ordered his car stopped, and backed up to assist Cermak, whom he then placed in the back seat of his own car en route to the hospital. Later that evening, he also displayed unusual courage when he betrayed no feelings of letdown or fear while discussing the event with his close friends.[52]

In those early days as president, he also empowered others repeatedly with his brave words. His forthright guarantee in the inaugural that the country would revive and prosper, and his willingness to assume wartime powers of the presidency if all else failed were compelling. The conclusion of his first Fireside Chat calling for confidence in the reformed banking system had the same effect: "It is your problem no less than it is mine. Together we cannot fail."[53] Just three months later he introduced his third Fireside Chat with the remarks, "When Andrew Jackson, 'Old Hickory' died, someone asked, 'Will he go to Heaven?' and the answer was, 'He will if he wants to.' If I am asked whether the American people will pull themselves out of this depression, I answer, 'They will if they want to.' "[54] Large numbers of Americans probably already shared the views of E. Francis Brown, a writer for *Current History*, in April 1933, when he wrote, "No President, unless it was Abraham Lincoln, ever took office in a more far-reaching crisis than did Franklin D. Roosevelt; yet it is difficult to recall any who have entered upon such great responsibility with more calm, with more self-assurance and courage."[55]

Personal caring, a seemingly unfailing interest in others, was another feature of Roosevelt's personality and this, too, registered very positively with the public at a time of national distress. This offset his activist strengths and assured him even wider circles of confidence among the public, prompting millions to regard him as the right person in the right place at the right time. And his caring like his courage was quickly sensed by the public because it, too, was central to his personality since childhood.

The following excerpts, taken from random letters to the president in a brief time span, are representative of unusually strong public confidence evoked by perceptions of his humane words or attitudes.

That talk [March 13, 1933] was the most human and encouraging one I ever heard a president utter . . . it won my absolute confidence and trust and made me one of your hundred per cent backers.[56]

Your attitude is so vastly different from the previous administration that you inspire confidence.[57]

Your speech last night on the radio was homey and human and was just what the country needed.[58]

I was one of those misguided Republicans—having voted Republican for the last 35 years . . . but through the events of the last ten days have come to feel the most profound and tremendous admiration, not only for what you have done, but for your courage and ability and, in addition, for your consideration for the individual citizen.[59]

I am sure the president, if only he knew, would order that something be done, God bless him.[60]

I think you Should investigate this matter yourSelf. The way they are treating the Darkies here [Vicksburg, Miss.] is A shame.[61]

We have no one to give us a [*sic*] Christmas presents.[62]

What was most heartening about your radio address last Sunday was your great sense of humanity. It is indeed most comforting and cheering to those of us who have been caught in the maelstrom of the depression . . . to know that we have a leader who holds out to us the assurance of equal opportunity to all.[63]

At times the president or a member of his staff did provide Christmas presents for poor children and the public learned about his generosity. Fifteen-year-old Nola Hall of Aurora, Missouri, wrote him: "I have just found out there is no Santa Claus and since you are the next best person, I thought I would write to you and ask for a plaid dress." Just before Christmas she received her present, postmarked Washington, DC, with the message, "In answer to your prayer to President Roosevelt."[64] Occasionally, Mrs. Roosevelt would also be asked by a letter writer for the same type of omniscience and benevolence as her husband. A woman writing from Eureka, California, informed the First Lady that her family was in danger of losing their home. But she expostulated, "We can't lose that [the home] because our baby will need it, and I can't wait until the depression is over to have a baby. I will be 31 in October and I'll soon be too old."[65]

Young Franklin Roosevelt probably had little choice to be other than pleasant, amiable, and sensitive to the needs of others; these qualities were essential to the character of young gentlemen toward which his mother steered him so relentlessly. What is remarkable is how early he developed this type of personality and how consistently he demonstrated it as a child.

His grandfather Delano referred to him when quite young as "a very nice child."[66] When an aunt, impressed by his social skills, remarked, "Franklin, you really have a great deal of tact," the four-year-old boy was so eager to please his adult audience that he replied glowingly, "Yes, I'm just chock full of tacks."[67] At age nine his schoolmaster in Nauheim in the Rhineland, where his family visited during his father's convalescence, described Franklin's polite and mannerly ways contributing to his being "one of the most popular children in the school."[68] Later at fourteen when he left home to attend Groton, he refrained from getting any black marks against his name for misconduct, although he finally relented in his senior year because his austerity was making him unpopular with the other boys. Although Sara wrote him letters soon after he left home expressing anxiety for his well-being, he responded, despite discomforts, with uniformly cheerful letters, showing how "not making a fuss" for his mother consisted not merely of repressing pain when his teeth had been badly damaged and nerve exposed; it also meant being genial, comforting, and free from problems of any type.

Surely, Sara adored him. It would be difficult to resist such blandishments from her as these, in her letters written while he was at Groton:

We miss you every moment my darling.[69]

We were made happy yesterday morning by your dear letter of Thanksgiving. I carried it in my pocket all day and read it over every now and then when I was alone as I do all your letters.[70]

When he is a junior at Harvard her letters include such affectionate lines as, "I feel fully repaid for my trip to Boston by the happiness of those few hours with you,"[71] and, "I have followed you in my thoughts ever since you left me."[72]

There was a high cost for her unrestrained though always highly conditional affection. While very young he learned to please others, especially his mother, by suppressing his own feelings. In effect, he acted as though he were continuously amiable and solicitous about the well-being of others, especially his mother. Roosevelt's great interest in acting while at Groton, even to playing a girl's role in one production, and his invariable showmanship as president, perhaps most strikingly exhibited in his press conferences—unofficially dubbed "the show"—illustrate that this trait became part of his character. It was also fully disclosed in his supposedly humorous remark to Orson Welles while president, "You know Orson, you and I are the two greatest actors in America." And at least one Hollywood wit described him as "the Barrymore of the White House." As his biographer, Hugh Gallagher, underscores in *FDR's Splendid Deception*, Roosevelt's ability to convey the impression that he had not been "disabled" from polio represented consummate acting skills. He never lost this effect, particularly his ability to charm others and win their confidence. He may have developed it even more keenly after he succumbed to polio in 1921. In 1924, under wearying and exhaustive conditions reaching the rostrum by means of crutches, he was still able to captivate delegates at the Democratic convention in Madison Square Garden. One senator then called him "the most popular figure in the convention" and another delegate quoted Tom Pendergast, a political boss from Kansas City, as saying "he had the most magnetic personality of any individual I have ever met." Ira R. T. Smith, who managed the White House mail room, would later observe about him as president, "He could turn on his dazzling smile as if somebody pressed a button and sent a brilliant beam from a lighthouse out across the sea—shining on whatever ship happened to be there."[73]

And so the pattern persisted. Roosevelt believed as an adult what he had learned as a child; praise and love were forthcoming when merited by his good spirits, charm, and thoughtfulness. What made his life difficult was that he was thereby denied the self-confidence that could only have come from genuine self-acceptance. If his "ungentlemanly shortcomings" had been permitted, he might better have grown through his own trials, errors, and successes. He might then have won affection based on his real self, his seeming weaknesses as well as his spectacular strengths. Unfortunately, he felt a continuous need, repeating a successful formula of his childhood, to display only his strengths for purposes of singular recognition and outstanding praise. This posture probably left him lonely, with the need to attain his idealized self leaving his real self famished and alone. His wife intuitively recognized this when she remarked to her son Elliot after her husband's death, "He was a very lonesome man. I wish I had been able to be closer to him, to comfort him some times, but I suppose that could not be."[74] James Roosevelt, his eldest son, perceived this quality as well, writing a memoir of his father entitled *Affectionately, FDR: A Son's Story of a Lonely*

Man.[75] James reports his mother's observation about his father, "He no more knew how to get along with boys his own age than the man in the moon," hence, he was always that way, "a lonely man . . . wanting terribly to be one of the boys."[76] Marguerite (Missy) Le Hand, the president's closest work companion as his personal secretary, who spent countless hours keeping him company as well as working for him, also picked up on his loneliness. She told writer Fulton Oursler, an author who visited in the White House, that he "was really incapable of a personal friendship with anyone."[77] Although people loved his bonhomie and champagne ebullience, Roosevelt was admired more for his show than his real self.

Franklin Roosevelt, having run for vice president on the Democratic ticket in 1920, was on his way to being a presidential contender when polio struck in 1921. Although he obtained great personal satisfaction operating a rehabilitation center for polio victims at Warm Springs, Georgia, in the mid-1920s while recovering some strength in his limbs, he decided in 1928, at the insistence of Governor Al Smith of New York and with financial inducements for Warm Springs, to run for governor while Smith ran for president. Roosevelt was extremely ambivalent about acceding to Smith's request, but, of course, the critical point is that he agreed and became governor of New York in 1928 and again in 1930. That decision meant an end of his personal rehabilitation at a time when he still hoped, emotionally at least, that he might achieve full recovery in the use of his legs through hydrotherapy and exercises.[78] It also meant grueling campaign schedules and personal exhaustion. Perhaps he might be severely embarrassed as he was carried up stairs, or fall while moving on a platform, or as he stood in front of a crowd because the podium had not been correctly bolted in place. But all these considerations, which probably would have diverted individuals less resolute about such grand achievements, did not deter Roosevelt.

Franklin Roosevelt's decision to run for governor of New York was probably influenced by the fact that other opportunities for the recognition and love to which he aspired had come to be severely circumscribed by the circumstances of his life. His mother remained, of course, full of ardor for him, though of necessity incapable of filling his major emotional needs. His wife, Eleanor, a respected partner in a Victorian, probably even sexless, marriage by the 1920s, could not fulfill all those expectations either. Lucy Mercer, married, and in 1932 some fourteen years removed from those impassioned days when Franklin Roosevelt had first experienced love as a mature man, was also distant. She apparently had never changed her loving feelings, fondly remembering him as a wonderful man, but she, too, could play only a minor role, if any, in his life in the future. These losses plus the effects of polio placed him in the position where he was unlikely to turn again to a woman for fulfillment, though he admired his working companion, Missy Le Hand and found pleasant company with cousins Laura Delano and Marguerite Suckley.[79] The gravity of this loss may be measured by his observation noted by his son, James, "Nothing is more pleasing to the eye than a good-looking woman, nothing more refreshing to the spirit than the company of one, nothing more flattering to the ego than the affection of one."[80]

It seems likely that his affliction with polio as well as therapeutic work with fellow polio victims at Warm Springs taught him to become, as his wife contends, more patient and perhaps more sympathetic to the needs of the unfortunate, a quality noted by his Secretary of Labor, Frances Perkins. It is even more likely, however, that his personality so deeply etched in youth—his courage and caring, stupendous exertions for recognition and attention, and rigorous denial of weaknesses of character—all triumphantly carried on with these qualities as important enrichments. His attention-seeking as recompense for accomplishments and charm surely continued. Even as he put himself through painful exercises, exhibiting his shriveled legs, he insisted that visitors and family members watch. At these awkward times, he would tell humorous anecdotes and stories as if these represented his part of the bargain. His indomitable spirit persisted as well. He expended inordinate energy exercising to recover his mobility. Even when it became unrealistic, clinically speaking, that he would make further progress, he would never concede that he would not walk again. When Roosevelt finally decided to seek the governorship of New York and later the presidency, he persisted in the formulaic use of denial—in this instance a denial of polio's incapacitating effects on his ability to govern. Even though he could not stand or walk by himself and despite the public's fears of polio and phobias about seeing and associating with polio victims, he was convinced he could deny polio's liabilities as governor of New York and president of the United States. To do so he would have to display unflagging vitality, to impersonate someone who had basically recovered from the effects of the disease.[81]

Franklin Roosevelt decided in 1928 for an active career in politics with all its trials and his vulnerability because he could there best realize his unmet personal needs; he would pursue that career for the remainder of his life. His most direct personal statement confirming his deep personal investment in being president occurred when he disclosed to his son, James, why he would run for an unprecedented third term in 1940, " 'I think I'm needed,' he said to me one day, 'and maybe I need it,' he smiled."[82] But, of course, disclosures of this type are seldom stated directly because participants usually seek more dignifying reasons for their commitments. It was in his actions and affections that he best exhibited that politics was the vitalizing influence in his life.

Many observers noted how much Roosevelt felt at home in the presidential office. They usually attribute his nonchalance to his aristocratic background, but it is probably more accurate to report how well the presidency framed his personality. Eleanor observed how campaigning was for him an exhilarating experience and how he derived confidence from the acclaim of crowds. Raymond Moley, who often campaigned with Roosevelt, stressed how much he liked to charm the crowds and thereby win their approval. He described the pure pleasure these trips held for Roosevelt, especially from the people he contacted and the approval they conferred. "It was broad rivers, green forests, waving corn, and undulating wheat; it was crowds of friends, from the half dozen who, seated on a baggage truck, waved to the cheery face at the speeding window, to perspiring thousands at a racetrack or fairgrounds; it was hands extended in welcome, voices warm with greeting, faces reflecting his smile along the interminable wayside."[83] The activities of the White House itself also served as ongoing therapy for the president; probably no one enjoyed the office, its duties or potentiality for social pleasures, more than he. John Gunther noted in the mid-1930s that despite its heavy responsibilities and mountains of work, Roosevelt never seemed tired. He appeared to feed off the demanding routine of appointments and the different people he met and almost uniformly charmed. It was, in fact, difficult to keep him on schedule, usually fifteen-minute appointments, because he wished to spend more time with his visitors. Gunther recalled that the president spoke forty-six minutes to him, time completely devoted to exhibiting his special knowledge of Latin America, even though Gunther just completed an extensive tour there.[84] Lunch was usually with a guest or guests. The day was capped with "the children's hour," cocktails for guests and select White House employees with Roosevelt doubling as mixologist and raconteur, always a grand success despite a consistent overreliance on vermouth for his martinis. The White House staff, considered family, also made life interesting as did members of the press corps whom he invited to the White House for dinner and for picnics at Hyde Park or Warm Springs or the White House. In the middle of it all, smiling, laughing heartily, was the president, the undisputed center of attention, returning admiration and adulation with unrestrained joy.[85]

It is small wonder that President Roosevelt loved his position or why he clung to it tenaciously. It was too busy and too exciting to permit boredom or to be diverted into self-doubt, unacceptable since childhood, but now more possible since polio. As president he could operate a familiar system of achievements and rewards, and the rewards would be enormous—the admiration of most of his fellow citizens. Although politics inevitably created divisions of opinion, he would strive to be president to all the people with favors for all groups. This would require extraordinary skills, almost magical charm, but it was his firm intention, and if accomplished, his rewards would be that much greater. By becoming president at a time of mass suffering and disorder, he could draw on his heritage of noblesse oblige and sensitivity to the needs of others to guide him. He had a lifelong commitment to work for a more just and decent society for everyone, and he also instinctively knew—indeed from his earliest days—that if he was considered good by others, he as well as they would benefit.

A champion in profile—confident, mirthful, and happy to be president of the United States. AP/Wide World Photos.

Franklin Roosevelt was the first president to utilize media-made psychological politics; he was the first chief executive to exploit the outreach provided by modern media, especially press, radio, and movies, to foster close personal ties with the public.[86] The 1930s were the right time for him to be president in the sense that the pervasive impact of national media provided him with an unprecedented opportunity to communicate his convictions and the magnitude of the crisis allowed him as president to preempt the attention of those media. But it is also true that he not only had an exceptional opportunity to use the media for effective political communication, he had an urgency to do so. He would work incredibly hard to portray himself positively through the media, and to personalize that contact so as to be regarded by the public as a warm friend, even a family member. In fact, as his adult daughter, Anna, noted, he was more successful reassuring others in distant communications than in relationships in his own family.[87]

Both the president and media representatives had much to gain from a harmonious relationship. Roosevelt needed a forum to educate Americans in order to modify their individualism, thus allowing for social reform and greater government regulation of business. He wished public approval of his humanistic values and the government's responsibility for the welfare of those less fortunate, and acknowledgment as well of the quality of his personal leadership. The media could render public service by providing their best news reporters and offer free radio time, but, of course, he was the outstanding newsmaker in the United States in the 1930s.

From Roosevelt's first press conference, March 8, just four days after his inauguration, it was clear he intended a "new deal" for the press, supplying special favors to the reporters. He met the hundred or so reporters, shook hands with each one, and called several by their first names. After establishing boundaries on what reporters could use from the conference, citing "off-the-record" information as confidential and hence not printable, Roosevelt told them what they wanted to hear. He would meet with the press twice each week and respond spontaneously to questions reporters asked during the conference. No more written questions were to be submitted to the president before the news conference as in the Hoover administration, unacceptable to the reporters because it was impersonal and gave Hoover an opportunity to prepare and hence distort his answers. The president then proceeded to be candid about the banking crisis, providing good background information. The conference ended with the reporters so pleased that they applauded spontaneously.[88]

Although most Washington reporters were sympathetic to the president's programs, and nearly all greatly appreciated the access he provided for the news, the president's charm was also a factor that cemented their relationship. With the sound of "all in," they went to his office twice a week for what they knew would be both an informative and entertaining time. As they settled in the Oval Office for one of the 377 press meetings in his first term, he traded small talk, kept up a repartee on their activities, and provided them with useful information interspersed with a few good laughs. Reporters noted how poised and confident he seemed and admitted that his charm was beguiling. Raymond Clapper, a senior Washington correspondent, declared a reporter's admiration for Roosevelt was "like admiration for Babe Ruth, Man of War, a skillful surgeon, for the man who knows how to do his stuff."[89] The press conference became "the greatest regular show in Washington."[90] One reporter confessed that being called by his first name by the president left a glow that stayed with him even as he later wrote his article. Indeed, Arthur Krock of *The New York Times* sensed that Roosevelt's favors and his "show" had the effect of manipulating the news and so he refused to attend. He told the president, "You charm me so much that when I go back to write comments on the proceedings, I can't keep it in balance."[91]

Apart from the press conference, Roosevelt courted the press in other ways. With the end of prohibition, the president diverted kegs of beer sent him by distributors to the press club. Favorite reporters were invited to the White House for Christmas dinner.[92] Each year the president and his wife were at home for the newspapermen and women and their best friends if they were not married.[93] Newsmen accompanied the president to Hyde Park and Warm Springs, but the merriment was not allowed to interfere with the regularly scheduled news conference that was then conducted on the recreational site.[94] He also actively participated in the skits of the Gridiron Club, made up of Washington correspondents.

The president's program of friendly persuasion had many beneficial effects.[95] He probably did influence some reporters to follow the slants he provided in the news conference and therefore to adopt his point of view in their stories, and when rumors of the Lucy Mercer episode began to buzz

around Washington in 1933 they never surfaced in the press. Personal respect for the president might also have been another factor that deterred
photographing him in ways that showed him handicapped. Such respect
surely helped dissuade reporters from mentioning his fall as he moved to
the podium to give his acceptance speech for the Democratic nomination
at Franklin Field, Philadelphia, in 1936.[96] The honeymoon with the press
was not fully satisfying, however, to either party. Each had different goals
that could easily conflict: the press to report the news as fact and to interpret
the facts, and the president to put a slant on the information that furthered
his political and personal ambitions. Furthermore, despite his characteristic
friendliness and cultivation of an atmosphere of family in his press relations,
Roosevelt saw himself as the authority figure in the family, believing that he
knew best what reporters should write. Even during the honeymoon years
1933 and most of 1934 he employed various techniques of control over
information in the news conferences. "Off the record" was a common defense, as were diverting humor and evasion of questions.

The reporters covering the White House were basically favorable to the
New Deal and most continued to be fond of Roosevelt.[97] But when conservative criticism of FDR mounted with attacks on the wastefulness and
inefficiency of the New Deal, its deficit spending, and seeming similarities
to totalitarian countries, the president showed increased sensitivity to reporting that he judged biased in favor of conservative interests, the newspaper publishers, against himself and the New Deal. His first salvo was fired
during the 1934 congressional election campaign when the New York *Sun*
published a story captioned, "Here are the Focal Points of Depression-Bred
Ferment Throughout the Nation" and then announced "Spirit of Unrest
Grips the Nation." Roosevelt was convinced that these remarks represented
an effort by persons hostile to the New Deal "to inject fear into the population," and that they bordered on "conspiracy."[98]

In the same year, the president launched a scathing attack on the press at
their Gridiron banquet, startling the newsmen and guests until they realized
he was repeating word for word an earlier piece by H. L. Mencken, so that
his strident criticism was amusingly masked in the clever words of an acknowledged iconoclast. As the New Deal lost public favor in Roosevelt's
second term with the president's proposal to reform the Supreme Court
(1937) and to substitute persons loyal to him for incumbent Democrats in
the primary elections of 1938, his suspicions and accusations of the press
grew. He became more convinced that publishers coerced reporters to be
critical of his policies and his relations became testy, even with key journalist
Eric Lindley of the New York *Herald Tribune*, a friend who had often been
invited to the White House for Christmas dinner. He openly raised the issue
of newspapers being one-sided in his press conferences and even threatened
to withhold news from individuals like Lindley.[99] When the venerable Wil-

liam Allen White, editor and publisher of the Emporia *Gazette*, suggested to FDR that Herbert Hoover had complained to him in a similar way about the press, he responded that the press should eliminate the "petty stuff," and newspapers get "their shoulders in behind national recovery"; in effect, of course, to support his policies.[100]

President Roosevelt demonstrated extreme manipulative intent in his relations with the press. While he presented newsmen special access to White House information twice a week, replete with his debonair style, and regularly invited them to his dinners, picnics and parties, he expected in return that they would be factual—that is, noncritical of him. When gratuities and charm failed, he became unreasonably angry. Having done everything in his own mind to produce a supportive response by reporters, he was finally forced to attribute their mild abstentions and open questioning to malign powers beyond his control—the publishers. Roosevelt's ingratiating dealings with the press sharply recalls his predictable reliance on similar methods to achieve recognition in childhood, though they were ineffective in this context and hence his spleen. But his intemperate reaction also illustrates the importance the president attached to being successful in the White House and just how much he invested personally in the successes of that office.

FDR felt more comfortable with radio than the press because it provided a direct contact with the electorate, one that he could better control. In his twelve years in office, the president delivered over 300 radio addresses, of which twenty-six were considered Fireside Chats, theoretically broadcasts of a nonpolitical nature dealing with the state of the nation. The streets of America were often empty when he gave his Fireside Chats. In his first on the banking crisis, March 12, 1933, Roosevelt reached an estimated 20 million homes and 60 million people, and he consistently scored high numbers for each broadcast. His successes in radio were attributable once again to his mastery of the art of communication, his disarming sensitivity to what pleased and reassured the public, effective dramatic emphasis, and his ability to personalize friendship despite physical distance from his audience. Here, too, he put himself wholeheartedly into his undertaking, even overworking, to reach out to people and become their friend. This, from his salutation, "My Friends," through his carefully prepared peroration that he wrote himself because he wanted each Fireside Chat to end on a high note. Finally, he added an expert dramatic reading that was designed to simulate naturalness and easy, friendly conversation. Francis Perkins, who witnessed his talks on the radio, was struck by the impression the president gave—that he was actually speaking to people in their parlors, listening with their neighbors. As he talked his head would nod, his hands would move in simple, natural, comfortable gestures. His face would smile and light up as though he were actually sitting on the front porch or parlor with them. He was making a personal contact with everyone, everywhere, at the same time.[101] People felt this and it bound them to him in affection. The president often achieved precisely this result as these random replies to his Fireside Chat, March 12, 1933, attest:

Just last night as we listened to you I thought how human and natural you were. You weren't talking down to us from your lofty height but shoulder to shoulder.[102]

It warmed the heart to feel that we had somebody in Washington that understood and appreciated our problems and our troubles.[103]

We certainly enjoyed your talk with us last night. I say this because this was the reaction of my family as we sat around the radio Saturday night. "It seems like he is here talking to us" was the way Mrs. Harris (wife) put it. "He is" was my reply.[104]

Franklin Roosevelt seemed like a providential president because he made such a timely appearance. Herbert Hoover's responses to the Depression were not reassuring when large numbers of poor Americans began to live marginally and many in the middle class were threatened with poverty. Roosevelt rekindled faith when he declared his determination to experiment and promote change through vigorous action while assuring that no one would starve. When many of his programs, including those for relief, were adopted in 1933 and 1934, many Americans were so thankful that he became their "champion." Indeed, in a culture still fundamentally religious, many conferred on him their ultimate tribute: he was a godly man. It is doubtful if he would have achieved such tributes without both his useful social programs or the confident, brave, and caring personality that could embellish his personal and media contacts with the American people with his own special ardor. Roosevelt did all these things well because he felt a need to enlist in the well-being and comfort of others and sought their admiration in return. He was a timely president because, as Robert Frost once noted, "It was only when one's avocation joined one's vocation that the deed was ever done for heaven or the future's sake."

3

The New Deal

Despite a sharp yearlong reversal in 1937–1938, Americans of the New Deal era generally fared better in the middle and late 1930s than in the early years of that decade. They also seemed more positive about their lives and their futures. The long breadlines and numerous Hoovervilles now virtually disappeared in the cities with the salutary effects of the New Deal relief, work-relief, and other social programs providing numerous Americans with unprecedented security. The great fear of economic collapse also subsided, with concerns now centering more on how best to facilitate recovery. Walter Lippman detected that this fundamental shift occurred by the end of Roosevelt's first year. He wrote:

Today there are still grave problems. But there is no overwhelming dangerous crisis. The mass of the people have recovered their courage and their hope. They are no longer hysterically anxious about the immediate present. They have recovered not only some small part of their standard of life but also their self-possession.[1]

Gross National Product (GNP) in the United States spurted to 90 billion in 1937 and 1939, a significant improvement over the 65 billion of 1934, though still well below the 103 billion figure for 1929.[2] Personal consumption of goods and services improved to 67 billion in both 1937 and 1939, considerably above the low year of 1933 when 46 billion was spent, but still well below the 77 billion goods and services consumed in the last year of the 1920s.[3] Personal income also made an impressive, near-50% recovery between the period 1933–1934 and 1939, but again was still 13% below figures for 1929.[4] Similar patterns held for the numbers of used and new cars on the roads yet actual expenditures for gasoline and miles traveled

exceeded sums every year from the mid-1930s to 1939.[5] Still another likely
index of Americans beginning to enjoy their lives was that gallons of ice
cream of all kinds produced in 1937 exceeded comparable numbers in
1929.[6] Movie attendance broke all records after 1936, albeit with the aid
of reduced prices and frequent prizes for patrons.[7] In fact, overall, Americans
with shorter working hours were estimated to be spending 5.2% of their
income on recreation in 1939 whereas that figure was only 5.6% in 1929.
The explanation for this growth was probably not primarily the result of
New Deal programs, but possibly a large increase in the money supply between 1934 and 1936—a consequence of an increase in the nation's gold
reserves translated by the Federal Reserve into monetary expansion. When
Congress passed a $2-billion bonus to veterans over Roosevelt's veto in
1936, this also helped put extra dollars in circulation.[8]

There was much less reason to be sanguine about the New Deal's efforts
to end other major effects of the Depression. Farm prices in 1939 were still
more than one-third below and retail prices one-fifth below those of 1929.[9]
Unemployment never fell below 16.9% from 1933 to 1939, except in 1937,
though this surely was an improvement over the estimated 25% in 1933,
nor did the estimated numbers of unemployed decline below 9 million with
the exception of 1937 when 7.7 million were unemployed. The high figure
of the unemployed, 19% in 1938, was by 1940 significantly reduced by the
impact of war in Europe and the Far East, but unemployment for that year
was still 14.6%.[10]

Despite the New Deal's relief and work-relief programs, poor people did
not benefit significantly in terms of their standard of living. By criteria employed in a Brookings study in the year 1929, when analysts estimated that
an income of $2,000 was required for strict necessities, the situation of the
poor in the New Deal years, even with allowance for a 20% drop in the cost
of living, was disconcerting. Probably 60% of American families earned less
than $1,500 from 1933 to 1939 and of those it is likely that 35 to 40%
received less than $1,000 a year when $1,200 per year was regarded as a
minimum subsistence income for a typical family of five.[11]

The following brief treatment of the policies and effects of the New Deal
is intended to demonstrate that political considerations alone cannot explain
the nation's resiliency and stability in the 1930s; the limitations of New Deal
programs suggest the supplementary role of America's social and cultural
resources as additional steadying influences.

One important explanation for the New Deal's failure to end the Depression or significantly reduce unemployment is that there was no assured
formula to do so. Besides, its efforts were undermined by circumstances that
it could not control. The reluctance of venture capitalists to invest severely
hurt job opportunities. There was also an unusual increase in numbers of
work-age Americans in the 1930s; more than 500,000 a year were reaching
age eighteen, while longevity increased by several years, thus assuring a large

number of available, though often unemployed, older workers.[12] Manufacturers, meanwhile, confronted with uncertain markets while being forced to pay minimum-hour wages, chose to apply advanced technology and reduce their dependency on manual workers. Thus, even when production levels were maintained or improved, workers suffered technological unemployment. The number of tractors in use in 1939 doubled from those in 1930 and usage of electric power quadrupled from 1926 to 1938. As of 1936, when both employment and production in manufacturing were only 10% below corresponding numbers for 1929, the number of manhours worked was still nearly 30% below 1929. This meant that to achieve the unemployment levels of 1929, there would have to be much greater production than in 1929. One group that studied the problem in 1937 estimated that only a 20% increase in production over 1929 would restore the unemployment level of that year.[13]

The New Deal's efforts to reduce unemployment also fell victim to the novel problem that many unemployed workers, though theoretically employable, did not have the qualifications to be employed in what had become a highly selective job market. Despite the popular notion that employers paid low wages during the Depression because of numbers unemployed, wages for those employed in 1935 were virtually on a par with 1929, and they continued to improve through 1939 when they were almost ten cents per hour higher than in 1929. This figure was even more impressive when one remembers that the cost of living declined about 20% from 1932 to 1939. With excellent wages, employers could be extremely discriminating in whom they hired. They preferred the most efficient workers to handle the new technology or speed up the tempo of work. Those without skills were dismissed and often not hired again for long periods, if at all. Young people coming out of schools without job experience were disadvantaged, as were older men once laid off. Similarly, men who had not finished elementary school were much less likely to be employed than those who did. Indeed, by the mid-1930s, when the new personnel policies in business were firmly in place, only massive work-relief programs that were larger than any attempted under the New Deal would have substantially reduced this hard-core unemployment.[14]

The other major reasons the New Deal did not spend sufficiently to end the Depression or significantly curtail poverty lay in the preferences, policies, and effectiveness of Franklin Roosevelt together with the country's characteristic conservatism. Although a pragmatist in his methods, Roosevelt never altered his view that government's rationale was essentially moral. One finds here once again the overarching influence of his happy, though highly disciplined, home environment. It was at Hyde Park that he witnessed his father's noblesse oblige toward employees and community, and the way residents tipped their caps to Master James, and he was constantly reminded later by his mother, after his father's death, to live up to his example and noble character. It was there, too, that he developed a remarkable sensitivity to the needs of others, a condition of his mother's lavish attention and love. This background, one of benign gentry, also assured Roosevelt's respect for property and "the economic status quo," which, as Frances Perkins once observed, were for Roosevelt "as much [taken] for granted as his family."[15] In addition to being confident of the virtues of capitalism as an economic system, he practiced, as did his Dutch Calvinist forebears, the ethic of thrift privately and personally in his daily life and later when president as manager of the government's resources. As a young family man he consistently sought to dine at home in preference to expensive restaurants. Later as president he sent away for mail-order shirts on sale and switched tailors for reasons of economy.[16] And to his secretary Grace Tully, he would inevitably remark each year when preparing his income tax forms, "You know, Grace, taxes this year are pretty heavy."[17]

Franklin Roosevelt repeatedly stated in public the major tenets of his mature political philosophy evident in his acceptance speech for the nomination in 1932 and his campaign, and he often restated them at critical times during his first two terms. He repeatedly returned to two major concepts: the moral preeminence of the common good (community) and the importance of constructive, hence orderly, change when that community was threatened. Their reiteration provides the New Deal's best definition of intent. In a speech before the Commonwealth Club in San Francisco during the campaign of 1932 he declared

that the responsible heads of finance and industry instead of acting each for himself, must work together to achieve the common end. They must, where necessary, sacrifice this or that private advantage; and in reciprocal self-denial must seek a general advantage. It is here that formal Government—political Government, if you choose—comes in. Whenever in the pursuit of this objective the lone wolf, the unethical competitor, the reckless promoter, the Ishmael or Insull whose hand is against every man's, declines to join in achieving an end recognized as being for the public welfare, and threatens to drag the industry back to a state of anarchy, the Government may properly be asked to apply restraint.[18]

In his acceptance speech at the Democratic National Convention in Philadelphia in 1936, Roosevelt underscored the dangerous antisocial quality of the supreme individualist; he was convinced that "private enterprise [in the 1920s], indeed, became too private. It became privileged enterprise, not free enterprise."[19] He summarized this position succinctly in a speech in Chicago on October 14, 1936: "I believe in individualism," he declared, "up to the point where the individualist starts to operate at the expense of the society." And again, "I do not believe in abandoning the system of individual enterprise . . . the freedom and opportunity that have characterized American development in the past can be maintained but only if we recognize the fact that individualism needs reform, and the collaboration of all of us to provide security for all of us."[20]

In Roosevelt's mind government was the moral agent of community; it served society by assuming responsibility for an equitable balance of interests. In so doing, government sought ideally to preserve the effectiveness of all interests and the freedom and opportunity of all individuals. Given the destabilizing effects of powerful business interests that imbalanced American society in the 1920s leading to the Depression, it was incumbent for government to restore that balance. Effective community also depended on government protection of ordinary citizens, not merely in the Great Depression, but by ongoing guarantees for their reasonable security. And so the essence of Roosevelt's political thought was to regulate the strong and protect the weak.

Whether liberal or conservative or, as one of his critics asserts, using "liberal means to achieve conservative ends," Roosevelt considered this balance the best guarantee of a free, progressive, yet orderly society. "Democracy can thrive" he insisted, "only when it enlists the devotion of those whom Lincoln called the common people. Democracy can hold that devotion only when it adequately respects their dignity by so ordering society as to assure to the masses of men and women reasonable security and hope for themselves and for their children."[21] Although the president defined himself as "a little left of center," Edmund Burke would probably have approved his programs during the Depression. Like the great British conservative who struggled to distinguish fastidiously between a liberal-conservative and a conservative-liberal, Roosevelt expressed the dilemma of attempting to find labels for his moral purposes.

The true conservative is the man who has a real concern for injustices and takes thought against the day of reckoning. The true conservative seeks to protect the system of private property and free enterprise by correcting such injustices and inequalities as arise from it. The most serious threat to our institutions comes from those who refuse to face the need for change. Liberalism becomes the protection for the far-sighted conservative.

He then expanded on this theme:

Wise and prudent men—intelligent conservatives—have long known that in a changing world worthy institutions can be conserved only by adjusting them to the changing time. In the words of the great essayist, "The voice of great events is proclaiming to us, Reform if you would preserve." . . . I am that kind of conservative because I am that kind of liberal.[22]

To fail to change constructively was to invite violent and irrational change from those who felt themselves outside the effective community. Roosevelt stated this conviction unequivocally in his acceptance speech at the Democratic National Convention in 1932:

Wild radicalism has made few converts, and the greatest tribute that I can pay to my countrymen is that in these days of crushing want there persists an orderly and hopeful spirit on the part of the millions of our people who have suffered so much. To fail to offer them a new chance is not only to betray their hopes but to misunderstand their patience.

To meet by reaction that danger of radicalism is to invite disaster. Reaction is no barrier to the radical. It is a challenge, a provocation. The way to meet that danger is to offer a workable program of reconstruction.[23]

The New Deal, though a lineal descendant of Woodrow Wilson's New Freedom, differed markedly from the latter in its methods; Wilson's basic view of good government was to regulate effective and fair competition between interests and deny them any manifestation of government favoritism. The New Deal, however, sought to overcome what it considered excessive individualism in American society and substitute an ethic of greater social unity and useful cooperation between groups.[24] To achieve a disciplinary framework for its "associative vision," the New Deal was prepared to offer a cornucopia of favors to all interests and classes and all sections of the country.[25] President Roosevelt's vision of a united America even included a bid for a nonpartisan alliance with Republicans. When, in 1934, he refused to attend a Democratic celebration for Thomas Jefferson, the party founder, he did so on the basis that it would serve unacceptable divisive purposes because "the recovery and reconstruction program is being accomplished by men and women of all parties."[26] Although Roosevelt's ideal of cooperation was more insistent in his first term, he never abandoned it entirely.[27] Roosevelt believed that the cooperative approach promised the most effective results for national economic recovery.[28] It also served his personal and political interests.

By exhorting and abetting a concert of interests, the president found a strategy to wield what he regarded as the necessary compromises to restore the economy. Under government supervision each interest group would receive benefits for which corresponding concessions would be offered to other interests. He would protect the capitalist system as the main player on his "All-America team" by restoring the traditional banking system with safeguards and encouraging compromises between capital and labor, usually favorable to management, in an effort to restore maximum, healthy productivity.[29] Indeed, Roosevelt would do so even in capitalism's most vulnerable moments in the early months of 1933, when one lawmaker conceded he would have passed "Mother Goose" if the president had so wished.[30] But correspondingly, he would initiate a significant and unprecedented benefits package at the federal level for all Americans, including by

1935 sustained programs of relief, protection of home owners with low cost mortgages, security for the elderly, and unemployment compensation.

There can be little doubt that Roosevelt's early policies represented his priorities in dealing with the Depression and that he then wished to be "President of all the People."[31] This strategy of favoring every group was not merely feasible on economic grounds; it also satisfied Roosevelt's needs to be useful and popular and his strong motivation to achieve extraordinary feats in return for appreciation. It was also compatible with his patrician background—his sense of social responsibility for all classes and disdain for irresponsible business leaders who needed to be disciplined in the name of community. These powerful personal interests also helped formulate New Deal strategy.

The New Deal's moderate policies, inherent in its advocacy of a "concert of interests," were dramatically underscored in its adoption of key social programs. Although the National Recovery Administration (NRA) and the Agricultural Adjustment Administration (AAA) produced handsome gains for the propertied and the powerful, the NRA provided merely modest gains for the worker and the AAA held generally adverse consequences for share-croppers and tenant farmers. The NRA and AAA, both enacted by Congress in the first hundred days, also illustrated Roosevelt's governmental thrift, a stance welcome among business interests, though obviously unattractive to the unemployed. Neither program was costly. Roosevelt exhibited similar preferences for cost-cutting during this period in reducing veteran's pensions and slicing salaries of federal workers.

The Agricultural Adjustment Act was designed to raise farm prices by restricting agricultural production. Because government subsidies were based on the size of farms under the AAA, only farm owners benefited and large owners received the largest compensation. Although the AAA made provisions for tenants and sharecroppers with small subsidies, the program at the local level worked through landowners who usually denied or reduced their shares; landowners preferred to replace them with now affordable trac-tors or rehire them as agricultural laborers without the cabins and supplies that constituted their job security. In 1934, when liberals in the Department of Agriculture, including Jerome Frank, insisted that the federal government honor its contract with the nonlandowning farmers, they drew fire from southern farm owners and were dismissed. Roosevelt explained to the so-cialist Norman Thomas who criticized this outcome, "We've got to be pa-tient."[32]

Although net farm income doubled between 1934 and 1940 in response to New Deal farm programs, farm owners were the principal benefactors. The AAA did little to redistribute agricultural income; tenants and share-croppers were often forced to live on relief or with low incomes. The Re-settlement Administration (1935) and the Farm Security Administration (1937) helped a small number of displaced landless farmers to rent or own land, but these programs were on short rations and not advanced vigorously by the administration, probably out of fear of offending landowners and their powerful representatives in Congress.[33]

The National Recovery Administration was also an embodiment of President Roosevelt's concert of interest thinking, with consequences favoring owners and lesser gains for workers. A perceptive student of the NRA, Ellis Hawley, described as one of the major goals of proponents of the NRA a "government-sponsored" business commonwealth.[34] Business was encouraged by the Roosevelt administration to devise self-regulating codes to set standards for industrial output, the intent being to raise prices by stabilizing production and thus avoiding overproduction. This was accomplished by planning within each industry and eliminating "unfair competition" (i.e., competition that did not live up to codes). These were then ratified by the government that pledged in return to suspend antitrust laws. Given these benefits, businessmen agreed to Article 7A recognizing labor's right to organize and bargain collectively through "representatives of their own choosing," a minimum wage and maximum hour regulation for labor, and to the establishment of a federally financed job program, the Public Works Authority (PWA), with an initial appropriation of $3 billion.[35]

Businessmen gained handsomely. They raised prices even before the codes were in place and continued to do so after the NRA began operation by controlling production and price-fixing.[36] Conversely, Article 7A, as applied, had an uncertain effect on labor's bargaining powers. When businesses complained about favorable interpretations to labor of 7A by the National Labor Board, allowing secret elections by workers to determine their labor representatives, with a majority of their committee empowered to negotiate with management on plant administration operations, Roosevelt hastily intervened. As a consequence, the administration watered down labor's bargaining strength by endorsing proportional representation and even company unions.

The NRA had other negative effects on workers and persons on relief; the new higher prices on manufactured goods offset efforts in other New Deal programs to sustain recovery by increasing the public's capacity to consume.[37] And although provisions for minimum-wage and maximum-hour laws theoretically reduced worktime and protected workers income, when challenged by business, especially in the South, the New Deal relented and permitted geographical and racial variations in the wage scale favorable to owners.

There were genuine benefits for labor in the NRA package as well; it protected southern cotton textile workers from their eleven-hour days and sixty-hour workweeks, although the shorter workweek, usually thirty hours, also produced hardships.[38] The NRA also terminated child labor in the cotton textile industry, a notorious violator in the past, and it facilitated drives for union membership by farsighted labor leaders like John. L. Lewis of the

United Mine Workers. More might have accrued to labor's benefit under the NRA had the PWA been more forthcoming in its spending for public works in 1933–1934. Honest Harold Ickes, its director, was so conservative in investing public monies, however, that one of his colleagues declared he spent PWA funds as if they came out of an eyedropper. Nevertheless, inexact figures show that one and one-half to two million more Americans were employed in 1934 than the previous year.[39]

The government programs with the most positive consequences for the poor, the needy, and the threatened in 1933–1934 were those enjoined "to prevent physical suffering and to maintain living standards." These were the boldest statements of Roosevelt's determination to be president of all the American people. In so doing, he saved lives and reduced personal suffering of countless Americans and was an important contributor to the country's social stability. Never doubting that people had to eat every day, he unhesitatingly risked political backlash by maintaining welfare programs throughout the 1930s, long after the period of acute danger to the nation. Beginning in early 1933, when Congress appropriated $500 million for direct relief, the New Deal's principal relief agencies—the Federal Emergency Relief Administration (FERA), the Civil Works Administration (CWA), and the Civilian Conservation Corps (CCC)—together provided income that year for 8 million households consisting of 28 million people, more than 22% of the population—a high in the history of welfare in the United States (13 to 15 million were then unemployed affecting perhaps 45 million people).[40] As late as June 1939, nearly 19 million Americans still received public assistance, then nearly 15% of the population.[41]

The funds dispensed in these programs were seldom adequate to raise people above poverty even when supplemented by government programs to purchase surplus foodstuffs and distribute them to the unemployed.[42] Monthly FERA relief payments averaged $25 to $29 in 1934–1935, hence approximately $350 for an unemployed person for a year (remember: $1,200 dollars was considered the minimum essential year's income for a family of five).[43] The CWA, a short-term work-relief program for the winter of 1933–1934, offered attractive wages (twice those of the FERA and greater than minimums in NRA wage scales) for 4 million workers, averaging $15 a week in early January 1934, but CWA programs were cut back and phased out shortly thereafter. The CWA prompted business to complain that its high wages discouraged workers from seeking private employment. Opposition in the South centered on the evil consequences of higher wages on blacks and race relations. The president, ever prepared to economize and susceptible to the idea that relief, even the work relief of the CWA, might become "a habit," decreed its demise. As spring 1934 approached, he confidently told CWA administrator Harry Hopkins, "Nobody is going to starve during the warm weather."[44]

Although relief recipients were provided no more than minimal support and a hopeful work-relief program was dismantled, Jesse Jones, director of the Reconstruction Finance Corporation (RFC), dispensed massive financial support to restore capitalism by stimulating the recovery of business.[45] The RFC expended approximately 1 billion to rescue failed banks by investing in their stock in 1933–1934, a measure that would eventually prove necessary to meet the needs of over 6,000 banks. Along with Federal Reserve Banks, the RFC also contributed most of the original capital stock in the Federal Deposit Insurance Corporation, thus guaranteeing holdings of depositors—again a remarkable move to restore public confidence. During the balance of the 1930s, it also performed other valuable social services by lending $1.5 billion to financially shaky railroads, $90 million to insurance companies, an additional billion and a half to farmers and abetting Rural Electrification. By 1935, in only two years, the Roosevelt administration had loaned $10.6 billion to businesses and government agencies assisting business to restore liquidity and raise the country out of the Depression.[46] It is instructive to compare that figure with federal expenditures for the unemployed from 1933 to 1939 when cumulative allocations for the major programs (FERA, CWA, and WPA) amounted to $11 billion, only slightly more.[47]

The president continued to be very popular in 1934, still steering from the center.[48] As late as October 1934, he appealed to the American Bankers Association for an "alliance of all forces intent on the business of recovery . . . business and banking, agriculture and industry, and labor and capital. What an all-America team that would be!"[49] But the slight recovery of the economy in 1934 and 1935 apparently undermined Roosevelt's grand strategy. At least, as fears of economic collapse and social dislocation receded, typical partisan, individualistic attitudes and loyalties revived and these dashed the spirit of cooperation necessary to maintain a popular front.

Once beyond the danger point for capitalism, businessmen resented the New Deal's regulatory intrusions and reminders that the New Deal–managed recovery would require subordination of market interests to purported national interests.[50] Besides, the New Deal threatened to redistribute income by supporting labor and even competing with free enterprise in supplying electric power through the Tennessee Valley Authority (TVA). Although businessmen accepted benefits from the RFC, they continued to mistrust Roosevelt's intentions and generally held back from lending or spending because of uncertainties. Their fears and anger generated organized political action and large campaign contributions to the Republican Party. They were also responsible for a vicious attack on the president's ability, health, and character, and that of his wife ("We don't like her either"). Insidious rumors from this whispering campaign sometimes surfaced in the press, but their heartlands were country clubs and dining cars.[51]

The president with excellent connections in both places often heard these stories. He affected a humorous indifference, but such severe criticism deeply hurt. As his New Deal aide William O. Douglas stated, "FDR expressed over and over to me as well as publicly his amazement at the charge of business that he was its enemy. . . . He truly thought he was capitalism's best friend, pointing out the way for its survival."[52] Even so, he did not immediately relinquish his ideal of an all-America team. The coup that had ousted Jerome Frank and his egalitarian followers from the Department of Agriculture in 1934 may have represented a bid to remain on course, a response to the hailstorm of criticism from business interests.[53] When the NRA was declared unconstitutional in May 1935 on grounds that Congress had exceeded its power to delegate authority, the president objected, in the spirit of being everyone's president, that this would thwart the government's resolve to assist all groups.[54] Roosevelt retained hopes, however, for a future government–business partnership.[55]

Historians often ascribe Roosevelt's swing to the left to the powerful new forces generated in 1934–1935: the liberal Congress elected in 1934; the turbulent strike activity in several cities in the same year; and especially the programs for wealth redistribution by Huey Long, Father Charles Coughlin, and Francis Townsend. Since the president's program for 1933–1934 provided little for labor and less for landless farmers, he was vulnerable to the lavish appeals via radio to these groups by Louisiana's Senator Huey Long. Long promised to provide every American family with an annual income of $2,000 to $2,500 a year and a household estate of $5,000, and, as a start, "enough for a home, an automobile, a radio, and ordinary conveniences" to be paid for by taxes on personal fortunes exceeding $2 million (1% tax) scaled to 100% tax on $8 million a year.[56] Faulty economics notwithstanding, Long claimed more than 7 million members in his Share Our Wealth Society. Roosevelt reacted with alarm, encouraging an investigation of Long by the Internal Revenue System.[57] An assassin's bullet in September 1935 would eliminate Long from seeking the presidential office to which he probably aspired in 1940. Although Long was the most threatening of the dissidents to emerge on the left in 1935, Francis Townsend, with an equally unrealistic formula for funding, was winning support from large numbers of retired persons. Townsend devised a wishful plan whereby every retired person would receive $300 a month on the provision that the recipient would spend his or her pension.

After the dissolution of his alliance strategy, Roosevelt had to rely on putting together a smaller coalition made up of moderates and those left of center and preempting the ploys of Long and Townsend. A strike wave in several cities in 1934 and protests from Farm Labor Party leaders in the Midwest merely reinforced his need to espouse bolder, more inclusive social programs. Heading off "The Rumble of Discontent," a term used by David M. Kennedy to describe this period, Roosevelt lost no time to assume the offensive; as early as May 1934, well before the congressional elections for that year, Roosevelt publicized his legislative agenda for a Congress not

scheduled to meet until January 1935. He called for sweeping liberal legislation, unemployment insurance, an effective labor board, pensions for the
elderly, medical insurance, a program for public housing, and a continuous
public works program.[58] Roosevelt's activist and partisan stance became
more pronounced in his presidential message to Congress on January 4,
1935. He declared that America was still a country with too much in-
equality; the problem of unemployment could not be solved merely by encouraging private enterprise but by government-sponsored work programs
among the underprivileged. He also called for regulation of utilities and tax
reform, the latter an obvious steal from the then still vibrant Huey Long.[59]

The actual legislation, 1935, however, was basically conciliatory to business while it provided less than promised advantages to ordinary Americans.
Roosevelt probably never doubted that the revival of free enterprise held
the key to America's economic recovery and probably was still balancing
interests in his own mind. His programs were also modified because business, now emboldened by an improved economy, challenged them and influenced lawmakers to do the same. Open repudiation of the president
occurred in the House when George Huddleston, a modest Alabama congressman, arose to protest the president's proposal to eliminate holding
companies in giant electric utilities; he declared, "I will do what I think
right, and all hell cannot stop me." Huddleston met with standing applause
lasting for several minutes from House members.[60] Professor Freidel observes that by the end of the 1935 legislative session, that hot summer before
air-conditioning was in wide use in the nation's capital, "There had been
ructions and rebellions enough in the defiant congress to lead the press to
hail a Republican resurgence and predict Roosevelt would have difficulties
in the 1936 election."[61] The conservative coalition of southern Democrats
and Republicans, which would thwart New Deal legislation in Roosevelt's
second term, was already showing strong signs of life.[62] Walter Lippman,
observing this reaction by Congress, concluded that he was witnessing the
"closing days of a period in American history."[63]

Among the most far-reaching legislation of the 1935 congressional session, the Wagner Labor Relations Act provided unequivocal government
sanction to labor's right to bargain collectively without interference by employers. The president withheld support because he preferred the NRA's
labor policy that he hoped would be sustained. This way labor would be
beholding to the government, and to Roosevelt personally, for its improved
benefits in wages and hours, unlike Wagner's bill that empowered labor to
obtain its own benefits through collective bargaining. Although Roosevelt
had refused Wagner permission to introduce the bill in 1934 when labor
was complaining about the harmful effects of the NRA's formulas for bargaining, he assented in 1935. Most of the credit for final passage, however,
must go to Wagner's ability to organize an effective coalition. His bill, deservingly cited as labor's Magna Carta, became the basis for labor's robust

organization in the late 1930s, and a genuine improvement in income for union workers.[64]

The Social Security Bill, by way of contrast with the Wagner Bill, had the president's unqualified approval through congressional passage in summer 1935. In fact, with the possible exception of the CCC, Social Security was the New Deal program that probably pleased him most. He confidently and correctly anticipated that his proposal for Social Security would be part of the New Deal's enduring legacy to America. The president argued that payroll taxes by each contributor to the Social Security system would assure its continuance; "With those taxes in there, no damn politician can ever scrap my social security program."[65] The legislation met with wide public approval and passed the Congress easily despite oppositions from the National Association of Manufacturers and disgruntled Towsendites. The Social Security Bill had three major features: unemployment insurance financed by federal payroll taxes, though administered by the states; the keystone provision, an old-age insurance system financed by both wage and payroll taxes providing $10 to $85 per month for persons over sixty-five to begin operations in 1942; and, finally, federal grants to states that provided direct relief for handicapped persons—those already old, the blind and orphaned, and so on.[66]

Although unemployment compensation and aid to the disabled were quickly put in place, the Social Security Bill, with its main feature operational in the 1940s, was more of a credential of hope than a palpable gain for Americans of the 1930s. Struggling young and middle-aged parents, who were quite possibly living with their parents during the Depression, experienced relief that they would not have to shoulder the whole responsibility for their care in the future. Unlike Great Britain, however, where general taxes paid for old-age assistance, Americans were expected to help themselves prepare for old age through regressive payroll taxes.[67] These added to the financial problems of individuals with small incomes who were already paying, or would soon pay, escalating state sales taxes. The several millions removed from payrolls for old-age assistance, together with a cutback in work-relief funds engineered by Roosevelt in 1937, are regarded as basic causes for the severe recession late that year and in early 1938. Nor were benefits generous under the plan even by Depression standards or even comprehensive because at least one-fifth of workers (mostly the poorest) were still deprived of coverage. Also, Roosevelt's earlier call for medical insurance was dropped.

Surely, the tax policies of the Second New Deal were more advantageous to the well-to-do than the "forgotten man." The Revenue Act of 1935, almost immediately described as a "Soak the Rich" bill, sounded like a clarion call in Roosevelt's leftward swing. On closer inspection, its effects, while providing a clever backdrop for the election campaign of 1936, were inconsequential for wealth redistribution. The fact that the president did not propose in 1935 or at any other time in the 1930s a tax bill requiring sizable contributions from the middle class explains the New Deal's funding inadequacies for its national planning, work relief, and relief programs. In other words, Roosevelt never pursued the course that had the best immediate chance of reducing the poverty of that third of the nation's ill-fed, ill-housed, and ill-nourished.[68]

Roosevelt's tax message on June 19, 1935, was worded as if he were an advocate of social democracy. He called for a "wider distribution of wealth" and cited the damaging effect of current concentrations of wealth on social unrest. He also condemned fortunes acquired by inheritance as inconsistent with democratic ways. Further, he exhorted big corporations to shoulder a larger responsibility for the benefit of society and declared that the prime purpose of his proposed legislation was "to increase opportunities for young men and women reared under more modest circumstances."[69] Even Huey Long was impressed, but the finished legislation made a folly of income redistribution. All together, the bill's provisions for estate and gift taxes, excess profits and dividends tax, and income tax increases were estimated to produce an additional $250 million a year in revenue, with the new income taxes only about 16% ($45 million) of that sum. In fiscal year 1936, the first year the new law was in effect, the government derived only 17% of its revenues (the average per year for the 1930s overall) from the income taxes. To illustrate that this remained a paltry sum, excise taxes with levies on such items as alcohol, tobacco, radios, and cosmetics contributed in the same year 40% of the government's revenues. Excises taxes were, as Professor Mark Leff described, "the revenue work horse" of the New Deal. In effect, these were sales taxes on goods heavily consumed by lower income groups. These skewerings not only absolved the broad middle class from paying taxes (only 5% of the population did so), but led "the forgotten man" to pay for a substantial part of the limited welfare he received. After 1937, he also paid for a share of his social security.[70] The long-range effects of this tax policy sealed the fate of lower-income Americans in the 1930s. In the immediate period, however, Roosevelt solved many political and personal needs with one blow. He silenced Huey Long temporarily at least and won widespread popular support. The large turnouts and stupendous enthusiasm that greeted his presidential campaign everywhere in 1936 also demonstrated that he found a campaign theme in the Wealth Tax Act (Revenue Act) of 1935. True, there would also be negative repercussions to Roosevelt's escalation of a war of words with the "economic royalists." Business opposition intensified and as a consequence congressional conservatism deepened.[71]

In 1936, President Roosevelt would liken his situation to that of Andrew Jackson. "It seemed sometimes that all were against him—all but the people of the United States." They knew, however, his true worth and so "they loved him for the enemies he made."[72] Roosevelt was too polite to describe himself that way, but the inference was obvious; he, like Jackson, was doing the right thing supporting ordinary Americans. In fact, however, his contribution was the more modest, though important one, that of including them in the benefits package.

The Works Progress Administration (WPA) is the last major program of the "Second New Deal" with important social implications. Carrying the bulk of the New Deal's relief responsibilities after 1935, it was the largest federal relief program in the 1930s. It expended $6.7 billion, about twice that of FERA or PWA and more than three times the amount spent on the CCC, all instituted in 1933.[73] The WPA, product of the Emergency Relief Act of 1935, was intended to reduce President Roosevelt's discomfort with federal relief programs on the grounds that these would sap the initiative and independence of its recipients. In January 1935, he declared an end of direct relief, calling on Congress to sponsor a work-relief program strictly for employable persons. All direct or home relief was henceforth to be distributed to unemployable persons—the elderly, blind, handicapped, and so on—with funding coming from state funds and federal grants. This division of responsibilities served to silence his critics who complained about big and inefficient federal programs wasting taxpayers' monies and to relieve fiscally constrained relief agencies in Washington.

Many of the problems associated with the WPA stemmed from its inadequate funding.[74] The WPA was funded yearly and hence subject to uncertain appropriations. Roosevelt intended the relief program to employ 3.5 million workers, but even at its peak periods—February 1936 (3,019,000) and November 1938 (3,238,000)—it fell short of that goal, and at other times it was offering employment to less than half the number the president envisioned, again a consequence of inadequate funding.[75] Although unemployed workers numbered 8 to 10.7 million between 1935 and 1940, the WPA generally provided work and work-relief funds for only about 30 percent of that group.[76] Many of the remainder would try desperately to be taken on the state's rolls for the unemployables, but state relief officials were not overly generous and often withheld assistance. They justified their refusal on grounds that state legislatures failed to provide necessary funds or because their grants from the federal government were insufficient. The able-bodied unemployed experienced particularly serious problems during the yearlong national recession beginning the summer of 1937, caused in part by a severe slash in WPA appropriations by Roosevelt.[77] Several states attempted to meet this impasse by adopting or hiking sales taxes and then offered aid to the employables, but at low levels even for relief recipients.[78] So, near the end of the decade, large numbers of Americans formerly middle class as well as workers were still without employment and adequate work relief—or indeed any relief. In 1938, Edith Abbot, a veteran in the field of social work, estimated that a million Americans were still awaiting regular work relief from the WPA and most of them were without relief of any kind.[79]

The circumstances of those on the WPA and state relief were, of course, better, but not exactly an occasion for jubilation. Not only was the WPA worker's tenure insecure, pending yearly congressional funding, but wages were paltry, averaging around $52 a month, though many rural workers received even less, only $21 a month.[80] Strict rules forbade employing persons who were not heads of families (a condition that hurt women's chances for employment) and blacks were discriminated against in the South.[81] The effects of meager WPA wages produced miserable conditions for many families. A family in Illinois observed by Edith Abbot lived on $65 a month earned by a father with the WPA. All five children, on medical examination, suffered from malnutrition and had serious physical maladies.[82] Families on state and local relief were also threatened by cutoffs in relief when times became difficult. Also, some states spent much less on relief than others. Even when fully supported, those on home relief in 1939 received an average of only $24 a month, several dollars less than sums spent by FERA four years earlier.[83] In a conservative farming area, Otter Tail County, Minnesota, a local relief board supported a family in late 1937 and early 1938 allowing $6 for rent, $14 for groceries, and $3.60 for milk each month. In May 1938, the case came up for review and "the board did not cut the relief funding level, but ordered the grocer not to allow the purchase of canned milk, Doan's Pills, or salad dressing, and requested that the family use lard instead of butter in cooking."[84] Those dropped from relief rolls in Cincinnati—an estimated 24,400 persons in 1939—were "entirely without resources." Some "had practically nothing to eat, except occasional surplus products food supplied by friends or neighbors and fruit salvaged from garbage at markets." One family was reduced to eating scraps from a nearby restaurant; the proprietor thought they were being used to feed a pet.[85]

Because Cincinnati's problems were probably not unique, one is left to ponder the numbers of similarly distressed Americans living hand-to-mouth at the very end of the Depression decade, after two full terms of Franklin Roosevelt and the New Deal. Pivan and Cloward have concluded, based on WPA surveys, that "for many people, the years after 1935 were as bad as any during the depression."[86] One of the best sources to gauge the accuracy of that statement is in the photographs of the Farm Security Administration. Its pictures of awful shacks and tubercular-looking people in the Ozarks of Arkansas,[87] families living in tent houses in Oklahoma,[88] evidence of people without teeth,[89] homeless families on the road,[90] gaunt and half-deserted towns in Williams County, North Dakota, being blown away by dust storms,[91] former miners living in shacks and abandoned stores in Ziegler, Illinois,[92] and the agricultural workers' shacktown in Oklahoma City on Mays Avenue strategically located next to the city dump where families scavenged while living in cardboard houses,[93] all provide mute testimony to the troublesome times still confronting countless Americans in the late 1930s.

Major studies on the New Deal regard Roosevelt's second term as disappointing. Chapter headings in these works declare "The Lion at Bay," the times as a "Sea of Troubles," or at best a period of "The New Dealer with Brakes On."[94] This, following one of the most convincing—indeed stunning—electoral triumphs in American history when Franklin Roosevelt carried every state in the union except Maine and Vermont and polled nearly 27.5 million votes—an increase of 5 million over his total in 1932—while the Republican candidate, Alfred Landon from Kansas, managed only 1 million more votes than Herbert Hoover. Roosevelt's surprisingly easy victory also helped produce smashing Democratic majorities in the Senate and the House, the largest by a single party since the mid-nineteenth century. The president consolidated the effect by running very strongly in all sections of the country and made spectacular gains among urban voters, especially northern blacks and ethnics.

The victory meant much to Roosevelt and must have been one of the genuine epiphanies of his life. For a man who passionately sought love and respect through politics, who once said, "I regain strength by just meeting the American people," this was a validation.[95] When challenged, as he would be many times in 1937 and 1938, he would find his justification in "the people are with me." The popular vote apparently, however, meant something else to the voters as indicated by their quick and decisive turn from New Deal policies in Roosevelt's second term. In retrospect, the size of Roosevelt's victory in 1936 meant that voters were willing to support the New Deal as far as it had gone and prevent its being dismantled by Landon and the Republicans, but their conferral was far from a blank-check endorsement for the future.

It now appears, given the results of the second term, that the New Deal led a more precarious existence than contemporaries supposed because it was working against powerful historical and social currents. Even if one supposes that the Depression decade, Roosevelt, and the New Deal were all oversized, the liberal policies of the New Deal still represented aberrations from American traditions, destined to be challenged and diluted by the nation's long-standing values and institutions. The United States typically had a minimum government and provided its citizens with unexcelled personal freedoms, which ran counter to the New Deal's regulatory apparatus for industry and agriculture and its system of mass welfare supplied by public borrowing and taxes. Although American presidents in the twentieth century were, with few exceptions, strong presidents, no one had ever dominated the Congress so decisively as Roosevelt from 1933 to 1936; Congress could be counted on to reassert its authority under separation of powers. State's rights and local decision-making in government were also formidable traditions certain to be revived once the great danger of Depression and unemployment peaked and conditions improved, allowing smaller units of government to assume efficient responsibility.

Roosevelt's ability to lead so effectively in his first term was predicated on adversity. North Carolina Senator Josiah Bailey, a critic of Roosevelt, correctly declared, though with exaggeration, "Mr. Roosevelt belongs to that type of man who lives on hard times and discontent."[96] Roosevelt's confident leadership and caring were most effectively expressed at a time of great human need; that was also an optimal situation for him to formulate a strategy of favors to all groups, hence protecting all, including, of course, the poor and the wretched. As the economy improved in the period 1935 through the summer of 1937, and again after summer 1938, several groups became less dependent on the president's favor, appropriations, and patronage. The New Deal was a creation of hard times, and the successes of partial recovery magnified its weaknesses. Never a stable entity, Roosevelt's coalition began to collapse into its discordant elements.

Congress increasingly reflected controversies with the executive just as it mirrored cleavages between social groups that once worked in tandem with the New Deal; it was not a pushover for the president even in the first term, but in Roosevelt's second term the historic conflict between branches of government was fully resumed. By 1939, according to James T. Patterson, an anti-administration bloc existed in both houses of such size that it could stymie legislation. In each case, a shifting group of Democrats, largely from the South, joined Republicans to form the coalition. The Republican contribution was, of course, enhanced by the 1938 elections when they picked up eighty-one seats in the House and eight in the Senate. Some Republicans, convinced that Roosevelt sought a third term, were now especially adamant to reduce his eligibility by demonstrating his ineffectiveness with Congress.[97]

Congressional conservatism also received a big boost from rural representatives. Although they tended to work closely with the New Deal in the first term, once real farm prices were nearly restored in 1937 to 1929 levels, they demonstrated less interest in the broad issues of New Deal legislation and concentrated more on their own specific concerns. Thus, groups in the former coalition not only no longer cooperated, but they also began to engage in conflict.[98] Urban representatives of the Democratic Party, conversely, had their own specific agenda for the party programs. After the whopping vote for Roosevelt by northern blacks in 1936, this group declared for civil rights, especially anti-lynching legislation, bringing further discord to a party with one of its principal bases in the South.[99] Similarly, this group's support for additional relief spending, housing, and labor benefits met with little enthusiasm from Democrats from the South or the West. Unity could still be obtained "on the make-or-break issues"—national elections, relief spending, and public housing, and a diluted wage and hour legislation, the Fair Labor Standards Act, the last major New Deal measure to pass Congress (June) during the recession and election year 1938—but overall the New Deal was virtually immobilized or, in the description of Professor Leuchtenburg, "stalemated" by Republican opposition and Democrat's factionalism.[100] In

1939 Congress was actually attacking the New Deal, cutting its relief appropriations and rejecting the president's initiatives.[101]

The conservative reaction in Congress was facilitated because the New Deal and Roosevelt had suffered sharp drops in public esteem. Although America's history, with its emphasis on individualism and local and state's rights, prophesied ominously for the extended future of the New Deal and its leader, he had served the country well, a fact fully acknowledged in the election of 1936, and had built a storehouse of immediate favor. The rapid decline in public support in 1937 resulted from the president's ill-advised efforts to reform the Supreme Court, his seeming tolerance of sit-down strikers, and a simultaneous faltering in the national economy.[102]

If economic successes had unfortunate political consequences for the New Deal, resulting in discord among Democrats and a resurgent Republican Party as well as heightened concern over preserving traditional American freedoms, its economic failures in the late 1930s were also prescriptive. When Roosevelt was unable to prevent the sharp recession from the summer of 1937 though the summer of 1938, his credentials as hero and economic miracle worker were seriously impaired and the New Deal became an inviting target for growing numbers of the discontented. Roosevelt's decision to cut $2 billion in federal spending from WPA programs along with the removal of $2 billion more from the economy on behalf of Social Security in payroll taxes led to a sharp reduction in consumer spending and an increase of 2.5 million unemployed in 1938. Production levels in factories and farm prices, meanwhile, hovered temporarily in the vicinity of their numbers for 1933. The president was able to help restore the economy with a huge infusion of government spending backed by an anxious Congress concerned about the 1938 elections. He received $2 billion for spending for federal programs, and $1 billion for loans and put $2 billion more in circulation by employing gold reserves. In addition, Congress passed legislation providing $1.5 billion to business in RFC loans. By 1939, even before defense spending was a factor, recovery was evident, but the damage had already been inflicted on Roosevelt's reputation.[103]

Although American people from all classes polled in 1938 still liked Roosevelt as a person, fewer than half favored his economic goals, and Americans in both the lower middle and upper middle class were opposed, in sizable majorities, to his methods. Only blacks and the poor kept the faith on every question. In the summer of 1939, slightly less than half of Americans polled in a national survey declared they would vote again for Roosevelt.[104] Indeed, the polls suggest that he would not have been elected again in 1940 were it not for the desperate state of international affairs.

On March 4, 1935, General Hugh S. Johnson, ebullient head of the NRA, described the state of the country during the first days of the New Deal two years earlier as being "in a national gloom as deep as that of the days when Washington stood in the snow at Valley Forge."[105] One need only recall a few details of that time to conjure up grave possibilities. On the day of Franklin Roosevelt's nomination, March 4, 1933, almost all Americans had either lost a job, were working part-time, or knew someone who was doing one or another. Many had lost money, even life's savings, or were threatened with major losses from an apparently insolvent banking system. Nearly every adult had seen breadlines in public squares or responded to a panhandler or to a knock on the door by a person who was hungry. No one in a position of authority seemed to have an effective solution, least of all the president or the Congress. As the nation was emerging from its fifth winter of ever-deepening depression, its cherished traditions of democracy, capitalism, personal freedom, and middle-class dominance seemed to be in potential jeopardy.

Hugh Johnson's assessment of peril to America reflected his fears that demagogues Long and Coughlin were emerging from the wings with beguiling promises, appealing to Americans regardless of the cost for democracy. Although political parties on the left, whether communist, socialist, or labor, posed no serious threat to capitalism or personal freedom in 1933, it was realistic to wonder what would have happened if conditions worsened. In 1933, some middle-class Americans were already apprehensive about their future, given the possibility of class strife. Some poor Americans were then taking militant action against authority and property.[106] There were also signs of labor–management violence in the communist-inspired workers' march on Ford's Rouge River plant in March 1932, loss of life there and in public demonstrations, and rent evictions. Similarly, General Douglas MacArthur had described the Bonus Army in Washington in the summer of 1932 as animated by "the essence of revolution."[107]

It is impossible to identify a political figure better suited than Franklin Roosevelt to the task of providing stability at this critical time. His presidency was a fortunate one for the times; he radiated confidence, courage, and warmth mainly because these qualities were basic to his own personality. He was without peer in politics in his ability to communicate to the American people because he used the media with disarming skill. His personality was also especially suited to devise a coalition of interest groups, the best possible strategy both for preserving America's most important traditions, democracy and capitalism, and for creative innovation, the setting up of unprecedented relief and work-relief programs for the poor and failing. Business defected early from Roosevelt's all-America team, but workers and the fallen middle class experienced a deepened sense of American identity that precluded their radicalism.

Although New Deal programs protected Americans from starvation and undue suffering and fear and helped to keep alive their faith in American institutions, thereby exhibiting a remarkable degree of humane concern, they failed them in other critical areas. The New Deal was unable to overcome many economic effects of the Depression: numbers unemployed remained large; monies for work relief and relief were barely enough to hold persons or families together; and millions of Americans suffered as intensely in the late 1930s as they had in the first years of Roosevelt's presidency.

By Roosevelt's second term, the New Deal found itself in a situation of double jeopardy. It began to fail because it had succeeded and because it also made serious mistakes. Although thoroughly pro-capitalist, the New Deal's yoking of capitalism with welfare, its regulatory policies toward business, and support for labor all seemed at variance with the country's traditions. With a firmer rostrum, based on recovery, business attacked the New Deal and Roosevelt personally. Better economic conditions also dissolved an alliance of need between urban and rural interests. And across the country, once stability was assured, more and more Americans began to turn on the New Deal, even though they had been happy to accept its benefits earlier. The remarks of Catherine McNicol Stock about Dakotans might be repeated for countless Americans in all sections of the country when she wrote, "Even though they voted for Roosevelt in 1932 and 1936 and thought of his aid as a 'God-send,' most Dakotans never fully embraced the means and ends of the New Deal."[108]

How was it possible for President Roosevelt and the New Deal to neutralize the revolutionary potential of the times without dealing effectively with some of its major social problems? The answer is, of course, that conditions were never revolutionary. This, because Roosevelt did respond positively and effectively in many instances and also because the American people were then endowed with values and institutions that afforded unusual strengths to deal with serious social problems. Roosevelt's role in promoting confidence and hope by words and deeds cannot be minimized, but great strengths of the nation at this time lay in the social and cultural resources of its people. They demonstrated remarkable endurance and optimism even in that third of a nation that remained poor under the New Deal.

4

The American Scene

Despite the severity of the Depression and insufficient sums allocated by the government to allay public distress, the American people, as a whole, showed remarkable strength amid their adversities. An unusual array of useful indexes of national opinion—literary, photographic, artistic, and statistical—all verify that most Americans, even in their most difficult times, maintained essential confidence in themselves and the future of their country and its institutions. In a phrase, they continuously displayed hope.

We often speak of hope as a virtue or personal asset, but we also often minimize its dynamics and may therefore underestimate its salutary effects. For Americans in the Great Depression, it is the key that explains their positive outcomes, and it is therefore important to understand in general terms its psychological underpinning.[1]

Hope is described in a wide corpus of Western literature and experience from Greek myths to contemporary studies of mental health. When Zeus was angry with Prometheus for giving man the ability to make fire, heretofore an exclusive secret of the gods, he chose to punish not only Prometheus but also humankind. He commissioned Pandora to bring hideous things in her box and then unleash its contents to plague everyone's lives forever. And to assure that the effect would be devastating, he enjoined her to keep Hope out of the box. Men without hope would be desperate, and, Zeus apparently thought, deservingly so. Hope thus appears central to positive outcomes—or to reverse the time-tested cliché, "Where there is hope there is life" (i.e., good adaptive life). One group of psychologists noting hope's facilitating role in mental health have defined hope as a state of mind that results from the positive outcome "of ego strength, perceived family support, religion, education and economic assets." Still others have noted the therapeutic effects of hope in dealing with personal problems such as illness, alcohol treatment, taking examinations, and weight reduction.

Hope is more than a comforting abstraction. When present, it helps us with our life's course; it is, in effect, a "gifted understanding of our predicaments" that assumes thoughtful, positive outcomes. People with hope believe that good things will happen to them and are able when confronted with problems to use their energies constructively; indeed, they are likely to regard obstacles as challenges and attempt to find a variety of useful coping strategies. Instead of being flattened by temporary reversals, they find other ways to achieve their goals. Their very persistence tends to assure them a way. And by using their energies positively in pursuit of favorable results, they are likely to succeed and hence enhance both their sense of what they can do and stimulate their hopes for other favorable results in the future. One better understands the function of hope in the 1930s by considering the desperate plight of hopeless people, those bereft of energy to plan or maintain a viable strategy to find alternatives for what proved unfavorable. In extreme form they are suicidal, with lives made more effective only by the chemical equivalent of hope—the antidepressant.

Canvassings of the American scene—American opinion nationwide in the 1930s—came from several distinct groups of travelers. These included individual writers resolved to measure the impact of the Depression by observing its effects on Americans in cross-country trips and by employees of government agencies, fact finders for Harry Hopkins, or photographers and muralists who also traveled throughout the nation and reported directly or indirectly on the state of public morale to other New Deal agencies. Those reporting to Hopkins also provided bright, perceptive observations in letters that collectively amount to an overview of the country.[2] At the same time, photographers of the Resettlement Administration and the Farm Security Administration (FSA) pictured the country as a whole, producing over 60,000 prints and 200,000 additional negatives. Collectively, they render a description of the American scene with astounding and fruitful abundance and, when pieced together, constitute an imperfect though strikingly useful picture of the country at large. Still another symbolic picture of America and how Americans saw themselves developed in the post office murals painted in hundreds of its towns and cities by itinerant artists. Apparently, all these peripatetics were numerous and bothersome enough to force one gasoline attendant to print a card to defend himself. On that card he declared that he smoked a pack of cigarettes a day, liked beer and pork sausages and rice, as well as President Roosevelt, disliked Hitler, and regarded himself as being in the gas, not information business. Apparently, no circumstance of the Depression was as irritating to him as the time he had to spend with the varieties of intellectuals then conducting people surveys.[3]

Those traveling with pen or camera to report on Americans often witnessed people in distressing situations. Henry W. Francis wrote Harry Hopkins about conditions in West Virginia in 1934, "I have found worse living conditions and more cause for discontent than I have seen anywhere."[4] And Lorena Hickok was forced to fight tears when she asked a farmer in North Dakota in 1933 how he and his family were fixed for the winter, and he did not answer except for tears that he brushed away with the back of his hand. Her sense of living in the rural areas of South Dakota was foreboding.[5]

Yet, despite these conditions and many other reports just like them, those who traveled the country to investigate how Americans were doing discovered, almost disbelievingly, that their spirit was more positive than their circumstances. "I have heard amazingly little whining," Sherwood Anderson noted in summing up his experiences talking with Americans everywhere. So, too, radical authors Anna Louise Strong, John Spivak, and Maurice Hallgren found little upset among working people and the unemployed, surely not enough to justify a revolution.[6] Lorena Hickok, a supreme realist, is continually surprised by the stamina and pride of the Americans she meets. On her ten-day trip in Maine in 1933, the worst year of the Depression, she described the unemployed as "almost tragically patient" with "seldom any bitterness." In New York City where over 1 million people depended on an inefficient public assistance program, Hickok reported protests were reasonable.[7] In North Dakota, despite many needy people, she found no radical protest; she was told by the editor at the Fargo *Forum*, "I don't expect to see North Dakota farmers 'blowing up bridges' this winter."[8] Conditions in South Dakota's farming areas with similar farm problems and weather were no better. Hickok labeled the area "Siberia," but noted that most South Dakotans took conditions for granted.[9] And despite farm discontent, Hickok was convinced that Iowa and Nebraska were relatively quiet.[10]

In other areas of the country, her reports were nearly identical; Hickok, ever concerned about the degree of poverty she encountered, was continuously surprised by the relative composure, even good spirits, among the impoverished. In North Carolina, a displaced tenant farmer's family life was described by a sixteen-year-old daughter as "just going lower and lower." Nevertheless, the daughter wore a campaign button with a profile of President Roosevelt as a brooch.[11] In Nevada, where cattle prices were down as well as tourism, Hickok reported in 1934, "They don't seem to be the downcast lot you'd expect them to be" and in western Kansas, stricken with drought for three years by 1934, Hickok concluded that morale could best be summarized "But what optimists!" She found them skeptical of government-sponsored programs; "All we need is a little bit of rain!" they said.[12] Across the state line, Coloradans were inbred with the same nonchalance despite shoddy living quarters and widespread unemployment. When one young father there was asked how he could extract enough heat from burning cow chips as fuel, he reminded Hickok that he and his wife were "Short-grass" people and were accustomed to the problem. The "short-grass boy" left the veteran urban reporter talking to herself; she was forced to conclude, "Now what are you going to do with a guy like that?"[13]

She also found unflappable resilience among the unemployed once their lives were modestly bettered. When the CWA improved the lot of some unemployed in winter, 1933–1934, it paid workers with money rather than the grocery orders typical for those on home relief and also provided slightly more income. Yet Hickok noted how workers in Des Moines after being switched over to the CWA "greeted us with broad grins and a wave of the hand." She reported from Sioux City, Iowa, after the CWA began, "Everywhere I've gone in the last week the story has been the same. They are all most enthusiastic about the CWA." And from Minneapolis, she concluded, "You get a feeling of optimism all through the area."[14]

The experiences of Henry W. Francis in the mining towns of western Pennsylvania and West Virginia, one of the hardest hit areas in the country, corroborated those of Hickok. He recalled radio commentator Lowell Thomas's description of one of those communities, Scott's Run, as the "foulest cesspool of human misery this side of hell." What he found were attitudes quite different from those one might expect in such a place. Men coming off their shift in the mines (working two or three days, sometimes four) were "doing pretty fair they said and they actually laughed." And when he visited children at the playroom provided by the coal company that was supplied with milk, he concluded that Thomas had been in error because "the children felt they lived in a nice place." He continued, "The air was a bit thick about the bridge but, in spite of that, it carried the intangible chemistry of happiness and hope and, breathing that, the children felt no need to use their pretty clean handkerchiefs as they crossed the creek on the way home. I felt like waving mine."[15]

Further down in West Virginia coal country in Logan and Mingo Counties, Francis met people whom he was led to believe were angry, rebellious, and poverty-stricken. He was advised by a West Virginia relief worker, "They're bad and they're proud of it. If you don't believe they're bad they'll prove it to you. If they don't like you they'd just as soon shoot you as not. . . . And down in 'Bloody Mingo' it's worse still." But they proved positive and steadfast, Francis discovered, despite their reputation:

For six days I have been traveling in Logan and Mingo. . . . I have found worse living conditions and more cause for discontent than I have ever seen anywhere. But nowhere have I encountered hostility—even sullenness has been rare. . . . I leave Mingo amazed at the docility and capacity for suffering of most of these people who, I had always understood, were hot-headed and temperamentally given to unreasoning revolt.[16]

In Uniontown, Pennsylvania, Francis found the nadir of depression. Here sewage leaked into the town's creek, housing conditions were "unspeakable," and there were no prospects for work. Francis was so distraught by the needs of residents that he asked a half-dozen unemployed miners in a group what they wanted. He described their response:

There is a moment of puzzled silence. All regard me questioningly. One man says he needs underwear, another shoes and a torrent of requests for stove repair parts, bedding, sweaters, clothes for the children, etc. "What do you need most of all?" I ask. "Work," says Zosky [one of the miners]. "That's what we need most; work under living conditions, don't we, fellows?" The roar of approval which meets this is deafening and Mrs. Zosky, drawn from the little kitchen by her eagerness to confirm the general sentiment, says excitedly: "New Deal give man work; that's all; no want relief if get work."[17]

The colleagues of Hickok and Francis also sent reports to Hopkins that testified to the essential steadiness of America's unemployed.[18] Hazel Reavis, commenting on Youngstown, Ohio, a steelmaking city of 170,000 people with one-third of its work population on relief, noted, "However, morale is surprisingly good with patience and hopefulness in the ascendancy."[19] About Homestead, Pennsylvania, a center for Carnegie Steel where many workers received only one day's work a week, she observed, "The patience of those on relief and the others managing to get along somehow on drastically reduced earnings is very impressive."[20] Thomas Steep, reporting on conditions in Chicago, professed that attitudes among the unemployed were "bad," but he also noted that more than 5,000 applicants had lined up for 500 unadvertised job openings at Sears Roebuck; the unemployed in Chicago still responded hopefully to rumors concerning jobs.[21] Martha Gellhorn was confounded by the peaceable attitudes of destitute workers in South Carolina:

These men are faced by hunger and cold, by the prospect of becoming dependent beggars—in their own eyes: by the threat of homelessness, and their families dispersed. (What more a man can face, I don't know.) You would expect to find them maddened with fear; with hostility. . . . And I didn't find it. I found a kind of contained and quiet misery.[22]

Not only did Depression-era Americans maintain an upright spirit in the face of negative experiences, reporters and investigators also found that they retained their faith in individualism: some persisted in this uncompromisingly, despite bitter adversity; others finally accepted government intervention reluctantly, usually preserving a preference for work relief over the dole, but an overwhelming number, regardless of circumstances, continued to see themselves as self-reliant people who still had opportunities to achieve the "American Dream" of freedom and opportunity—this, after nearly a decade's battering from the Depression.

Observers frequently reported that Americans retained a personal responsibility for the success of their lives despite the paralyzing reality of mass unemployment. When James Rorty invited a hungry, young hitchhiker to dine with him, he declined. "Why?" Rorty asked himself. "Had I offended him? No, not at all. He wasn't really hungry; also he had never begged and didn't intend to begin. I spent ten minutes trying to persuade him."[23] Sherwood Anderson faced a more daunting prospect of unbridled individualism with a hitchhiker who professed that the poor in America would have to be exterminated by the well-to-do, even though that meant he would be one of the first to go. His reasoning: "You see I haven't succeeded. I don't believe I will ever succeed," and so "I might as well be put out of the way."[24] Almost as poignant, Lorena Hickok reported that a young woman in New Orleans, a former teacher with a college education living in reduced circumstances, informed her case worker not to bother to encourage her because she was not worth helping.[25]

Although many of the unemployed compromised their rigid self-help convictions when confronted with threats to survival, they remained reluctant to accept welfare until conditions became grave. Hickok found "a Maineite . . . would almost starve rather than ask for help."[26] When, in 1933, she visited Otter Tail County, in one of the most severe drought-stricken areas in central Minnesota, she was astonished to discover that the local relief committee didn't have their first meeting until just before her visit. As for Kansas farmers, "They didn't want to be rehabilitated."[27]

The white-collar middle class found the idea of being on relief especially repugnant, even when "dumb with misery."[28] In one instance in Birmingham, Alabama, a white-collar family, on the verge of collapse, had pawned the wife's engagement ring, jewelry, and the bulk of the husband's clothes; most of the time they were without enough to eat, the wife was ill and losing her teeth because of her poor diet, yet she continued to breast feed their seven-month infant because the family could not afford to buy milk. But Hickok found they had the will to persevere.[29]

By 1934, "the stigma of [being on] relief" was past in all but white-collar groups—it had become a fact of life; unemployed families became more and more dependent on relief and more insistent about having their checks on time.[30] As Lisa Wilson observed from talking with relief caseworkers in the Detroit area, "They cry the first time they ask for relief. By the third time they become demanding."[31] However, even this discrepancy with the work ethic can be exaggerated. One FERA commentator reasoned that home relief, though a dole, could be construed as self-help because recipients were able to gain dollars by convincing social workers that they deserved home relief, and yet they could still pick up odd jobs on the side for spending money.[32]

Reports by aides to Harry Hopkins also revealed, however, that most unemployed Americans preferred to obtain work relief rather than depend on the dole. In reporting on conditions in Gary, Indiana, Thomas Steep observed the large number of applicants for work-relief jobs.[33] "Home relief" he remarked, "meant staying at home, having nowhere else to go and could lead to quarrels with wives; husbands often appreciated work as a basis for both income and independence, and wives now often found their husbands whistling instead of quarreling."[34] "You can hardly appreciate it without having known them before," a county relief director informed Lorena Hickok. "They're off [home] relief now, and there is in them a new kind of independence and self-respect."[35] Based on discussions with relief workers, Wayne Parrish reported to Harry Hopkins that the percentage of white-collar people who preferred work relief to home relief in New York City was in the magnitude of 95 to 99%. The rate for the city overall, including all classes, he believed, was 80%.[36]

Pollsters also underscored the fact that most Americans, despite the effects of the Depression, continued to see themselves as individualists and their country as a land of opportunity. The basis for this conclusion may be found in two separate surveys of over 2,000 people by Elmo Roper for *Fortune* in 1939.[37] Roper's polls are especially diagnostic because they reveal popular attitudes about the responsibility of government to provide relief and jobs across the class spectrum including unemployed workers. Since the Roper polls asked about class self-identification, they also measure the degree of class consciousness of Americans after a decade of depression.

On Roper's queries regarding the government's responsibility to provide for those in need (including a minimum subsistence level, relief, and guarantee of job responsibilities) all classes registered approval (67% in composite), with the upper white-collar class least likely and the unemployed most likely (75%) to support the programs. On the defining question, "The government should confiscate wealth beyond what people need," a mere 6% of upper white-collar approved, but only 24% of employed workers agreed and, even more revealing, only 28% of the unemployed were in favor. The number favoring a complete change in the constitution was also very small, less than 10% of workers and 7% of the unemployed.[38] Clearly, even those workers who experienced the most severe consequences of the Depression were not very radical. When respondents were asked to identify themselves according to class, they confirmed conservative views; all classes saw themselves predominantly as middle class, including the unemployed with only 27% of the latter defining themselves as lower class. The fact that nearly 30% of the unemployed and 25% of the employed workers did not answer the question probably indicates that they considered themselves middle class in fact, fantasy, or potentiality. Less than 3% of all whites polled identified themselves both as working class and believing there was a basic conflict between management and labor, a perspective that could be construed as radical, or at least class-conscious. And this view was held by only 12% of employed workers and 10% of the unemployed.[39]

In contrast to these small numbers of potential alienates, an overwhelming number of respondents from all classes were optimistic about the future; they still perceived themselves in 1939 as either able to advance in the society or convinced that "their children will have a better opportunity than they." Among the employed working class, nearly two-thirds (64%) believed that "the future holds opportunity for advancement" and 76% saw their children as having a brighter future than their own. Among the unemployed those figures were, respectively, 45 and 64%.[40] Thus, the statistical data offer corroboration for evidence presented by the official and unofficial itinerants who traversed the country; despite the Depression, Americans preserved their historic values, especially confidence in democracy and opportunity for betterment in the future. Further evidence is displayed in the treasury of photographs and negatives taken principally in the 1930s by the Historical Section of the Farm Security Administration.[41]

The mission of the FSA's Historical Section, with its photographic unit headed by Roy E. Stryker, was to educate Americans about rural social problems. Or as Arthur Rothstein, an FSA photographer, later observed, "It was our job to document the problems of the Depression so that we could justify the New Deal legislation that was designed to alleviate them."[42] Dorothea Lange, one of the most gifted photographers with FSA, confirmed this point of view when she wrote Stryker in words he understood and wished to hear: "You are loaded for a really good photographic report, aimed at the place it counts most, Congress."[43] Stryker expanded the scope of FSA's photographs in 1938 from poor, rural America to the broader preservationist purpose of creating an authentic pictorial record of America, particularly rural and small-town America; the FSA's new focus became town scenes, courthouses, barber shops, parades, and so on.[44] This segment became the FSA's outstanding legacy for a study of the American people in the late Depression years.

Stryker operated a tiny kingdom within FSA, essentially a film lab, a darkroom, and control over eleven photographers, though seldom more than three at a time. Among them were Rothstein, Russell Lee, Ben Shahn, Marion Post Wolcott, and, in addition to Lange, the very talented Walker Evans. They were compensated from $2,300 to $3,200 per year for their work. Stryker supervised the group, suggesting locations and subjects, and then disseminated the photos to newspapers and magazines, including *Time* and *Fortune*, and to exhibits in New York City—one at the Museum of Modern Art—and on college and university campuses.[45]

Given the meliorist spirit of the FSA, one shared by all its photographers with the exception of Evans, it is not surprising that critics have raised questions about objectivity. Dorothea Lange's haunting "Migrant Mother" pictures her subject forlornly in a half-tent with three children clinging to her. It is a masterful depiction of human need and all the more so when one inspects the five other pictures Lange took of Florence Thompson. In these we learn that she has older children who might assist her and still other

Dorothea Lange, "Destitute Pea Picker in California, Migrant Mother of 6," 1936. A photograph of Florence Thompson with three of her children. She is often described as the "Migrant Madonna." Reproduced from the Collections of the Library of Congress.

children who are not so overwhelmed that they cannot smile.[46] Purists therefore object to the implied exaggerations of poverty in "Migrant Mother." Nevertheless, despite the obvious arrangement of this classic, were these not perilous moments when children might cling to their mother, especially then, just after the family was forced to sell its car's tires for provisions? Nor does Thompson's pensive concern for her family's future seem exaggerated. "Migrant Mother," though not literally correct, retains its value as an essential pictorial representation of the period.

Each FSA photographer also has a specific camera style representing his or her sense of reality and, of course, this also produces some photographic subjectivity. Evans provides clear pictures with hard lines and artistic order. He wishes to capture the essence of what he sees and avoid pedestrian aspects of objectivity. Although he adds nothing to his camera scene, he organizes the picture to give its clearest possible essence, not its accidental attributes. This is distortion for those who demand literal truth from the camera, but could be considered insight for those who seek a deeper meaning than surface description.[47] Those who have questioned the validity of FSA photographs, beginning with William Stott (1973), have served the best interests of scholarship by establishing that cameras are not scientific tools: people, after all, use them to take the pictures. In very recent revisionist scholarship, however, particularly that of James Curtis and Moren Stange, critics invest FSA photographers almost exclusively with negative and iconoclastic goals, and a "suspicious determinism" that discredits this vast collection despite the fact that it transports viewers into places where descriptive words have sometimes never gone or gone only clumsily.[48] It almost seems that the new criticism has turned the camera on the photographer, minimizing the value of the photographs. Walker Evans's love of form is supposedly superimposed on the lives of Alabama sharecroppers, yet how much could be altered or refined in Floyd Burrough's minimal house? Even if Evans placed a few objects in closer symmetry, he couldn't alter its essential poverty, its sparse furniture or mantelpiece, or bare look. That Evans allowed his subjects to preen for their photographs is also seen as producing distortions, yet he is actually picturing another reality; people having their pictures taken often wish to look attractive, especially if they have personal pride. Evans captured that attitude for posterity along with their meager household interiors. His "touch-up" irritates James Curtis, who believes that photographs of people off-guard are somehow more objective.[49] But Evans recognized an enduring quality in the Burroughs family. Their disciplined patterns of life and the plain workmanship of their household objects were consistent with wanting to make themselves presentable for the family picture—an insight that a mere amateur photographer might have overlooked. For Curtis, Dorothea Lange's search for adulation and publication possibly accounts for the fact that there were only three children appearing in "Migrant Mother," instead of the seven she had.[50] This, because Lange wished to seek favor with middle-class readers who had small families, though this conjecture is unsupported by evidence. She may have decided, however, for aesthetic reasons, that three frightened, dependent children in the scene were quite enough to convey the emotional intensity of her photograph. Curtis also ascribes Russell Lee's pictures of attractive, small American towns in the 1930s to Stryker's compensatory needs to prove that older America was not succumbing to commercialism and impersonality.[51] Yet, nearly half of Americans lived in these types of towns and, on this account alone, the motivation for Stryker's decision is amply justified.

FSA photographs, despite their limitations, usefully depict how Americans lived. Collectively, they record the experience of hundreds of thousands of persons and leave the viewer with an indelible sense of how they looked, what they did, and the kinds of people they were. Dorothea Lange's "Migrant Mother" has been reduced materially to a half-tent, but she gives the impression she is resourceful and will somehow survive and does. Lange's "Former Nebraska Farmer, Now a Migrant Farm Worker in Oregon" is similarly situated in what appears to be a tent with the starkest interior, but this young migrant sports a confident smile, a dapper pipe, and muscular shoulders on which his suspenders ride. He seems for the moment thoroughly content with his apportionment of life's opportunities as he sits on a narrow bench with arms folded. His pretty wife, wearing lipstick, is seated behind him looking directly and easily at Lange from a bed that appears to be the couple's only furniture.[52] The Burroughs' family, Alabama sharecroppers, with whom Walker Evans and James Agee lived for several weeks, led destitute lives with less than $100 cash income in the middle 1930s. Still, they wished Evans to photograph them in their best clothes, smiling, and with their arms around one another.[53] Although they lacked running water, they could be clean and they were proud.

Despite depicting the insecurities of the migrant life, the FSA photographs also instruct us about poor people's hopes and pleasures. The Okies en route to California found time after lunch for guitar playing and singing while seated on the ground near their car.[54] Migrant Indian blueberry pickers in Little Fords, Minnesota, play guitar and fiddle.[55] Mothers smile rapturously with their newborn in their arms in the most primitive and desolate surroundings.[56] A migrant farm family in Berrien County, Michigan, despite the difficulties of long trips to locate temporary employment, proudly proclaimed the value of another work site on a small auxiliary license plate. It declared, "Belle Glade [Florida] Her Soil Is Her Fortune."[57] The very poor often wear their "Sunday best" for photographers. A black tenant family of nine in Jefferson, Texas, poses for FSA photographer Russell Lee all neatly and cleanly dressed as they stand in their living room with newspaper-lined walls.[58] In Creek County, Oklahoma, another grossly impoverished area, black schoolchildren are dressed in their best clothes for school the day the photographer came.[59] An FSA borrower's family at Dead Ox Flat, Oregon, stands on the steps of its basement home in a finery of dress-suspenders, ties on the older boys, and girl in blouse and dress.[60] In the poorest circumstances there were tricycles and wagons for kids. Although families lived in trucks and tents as migrant berry pickers, children hugged and laughed.[61] Perhaps their pet dogs explain the smiles of little girls seated on old automobile seats in the sparse camps of agricultural laborers.[62] The daughter of a sharecropper in the wretchedly poor area of New Madrid County, Missouri, sits seemingly oblivious to her poor surroundings proudly holding her large doll.[63] In the dirt-poor lands of Lake of Woods, Minnesota, a farm boy presses his nose affectionately to that of his friendly collie.[64] Dogs supplied fun and good times regardless of the income of their owners.

Photographers from FSA who took these pictures retained vivid memories of those whom they photographed and confirmed that their subjects were indeed a strong and enduring lot. Jane Lee, the wife of Russell Lee, FSA's most prolific picture taker, recalled with Russell after all their travels, "a tremendous pride and tremendous courage among Americans." They met many people who didn't have anything "but seldom a person who really felt whipped." Dorothea Lange had compassionate feelings for her subjects who often appeared abject and hungry, yet she noted they invariably responded with "real courage, undeniable courage."[65] As photographer critic John Szarkowski observed, Lange's pictures are "primarily of people . . . of exceptional value, proud, and independent and competent, who are unlikely to ask for help, but who clearly deserve it."[66] Nor did the Americans photographed by Walker Evans fold in the face of the Depression. The director of the FSA's photographic division, Roy Stryker, came to the same conclusion after reviewing thousands of pictures from his photographers. "Many of the people [in these photographs] were sick, hungry and miserable," Stryker wrote, "the odds were against them. Yet their goodness and strength survived."[67] The subjects in these photographs had the same worn faces and torn clothes noticed by FERA investigators sent out by Harry Hopkins, but they also displayed the same wiry resiliency.

Clear evidence of positive attitudes across the nation is also illustrated in the more than 1,000 post office murals commissioned by the Section of Fine Arts of the Treasury Department in the 1930s.[68] The mural program for the nation was organized, with extensive participation by residents of each recipient community, and it therefore became an important symbolic statement of how Americans viewed themselves.

Muralists would vie to win competitive prizes to paint local post office murals, often $1,500 for a large mural, a handsome reward on the order of a year's creditable salary. They were obliged by the Section to express one of three themes: the postal service (seldom used), the local scene, or considerations of local history. Mural art as a genre usually has significant social meanings. Intended for large numbers of passers-by, it is likely to express— or at least aspires to express—public truths and values. The murals authorized and paid for by the Section were especially reflective of this because prospective muralists were cautioned to be conscious of "local interests, aspirations, and activities." Artists were advised to visit the community they were to depict and accept advice from its residents. Instructions read: "While the aesthetic quality of each completed design rests with the personal interpretation and ability of the artist, the content is determined by the community for which he is working." The finished mural is interwoven with positive and negative comments by local viewers as well as their letters and newspaper observations. Thus, the effect one finds on these diverse post office walls is how Americans perceived their history and how they saw themselves in the 1930s.[69]

When the murals spoke, what did they say? They described a winning people, healthy looking, muscular individuals, a country of husky shoulders working and achieving, forging new communities, then improving them, tending clean-looking farms with fields of abundant corn, cotton, or wheat. The people portrayed are never pathetic—indeed, they seldom lack dignity. Blacks are usually depicted in southern murals as productive workers, though rarely in the foreground. A few are represented as merely fun loving, playing banjos while others worked. Indians are strong and sage, but sometimes are depicted as menacing to the survival of families and communities. White men and women are depicted settling and farming—men doing the hard physical labor, while women were identified with the town or farm's abundance by its conservation.[70]

Another leitmotif of the murals was pride in community, communicating the sense that a great latent strength existed in each community that assured its future progress. This pride was not based merely on standards of material growth and plenty. The murals often highlighted a spiritual inspiration at some critical moment in the community's evolution, perhaps even the implication that its subjects were collectively a covenanted people.

When Elizabeth Terrell submitted a design for the post office at Conyers, Georgia, and residents discovered its contents, they were "outraged." Not only had it been submitted earlier in the competition for a town in Kansas, it depicted a farmer using horses instead of the mules customary in Conyers, but, even worse, the farmer was plowing without regard for the contour of the land. Since people in Conyers were "rather proud" of the fact that "they originated the idea of terracing of fields with the contour of land," in their area they felt cheated of their claim to fame. The mural illustrated that Conyers was a special place.[71]

Seventy prominent residents of Amory, Mississippi, gave a reception for the muralist who completed their post office tableau because he had harkened to their advice and presented their town as they wished it to look in 1888. The scene shows a locomotive passing some distance behind citizens on the main street, perhaps a reminder that prosperity depended on the railroad. The mural also sends a message to everyone that responsible citizens then as now still hold the key to the community's future. A group of leading citizens have drawn guns on a man who has just stepped off the train, warning him to depart. A sign behind them reads "Amory wants no yellow fever. STRANGERS KEEP OUT."[72] These townsmen were protecting their city from epidemics that then ravaged the South. The mural extolled the optimistic faith of Amory townsmen who apparently believed their town would progress in the future as in the past with a healthy economy and vigilant leaders.

The mural for Granville, Ohio, provided a more complicated explanation for progress. Wendell Jones completed *First Pulpit in Granville* for the local post office in 1938. Jones originally intended to depict the founding of Granville, in central Ohio in 1805, by a band of Presbyterian pioneers from Massachusetts. His first design pictured members of the church amid natural abundance, as if a tribute to faith and hard work. When he heard from a local history buff that a Welsh pioneer, Theophilus Rees, was living in a distant area of the township even before the Massachusetts settlers arrived in Granville and that he had chanced upon their first service and had worshipped with them in a language he could not understand, Jones modified the mural to include Rees. This completed a sensitive statement about the genesis of Granville and provided residents with a cherished recollection of their special resources as a community. The final mural is laden with images of abundance, fat babies, lush vegetation, a plump turkey, and the Welsh settler peering from the upper left corner, a party to the scene's abundance and, most important, a participant in its brotherhood. Wendell Jones consciously recognized the message disseminated by his mural: "The brotherhood of man can weather another storm." That message was readily accepted by residents who recognized that they controlled their destiny if they remained faithful to their early principles.[73]

Conversely, there is a striking absence of pessimism in the murals. One that depicted the effects of a mine disaster on workers in Kellogg, Idaho, was explicitly rejected by residents as too pessimistic and was withdrawn.[74] And when Stefan Hirsch, from Bennington, Vermont, submitted a mural for Aiken, South Carolina, depicting a dark-skinned woman as the goddess of justice, and an aroused citizenry could not convince the Section to remove it on the grounds it was negative and critical of their way of life, they put up a curtain over the mural and simply refused to unveil it again.[75] When it came to historical motifs, Americans overwhelmingly preferred to depict their communities as demonstrating the great and ongoing potentialities of their people.

Another large cluster of mural paintings even more explicitly heralded the role of America's boundless technology in the country's continuous progress.[76] It was the train that made possible Amory's prosperity in 1888, evidenced by the fine ladies cavorting on the town's main street, the steamboat's arrival that produced the joyous dance on the docks in Grand

Rapids, Minnesota, on the upper Mississippi, and the steamboat a propelling factor in the growth and affluence of Poughkeepsie, New York, on the Hudson River. The latter mural, a five-part historical layout, was installed in Poughkeepsie's post office between 1937 and 1940. It was an especially generous mural because Franklin Roosevelt, himself a resident of Dutchess County, took an unusual interest in the project. Karal Marling, perhaps the foremost student of the iconography of post office murals, concluded "Depression America believed passionately in a verifiable, usable past of happiness and plenty, and in a future that would once again fulfill the primal needs of the forgotten man."[77]

Those who explored the American scene in the 1930s also noted the strong attachments of Americans for their country and president. Their sense of America as unique or especially endowed and led by a caring and courageous head of state constituted important additional reasons for their optimism. It also explains, of course, why protest movements, let alone revolutionary forces, seldom attracted numbers of people even in those perilous times.

Many Americans were unabashed president and country-worshippers. They often referred to the United States in exalted terms, though nonchalantly ("this great country of ours," "our great and noble nation," "our beloved country," "our great nation," "the greatest nation," etc.) as if these descriptions were so indisputable as to require no qualification. The same letters, sampled at random in the Roosevelt Library, show that this confidence was dramatically strengthened by the new president especially in his first term.

The way you stand for our great nation.

God's President of God's country.[78]

Dear Mr. President, we are with you 100%. We love our country, we love you. We have confidence in our country we have in you.

. . . your sincerity and call to action have renewed my confidence in the future of this country, have increased my courage in facing the present, and have prompted me to pen this letter to you.[79]

Though I am on the borderline of destitution and loss of self respect, your speech has imbued me with a desire to hold on and keep faith.[80]

I add my own thanks and congratulations to the man who has revived the old American spirit.[81]

You have once more talked to us, as you always do with faith renewed in God and country. It helps us much to do likewise.[82]

While listening to your heartening and inspiring talk over the radio this evening [April 28, 1935] I often looked up at a small American flag which our children have put up in the living room. Whenever I looked at the flag, I instinctively had more confidence in the future and in our country than before.[83]

And from immigrants:

Proud I am indeed to be an American citizen yet more happier my beloved adopted country is led by an American like you—(The English is poor I know but I want to write from my heart myself).[84]

From a recent immigrant:

I want to thank you for your wonderful speech in Philadelphia [June 27, 1936]. I came to America as a German-Jewish immigrant in December 1935, and am proud now to live in a country the government of which stands not only for the good of the whole nation but also for human civilization in the world.[85]

   This love of country is also evident in FSA photography. Numerous pictures from that collection show how patriotic symbols and ceremonies characterized the lives of Americans in towns and cities. War memorials dotted the landscape usually in or near town squares. Parades were an important feature of civic life invariably led by flag bearers with "Old Glory." As the flags passed in Cincinnati's sesquicentennial parade in 1938, young men watching are at attention, with arms held firmly to their sides. Spectators of all kinds massed for that parade—men, women, and children, blacks and whites.[86] The American Legion, then mostly made up of men in their vigorous thirties and forties, marched in many parades, particularly on Armistice Day. A photograph of their parade in Omaha, Nebraska, shows thick crowds attending, including some watchers on rooftops to get a better view.[87] The state commander of the American Legion, along with "the colors" and many large American flags, were also in the vanguard for the celebration of state fairs.[88] And flags were, of course, a feature of Fourth of July celebrations in parades, the town square, storefronts, and on grounds and porches of homes.[89] The flag's prominent place in schools underscores the classroom's auxiliary function to promote patriotism.[90]

   Since submitting pictures to illustrate patriotism was not a primary goal of FSA photographers, one must infer the depth of that sentiment by its unexpected symbolic presence often in the lodgings of the very poor. The Scarborough family, with its eight children, sit in a sparsely furnished room near Laurel, Mississippi, in 1939, under two small American flags.[91] An enlarged painted copy of a letter from President Roosevelt to a local citizen was publicly displayed in the town of Port Gibson, Mississippi.[92] In New Madrid County, Missouri, the only embellishments of a tenant family shack in this cotton-growing area were family pictures, a Bible, and a sketch of the first president. A photograph of the interior of a modest house in Warner, Oklahoma, revealed a quilt made of American flags.[93]

National statistics round out a more sanguine picture of the American scene by the mid-years of the Great Depression. These demonstrate, for example, that Americans lived longer in the 1930s than the 1920s; life expectancy in 1929 was only 57.1 years—in 1939 it had reached 63.7 years.[94] Dramatic gains were also recorded in the 1930s in the fetal death ratio, infant mortality, and maternal mortality rates, and spectacular gains in the survival rates of infants under one year of age.[95] Although such improvements reflected advances in medical knowledge and practices, particularly combating epidemics, they also resulted from better access to physicians both from expanded national health care programs provided by the New Deal and increased personal health care expenditures, most notably after 1935.[96]

Nutrition experts probably also had a hand in the improving health of Americans. Comparative figures from a Bureau of Labor study with persons of identical incomes in twenty-seven cities revealed that there was a larger per capita consumption of milk, oranges, lettuce, spinach, and canned tomatoes "in every one of these 27 cities" in 1934–1936 than in 1917–1919.[97] Americans from 1935 to 1939 consumed more than ten pounds more grapefruits, oranges, and lemons per capita than in the 1920s, more than fifteen times the amount of fruit juices, and twice the amount of frozen foods and juices.[98]

There were still other reasons the 1930s stood for progress as statistics demonstrated. Young people were more likely to remain in school and to graduate from high school and college than in any decade in the American history. Numbers of students and graduates in high schools nearly doubled and numbers of college students greatly exceeded those of the more prosperous 1920s.[99] Much of this came from reduced options, some from the guidance of the National Youth Administration. At the same time, new book publications by 1936 outnumbered those for 1928 and 1929 as did newspaper circulation and the average number of conversations on the local exchange of the Bell system.[100] Meanwhile, the town and city street scenes, day and night, were filled with parked automobiles.[101]

Even though the 1920s are sometimes described as the "Age of the Automobile," the title in some ways applies more fittingly to its successor. Although new car sales in 1925–1929 averaged 3.3 million to only 2.8 million sold on average from 1931–1938, when used cars sold every year are added, the totals are almost identical.[102] Lorena Hickok noted that, despite the drought in Kansas in 1934, the crowds packed the fairgrounds of the Kansas State Fair in Topeka and observed: "You never saw so many new Chevrolets in your life."[103] Automobile registrations during the Depression period far exceeded counts for the 1920s (in 1939, 26 million cars were registered, doubling the number for 1924). Similarly, the 1930s posted larger numbers for miles of surface road, miles traveled by cars, auto operating expenses, and filling-station sales. People traveled by automobile during the early years of the Depression nearly as much as previously and by 1935 through the remaining years of the 1930s much more than comparable years in the 1920s. In 1935, Americans were already spending more on vacation travel by car than 1929, the banner year of prosperity.[104] Lorena Hickok commented on tourism in Florida in 1934, "The streets of Miami are a mess what with hundreds of out of state automobiles," and Marion Post Wolcott's photos of Miami in April 1939, with its sunbathers asleep in deck chairs on the beach and the large crowds at Hialeah race course with women cashing tickets at the five-dollar window, illustrate Miami's ongoing appeal for the period.[105] Since little was spent on railroads or air travel for vacation travel, cars were responsible for the new travel experience.

Cars also supplied enthusiastic customers for the boomlet in spectator sports after 1935. The 1920s have been eulogized as the "Golden Age of American Sports," celebrated for its crowds and performers and deservingly so for Babe Ruth, Jack Dempsey, Red Grange, and Bill Tilden, but fans at sporting events in 1938 doubled their number when compared with the turnout in 1925, and were nearly a third more numerous than those who attended in 1929, the peak year for sports in the 1920s.[106] Apparently Joe DiMaggio, Joe Louis, Nile Kinnick, and Don Budge also brought out the crowds. World Series attendance between 1925 and 1929 averaged less than comparable years in the 1930s, and, despite the explosive quality of the 1927 Yanks and their unquestioned appeal to the fans, the 77,000 who attended a doubleheader between the Detroit Tigers and the Yankees, August 14, 1934, broke the attendance record at Yankee Stadium while an additional 20,000 had to be turned away. A reporter on the scene quickly spotted the automobile jam that accompanied the crowd as it tried to enter the lower Bronx for the game. "For the first time, too, automobile traffic got itself hopelessly entangled as every inch of the usually ample parking space about the arena was exhausted long before game time."[107] For some, the great games seemed to take precedence over conversations about social problems as James Rorty acknowledged when he found in California a lad from Michigan who, "tormented me with his frantic longing to get to Los Angeles to see the Southern California–Notre Dame football game."[108]

The ubiquitous car of the 1930s also triggered an enormous rise in movie attendance since most movie houses were in the downtowns of towns and cities. Moviegoers, like purchasers of electrical appliances, exploited Depression prices. By 1935, they were attending in numbers that compared with the best years of the 1920s. Thereafter they exceeded those numbers by a wide margin every year.

The shocking and hurtful economic conditions of the 1930s prompted many thoughtful Americans, including numerous workers for New Deal agencies, to survey its effects on the American people. More than at any previous time in the country's history they were questioned, polled, pictured, and painted in community after community. These reports are impressively thorough: numerous traveling journalists and writers wrote descriptions of their search and findings; hundreds of reports from all parts of the country were forthcoming from discerning legates of government. National polls were widely employed to corroborate these findings. Our understanding of how Americans responded to the times is also greatly enhanced by visual materials—over 60,000 FSA photographs and more than 1,000 post office murals. It is this juxtaposition of words, numbers, and pictures that makes these surveys so cogent because their findings are virtually identical.

The statistics on unemployment, even after 1935 when life was improving, remain grim. Many Americans were hurting and living miserably, and many more experiencing insecurity. What is surprising is the unanimous testimony of these varied sources, illustrating how even-tempered and confident Americans remained during their Depression decade. Some of the reasons for this anomaly surfaced in these national surveys. Based on their country's and their community's sterling achievements in the past, the broad masses of the American people retained their confidence in the future despite troublous times. They were mindful that they had succeeded far better in America than they or their families had anywhere else, and they assumed this would be true of the future as well. Although often discouraged, they almost never felt downtrodden. The presence of a solicitous, compassionate president determined to improve the fate of the "forgotten man" also helped to sustain those who might otherwise have wavered, especially in President Roosevelt's first term, and the slow but perceptible growth in the economy and gradual improvements in the standard of living helped thereafter.

Overall, however, the benefits from an exploration of the national scene are more descriptive than analytical; we learn that Americans did not despair or defect from the American Dream, yet we do not fully learn why. Beneath their faith and hope in the future of their country was a projection of the faith and hope they had in themselves. Granted that America's positive national historical experience bolstered self-esteem and personal prospects of individual Americans, the opposite was also true—a confident people was predisposed to believe in the future of their country. Ultimately, it was because Americans of the 1930s still lived their daily lives in a network of inspiring precedents, institutions, and values that they could find psychological and characterological resources to cope with their predicament. This cumulative effect of their confidence in themselves contributed importantly to America's smooth landing in the Depression.

5

Small Worlds Sustained

That those living on farms, in small towns, and county seats embedded in farming areas were relatively calm in the 1930s was one of the most impressive findings of the investigators of the Depression's reverberations across the nation. Although feeling the effects of the Depression, sometimes even dependent on garden produce and small business sales of farm women for butter, eggs, and poultry, rural Americans generally managed, despite uneven New Deal benefits, to maintain themselves without radicalism or cries of desperation.[1] Since nearly one-half of Americans (49.1%) still lived in communities of less than 8,000 in 1930, with 45% living in rural territory (less than 2,500), their number is critically important in explaining the response of Americans to the Depression. Yet, we have not effectively credited this information.[2] Perhaps the impression of declining rural life in the twentieth century is so pervasive that we underestimate its ongoing strengths. Rapid growth in American cities since the 1930s and the consequent urban domination of rural life may have confirmed our misunderstandings. There is also no denying the formidable challenges that threatened the integrity of rural life in the 1930s: the depopulation of rural villages, increasing impingement of national culture on rural small-town life, or growing restiveness among rural youth. It is historically correct, however, to acknowledge rural culture's formidable residual strengths in the 1930s as well. These included values and practices so integral to rural life that they helped sustain its people during the Depression and thereby contributed importantly to the equanimity of the nation.

Farm families and persons and their suppliers in nearby rural communities in the 1930s lived quite differently from their predecessors a generation earlier. In 1900, farmers spent more time at home or with farm neighbors than in villages or towns because of problems of access with buggies or teams of horses, though their limited public information did come mostly from the town's small newspaper or conversations with local shopkeepers. Together, the farmers and their mutually dependent villagers or townsmen, who provided farmers with markets, goods, and information, constituted close-knit "island communities." With the advent of automobiles, movies, and newspapers with national and international wire services and abundant use of photography, typical of the period 1900 to 1930, farmers' relationships with their nucleated villages and towns changed significantly. Farm families were still attached to their original "hometown" economically and psychologically, but they were also willing to embark on island hopping for specialized consumer goods and unique services if these were more amply or more cheaply provided in another community. Irwin, Iowa, a rural hamlet at the turn of the century, sixty miles from Omaha, Nebraska, made the necessary adjustments and remained the town center for its rural population in the 1930s. A veteran student of rural life and one-time resident described its effective transition: "The Irwin Village has a population of 345, but it serves a thousand members of farm families who live around it. They buy in Irwin. They sell in Irwin. They attend school, church, and lodge there, plus dances, movies and other community activities. They visit in Irwin and loaf there when they have time."[3]

Many small communities could not adjust. "Possum Trots," often the smallest and once most convenient of old-time places, began to disappear in the 1930s, leaving only memories and a few old people who had no place to go. One man was left to mourn the effective demise, even anonymity, of his home community where all four of his grandparents were buried. This community in the vicinity of Anniston, Alabama, "was located near such rural points, past or present, as Angel, Webster's Chapel, Hopewell, Ball Play, Bold Hornet, and Rabbittown."[4]

Rural villages (population 250 to 2,500) and small cities (over 2,500) in rural areas were more likely to survive, especially those with automobile services and sales, specialty stores, consolidated schools, and appealing ministers. The county seat, with myriad governmental services as well as numerous stores and possibly moving pictures, attracted special attention from farmers who could regularly be seen there on Saturdays in the vicinity of the courthouse. Meanwhile, the country store was being bypassed and small chain stores were making their appearance in the villages. By 1940, "going to town" was no longer a big experience for farmers and their families; visits on Wednesday and Saturday nights were becoming customary.[5] At the same time, farmers began to shop for specialized goods and services in larger towns and even cities. One commentator's description of residents of "Plainville," a community of 300 in the Ozarks in the late 1930s, can be readily duplicated by students of other rural communities. He observed:

Arthur Rothstein, "Saturday Night, Main Street Iowa Falls, Iowa," 1939. Reproduced from the Collections of the Library of Congress.

But Plainvillers also "go outside" nowadays. They go to "X," a county seat of 1,000 inhabitants, situated thirty miles north of Plainville, on the gravel road which runs through Woodland County. They go still more often to "Y," another county seat about the same distance south, likewise "on the gravel." The population of "Y" is 2,600. At both "X" and "Y" there are modern movies, chain stores, and larger stocks of merchandise of all kinds than in any of the home towns. For really important purchases, entertainment, or medical care, Plainvillers often travel to Largetown, a regional metropolis of 60,000 people in the hills seventy miles south; or even to Metropolis itself, an important Midwestern city with a population of nearly half a million.[6]

In some rural communities such as Sublette, Kansas, persons felt so expansive as to define their locality as being 100 miles in diameter. A rural sociologist who carefully studied Sublette in 1939 described the freedom of farmers to choose from villages, towns, and cities "as not unlike that of the urban shopper."[7] Whereas the unique qualities of earlier rural life had been strengthened by its isolation, this expansion of living area and experience diluted neighboring, as well as the constraints of a watchful home community, formerly key ingredients in rural life.

The depopulation of farms and hamlets with many of its residents, especially its youth, preferring towns and cities also threatened the traditional integrity and vitality of rural life. Migration of surplus population from rural areas to cities typified American life in the twentieth century, but in the 1930s the phenomenon was quickened by New Deal policies, large numbers of children in farm families, increasing mechanization of farm work, and, of course, depressed economic conditions on American farms then extending for a second decade.[8] In better times, farm parents might have helped a second or even third son make a down payment for a farm of his own. But in the 1930s conditions were such that parents were more likely to provide merely a mortgaged farm to only one child who would then be responsible for their care when they were old.[9] Other children had almost no hope for an inheritance in farmland. In Irwin, in Shelby County, Iowa, the majority of parents were able to pass on only a few farm implements and household goods. This poverty probably explains why more than half of Irwin's high school graduates moved out of Irwin in the 1930s. In the Dakotas in the 1930s, "Youth turned away from agrarianism and small town life at a rate even higher than their parent's generation." In Sublette, Kansas, only one of the forty-three male graduates of the high school between 1936 and 1939 was farming for himself, though eleven were still at home working on the family farm. In the hilly, northern New Hampshire community of Landaff where returns for farming, largely dairy farming, were marginal, it was assumed that young people would leave for the city; they were rewarded with praise by the community for their initiative even though their migration weakened family and community solidarity.[10]

One feature of young people's migration from farm areas was the departure of many of its marriageable women. Young farm women who sought independent income were forced to leave rural communities where men were mostly responsible for cash earnings unless they found scarce jobs at home such as teaching or nursing. Nearly half of the female graduates of Sublette High School in Haskell County, Kansas, between 1920 and 1935 were residing outside that county in 1939, while only 20% of the 102 female graduates were married and residing there. Similar patterns were noted in Boone County, Nebraska, especially where educated young women were concerned.[11]

The increasing use of farm machinery expedited these processes. Mechanization of agriculture accelerated in the Midwest in the 1920s and 1930s and began to make inroads in the South where it is estimated that as many as one-third of that region's farm operators gave up farming because they could not afford new agricultural machinery, mainly the tractor. Special impetus to depopulation and further mechanization there also came from subsidies to farm owners under the New Deal's AAA crop reduction and soil erosion programs. Some owners invested their federal subsidies in tractors to rid themselves of their sharecroppers; they substituted hired hands when needed, thereby saving year-round maintenance costs of the croppers and the feed required for their mules. Midwest farmers relied even more heavily on machinery, using only occasional outside help from neighboring farmers or hired labor. They dispensed with their former help, in this case often members of their own families, for whom there was insufficient work to stay on their family farm.[12]

Popular culture coming from Hollywood and media from the big cities, available in a variety of forms and in various degrees in rural areas, also appeared to weaken ties in rural communities. Whereas faster and more efficient automobile travel provided opportunities for country folk to learn about cities firsthand, urban-based entertainment and information also began to saturate rural America even for stay-at-homes. For rural persons in the vicinity of Brattleboro, Vermont, in the summer of 1936, Toto's Zepplin promised "Dancing to Dawn" while Wingy Manone offered "to swing" with his band in a nearby roadhouse.[13] Small towns and cities featured the current sensational films. *The Daily Gazette* in Augusta, Kansas (population 4,000), advertised *George White's Scandals* for its silver screen, and Sycamore, Illinois, ran an ad for Clara Bow in *Hoopla* that declared, "She has what it takes to get what she wants," with Clara dancing provocatively in the corner of the advertisement.[14] "Pinups" made their way into country stores while small-town drugstores displayed such titles in their magazine racks as, "Parisian Snapshots," "Spicy," "Allure," and "Silk Stockings."[15] Miss America contestants were also being selected in small rural towns and paraded for the local newspaper photographer in bathing suits.[16]

The most important effect of the car and new forms of entertainment, dancing especially, was that more young people made private choices about their lives, outside their families and without the supervision of chaperones. Although parents in "Plainville" continued to plant persons who would report on recreations of teenagers, they agreed it was hard to restrain them once they were "at the sparking age." One resident declared, "Nowadays, it is the age when girls like to read love stories and see them fool movies, and boys like to see just how fer and how fast they can drive."[17] In Irwin, Iowa, young people justified their interest in dancing on the grounds that, if they didn't dance, they would be unable to enjoy the company of other young people, and so they were known to drive fifty or seventy-five miles to attend a dance and return very late to their community. In at least one small rural community, Indianola, Mississippi, the outcome for youth seemed explicitly transformed. Hortense Powdermaker reported, "Much of what they do and say is modeled after what they see in movies and read about in popular fiction magazines. Their world view was made in the city rather than from parents and the example of persons in their home town."[18]

The aggregate effects of these significant social changes in rural areas—a more open neighborhood, depopulation and a partial urbanization of rural cultural patterns—convey the impression that older values and attitudes in country areas were sliding into oblivion. Closer inspection reveals, however, that people in these small worlds were able to sustain important features of their older ways even as these were being gradually transformed. This was even true for many rural youth, seemingly consumed in media culture. In some rural communities, dancing and drinking were frowned on, with the drugstore remaining the center for socialization. Again, farm and small rural town youth often did not have the money to attend movies or dances—the monies available had to come from the "family purse" at a time when what was considered frivolous was unacceptable. Movies, unlike radio, invited individual choice instead of family group entertainment, but families in rural communities often attended movies together as part of their trip to town. Or if young people went with peers, they were in the company of friends from identical rural backgrounds, which shielded the group from the cinema's modernizing features. Furthermore, not all media served to destabilize rural patterns. Radio had a distinct homey touch in the 1930s. Family members on farms and in the rural towns still spent a great deal of time listening to programs together. Moral standards were surely not compromised when millworkers, usually with rural backgrounds, in Gastonia, North Carolina, petitioned their company to begin work fifteen minutes earlier so they could be home to hear *Amos 'n' Andy*.[19]

An "apprenticeship for life" was the way one gifted participant described the effects of rural family life on those who were raised on farms.[20] Surely, it was a vital educational experience for young people because it typically fostered expectations for hard work, self-control, cooperation with others, and modest personal gains.

Overwhelmingly, most farms in the 1930s were family farms where parents could still effectively transmit their heritage to a younger generation.[21] The farm family's residence was a center for joint enterprise of all its members, except only small children. Unlike most urban families where fathers left home to work and often found their job foreign to the activities and even interests of other members of the family when they returned home at night, members of farm families worked together in full view of one another. The situation was unparalleled for educational advantages; working beside their children afforded parents opportunities for continuous instruction of children through example as well as precept. Furthermore, farm families were stable, assuring continuity in message, at least until some of the children decided as young adults to leave farm life for the city. Married farm women were much less inclined to divorce than their urban sisters. Those widowed or divorced, twenty years and over, were only 11.2% of the rural farm population, but 16.2% in the urban population.[22] The fact that many children raised on farms lived there throughout their childhood also strengthened the meaning of their parents' teachings. Harry Crews testifies from the background of his rural raising in Bacon County, Georgia, to the importance of "the home place for farm youth." For Crews it was "that single house where you were born, where you lived out your childhood, where you grew into young manhood . . . your anchor in the world."[23] To be sure, even though farmers were now traveling more by car, with their visits once or twice a week to town, they still lived the rest of the time on a relatively isolated farm. As one young woman described the situation in rural Nebraska, "We only went to town to get the groceries we needed. That's all. Then we stayed home. . . . Dad wanted me out in the field."[24]

The continuing relative isolation of farm life assured that parents and children would be less influenced by peer and national culture than young people in cities. Officials from the Department of Agriculture noted numerous activities shared by family members in Shelby County, Iowa: "Family customs and events such as taking meals together, holding family prayers, reunions, weddings, funerals, picnics, festivals, letter writing, and inheritance are important parts of associate patterns within Irwin families. Family mealtimes are definitely set and all members are expected to be present when the meal is blessed on the table." Young people were also frequently at home in the evenings. As late as the 1930s, dating between young men and women was still largely an urban institution. Even at ages eighteen to twenty, most young women in rural New York were not dating on a consistent basis. And in a rural Kansas high school, boys and girls still went to the movies separately in groups, their social lives seldom including the other sex.[25]

Hard work with its implications for the responsibility of each person for the welfare of the family group remained the norm of farm life in the 1930s and was probably the most important lesson children learned there. The workday for sharecroppers in the Cotton South was "good sun till good dark"; the farm family was already positioned to work by the time they could see and only departing after they could no longer do so. When a farmer in New England didn't need to work hard for his own survival and that of his family, he still felt obliged to do so to win respectability from his neighbors. A typical workday there began before breakfast at 5:30 A.M. and ended at 8:00 P.M. unless additional work was required to keep the books or repair a harness. In Landaff, New Hampshire, in the late 1930s, "Hard work and thrift are [were] considered basic virtues" because "they have always been essential to the life of the community." In the Dakotas work was considered the "core of the moral life" by farmers and the villagers with whom they traded. In Iowa, farm work was more seasonal with high work points during plowing and threshing and corn picking, but "the kind of farming we do here" explained a young farmer, "is a long hard job. We're never through." "And in June" another farmer there observed, "we want to drive ahead and get things done; we get keyed up going to the field just like athletes do before a big game."[26]

One of the most engaging descriptions of the work life of parents as farmers and its effects on their children comes from James Hearst, a young farmer raised near Cedar Falls, Iowa, in the 1920s and 1930s.

We boys were mother's "hired men," helping weed and pick and carry in all the vegetables and fruit needed for a family of six, eight, ten—depending on the number of hired girls and hired men that lived with us. No one ever went hungry, but almost everyone complained of the work necessary to bring the produce to cellar and bin. It was an autumn of discontent and a winter of fulfillment. . . . Granted, father worked hard—put in long days of labor, taught us patiently how to harness a horse, milk a cow, help a sow deliver her pigs—but he vanished into the barn before the threat of helping around the house. Mother depended on her children—and a hired girl, when she had one—for help.

About the boys and their work on the farm, Hearst recalled:

We might complain, but we did what had to be done. As soon as we were old enough, my brother Bob and I graduated to barn and farm work. We milked cows, fed the pigs, carried corn, and threw down hay. But so did all the other boys in the neighborhood. We just followed farm custom.[27]

"Hard work" was also a "basic virtue" in the cotton and dairy farming community of Harmony in Putnam County, Georgia. A government official who studied the community underscored that "most of them (farmers) have worked hard, long hours from light to dark." And the same could be said for the Amish farmers in the vicinity of Lancaster, Pennsylvania, where occasional visiting was "the only approved leisure activity." Although mechanized wheat farming in the Midwest confined intensive labor to the summer and fall, it also led to reliance on the farmer's family as a workforce and to the farmer's seeking outside employment when he was not working his own farm.[28]

For families accustomed to working together and working unremittingly, the Great Depression accentuated needs for cooperation. James Hearst recalled the response of his Iowa farm family:

By 1930 our family reached out all its hands to stay alive. We knew we had the muscle and we proved it. Father took a job with the Farm Bureau (he was President of the Iowa Farm Bureau for 13 years) and his paycheck helped bolster the bank balance. My sister, Louise, taught school and her check, when she got one—during the Depression school teachers were not paid regularly—went to the same place. Mother made cottage cheese and sold it and eggs to the Blue Bird restaurant in town. I had a small check from my army insurance. Chuck ran the farm, tried to keep worn machinery in action, the pigs healthy, the hired men paid.

Hearst concluded that his family "just dug in and faced what had to be faced and survived."[29]

In Iowa, Shelby County farmers acknowledged in the late 1930s:

Were it not for the comfort our family was to us, we wouldn't have been able to take what we did. Our children buckled in and helped. We all had to work together to keep going at all. We sympathized with each other, stayed at home more because we couldn't afford to go out very much, and got through it somehow. Some of our neighbors lost their farms. It was hard on their families but it would have been harder for them if it hadn't been for their families.[30]

Farm children made stellar contributions. From the time they were "big enough to tell weeds from beans," it was customary to expect labor from children in tenant farm families in the South. Some tenant farmers in the Piedmont even approved of their children going into the field of work when they were babies because they would then learn what their parents were doing.[31] Later, large numbers of children there, nearly half in some areas, would be working their family farms rather than attending school.[32] Dorothea Lange's photographs of farms and farmers often show children in responsible roles: a thirteen-year-old daughter plants sweet potatoes; a son and grandson bring in their mules from plowing for water; all the children feed the pigs while a younger daughter takes care of the chickens. Near Sublette, Kansas, farm boys helped their fathers as partners. If boys of school age were not needed to work at home, they were expected to work as farmhands for someone else. Grown-up children, even those no longer living at home, still contracted to support the economic welfare of their parents and family of origin. One woman, a teacher in rural Nebraska, bought a tractor so her father could continue to farm. Another from the same area, who worked as a domestic in Chicago, bought clothing for her brother and sisters without requests from her parents. Young men often entered the CCC so that their families would accrue the sum of $25 dollars from their monthly paycheck of $30.[33]

Farm wives generally contributed substantially to the farm economy during the Depression. They did so with practical economies—making things do, canning and preserving, caring for chickens and selling the eggs, selling butter, and having special responsibility for the family garden that often provided the entire supply of food not purchased at the store.[34] And they usually did so despite large numbers of children when they were young, and without or with only limited household conveniences. Margaret Hagood marveled in 1939 at "the emotional maturity" of the white tenant farm women she interviewed in the South as "evidenced in their acceptance of economic hardships." She was surprised that "they are able to keep up the level of energy output during almost every waking hour, day in and day out, year after year, which is demanded for getting big families fed, cleaned, washed and sewed for, with such meager and inadequate equipment, and with such antiquated methods." Hagood noted that these women also helped in the fields with hard manual work as a matter of custom.[35] In the Dust Bowl areas in the 1930s, wives were lifesavers, producing even more eggs and butter to obtain cash while their husbands' income was blown away year after year by wind storms. Furthermore, mechanized farming in the Midwest led to short periods of intensive work for mothers and daughters in the fields during corn-picking, cutting oats or wheat, and in the haying seasons.[36] Indeed, women's economic contributions "often became the mainstream that provided life and sustenance for all concerned."[37]

Fathers in farm families gave examples to their children, as did their wives, by their hard work, personal responsibility for the family's well-being, and frugality. They also generally retained sufficient patriarchal presence as prime workers to make their wishes known effectively. Although there were numerous exceptions when a wife had the stronger personality and would have an important voice in decision-making, as a rule, fathers remained leaders and arbiters; motherhood was the principal area of the wives' identity. Some wives even referred to husbands as "the boss," and were most reluctant to challenge their husband's authority on major issues. Even a young woman with the extraordinary vigor and independence of Ann Marie Lowe, a daughter in a congenial farm family in North Dakota in the 1930s, felt powerless when dealing with a family's economic crisis in 1932, observing, "But what can a woman do? Who will listen to her?"[38]

In photographs of rural families, father invariably sat at the head of the table or as the head of the family walking down a road. His body posture is one of authority, even in this depressed period that often mocked his ability to produce needed income. Unfortunately, that authority was sometimes used to be brutish, alcoholic, and cruel.[39] However, lingering patriarchy served many useful purposes in times of economic uncertainty. The White House Conference on Child Health and Protection in the early 1930s discovered that rural children were especially raised to accept discipline, authority, and responsibility. This, because conditions of survival warranted those goals, but also because fathers were generally inclined to raise by rules rather than sentiment. They considered disciplined performance by their children an effective preparation for their futures, and their children performed nearly twice the number of tasks undertaken by urban children. The father's touch is also suggested by ready use of punishment, avoiding less demonstrable occasions of affection such as kissing, and a careful curbing of the children's social life outside the family. These techniques of child raising according to conferees on child health were quite different from middle-class urban patterns, more influenced by mothers whose close emotional and affectionate ties were more apt to be the rule of family life. Acceptance of hard work, self-discipline, collective responsibility for welfare of family, and consequent strengths to live with a degree of deprivation without complaint—the norms of farm family life—explain much about the absence of chronic turbulence in America's farm areas in the 1930s.[40]

The farm family's ability to sustain itself was not just the result of cooperative work among its members. It was also strengthened by expectations of cooperative relations with farm neighbors and people in the nearest village. At times during the 1930s, these bonds would be strained by the concerns of each family for its own interests. Wives might inquire of husbands who sought to assist a poor neighbor or farmer who traded at his store whether charity was affordable at these times. Nor could village merchants expect locals to automatically patronize stores in their hometown (the village closest to them) because prices were sometimes better in other places.[41] Yet for all that, and given the fact that automobiles and phones made neighboring a more selective process while farm equipment on many farms reduced needs for a cooperative workforce, there was still an impressive amount of neighborly goodwill and cooperation among people living in farm areas. This was especially true among farmers who still "lived at home," those producing most of what they consumed. In the Ozarks, houses were still raised by groups for individual families. Everyone in the area participated, "the men and boys worked on the main project. The women and girls prepared a bountiful meal." And when the neighbors departed they didn't say "Good-bye," but "Now let us know when you need anything." And, as one participant noted, "At the end of such a day there glowed within the breasts of these mountain dwellers the deep-seated satisfaction and contentment which comes to those who do good."[42] This type of life where little cash changed hands—one dependent on cooperation with others—still typified the upland cotton country of Georgia, Alabama, Mississippi, Louisiana, and Arkansas and "even the coastal flatlands in sections of Virginia, North and South Carolina, Georgia, Florida, Alabama and Mississippi."[43] "Being willing to share to the last string-bean" was the way Lorena Hickok described Kentucky mountaineers in the 1930s. Men still cooperated in cornshucking in the Piedmont of North Carolina where it was an obligation to return service for everyone who worked on behalf of another.[44] Cooperation between farmers also occurred in the corn belt of Iowa, largely in haying, threshing, and cornpicking, and remained critical in threshing wheat in the Midwest, and occurred in New England, though usually on a smaller scale by farm neighbors.[45]

Situations in which farm families met with disaster, such as the illness or loss of life of a parent, a fire, or a problem of making ends meet, virtually guaranteed support from one's farm neighbors in every area of the nation. Two veteran observers described this bonding in Iowa:

Such behavior is expected. Mutual aid and visiting become conjoint activities. It is not unusual for 5 or 10 farmers with tractors to gather on the farm of a farmer who is too ill to prepare the ground and plant his entire crop. Occasionally 15 or 20 farmers with as many tractors turn out to help, and village dwellers also do what they can, such as driving tractors or operating planters, to relieve the burden on the owners of the machinery. Persons in difficulty are expected to accept help graciously and to pay their obligations by similar conduct toward others in difficulty.[46]

In 1938, when a father and son in Iowa were killed by lightning while harvesting their crop, more than 100 men with sixty wagons appeared and gathered the corn to support the bereaved family. Lyndon Johnson once remarked about his neighbors in the cotton farming area of Johnson City, Texas, "They knew when you were sick and they cared when you died." This observation was still applicable to most areas of rural America in the 1930s.[47]

Rural people also seemed especially inclined to join churches and demonstrate the impressive influence of religion in their lives—the effect being to espouse still another institution that generally fostered stability. A random study suggests that rural communities had their share of nonbelievers.[48] But churches, which usually appealed to rural Americans, experienced noteworthy increases in membership in the 1930s. Reliable figures for Gastonia, North Carolina, a milltown with a large influx of population from rural areas, showed nearly a 20% growth in white church members, mainly Baptist, Methodist, and Presbyterian, between 1930 and 1938.[49] Overall, the Southern Baptist Convention reported an astounding increase in membership of 25% between 1925 and 1935, an increase from 4 to 5 million members. Numerous smaller evangelical and Pentecostal churches also experienced similar, unprecedented gains in members during the same period.[50]

What the Christian faith meant to rural Americans in the Depression is probably best reflected in their own words. A major conclusion from impressionistic data in thousands of interviews conducted with rural southerners, gathered under the auspices of the Federal Writer's Project, is the critical if not decisive role of religion in their lives; religious convictions explained away their big problems and minimized their frustrations and deprivations and, above all else, was a major source of their confidence.

By way of example, Silas Harmon, a black handyman raised in a tiny rural place, declared to an interviewer, "God, He got his eyes on all us poor folks. He kno we have to go exposin' in de cold, wid mighty little rashions sometime, an' no shoes. Here I sets wid not a sock to my foot. But God says my foots is jes' as good as them what's got de cover on 'em." Another black in Seaboard, North Carolina, professed, "I ain't lost heart" because "the Lord has blessed me in a lot o' ways" and because "my religion gives me more pleasure than anything else." Fleety Dodson, the white wife of a sharecropper and mother of thirteen children, also found a satisfactory explanation for the major problem of her life:

First there was Charles, and he's goin' on 20 now, and after him there was one purty near every year till they was the whole 13. Younguns was never no bother to me. Charlie and me both come from big families. I had nine brothers an' sisters and after I'd helped raise most o' them it seemed natural for me to be raisin' some o' my own. I never felt they was a burden. If it was the Lord's will for us to have em, I done my best to raise 'em right. I don't hold with talk about not havin' the babies it's the Lord's will to send.

To which she added, "Yes, we've had it some hard at times, but I believe in the Lord and his power an' if we live a Christian life like the Bible says, He will provide."

A black sharecropper's wife in Dillon, South Carolina, interviewed in 1939 found in religion a way to settle the most serious scores in her life—those with her landlord, Mr. Stores:

When we gits up before dat golden throne de Lawd gwine say to Mister Stores: "Stores, yo' ain' treated people right, nawsuh, dat yo' sho' ain't!" An' de Lawd gwine call St. Peter an' tell him to throw Mister Stores in de bottomless pit! Yassuh! Mister, dey's gwine be a scatterin' er black an' whites up dere near de throne. Heaben gwine be full er dem dat's kept de law of de Lawd, an' hell gwine be packed to overlowin' wid dem what ain't, yassuh, dat hit sho' is!

Lola Rucker, a mother and common-law wife of a carpenter whom, she remarked, she could not afford to marry, lived in the mountains of Tennessee. They moved to Knoxville to make ends meet and were barely doing so. But, "as wore out as they was," religion provided perspective on their difficulties.

I know that Jesus Christ died to save sinners. All that me and Calvin have to do is trust in Him. And we do. And we believe in Him. I don't see where they's any way to keep me and Calvin out of Heaven. . . . Calvin and me ain't never harmed a living soul in our lives. . . . When me and Calvin gits there [Heaven] I'd be more than glad to do what I could to help others git in. They's some folks, not a thousand miles away from here, that are going to need a heap of helping. Ah Lordy, yes![51]

Another woman standing beside her husband in front of their shack in Oklahoma City in 1939 reminded FSA photographer Russell Lee from her doorway, "We may not have much of a home here, but we will have one in Heaven."[52]

When a tiny baby died unexpectedly in Elba, Alabama (population 2,500), in late 1932, its father and mother wrote the following words in her memory in the local paper:

Little Rubie Mae was almost six months old. She was sick only one day and one night with pneumonia. All that loving hands could do was done, but still dear Jesus saw fit to take her home with Him. Sleep on, sweet babe, for we know you are at rest. . . . Our home was filled with gladness and our hearts were filled with joy, with the smiles of little Rubie Mae—our precious household pet and toy. But our Savior sent an angel to carry our child above, to dwell with Him in joy and peace where pain and sickness never come and where death is no more.[53]

Christianity in rural America was more than a religious system that provided coping and solace. It was also a social and ethical mainstay and a dominant cultural influence, part of the essential atmosphere of rural communities because it effectively touched the lives of nearly everyone. Christians in these communities usually enjoyed a special status, something of an amalgam of being considered more moral, more purposeful, and perhaps slightly more well-to-do. The churches to which they belonged were centers of community activities and social life and hence newsworthy, as were the church members who participated. Both provided front-page news and usually evoked favorable editorial comment in the local paper. Also, the timely annual calendar of church activities was deeply etched into community life; Thanksgiving, Christmas, and Easter were virtually public observances and duly underscored in the local press. And, of course, the churches usually stood physically above the stores, banks, gas stations, and houses, the one or two-story buildings on Main Street, thereby enjoying in their home communities a small version of the stature of medieval cathedrals in European towns.

Christianity's influence was often so subtle and pervasive that people in rural communities actually lived in a type of Christian ethos whether or not they were believers or churchgoers. "From the first," according to consensus in Irwin, Iowa, "children should be taught the virtues of honesty, frugality, friendliness and hard work. They should be sent to church and should be taught to believe in God and to be good Christians." One observer, a resident, underscored the critical linkage between churches and community in Irwin. "The churches are the most important institution in Irwin today," he declared. "Were it not for them the community would not be a desirable place to live. Loss of the churches would be an irreparable blow to the community." Still another asserted, "Religious principles are important in governing the welfare of our community. With few exceptions, the people are fair in their dealings with each other."[54] When Christians became overly zealous and used backbiting and gossip to attack those who deviated from acceptable norms, this too probably represented an application of their principles, however misguided. Here too, Christians influenced and sometimes controlled the behavior of others.[55]

Furthermore, small-town editors often highlighted the message and activities of the local churches, thereby helping to consolidate religion's place in the daily life of their communities. The editor of the *Randolf Review* published in Elkins, West Virginia, epitomized this position when he wrote, "The greatest of all gifts was the gift of the Father of his Son, the Lord Jesus Christ, 1934 years ago. . . . All that is good and fine focuses around that event and the career of a Divine character who came to live among us for a few short years and who by His kindness and His common sense made this earth a better place in which to live."[56] In Grand Rapids, Minnesota (pop. 3,200), the editor of its *Herald Review* called attention to the inevitable progress of human values in the world, assured by the founder of Christianity. He wrote, "In Honor of the Master" that "the Babe of Bethlehem may not have achieved the great purposes for which He was born. But He is making progress. He has pointed the way. As generations and centuries pass many will follow Him."[57] In Augusta, Kansas (pop. 4,000), the editor of that town's *Daily Gazette* announced his "Kansas Editor's Faith" with consummate confidence that God would help Americans overcome the Depression. He stated, "I believe that American people will be calm in the hour of trial and have faith that a higher power will divide a Red Sea again if necessary, opening up the route to the greener shores on the other side."[58] In anticipation of Easter, the Bozeman, Montana, *Daily Chronicle* included an editorial, "I Am the Resurrection," with the editor asserting that statements in scriptures establishing Christ's resurrection amounted to "the living refutation of the prophets of doom and sentinels of perdition who would have us believe that civilization is poised perilously on the brink of oblivion, to be pushed at any moment into the chaos of nothingness."[59]

Editors of newspapers in rural areas often reminded readers of the importance of church attendance. In Marianna, Florida (pop. 3,200), the editor of one paper asserted, "By the way you know you should go to church every Sunday. Next Sunday [Christmas] is very important . . . your minister has a special message for you." The front-page message of a competing newspaper in the same locale declared, "Regardless of denomination you should plan to attend at least one of the numerous devotional services on Sunday."[60] The Taylor *County News* reminded subscribers in the small community of Perry, Florida, and vicinity, "Go to church Sunday."[61] Similar newspapers were also embellished with attractive illustrations such as, "The Story of the Bible Told in Pictures," "Easter," "The First Christmas," "Daily Bible Thoughts," and even "Sunday School Lessons."[62] The Beloit *Daily Call* (Kansas, pop. 3,500) included an instructive, lengthy death scene of a former resident and priest. The newspaper narrated the priest's last remarks and actions on its front page in great detail beginning with, "I am willing to die; I am willing to go," and ending with his last murmured words.[63] Other small-town newspapers used special terms on their front pages that described deaths of townspeople in religious terms: "Malta Youth Is Summoned Late Thursday" refers to a young man's death, not his court appearance. In another paper the caption read, "Former Resident Is Suddenly Called."[64] The same ethos was sustained by the attention newspapers called to cultural activities sponsored by local churches. These might, for example, include information on special joint services by several churches, the presentation of "The Messiah," or a Christmas cantata.

Photographs also uncover a deep underlying Christian faith among farmers and villagers. Some posted pictures of saints or Mary or crucifixes on the walls of parlors, living rooms, or bedrooms. A sign, "I am thy Lord and thy

God," was stationed above a rickety bed in a destitute dwelling in Muskogee County, Oklahoma. Photographer Dorothea Lange chanced upon a woman named Mrs. Hill in her house, a one-room dug-out basement in Dead Ox Flat, Oregon, in October, 1939, and learned that her prize possession was a blackboard, something she had wanted for a long time, she said, "for my Bible verses, to keep them in our mind." Ben Shahn recorded a prosperous farmer who had pictures of Christ in his living room while the song sheet on his piano was "Little Old Church in the Valley."[65] FSA photographs of the South and the Southwest reveal those regions alive with religious statements or symbols: revivals in town squares, advertisements of religious services in post offices, a grocery called the Golden Rule Store in North Carolina, frequent biblical messages and signs along roads and highways, riverside baptisms, and itinerant preachers. You could even pay to have the "Lord's Prayer" engraved on your penny at the Louisiana State Fair.[66]

Farmers' capacities to deal confidently with the Depression were also enhanced by their association with the rural villagers and townsmen whom they resembled. By urban standards, rural townsmen and villagers, like farmers, were relatively isolated, struggling, and poor. Few rural communities had first-rate medical or dental services. Almost all were understaffed in public employees; their small population base meant too few people to deal with community social problems. They were also vulnerable to factors affecting farm income—the weather and market fluctuations. And, like the farmers, they developed personal resources emphasizing hard work and cooperation to compensate for their problems.[67]

They lived in "person communities" with people often seeing one another face-to-face, hence admitting close personal ties with one another. This closeness made it possible for them to organize opinion, foster goals, and even enforce conformity. They formulated prescriptions to accomplish necessary work; these placed special emphasis on mutuality—good neighboring, civic-mindedness, reciprocity, paying social debts, and assuming obligations to the community and each individual in the community. People living in these towns or villages also celebrated the importance of hard work for personal and community benefit and upheld a galaxy of virtues associated with the work ethic, especially frugality, temperance, and self-improvement. As a consequence, farm families now spending more time in the towns found resonance for many of their own deeply held beliefs. Reinforcement of this kind meant that there would be many similar types in rural communities, bound by a common language for good and evil. This left them with less than optimal tolerance for diversity, hence ethnic and religious minorities, but well positioned to defend against the large and immediate perils of the Depression.[68] Community was strength in rural American towns and villages, and many Americans who lived there were empowered by that strength.

"There is a very real attachment of the people to the community," a

Russell Lee, "San Augustine, Texas," 1939. San Augustine's population was 1,300. Small rural towns were places farm families went to shop, attend meetings, gossip, discuss crops, and attend movies. They and shopkeepers who serviced them in the towns thereby developed a sense of identity and belonging based on personal associations. Reproduced from the Collections of the Library of Congress.

seasoned analyst of rural life wrote about Irwin, Iowa, and this sentiment could be applied to most rural communities. That persons living on farms and nearby small towns experienced together a sense of community is revealed in numerous ways. One notices immediately from photographs a remarkable number of people on the streets of rural towns, especially on Saturdays. Arthur Raper describes the excitement and stirring of blacks and whites in the towns of Greene and Macon Counties, Georgia—some buying, some watching the parade of people, some listening to a banjo played by a black, and some playing games in an atmosphere resembling a people's fair. Farmers came to Marianna, Florida, the county seat of Jackson County, on Saturdays to buy and sell, share stories, and size up progress; they regularly occupied an area along one side of the courthouse on Saturday morning.[69] Similarly, farmers in Steele, Missouri, sat on the curb and bumpers of cars on a Saturday afternoon; they wore overalls, straw hats, and suspenders in several different groups. In Iowa Falls, Iowa, a community of 4,100 people and a center for farm families, Main Street was bustling with residents on

Saturday night; groups of men talking, women and daughters shopping, and
people going to the movies.[70]

The local newspapers, published for area farmers and country town readers and the chief source of news for them, exerted strong influence in defining and developing community attitudes; they did so through editorials,
front-page local news emphasis, and a prevailing tone that was confident
about the merits of their communities. The editor invariably projected an
image of his community as a place where people cared about one another
while his newspaper cared about everyone. One editor's credo in this regard
would have met widespread approval from other editors. It stated:

Here are set forth only that which uplifts a community—the activities of businessmen,
the church news, the civic good accomplished by women, school items, the happy
social gatherings of the people . . . all the thousand and one occurrences that make
up the simple annals of the great common people who are really the foundation of
this great country of ours.[71]

Another country newspaper editor in a similar vein defined community
as the willingness of an individual to accept responsibility for others. He
praised:

The unlauded men and women who are quietly attending to their own duties, every
day contributing something substantial to general industry, property, and progress,
rearing children in habits of useful work and right living and supplying examples that
elevate the moral and intellectual level of their little communities—these are the men
and women of real influence and power.[72]

These people, a small-town editor in Vermont noted, were mainstays of the
nation during the Depression. He wrote, "For millions of people this year
just past (1932) has not been a happy one; yet, when you speak to those
same people they greet you with joy and courage and wholeheartedly they
try to help each other to more happiness. Such people who are keeping a
stiff upper lip in the face of a dark time are the hope of the nation in its
crisis."[73] An editor for the Grand Rapids *Herald Review* lauded the character
of Minnesota's pioneers for their frugality and reminded his readers that
they should draw on those strengths of their communities at earlier times
to combat problems of the Depression.[74] Other newspapers praised those
contemporary persons and organizations that promoted self-reliance because
communities benefited from successful, hard-working individuals. They
lauded the Boy Scouts, Girl Scouts, and Camp Fire Girls for providing
young people with "The Right Start" through "character building" and
"citizenship training" because these organizations were "intended to sup-
plement and cooperate with parent, church and school." The Bismarck
(North Dakota) *Tribune*, which frequently cited biblical passages as "Inspiration for Today" on its editorial page, looked to American Legion baseball

as "Making Men Out of Boys" (and, of course, nearly every rural small town had a baseball team for which the town turned out and rooted rabidly). Still other papers honed the skills of its readers for self-improvement and responsibility with "Daily Lessons in English."[75]

Every conceivable distinction that reflected well on hometown residents was exalted by the local paper, usually with front-page coverage. Praise was conferred on winners of public speaking contests, students who achieved perfect attendance or who were on the honor roll, those graduating with the highest scholastic average, scouts achieving the highest ranks, students competing for high ranking in statewide examinations ("Wednesday's test will be the final Minimum Essential of the Year, and the local school [Hastings, Minnesota] will attempt to better the average made in the second test in February when the Hastings students placed second"). The rural press also congratulated Illinois national 4-H delegates from the local area who won prizes at the state fair for potatoes, and even victories by the local checker team. And almost as if they were carrying the town's ancient escutcheon into battle in every contest, local athletic teams and individual athletes were a continuous source of attention, pride, and morale. In Perry, Florida, distinguished students were inducted into the "Round Table," a ceremony duly reported in the center of the front page of the Taylor *County News.*[76] Perhaps the most inspiring characterological call to arms was a front-page report in Chillicothe, Missouri, about a boy who traveled twenty-two miles a day to attend school. The writer commented:

Up to a short time ago this boy walked this distance much of the time. At the present time he has secured transportation and is not walking. It is also interesting that after walking 22 miles each day that this boy helped with the chores on the farm. He was also a member of the football team and spent some time after school practicing football. This is a very good example of the determination of the youth of today to get an education.[77]

Another group of "sterling citizens" upheld by the local press were those who served the community with distinction; they were often commemorated in death with a front-page obituary accompanied by a photograph or a laudatory editorial. Without exception, this praise came in response to the former citizen's "neighborliness," "kindness," or "public service." Beloit, Kansas's "great and beloved bandmaster" lived on in memory because he was "Beloit's gleaming example of the truth that a man's works, if he merit it, do live after him." Another small-town newspaper celebrated a prominent woman for having a successful life because of "her loveliness of character and her consecration to the highest ideals . . . as well as her sympathetic understanding." A doctor who answered the "final summons" had contributed such kindness and service to his community that a reporter acknowledged he could not find words to express the depth of his sorrow and that of others. A city official in another small community was described as "always the same; friendly, congenial, warm-hearted. Everyone was his friend, and no one ever appealed to him for a favor—that was within his power to grant—without receiving an instant and whole-hearted response." And so it went with congratulatory statements for those who brought people together and helped to make the community work. They enjoyed "useful lives," and "exemplified in every way the real spirit of Christianity."[78]

The ideal of community as mutual responsibility was not only taught by exemplary citizens and newspaper editors, it was also widely practiced by a variety of local groups. Many small towns had sings and picnics and Christmas events with gifts for children, and virtually everyone supported the high school teams. Local plays by either a church group or an independent club of dramateurs were usually open to the public; likewise, concerts by high school and town bands, recitals, and fireman's balls.[79] High school faculty members lent their sobriety to gym parties on Saturday evenings with students, chaperoned students for away games in basketball, and sometimes put on a faculty show for students. Very active civic clubs such as the Rotary or Lions in the larger rural towns and small cities in rural areas usually adopted a project for civic improvement. "Courtesy Week" with all its prescriptions was sponsored by high school girls with rules inscribed in the local paper. Banquets for fathers and sons and mothers and daughters served purposes of socialization and reciprocity between generations. Many prepared Christmas boxes for the poor, others sang carols in the village, and each high school class assumed responsibility for sponsoring programs for the entertainment of the entire student body.[80] Despite the diversity of church groups and the variety of organizations for service, recreation, or entertainment, each one believed in serving the community.[81]

The three major institutions that shaped character in rural America—family, church, and community—all contributed to a way of life that made rural people resistant to the worst effects of the Depression. Still another was public confidence in the virtues of their country and its future. An editor in a small-town Kansas newspaper noted this faith and its effects most clearly when he wrote in the desperate year, 1933, "Yet in the face of appalling blight (the depression), our people have not lost hope. Their faith in America's institutions has not wavered. Their trust in the ultimate recovery of the country is sublime" and continued, "in no section of the country has that courage been more clearly demonstrated than in the small town and countryside."[82] Thanksgiving seldom passed without widespread reference in small-town newspapers to the Pilgrims, their bounteous harvests, and the continuous special blessings enjoyed by America's rural people. The editor of a newspaper in Bismarck, North Dakota (then a small city of 12,000 embedded in the country), declared on Thanksgiving Day in 1935 that America's largesse in history was a generous reward to a covenanted people. "This day, perhaps more than any other," he wrote, "emphasizes the brotherhood of man and the responsibility of the individual to a Guiding Power. It may be that we do not DESERVE to be a chosen people, but any dispassionate stocktaking reveals that WE ARE A CHOSEN PEOPLE."[83] Another editor restated this theme, and declared that this special gift to Americans in history assured America's economic recovery.[84] Still another wrote that America's achievements as a nation assured its future success. He reasoned reassuringly, "We must measure our lot by comparison. There is no nation on earth whose prosperity, general happiness and the outlook for the future compares . . . with the United States." He added, "The days that are to come will be marked by constant improvement in everything in which Americans take pride."[85]

In truth, a type of muscular patriotism pervaded the rural press—exultant praise of America's achievements and prospects along with vigorous denials of the country's shortcomings or grounds for pessimism. "We are not a decadent but an advancing people. We have had a setback but it will be corrected in due time," wrote the editor of the Pendleton *East Oregonian* on July 4, 1932, while another editor in Kansas observed in the same difficult year, "We know in our calm moments that a people who have gone through Valley Forge and a bitter Civil War are hardly going to flunk out because they can't put two cars in a garage until times get better."[86] "The American constitution is still solid as a rock" wrote another, "and it is still the hope of the world."[87] A large sketch on the editorial page of the Brattleboro, Vermont, *Reformer* was entitled, "A Word from Uncle." It depicted, of course, Uncle Sam, whose kindly hand is on a young man's shoulder, saying, "We've come through the like of this before, son"; the date of the newspaper was March 9, 1933, the eve of major New Deal reforms.[88] In 1932, in rural Jackson County, Florida, a gigantic parade was held in the county seat of Marianna to commemorate the 200th anniversary of the birth of George Washington. On that occasion girls sang the "Washington Ode" and a speaker eulogized the first president as the first great man since Genghis Khan to refuse a crown.[89] The editor of the local newspaper meanwhile condemned those who would find fault with American history because "There is nothing to be ashamed of in the history of America."[90]

Despite living in a decade of widespread use of automobiles and mass entertainment, rural Americans were still being educated primarily at home, by the realities of farm and small-town life. Survival of farm families then dictated performing tasks, long hours each working day, by all family members, even young children. It also required meticulous management to achieve economic goals, and hence disciplinary controls over the work and social life of individual family members, including teaching their unquestioning loyalty to family before self. Although cooperation among family members was imperative, the rural credo also declared that it was necessary for families living in such unpopulated areas to have good neighborly relations with other rural families and townspeople on whom they depended. Christianity, common to both farmers and townspeople, was also an important resource for dealing with problems and uncertainties and fostering mutuality. It offered meaning, confidence, and protection to their lives and lent instructive higher purpose to their other reasons for getting along with one another. The practice fell short of any resemblance to the ideal of a mythical extended family, sometimes professed or described by rural editors, but it did provide stabilizing collective strengths during the 1930s when individuals by themselves were especially vulnerable.

Rural Americans still heavily influenced and protected by traditional institutions—family, church, and community—and assisted by New Deal programs as well as confidence in their country's benign future, remained steadfast in the 1930s and waited for better times. As we shall soon see, even those forced to migrate as families to sustain their way of life retained essential confidence in a better future.

6

Rural Worlds Confirmed

In the public mind, no group better symbolizes the nadir of Americans in the Great Depression than the Okies who migrated to California. We associate poignant images with these poor wanderers from the central Southwest who trekked to California to escape poverty only to suffer seemingly repeated indignities there and even greater exploitation. Two extremely talented, creative artists contributed importantly to these images: Dorothea Lange and John Steinbeck. With the assistance of a movie director, John Ford, and folk singer Woody Guthrie and others, they succeeded until very recent times in turning the "Okie Odyssey" of the 1930s into an ideological as well as sentimental journey that substituted for reality.[1]

Although Lange's numerous photographs of the migrants to California are generally moving, none is more eloquent or attains such notice as "Migrant Mother." Photographed in February 1936, three years before publication of Steinbeck's *The Grapes of Wrath* would seem to endorse her essential image, "Migrant Mother" ("Migrant Madonna") was an extraordinarily moving document—a lonely, frail, sunburnt mother, pictured in a ragged half-tent with a forlorn pensive look; her three children clinging dependently to her—no work, food, or husband in sight. Lange's photographs of the Okies were so appealing that the public mistook them for the more significant contextual life of her subjects; her camera could not record their essential optimism, toughness, support in family and community, limited expectations, or confident belief in self-reliance, all typical of rural people. It was these characterological qualities that made them more resilient than her pictures of rootless poverty suggest. Although middle-class intellectuals like Lange showed a great capacity to empathize with poor folks living on the edge, they seem less well endowed to depict an abiding personal and cultural strength in their subjects. To do so, of course, would imply they could begin to help themselves.

The Grapes of Wrath (1939), a Nobel and Pulitzer Prize-winning novel which became a movie sensation (1940) directed by John Ford and starring the talented Henry Fonda as Tom Joad, was one of the most socially committed and effective artistic statements of the 1930s. The appeal of Steinbeck's novel (more than 400,000 copies were sold in the first year of its publication and many millions attended the movie) may be attributed to its excellent literature, the emotional power inherent in this victimization of poor, innocent people by the powerful and their underlings, and the author's ability to personalize the complex character of the Okie migration and resettlement in California. Again, unlike the pinpoints of time in Lange's photographs, Steinbeck provided a sweeping narrative that purportedly explained the Okie exodus as well as their experiences in California. To this John Ford added the magic of cinema's dream factory—Hollywood's special aptitude to render drama as reality.

Until the early 1970s, scholarly literature on the Okies was sparse, so historians could not begin to compete with the vested position of Steinbeck and others who shared his views. "As a consequence," historian Sheila Goldring Manes wrote in 1982, "Americans never knew the real migrants [from Oklahoma to California], and they still do not. They know the Joads." She continued, "Steinbeck was so impressed by the apparent powerlessness of his characters that . . . he never fully realized them as human beings."[2] Steinbeck's observations about the Okies are often, of course, imaginatively useful, but many are simplistic and many others simply inaccurate. He does effectively symbolize through the Joads the fact that the largest migration to California from any state in the 1930s came from Oklahoma, amply reinforced by smaller but significant numbers of migrants from Texas, Missouri, and Arkansas, all collectively called Okies.[3] Steinbeck makes no mention, however, of the large numbers from the Southwest who preceded them in the more prosperous 1920s, and who greatly influenced the decision of many latecomers.[4]

Although Steinbeck paints a vivid picture of the hazards of the Joads on Route 66, the Mother Road of migrants to California from the Southwest, he exaggerated some impediments of their trip.[5] The Okies benefited, after all, from the fact that most traveled in families, which provided a basic security for everyone who was uprooted. They had an average net worth of $268 when they arrived in California, with forty dollars in cash and a car worth roughly the same amount.[6] Most Okies were relatively young and many enroute had provisions aboard and slept out by the roadside. The trip could be made in three days, with gas costing only ten dollars. If they needed extra money, they could stop off and work the cotton fields of Arizona.[7] And, regardless of the trials of the trip, many reached California

Dorothea Lange, "Bound for California," 1936. The trek of most Okies to rural areas of California went better than that of the Joads, described by John Steinbeck in the *Grapes of Wrath*. Most traveled effectively as families, entered California with modest savings, and settled with friends and relatives. Copyright the Dorothea Lange Collection, The Oakland Museum of California, City of Oakland. Gift of Paul S. Taylor.

confident of their prospects for hospitality, jobs, or improvements in their lives.[8]

Steinbeck is equally misleading about the fact that most Okies, even from 1935 to 1940 when their migration peaked, went to California's cities and not into its agricultural economy. This was especially true of urban residents of the Southwest who found employment opportunities in California's urban centers; they met with little hostility, transferred skills, and seemingly dissolved into a mix of people with minimum adjustments.[9] It was the other Okies, those living largely in the San Joaquin, Imperial, and Sacramento Valleys, the rural migrants, who caught Steinbeck's eye and later, through his novel, became synonymous with the Okie experience in California during the Great Depression. It is, therefore, this group with which we will concern ourselves to establish that those whom Steinbeck mistakenly regarded to be most downtrodden had values, institutions, and successes that permitted them to cope with their problems and hope for a better future.

There were problems of relocation for Okies migrating to rural areas in California to be sure, especially in their first year, and especially for those who had no friends or settled family there to help with emergencies. Accustomed to being tenants or owners in Oklahoma, there was little chance for them to own their own farms in California where land for farming was largely controlled by corporations employing expensive hydraulic systems.[10] What is more, the rhythms of California farm production with different crops and fruits maturing and worked at different times of the year resulted in a large mobile workforce, which restricted wage levels for Okies even when employment was possible.

Despite the fact that relief was available only after one-year's residency in a California county, half the rural migrants from the Southwest, finding support from former friends or relatives or special opportunities, settled immediately in one town in California and continued to reside there. Most of the others also settled in a permanent residence within a year or two of their arrival in California.[11] Only a small minority continued to serve as farm laborers on circuit, traveling perhaps a thousand miles a year; these few sometimes experienced situations that Steinbeck attributed to the literary Joads: company-owned living quarters, poor one-room shacks, a single faucet or shower, one septic toilet for several hundred residents, guards patrolling the gates, trash on the ground, company stores with outlandish prices, and the threat of epidemics.[12]

One of the most severe tests for Okie newcomers, which Steinbeck aptly described, was the animosity they inspired among some Californians. Ma Joad was surprised when she first heard the word "Okies." She looked puzzled. "Okies?," she said softly. "Okies?" But Tom Joad had already learned by this time that Okie "means you're a dirty son-of-a-bitch. Okie means you're scum."[13] The term "Okie" and the patronizing and abusive behavior it often sanctioned were due in part, to the meager living conditions and lowly status of agricultural laborers in the agricultural valleys of southern California and the peculiarities of their speech and ways often offensive in California's different regional cultures. Okies frequently used "ain't" and "might could" and dropped the final "g" in words, pronouncing them "pickin" and "dancin."[14] There were also numerous economic and political reasons why Californians feared the Okies and therefore mistreated them. Population increase in California in the midst of a Depression naturally promoted fear for jobs. In some rural counties (Kern for example), the Okie influx added more than 60% to the existing population in less than five years.[15] The newcomers also meant increased taxes for locals with payments for relief, school enrollment, and health services. Meanwhile, their impoverished condition fostered aesthetic blight and threats for public health and sanitation. Finally, there was serious concern among Californians that the growing numbers of Okies would allow them to take over politics and lead California in a radical direction or, at least, turn the state over to Democrats.[16]

Schoolchildren of newly settled families from the Southwest faced particularly hurtful challenges. Many had worked with their parents in California's cotton fields and had fallen behind in school preparation. Not as well dressed as local children, forced "to drag out those two sandwiches full of beans for lunch," commanded to stand inspection for lice before the school nurse, they often faced unremitting peer pressure as well.[17] But for all this, there was no caste system operating against the Okies as the *Grapes of Wrath* seems to suggest. The social situation was sufficiently fluid, at least, to allow a few outsiders of character, ability, and income to shed the onus of being an Okie.[18] And because the southwesterners came as families, this not only served to refine their behavior and motivate them to improve their circumstances, their families also generated opportunities to communicate with those in the dominant group, especially through schools.[19] However, since incomes for agricultural laborers remained paltry, changeover to acceptance by locals was bound to be very slow. This, too, proved beneficial to the Okies, however, because it encouraged most to seek closer, mutually protective relationships with one another, allowing time and circumstance to determine whether their future allegiance would be in the California or the Okie California community.[20] Not only did the relation of outsiders to insiders admit of choice and change, it was also true that not all Californians were hostile to unreconstructed Okies, and not all Okies resented Californians given offsetting advantages of living in their state. In Modesto, a farm and orchard community in the San Joaquin Valley, where over 1,000 people lived in "Little Oklahoma," the reaction of locals to them was, at the least, mixed.[21] Sympathetic Californians in Modesto sponsored clothing drives for schoolchildren from "Little Oklahoma," and a careful analysis of themes written by 107 students in the local junior college on the subject "Little Oklahoma" revealed that more than half expressed tolerant opinions about the Okies, though the remaining 49% described its residents in terms of "poor white trash," "let them starve," or "should be on reservations." As for the residents of "Little Oklahoma," Lillian Creisler, an interviewer, reported, "All of them said they liked California better than the states from which they came." Some of the reasons were "free hospitals," "can see farther ahead," "good climate," "friendly neighbors," and "more money."[22] Benjamin Higginbotham, an Oklahoman before the Tolan Committee investigating interstate migration in 1940, one year after he arrived in California, was asked, "Do you consider yourself today a Californian or an Oklahoman?" Higginbotham replied evasively, "Well, I don't know. The California people have always treated me mighty nice." The questioner thereupon declared, "Then you consider yourself a Californian?" and Higginbotham replied directly, "Yes."[23]

When the *Grapes of Wrath* is viewed as social history, it may be credited with developing several useful themes of Okie experience in rural California, such as reliance on family, sensitivity to prejudice, and, for a small minority of the Okies, their difficult working and living conditions. Steinbeck is misleading or mistaken, however, on major considerations of their experience: the reasons for their exodus from the Southwest, their ability to deal with their problems with resiliency and determination, and their ability to succeed in California, noteworthy after World War II, but also evident to careful observers in the late 1930s when Steinbeck was writing his novel.

The sizable Okie migration to California in the 1930s suggests that great numbers of Americans moved across state lines to improve their lives in that decade, but a special census in 1940 asking where they resided in 1935 demonstrated that assumption to be erroneous.[24] Furthermore, farmers and rural nonfarm persons were particularly stay-at-homes compared with urbanites and were least likely of all Americans to migrate outside the state of their origin.[25] Migration from the southwestern states, Arkansas, Missouri, Texas, and especially Oklahoma, proved exceptional. Large numbers of Okies, probably in excess of 315,000, migrated to California in the 1930s and large numbers, over 40%, came from rural areas and settled in rural areas of California. Good data on the 1935 residence of interstate migrants living in the agriculturally rich San Joaquin Valley show nearly 71,000 came from four southwestern states. All other states were the 1935 place of origin of only 115,000 migrants.[26]

Recognition of this unusual surge of population underscores special elements in the history and culture of people from the Southwest.[27] Steinbeck understandably makes no mention of these statistical data or the inferences to be obtained from them. He accounts for the migration of the Joads with Dust Bowl references to soil blowing and crops destroyed, corporate greed, and exploitive banks, and the monster of their employ, the tractor. In fact, however, most Oklahoma counties reported more rainfall and lower federal drought relief than counties in Kansas, Nebraska, or the Dakotas.[28] Sallisaw, where the Joads lived, was located in one of Oklahoma's parts least affected by drought.[29] The only area in Oklahoma to suffer severe drought was the Panhandle, the site of Arthur Rothstein's surreal photographs of embankments of soil covering parts of houses and barns, but only a negligible number migrated from there to California. Although the press, and later Steinbeck, played up Dust Bowl conditions as responsible for migration, migrants from Oklahoma were questionable Dust Bowl refugees because drought was unlikely to be as severe there as in nearby states. Furthermore, tractors were seldom used in Oklahoma's cotton belt.[30] As for business conspiracies, Donald Worster wrote: "Great invisible corporations interlocked with banks supposedly controlled the land around Sallisaw. It made a good story and a familiar one. . . . In fact, however, there were few farming corporations anywhere in Oklahoma in the 1930s."[31]

Historians have recently reclaimed authority in assessing the nature of the Okie exodus beginning with Walter J. Stein (1973), Donald Worster (1979), Sheila Goldring Manes (1982), and, especially, James N. Gregory (1989). An array of valuable new explanations have been established to account for the attractiveness of California for southwesterners.[32]

Our information on the Okies is best for rural Oklahomans migrating to California in the 1930s. Many of them felt impelled to migrate from their state because of depressed cotton prices and the New Deal's devastation of tenant farmers under the AAA, allowing owners to hire former tenants as mere laborers. They also suffered from the failure of federal relief programs in Oklahoma to provide minimum standards for living. Most Oklahomans who chose to improve their conditions by leaving Oklahoma resettled in contiguous states, but for those prepared to travel farther, the largest number by far made the distant trip to relocate in California.[33] That seemingly exotic choice for Oklahomans and other southwesterners was, in fact, exceptionally well founded. Southern California's vast cotton agricultural system, centered in the San Joaquin Valley, probably appealed to them because they knew that crop best of all.[34] Again, Route 66, the main avenue to southern California from the Midwest, ran through the heartlands of the Southwest, splitting Oklahoma almost in two.[35] Most Oklahomans who migrated to California from rural areas came from locations close to that highway. The "golden glitter" from California's sun, purported abundance, better pay, and Hollywood culture simultaneous with the state's vestiges of being a last American frontier, undoubtedly provided additional elements of appeal, though these factors do not fully explain the large and disproportionate Okie migration from the Southwest.[36]

It appears that the large number of Okies already in California in 1930 (430,000) enticed those who followed in the 1930s. The decision whether to migrate is always a choice between the appeal of new, uncertain opportunities versus the limits of better-known conditions in the home area. The Okies, a clannish people, reduced the risk of moving by obtaining reliable information about their prospects in California from the large numbers of their friends and relatives already there. On arrival, the later migrants often found themselves in helpful circumstances or, as one former Oklahoman in California described the situation, "If you're from Paul's Valley, Oklahoma, you didn't have any problems out here because half the people out here are from Paul's Valley. I still know them."[37] This type of familiarity primarily explains why great numbers of Okies moved to California and remained there. A secondary consideration that probably also explains the phenomenon of large numbers of Oklahomans moving to California may be attributed to their perennial migratory patterns. In the early 1900s, they were moving from Alabama and Tennessee to Oklahoma; in the 1930s, to California. Many still remembered that earlier migration at a time when they were children, and many still identified with the adventurous spirit of their pioneering forebears; the title of at least one Okie camp newsletter in California was "The Covered Wagon."[38] Ever responding to adversity by moving, the Okies from Oklahoma merely "substituted cars for wagons" in the 1930s, thereby completing a phase of the ongoing westward migration of the American people, but one they were apt to repeat because of their recollections.[39]

All things considered, the rural migrants, especially from the southwestern states, made calculated decisions to go to California; they were not merely "blown out" or "tractored out"—rather, they had reduced their risks to tolerable, if not manageable, proportions. Those who were very poor generally did not go. Those who did would participate in a cotton farming economy with which they were familiar. Many were influenced by the reliable judgments of California residents whom they already knew. They brought their families with them to ensure their productivity. Their families of origin had made these kinds of moves before, and they, their heirs, were living proof of the foresight of those decisions. Furthermore, they brought with them confidence in their own rural-based cultural heritage—hard work, family cooperation, community with kindred folk, and prayer—that would work anywhere. The hopefulness of Okies going to California in the 1930s was something they brought with them.

The rural heritage of the Okies showed especially in their commitments to family. A careful enumeration of 8,000 rural persons moving out of Oklahoma in the 1930s (40% of whom moved to California) revealed that 82% were married and less than 3% had been divorced.[40] The size of families from the Southwest entering California, 4.4 members, was also unusually large considering that 3.9 typified Californian families and 3.6 for migrants from other regions of the country.[41] It was because the Okies were so family oriented that they promptly modified the patterns of agricultural labor in California. Until the 1930s, this type of work had been largely performed by Mexican families or single Philippino males who harvested fruits and vegetables on an eleven-month migratory circuit, often traveling more than 1,000 miles. They pursued a variety of routes that might include pea-picking in the southernmost Imperial Valley in the spring, potato harvesting later in the San Joaquin Valley, then fruit gathering in the more northern valleys in the summer, and back to the San Joaquin for grapes and cotton in the fall.[42] As we have observed, most Okies promptly rejected this approach as ruinous to family life; others quickly followed suit once they were eligible for welfare because relief benefits allowed them to live in a single community even through slack periods in the agricultural year.[43] Almost all Okies who had families then became residents of a single community while working a narrower radius, usually within a day's drive, with some exceptions when unusual work opportunities developed, such as during the summers. Even here, however, the family remained in its community while the worker temporarily extended his area of harvesting.

The migratory agricultural cycle was objectionable to family-minded people. They resented living in tents and squatting on the side of the road or an open ditch on the land of vegetable or fruit growers. They felt "like gypsies" and saw their children suffering from a lack of a homeplace, a regular church, a permanent school.[44] As one historian noted acutely, "Wives after all became pregnant, there were children to tend, and even more important, the children went to school."[45] Since parents in Okie families in California were no longer farm owners or tenants, they could not expect to endow their children with land on which to make a living; they looked now to the education of their children as a major responsibility. Residential living meant a permanent place in school for youngsters through high school, and medical attention in county service programs and local hospitals. One Okie who lived in Modesto aptly expressed the conviction shared by almost all Okies that life for them in California would go better once they had a home of their own. "This is the way I figured," he declared. "I'd get a few months work and then I'd lay by enough for a down payment. Once we had our own place, we'd be all right."[46] Having a house became such a priority that it may have taken precedence over other needs for food and adequate clothing.[47] Like prior rejection of the migratory farm labor cycle, their consuming desire to own land and build their own houses demonstrated the determination of Okies to mold their environment in accord with their values rather than become its passive victims.

They built their houses (they chose overwhelmingly to own rather than rent) in settlements called "Okievilles" or "Little Oklahomas" on cheap land on the outskirts of towns and small cities in California's rural valleys.[48] These were modest and finished only gradually, primarily distinguished by the determination of those who built them and their pride in ownership rather than quality of construction.[49]

The structures proceeded in carefully graduated steps as money came to hand. One Okie housebuilder declared his building strategy was "jest like the cat eatin' grindstone—a little bit at a time."[50] At first, residents lived in tents—sometimes attached to their automobiles—then there would be a quickening of construction as men, women, and children in families, bringing home building materials, would begin to raise a wooden frame, the father directing the operation with skills in carpentry obtained from his farmwork in the Southwest; a foundation was dug, cement mixed by hand, boards hammered together, and a house began to appear. Since the houses in Okieville were usually at different levels of construction, the effect, in the early days, sometimes gave the appearance of a "shacktown." In Modesto, a good number lacked running water and were without tubs, but owners found reasons to be satisfied.[51] "Jim did most of it, me and him," reported a wife who lived in one of these dwellings in Tulare County. "Well, it's not modern by a whole lot, but then I was never used to a modern house, no how; so what's the difference. I get by with it."[52]

Families building their own houses, with individual family members co-operating in their construction in their free time, were typical definitions of the rural heritage of southwesterners. Once these houses were completed, Okie families ceased to be migrants; they now had roots in California and could safeguard and transmit that heritage more securely to their own children. Lillian Creisler acknowledged other ostensible signs of their rural backgrounds in her careful study of Modesto's "Little Oklahoma." Writing about the several hundred people who lived there in the late 1930s, she stated, "In general, the people were sober, well-behaved, and industrious. They are a family-loving group whose home relationship is close. The children are wholesome, happy youngsters. The [Okies'] moral and religious standards are rigid." She noted as well, "There is prevalent among them a spirit of mutual aid."[53]

Few would disagree that the Okies in California were hardworking and industrious. It almost seemed as if these words had talismanic significance for them; they confidently believed that positive attitudes toward work would eventually overcome all obstacles. Observers marveled at their stamina and their pride in self-improvement.[54] A Modesto businessman observed that they were "of good character and industrious . . . they are a class that are [is] anxious to better their conditions both socially and financially."[55] A local real estate agent supported this view, declaring, "All they want is a chance to work and a home to call their own . . . and by their own efforts, they will quickly recover financially."[56] This spirit explains why Paul Allen did not complain about picking lettuce in California all day and into the night until nine or ten o'clock for seven dollars. He later returned to Oklahoma not because of unreasonably long work hours, rather because "I didn't like to work for the other fellow."[57]

Pride in toughness, physically and psychologically, and "refusing to accept defeat" were other important aspects of the Okie work ethic. Accountability to Okie codes meant one could never allow mere circumstances to interfere with one's ability to succeed.[58] Parents in "Little Oklahoma" communities consciously toughened their boys and girls to cope with a difficult world without complaining. "It ain't no use to sit and whine," one Okie song asserted; another mandated:

> You must take a blow and give one
> You must risk, you must lose . . .
> But you mustn't wince or falter
> Lest a fight you might begin
> Be a man and face the battle
> That's the only way to win[59]

It was unacceptable for boys to show pain back home in Oklahoma or Arkansas and that message was even more useful in California.[60] When Okies gathered for sport, boxing and fighting were featured recreations, including even an occasional boxing match for girls.[61] Boxing was so popular that an evangelist made a great mistake scheduling his revival on the same night as the matches; the latter were well attended, but the preacher was "left with a mighty slim congregation."[62] Okie young men in California were known to be quick with their fists when issues of family or community honor were at stake; one admitted his right hand was sore on this account the first three years he was in California.[63]

The same strict moral and religious standards and determination that Lillian Creisler observed among Okies was recognized by others. Helen Gahagan Douglas, a celebrity interested in the social conditions of the Okies, noticed even in their "tents with mud floors, there would be snowy white sheets on beds." She declared, "I have always felt from my experience . . . that they made this trek because they didn't want to sit down and take defeat." She found them to have "amazing good nature, politeness, and resistance to hardship." She also described them as very religious.[64]

On church attendance, which attracted large numbers from the Okie community, those who went to services did so enthusiastically, expressing unusual religious fervor. Few rural persons from the Southwest felt comfortable in established, middle-class churches; poorer folks required more dramatic victories over life's problems and could not achieve these in the song-sermon-prayer rituals of orderly religion. They wished to be with their friends in the Pentecostal and Holiness churches where believers expressed faith personally, relating publicly their trials looking for and finding God; they relished spontaneity among the faithful, the hands-on touch of evangelistic ministers, faith healing, and "amens" and shouts of faith, recitation of personal victories resulting from prayer and sacrifice, and the inner peace and joy that came from a believer's ability to renounce this world for the joys of heaven. The bonding of church members by these experiences, their solicitous regard for one another, whom they called "brother" or "sister," and their mutual aid when fellow believers were in need, made the churches the center for both the spiritual and social life of members.[65] What were the practical results of their faith and fellowship at a time of depression and resettlement? Oca Tathan, a migrant from Oklahoma in the 1930s, had a reply that he believed applied to the entire Okie community in California. "Did we need the church in the depression?" he asked. "You bet we did. What else did we have. . . . And you know something? We were full of joy . . . didn't have everything, but we had peace and joy." Thus, a title of a song in the Pentacostal church in Shafter, California, attended by Okies read, "There Is No Depression in Heaven."[66]

The Okies had, in fact, established a new and better life for themselves in California in 1939 when Steinbeck was portraying them in *The Grapes of Wrath* as victimized and deplorably poor. For one thing, they had transplanted themselves to California and, by all reports, their morale was good;

they pointed enthusiastically to the homes they owned and their children in schools.[67] Another continuing sign of their California identity was that, as a group, a large majority remained there despite occasional trips back and forth. The most careful study on their return is based on a tracking of 8,000 outmigrant Oklahomans from five rural townships. According to this study only 1 in 6.3 California Okies returned to Oklahoma to live.[68]

Their allegiance to California did not reflect sudden gains in wealth or power, though California's improved opportunities for wages and relief benefits undoubtedly helped convince many Okies that their choice to migrate was well founded.[69] They were still poor, but probably not as poor as they would have been staying in Oklahoma. The net worth of the 40% of migrant families who purchased land for a house among 1,000 migrant families to California averaged $465, only slightly more than their estimated worth of $268 in 1935 when the Okies first entered California.[70] Their median income for 1938 was approximately $650 when median income nationally was $1,500.[71] The modest increase in net wealth had come principally from their investments in houses, though substantial debts on them depreciated those houses as assets.[72]

The chief gains for the southwestern migrants in California came from having houses, and hence also gains in family security and psychic capital. One state official commented that three-quarters of the residents of Okie communities were in their houses within two and one-half years of residence, and another remarked that these houses were often whitewashed.[73] The Okies not only experienced a sense of progress with ownership, they also took pride in the consistent improvements in the attractiveness of their communities. Few matched the sweeping improvements of East Salinas, the lettuce capital of California. There, a reporter for *Current History* concluded, "In 1933, a dirty, unpainted, gardenless, ugly shanty town of approximately 200 persons, East Salinas has grown in the last seven years into a thriving community." The title of the article was appropriately "Grapes of Joy—Okies Forge Ahead."[74] But other Okie communities also made progress in a short time. Lillian Creisler observed about Modesto's "Little Oklahoma," "Today, one sees a pleasant, semi-orderly residential community of small white-washed houses, fronted by attractive lawns and vegetable gardens, and bordered by gay flowers. The tents, trackers, and privies have almost completely disappeared." A *New York Times* reporter who witnessed these improving communities titled his commentary, "Migrants Dreams of Owning Land Make Them a Conservative Lot."[75] These personal touches with their houses were subtle but significant statements of a growing contentedness and at-homeness of persons living in Okievilles. Each gave evidence of a determination to stay and, by inference, a statement that they were doing well enough to want to do so.

There were other salutary attributes of these communities. Their clotheslines abounded with freshly cleaned and starched clothing.[76] One woman who hung clothes to dry on those lines remarked, "We knew all about grandma's lye soap. We always were taught cleanliness was close to Godliness. We didn't have a dime but we cleaned up every day." And Okieville residents took pride in their personal appearance as well, the women especially. "They fixed their hair so nice," one of them remarked, "and all of them wore make-up—Coty make-up—that was the thing then."[77] The residents also earned favorable comment for their spirit of mutual help, again drawing on their legacy of farmlife in the South and Southwest.

By the end of the Depression decade, the rural Okies could look hopefully on their situation in California. A large majority regarded their resettlement as permanent and themselves as winners. In fact, a frequently repeated jest of the times was that the Okies had conquered California without firing a shot.[78] Public officials who had frequently interacted with them in their communities reported their morale as excellent—indeed, a county report found the Little Oklahomas "teaming [teeming] with hopeful life."[79] A Kern County supervisor was so impressed by their "hopes and aspirations for a better future" that he reportedly wrote President Roosevelt to that effect.[80] A specific, detailed study of Modesto's Little Oklahoma based on personal interviews found:

They have maintained an indomitable courage despite overwhelming hardships; they continue to be ambitious and optimistic; they have not lost their morale. Their simple little homes spell security to them; with ownership came the feeling of permanency. They have ceased to be migrants, becoming instead part of an established group, an essential for sane living and purposeful existence.[81]

The Okies did not go to California as hollow people to be tossed about by the Depression's uncertainties. Rather, they brought with them a corpus of intergenerational wisdom from farm life. Even before resettling, many, perhaps most, relied on information supplied by family members already living in California to determine whether they should attempt that distant migration. Once there, many decided immediately to settle in communities where family help would be available, and then, to facilitate their survival and success in new circumstances, they turned to the tenets of their rural heritage; they would work hard, yet expect only modest gains in a tough world for which they knew they had to be ready and to persist; stress each family member's responsibility for the well-being of the family as a whole and the value of mutual aid; and, for many, rely on religion to explain life's mysteries and persistent discrepancies. Despite California's large hydraulic farms with migratory labor forced to work vast distances, the Okies put the needs of the family unit first and sharply reduced their work circumference. This meant an unwelcome compromise with their work ethic by requiring that they accept relief when they were not working. Their premium on family loyalty also explained why family members cooperated to build houses and the advantages that later accrued from their having permanent residences. Although Okies benefited from an improving agricultural economy in California in the late 1930s, their heritage also played a major role in their successes in California.

African Americans in the Cotton South

The most abject of America's rural people were not Okies. They were the African Americans who farmed in the South, especially the lower Cotton South; they lived in the poorest region in the United States and were the poorest people living there. But beyond this, again unlike the Okies, they were ensnared in a comprehensive and exceptionally hostile racial system, designed and enforced to perpetuate their poverty. Rural African Americans in the Cotton South epitomized these disadvantages since the onus of the caste system fell heaviest on them. The fact that most of them remained positive about the future, especially in the decade of depression, is one of history's important legacies to the strength of human spirit.

In the 1930s, most American blacks still lived in the South and most of them in its cotton-growing black belt, stretching from the Carolinas through the lower South to the rich delta lands of Mississippi and Louisiana. Only a small number there, perhaps 10 to 12% of all blacks who farmed, owned their own land, usually small plots that produced smaller income than lands held by white landowners.[1] Even their independence was illusory because, on account of their mortgages, they often remained hostage to discriminatory practices of white bankers and moneylenders. They might "sacrifice morning til night, cradle to the grave and yet be busted."[2] Black tenants were slightly more numerous; they owned their own mules and equipment and paid fixed rates of cash or shares to farm an owner's land. Their incomes varied, but they usually extracted less income than independent farmers and more than sharecroppers. The latter comprised the typical black farmer, especially in the states of South Carolina, Alabama, Georgia, Mississippi and Arkansas, the location of two-thirds of the South's sharecroppers. Indeed, while white sharecroppers were more numerous than their black counterparts in the upper South, the reverse was true in the lower South, where, in the 1930s, black croppers outnumbered whites two to one. This situation would allow Arthur F. Raper, a skillful analyst of the rural South at that time, to declare that sharecropping in the South was a "Negro institution" while share-renting was "historically a white institution."[3]

The most conspicuous characteristic of black rural life in the South was poverty. This, despite the typical farm family's demanding work schedule from early in the morning until sunset and often including a half-day on Saturday. Their difficult living conditions are best described by Charles S. Johnson, a sociologist from Fiske University. His findings in the late 1930s emerged from a survey of 916 black rural families living in eight rural counties in the South, five in cotton-growing areas and three where mixed agriculture prevailed. He found the median income of most of these families only $452 a year, with appalling living conditions: floors bare, furniture sparse, and rooms unlighted. Only fifty-three families had running water and only nine of these were actual farm families; two-thirds had an "open privy" for a toilet, while ninety-three families (10%) had no toilet facilities at all. Less than 2% had electricity. One-third of the families had only two or three rooms, though more than half of these had more than six family members. Nearly another third had over eight family members, and most of them managed in four rooms or less. As for contents, these consisted of old couches, rickety beds, and sparse chairs. Although Johnson found few hungry people, their typical diet of cornbread, sugar cane distilled into syrup, and occasional smoked and cured ham from butchered hogs was monotonous and unhealthy. Johnson, who conducted a separate study earlier of Macon County, Alabama, came to an understated conclusion: black rural areas in the South produced "a cheerless condition of life."[4]

The New Deal, contrary to popular assumption, did not substantially improve the material life or opportunities for southern rural blacks. Its farm subsidy programs benefited largely white landowners while costing their black sharecroppers cabins and commissary security as owners cut back their production of cotton; many were forced to enter the labor market at lower levels as wage laborers with paltry incomes, and were employable only when the farm cycle required extra labor. Those displaced frequently moved into nearby farm towns and gradually began to improve their income with an occasional job in the off-season or supplements from New Deal relief or work-relief programs, though blacks were often underrepresented on relief rolls and often received lower relief rates as well. Still other blacks, 500,000 in all, many from the rural South, migrated to the North and Midwest, where they were also heavily dependent on New Deal welfare programs. The New Deal may have conducted a "very quiet revolution" for southern rural blacks in substituting federal paternalism for that of the white planter, but genuine choices and improved ability to participate in the country's social and economic system would, for once rural blacks, depend on later economic development and events.[5]

There are an unusual number of carefully researched and perceptive analyses of rural farm-serving communities in the South that attracted displaced black sharecroppers in the 1930s.[6] These attest that blacks in these places were also much less equal than whites who lived there. Although black residents of Cottonville (Hortense Powdermaker's fictitious name for Indianola, Mississippi) were free to enter the attractive part of town (population 3,000) where whites lived and owned stores on Saturdays to loiter, buy, socialize, and watch others, blacks, other than those employed there, did not remain at night. They were expected to be "across the tracks," a euphemism for the ghettoized black community separated from the main part of town by railroad tracks. Blacks living in that section owned small groceries, a cafe, a pool room, juke joints, and soda shops. Here, too, were offices and, of course, houses for a few black professionals, and also churches; the area as a whole was markedly different from where whites lived and shopped.[7] One commentator summed up a description of the black quarters in a typical rural community in a cotton area:

In general, the Negro areas have fewer paved streets and sidewalks (in fact, the only ones paved are those streets which carry a large amount of through traffic). Many of the Negro districts have no sewerage system; the streets are poorly drained and poorly maintained; and street lights are few or absent. In essence, this means that the Negroes generally occupy the least desirable residential areas and receive only a minimum of public services and improvements.[8]

Although there were occasional substantial homes for black professionals, if not equal to the best homes of whites, most blacks lived in rundown houses, lacking even such basic conveniences as inside toilets. Living conditions for blacks in Indianola prompted John Dollard to conclude that the community consisted of a white middle class and a "Negro group largely of the lower class."[9]

That none of these disparities were decried publicly by whites was a tribute not merely to their self-interest, but their confident reasoning that the caste system correctly implemented differences in the abilities of the races. Applied variously through the South, its credo was most insistently held in the plantation or Cotton South. The caste system may be defined as codes of law and conduct crafted to assure comprehensive and permanent domination of African Americans by whites. John Dollard summed up its emotional meaning for Southerntown with a couple of deft phrases and a striking example of attitudes:

Southerntown is a veritable Cheka [Soviet secret police] in its vigilance on caste matters. There are constant and potent pressures to compel every white person to act his caste role correctly. Once I was walking to a Negro home, one of the few on the white side of Southerntown, and had to ask directions. A white woman on one of the porches told me and then said, "You know that niggers live there, don't you?" She was at once expressing surprise and defining the situation so that I would be sure to behave correctly.[10]

Dollard noted that this caveat was typical of the special energy whites invested in preserving the rigidities of the system. He also understood the utilitarian advantages that explained their obsessive commitments. The caste system represented their best sense of peacefully managing a biracial society on terms favorable to themselves. As Dollard wisely reckoned, "In essence the caste idea," its "one absolute" was to prevent miscegenation because this was the part of the code that incited the most determined hostility. Miscegenation was enforced by laws that declared that a child born of sexual union of persons in the two castes was illegitimate and automatically consigned to the lower caste. But behind this seemingly impersonal formula Dollard noted a deeper meaning. "Caste in Southerntown is" he wrote, "a categorical barrier to sexual congress between upper-caste women (white) and lower-caste men (black)."[11] Since the system did not prohibit sex between upper-caste men (white) and lower-caste women (black), white males could enjoy women of both races, a gender as well as a racial gain.

Besides these benefits, whites achieved other substantial advantages by subordinating blacks, especially cheap labor, expectations of deference and obedience, and spatial separation insofar as that was practicable in small southern towns. To justify their dominance, whites held fixed ideas about the inferiority of blacks. Either God or nature determined their inferiority, but in any case the outcome was immutable.[12] Mentally and morally inferior, they were still acceptable if they remained in their place subordinate to whites, a lesson whites demonstrated to blacks continuously in their interactions. Even lower-class whites were superior to all blacks, including those of apparent distinction. The word "nigger" was the white community's code word to signify the inferiority of blacks and it could be used by any white to any black. Ned Cobb, a philosophic black farmer who spent a lifetime trying to figure out white folks, noted that even poor whites "seem to have thought they was a class above the Negro."[13]

All whites in rural areas of the South had much to gain from upper-caste solidarity, and this accounts for their tenacious group dedication to its implementation. Any white who balked at the caste system and attempted to initiate personal as against caste relations with blacks risked severe social ostracism, even being cast out of the community.[14]

Caste sanctions, however, proved an illusory mechanism for pattern maintenance between the races because blacks perceived the system's injustice, and whites, ever conscious of its incongruity with overall American mores, became defensive if they felt blacks were restive. This predicament sometimes reached the pressure point "for a bursting of the steam boiler over the white man's keeping the Negro in his place." Whites then felt impelled to exercise their ultimate weapon, lynching, as a resolvent of tensions. The sociologists and social anthropologists observing as residents in the small towns and cities of the South in the 1930s noted how slight violations of caste codes could magnify tensions and result in lynchings.

Finally, the hostility of the whites reaches such a pitch that any small infraction will spur them to open action. A Negro does something which ordinarily might be passed over, or which usually provokes only a mild punishment, but the whites respond with violence. The Negro victim then becomes both a scapegoat and an object lesson for this group. . . . The whites always say after such an outburst: "We haven't had any trouble since then."[15]

What was particularly likely to prompt a lynching was for a black to rape or have sexual relations with a white woman, usually construed as rape as well. This was a virtual call to arms to preserve caste dominance; the black offender had tested the ultimate taboo. If this behavior were permitted, the entire caste system would be jeopardized. Actually, southern white males were overly protective in this regard because chances for consummation were slight. Yet, the accruing caste and gender gains outweighed expenditures required to sustain the system. Rewards obtained (silencing fears, maintaining caste, supposedly protecting women, releasing aggression) over-matched fears of being caught for their desperate acts of vigilantism.[16]

Even though lynchers were often well known and could be identified, there was no effective opposition to the practice in southern rural communities as late as the early 1930s. To oppose lynchers would jeopardize the benefits of all whites and, consequently, would be tantamount to forfeiting one's place in the community. Nor did southern states enforce laws to punish these vigilante murders; only four had statutes prohibiting lynching and these obtained only a small number of convictions. In the state of Florida, with a cotton economy in its northern areas, there was not a single conviction for lynching as late as the 1930s, despite the fact that Florida had the highest rate of lynching of any state relative to the size of its black population.[17]

Effective opposition to lynching came not from local church groups, ministers, or civic-minded citizens, state governments, or generally even county sheriffs. Rather, it was precipitated by private agencies and people outside the immediate area of the crime. A major corrective influence came from the Association of Southern Women for the Prevention of Lynching (ASWPL), a group that resolved that white women of the South could protect themselves with effective police and government action; it worked especially to sensitize the public to the dangers and injustice of lynching. Another major factor contributing to the decline of lynching was the ex-

posure of the vigilantes by the national media, abetted by the indefatigable
efforts of the National Association for the Advancement of Colored People
(NAACP), especially when Walter White was its executive secretary in the
1930s.[18]

Young black males raised in the South in the early twentieth century were
still apprehensive about the possibility of being lynched; somewhere, somehow, they would be accused of something and find themselves in a circle of
unrelenting tormentors. Fears of being expendable in this way were underscored by the fact that on average nineteen blacks were still being lynched
each year between 1933 and 1935, and the realization that incitement might
proceed on a casual circumstance or merely a monstrous whim.[19] The im-
potence blacks felt at times of lynchings and the rioting by whites that frequently accompanied them aroused deep and desperate fears. Often without
guns, usually without means of redress through the sheriff, without white
friends who would stand up and denounce these events as outrageous, they
appeared defenseless. This, coupled with their poverty and poor educational
facilities, the aggressive determination of whites to enforce all precepts of
caste, the inability of blacks to participate effectively in the political system,
leads to the reasonable conclusion that these were America's most downtrodden people at a time of calamitous national misfortune—the Great Depression—truly a people without hope. But evidence contradicts this logic:
they used their weaknesses to advantage, mounted their own campaign of
diffuse aggression against the dominant caste whose actions, at least, spurred
solidarity among themselves, and they found relief from their afflictions in
religion as well as a sense of their own moral dignity. They scoffed at times
at their oppressors, enjoyed one another's company, found help from outside the South to define their image of themselves, and, above all, many
looked to a better future.

John Dollard acknowledges only a "passive solidarity" among blacks in
Southerntown, illustrating his position by establishing that they would not
testify against alleged criminal activity by fellow blacks. Although Dollard is
convincing when he maintains that caste sanctions prevented African Americans from active solidarity through politics, and that they diminished their
own chances of confronting whites with a common front by cleavages of
class among themselves, he underestimates their effective solidarity on key
issues that promoted their group interests.[20]

To begin with, most rural blacks in the South displayed solidarity in recognizing that they were dealing with a hostile, racially prejudiced system
foisted on them by whites. Many actually concluded that it was dangerous
or embarrassing to spend time with whites and decided to avoid them as
much as possible.[21] Speaking freely with fellow blacks, Charles S. Johnson
corroborated Dollard's conclusion that many blacks in Southerntown (Indianola, Mississippi, also), a representative small town in the Cotton South,
believed that it was dangerous to deal with whites. From a black raised as a

farmer in Alabama, Johnson learned it was wise to respect whites because "they will get you killed for disrespecting them."[22] The barbarous nature of lynching especially broke down trust for whites among rural blacks. But fears of lesser humiliations also prompted fear and avoidance of whites. "I just don't ride trains now," an upper-class black declared. "I use my car and drive anywhere I want to go. . . . I feel sorry for Negroes who have to ride trains and busses."[23] "I stay away from 'em as far as I can," declared one black youth and another asserted, "the farther they is [away] from me, the better I like it."[24] Maya Angelou, while growing up, learned from her family living in a cotton-growing area of Arkansas, "The less you say to white folks the better."[25] "I am not a white folks' nigger, and I try to keep out of trouble," declared a black farmer in Marked Tree, Arkansas. "I know, though, that I am in the South, and I know they can make it hard for me, so I just attend . . . to my business and see if I can dodge a lot of trouble."[26] Another black explained he liked whites "in their place."[27] Among black youth in the black belt, Johnson found a greater aversion to whites than that felt by their elders; two-thirds did not wish to contact them either from caution, discomfort, or active hostility.[28]

The wish of many blacks to remove themselves from the company of upper-caste whites was accompanied by their keen perceptions of the foibles of whites and assorted convictions that diluted the pretensions of whites to exert power over them. In effect, blacks often managed to right the imbalance between the races regardless of the caste system. When African-American church women in Cottonville put on a program for their club, one who impersonated Mrs. Roosevelt invited "some of her Negro friends to sing a few songs and the audience roared."[29] Since the skit occurred before Mrs. Roosevelt's genuine friendship for blacks was known to them, the issue was not to make fun of Mrs. Roosevelt—the notion that any white had any black friend was the source of hilarity. "Whites could never be real because they were always on guard," another black woman noted. "We know we are Negroes," she remarked to Hortense Powdermaker, "but when we're alone we sometimes forget it. But white people never let you forget it, they always make you stay in your place."[30] Airs of superiority of whites and their lack of "fairness" were held up for scorn by educated blacks. An upper-class Negro pointed out to Powdermaker, "Whites never respond politely to a Negro's 'thank you,' but make no reply . . . or else grunt 'all right.' "[31] And those who plumbed the meaning of laughter by blacks when whites unexpectedly approached, sensed that not a little of this had qualities of private, last-laugh derision of whites. "The Negroes always have the laugh on the Whites," one black asserted, "because the Whites are always being deceived by them and never know it." He believed this gave blacks "the upper hand."[32]

Awareness among blacks of the artificiality of caste relationships was also consciously expressed in their own racial pride. Maya Angelou, raised in

Stamps, Arkansas, declared segregation was so complete in this small town where her grandmother operated a grocery that black children "didn't know what whites looked like." Yet her memories are noteworthy for favorable comparisons of blacks with whites, and she concludes her segregated high school experience in 1940 with "I was a proud member of the wonderful, beautiful, Negro race." Albert Murray recalls the enthusiasm of children while singing "Lift Ev'ry Voice and Sing," often called the Negro National Anthem in a Mobile, Alabama school for blacks. He doubted whether the leitmotif for civil rights in the 1960s, "We Shall Overcome," could compare with the "aspiration and determination" rendered earlier in the "anthem."[33]

Henry Louis Gates's memoir, *Colored People*, focuses on the Colored Zone, a ghettoized community of 200 or so blacks who lived within Piedmont, West Virginia (population 2,500), during his raising in the 1950s and 1960s. Despite its seeming chronological incongruity for a study of Americans in the 1930s, this unusually frank memoir is useful for an understanding of the earlier period. The Colored Zone hadn't changed substantially and would not do so until integration became a fact of life in America in the 1960s; it remained until then ghettoized and virtually "self-contained," similar to blacks living in Cottontowns.[34] Interspersing accounts of the lives of his grandmother, mother, and nine uncles, all of whom lived in the Colored Zone, Gates attests to this continuity. For them as well as for him, the black world was the important world before integration.[35] One senses that Gates's own glorification of the superiority of blacks over whites was in part a legacy from his elder relatives. Heritage among blacks in the Colored Zone held that blacks were better in hunting and fishing, their food was better, and they had better values than whites; blacks also, unlike whites, had genuine community because of their good feelings and fondness for food, drink, and fun at get-togethers. They also had better cemeteries and funerals (where you could work over your grief) than whites. This bountiful and fulfilling isolation (segregation), Gates candidly relates, shattered on the occasion of Piedmont's first compulsorily integrated mill picnic.[36]

Racial pride was manifest in a variety of other ways. Richard Wright, raised primarily in Jackson, Mississippi, establishes how black boys whom he met or with whom he associated felt anger and resentment against whites and some of them relished the idea of becoming "bad niggers," even to terrorizing whites.[37] Although few in number, they demanded extraordinary vigilance from whites. For some whites the only feasible course was to lynch or "smash them down." "If they get sassy," a white employer informed Dollard, "hit them, that is all they understand."[38] However, the "bad nigger" might be "secretly endorsed" by the black community, and if he gave no quarter to his tormentors he might even become their hero.[39] Raper found that racial pride among rural blacks in Georgia was a factor in their prohibiting sexual relationships with whites.[40] Dollard heard reports in Mississippi about blacks beating up black women to assure that they not have sex with white men.[41] There were also isolated incidents of whites being gunned down from the bush probably for the same reason.[42] Young school-age blacks in cotton plantation areas, those most vocal about their racial affirmation and animosities for whites, twice hissed white speakers before student assemblies when they referred to the beautiful tradition of the "black mammy."[43] In Stamps, Arkansas, black students concluded their graduation exercises with James Weldon Johnson's "Lift Ev'ry Voice and Sing," a stirring call for the full emancipation of African Americans.[44] The animosity among Southerntown's blacks toward Italy for attacking Ethiopia was still another sign of racial solidarity.[45]

However, paradoxically, many rural blacks in the South also used caste rules to advantage against whites.[46] Whites readily conceded that blacks in cotton plantation areas often led happy-go-lucky lives with their assured cabins and food as plantation croppers and their permissive sexuality.[47] Whites, however, underestimated how much they themselves contributed to rewards for blacks by their imposition of the caste system. One black youth described his strategy to Charles Johnson, "When I'm around them [whites] I act like they are more than I am. I don't think they are but they do. I hear [black] people say that's the best way to act." Another black in a small southern city declared, "They [whites] all want Negroes to jump and pull off their hats when they are talking to them. . . . When Mr. Charlie [important white] has something I want, there is nothing I can't do to get it."[48] By appearing docile and pliant, blacks were often preferred over whites as sharecroppers by plantation owners.[49] Black cooks were allowed to take home food for their own families, even though white employers considered this practice stealing, because that was the way they were expected to behave.[50] Again, the same criterion justified their borrowing from employers without paying back. Similarly, blacks were unlikely to go to jail despite brawls and knifings among themselves.[51]

Jack T. Kirby relates how a shrewd black male, a horse trader, would play on the sympathies of white customers, irate over the broken-down horses he sold them. He would counter with how he was just a "poor old negro" sure that "good white men" would understand. Whites would then relent and he would be on his way to sell another flawed animal to another white.[52] Assumptions of the natural inferiority of blacks sometimes facilitated their release from responsibility, even from automobile accidents. In one instance, or so the story goes, a black man went ahead at a red light and convinced the arresting officer that he noted whites went ahead on green so he assumed "red" was the appropriate signal for blacks.[53] Lower-class blacks also exploited the view of whites that blacks were by nature animalistic and sexually promiscuous. This made for tolerant community attitudes among whites toward "fun places" in the black quarters, especially the gambling, racy juke joints, the kinds of circumstances that prompted one white viewing blatant black sexuality to chuckle and say, 'That is another good reason for being a nigger!'[54]

Some social scientists who scrutinized rural blacks in cotton-belt towns in the 1930s observed what southern whites were slow to realize—how much African Americans enjoyed life among themselves, what Henry L. Gates described as "the warmth and nurturence of the womb-like colored world."[55] Blacks who recall the spirit of their get-togethers such as picnics, church socials, or camp meetings do so with nostalgia.[56] Participants often remember these settings for their friendliness and easy communications. "In social groups of their own [Southerntown]," Dollard commented, "Negroes appear to have a kind of naturalness and lack of tension in personal relationships that is not characteristic of whites; they seem to fall easily into conversation and get in touch with a kind of charming directness." And those blacks who migrated from the Cotton South to the "Promised Land" of the North sometimes sadly contrasted their urban situation in an era of civil rights with the all-black world of their Cottontowns in the South, noting the city "broke down a lot of things we had going."[57]

Churches were especially instrumental in fostering social activities among blacks in the Cotton South. These included clubs and meetings, suppers, services, and revivals. The services and the greetings between families and friends (they often addressed one another as "brother" and "sister") before and after them were the most important weekly social experiences for many rural blacks. Services were conducted in such a way that the members participated energetically, with the minister engaging the congregation in dialogue. "Have you got the good religion," he would query. The replies would vary: many responded with "Amen," others "Certainly, Lord," and still others "Sure enough." As the emotional tempo escalated and the minister became more dramatic, some members fainted and needed to be carried outside for fresh air. Others shouted, and everyone sang enthusiastically.[58]

The importance attached to the celebration was evident from the dress of the worshippers and their special reception before services began. "On the hottest day in August the men wear coats and the women their hats" but with adaptations to summer with "a predominance of cool, white and light colors." Meanwhile, circulating through the congregation, helping members to be seated, scurried young women explicitly designated by their white gloves and headbands proclaiming USHER. The church not only fostered religious services that invited expressive solidarity and community, it helped establish clubs and lodges, the latter usually designed to look after the sick and bury the dead, organizations outside the church, but often led by churchgoers.[59]

Not all blacks in Southerntown, especially those in the lower classes, went to churches, and not all who did felt impelled to honor its disclaimers forbidding drinking, dancing, and promiscuous sexuality. Lower-class blacks (farm laborers, transient sharecroppers, and those doing manual work on odd jobs), though at times members of the churches, were more often variable or absent. Dollard observed they were not sexually inhibited, and Powdermaker that "they made no pretense of monogamy," instead flaunting a promiscuous sexual morality. Middle-class blacks informed Dollard that blacks in the lower classes were not satisfied unless "they had three or four partners on the string."[60] Life really began for them on Saturday nights when "they raised Cain" in the jukes where whisky was sold, gambling and dancing were wild, and the women were considered sexually available. Noise from the jukes blared through the black quarters—loud music from race records, animated conversation and accusations, boisterous laughter, and the sound of verbal skirmishing often a prelude to violence. The latter, usually in the wee hours of the morning, would invite the presence of the white sheriff who might be forced to close the place down if there were a shooting or a knifing. The revelers who crowded into these places week after week were not defeated people or pessimists. They had the illusion of all life's big options at their fingertips—power, sex, and riches. The jukes provided diversions for many who might otherwise have despaired.[61]

Religion was also an important source of collective strength and hopefulness among blacks in rural areas in the Deep South in the 1930s. Maya Angelou, from her recollections of that time, regarded Christianity as essential to their survival. She wrote, "People whose history and future were being threatened each day by extinction considered that it was only by divine intervention that they could live at all."[62] Most blacks in Cottonville belonged to a church that was usually Baptist or Methodist; both were churches in which women supplied most members—at times as many as two-thirds of those attending—though ministers and deacons or elders were men.[63] Most members were middle class and middle aged, with young people less numerous and less committed to the church's programs and social activities.[64] Sermons, described by both Dollard and Powdermaker, illustrate that blacks in Southerntown were spared a righteous and punitive God; the emphasis was placed on God as a loving and merciful Being who readily forgave the contrite and welcomed all for salvation.[65] God's mercy seemed to take special cognizance of sins of the flesh; sermons on those subjects were not common nor strongly condemnatory when cited. In this context, church members openly avowed that they might commit sinful practices for the time being, but they expected to reform later. In the interim, church members responded enthusiastically to the refrain "Come unto me all ye who are heavily laden," an appropriate theme for those with difficult lives.[66]

Christianity was a working resource for the black faithful in the rural South. It powerfully affected their immediate thoughts, decisions, and needs, and was, at the same time, an inspiration to sustain justifiable hopes despite rigors of the caste system. At numerous times and in countless ways, it provided them with a coherent and dignified message to deal with the

Marion Post Wolcott, "Jitterbugging in a Juke Joint on a Saturday Afternoon," Clarksdale, MS, 1939. Reproduced from the Collections of the Library of Congress.

burdensome and dangerous circumstances of their lives. Ned Cobb's life history illustrates this well. A black from Central Alabama, a man of towering abilities and strengths of character, he was cheated and exploited by whites through his early life as sharecropper and finally as a landowner. When he joined the Alabama Sharecroppers Union, a biracial organization intended to protect white as well as black croppers by collective bargaining, Cobb ran afoul of the law and was threatened with arrest. He engaged in a shoot-out with sheriff-deputies. Cobb was wounded and captured and, at age forty-seven, consigned to prison in April 1933 for what would become a term of twelve years. Cobb called this his "bluesey times." He was separated from his wife, identified in Alabama as a representative of a communist-led organization, known by white guards as a prisoner who had fired at a white sheriff, and housed in prison with "hellions" who intended to harm him. "And all of a sudden," Cobb related,

God stopped in my soul. . . . I just caught fire. My mind cleared up. I got so happy— I didn't realize where I was at. . . . I was a raw piece of plunder that mornin' in jail. God heard me and answered my prayers. . . . Well, they had my trial and put me in prison [12 years]. The Lord blessed my soul and set me in a position to endure it.[67]

Maya Angelou's grandmother in Stamps, Arkansas, was never confronted by problems of this magnitude (she faced aggravations from insensitive whites instead), but she too found the strength to deal with bothersome issues through religious convictions. On one occasion a group of poor white girls trooped in front of her store, with Maya watching from inside the screen door. They disparaged the grandmother, imitating her posture and puffing up their lips to mock her appearance, and one of them added further humiliation to the great amusement of the other girls. She performed a handstand showing thereby her bare bottom since she was not wearing drawers. The girls then departed, each saying good-bye insincerely to Maya's grandmother. She replied with her own good-byes while addressing each one by name and then humming softly, "Glory, glory hallelujah when I lay my burden down." Witnessing the entire exchange, Maya Angelou marveled at the fact that her grandmother was happy. Angelou knew her grandmother had won the contest.[68]

No secular institution could match the power of the churches to help those who felt afflicted. An elderly widow in Cottonville put her faith in the "Lord's help" and found her faith justified. Another was sure the Lord would not let her starve because she knew "the Lord would never let a Christian woman who leads a good life go hungry."[69] Others who prospered as farmers voiced "thanks to the good God with every other breath."[70] Personal misfortune in everyday life could also be explained by believers. When a woman reported to her friends in church that a man had recently been killed by lightning while plowing, she explained the incident with "the Lord did not mean for men to plough when it was lightning." This met with a reply from another woman in the group that "this was a lesson for all to be ready because we never know when our time would come."[71]

Another important function of the churches was to provide individuals with dignified purpose in important times of their lives. Baptism was usually celebrated in the quiet part of a river with immersion of those baptized and solemn statements by the minister as large numbers watched on the river-banks. The ceremony was marked by special dress for the ministers and church officials, hymns, and firm admonitions to "Go in peace and sin no more." Later the baptized would be called on to testify to their new faith. The ceremony was expressively joyous, celebrated by shouting, laughter, and happiness, especially the immersion of the baptized, usually adolescents, now more completely bonded to their families in faith.[72]

Funerals in the black Christian churches were rituals in grief, expressing that grief, being reconciled to the transience of life while remaining hopeful about its ultimate outcome. The service emphasized that a deep human relationship had been sealed by death. The deceased was gone, really gone, never to be seen alive among family and friends again. The minister consciously heightened grief by rendering touching personal statements about his or her life. Remarks by friends would then be introduced unless the mourner could no longer control grief and broke down. They would then play a "bitter-sweet song" such as, "When I'm gone the last mile of the way . . . and I know there are joys that await me."[73] The intense sadness of the service was offset by the hope that all would meet again as each walked the last mile toward heaven.

Christianity not only contributed to the personal strength and adaptability of individual blacks in parlous times, it could also serve racial pride and hence collective strength. Not a few blacks saw themselves as superior Christians to whites because they were a kind, warmhearted people while whites demonstrated mean-spirited natures as they attempted to impose their superiority over blacks; Some took solace from religious convictions that they would receive special treatment on Judgment Day. Maya Angelou recalled what she regarded to be the essential message of the big annual revival for blacks in Stamps, Arkansas, in the mid-1930s:

Even if the congregation were society's pariahs, they were going to be angels in a marble white heaven and sit on the right hand of Jesus, the Son of God.[74]

Angelou remembered the general tenor of the discussion among members of the congregation as they left the services:

Let the whitefolks have their money and power and sarcasm and big houses and schools and lawns like carpets and books and mostly—mostly—let them have their whiteness. It was better to be meek and lowly, spat upon and abused for this little time than to spend eternity frying in hell. . . . The Bible said . . . folks going to get what they deserve.[75]

However incongruously, for the ladies walking home and discussing lofty religious issues, they began to hear warning signals from Miss Grace's house, a juke joint where customers would be stamping their feet and making uproarious sounds to the strains of the blues from the early evening to the wee hours of the morning.[76] Truly, African Americans in Stamps, Arkansas, like those in most small towns in the cotton economy areas of the South, derived nurture from both the sacred and the profane; each gave something to its faithful.

That same enthusiasm for life's potentialities so clearly reflected in robust religious experience in church services, the boisterous music and stomping of the jukes, and in frequent testimonials to racial pride was also exhibited in the fondness of cotton area African Americans for their children. At minimum, having large families as they did expressed parents' confidence that new life served important purposes and that their future would be better with many children. A principal motive for producing large families was economic advantage—more hands for the field and hence improved production and greater economic self-sufficiency for the entire family. That the large family was seen as an expanded workforce may be inferred from typical roles of children in these families. They were seldom individualized; parents on several occasions even failed to recall their names or ages and deceased children were seldom remembered.[77] Clearly, however, as research sociologists noted, there were noneconomic considerations for having large families as well. Powdermaker found "a real love for children and a great joy in having them about."[78] Women were generally proud of the number of children they bore and those with large broods were admired. Some mothers saw this as a sign of their biological vitality, a claim proudly shared by fathers as well as mothers. Others reasoned it was the "Lord's will"; researchers found "little conscious birth control" in the black community.[79]

Southern rural blacks not only had large families of their own, but they also enthusiastically adopted children. Although family life among middle- and lower-class blacks was characterized by discontinuities, especially divorce and casual separation, often unrecorded, and numerous children born out of wedlock, the black community cared enough for its children to resolve the problem of finding a home for those jeopardized.[80] Grandparents often served as surrogate parents. Again, parents of a young unmarried woman would sometimes raise her child as their own, with the actual mother resuming her role as an elder sister.[81] A separated parent, if remarried, brought some or all of his or her children by a previous marriage to the new marriage, adding to all or some of the children of the other spouse by a previous marriage.[82] What was most notable about these arrangements for sociologists Johnson and Powdermaker was that the newly adopted children did not appear to be distinguished from the spouse's natural children.[83]

New sources of encouragement for rural blacks in cotton areas in the 1930s came from the effects of technology, and the new and better contacts it opened with the world outside their rural community. Technology's metamorphosizing powers in cotton areas are captured in Arthur Raper's description of the impact of the car in the 1930s in Georgia's black belt. He observed that whites and blacks both bought power when they purchased automobiles because they could go to town and ignore the plantation commissaries with their exorbitant price markups for captive buyers.[84] Temptations like these accounted for poor farmers spending extravagantly for secondhand cars that they often couldn't afford, but the psychic capital of independence and choice made the purchase price seem reasonable. In checking data on car purchases, Raper discovered that nearly two-thirds of white renters and over one-half of white sharecroppers had cars in the mid-1930s but so did half of black tenants and 40% of black croppers. Raper shrewdly observed the car's special appeal to black farmers for its dissolvent effect on the caste system because "only in automobiles on public roads do landlords and tenants and white people and Negroes of the Black Belt meet on the basis of equality."[85] Self-preservation dictated that each driver retain his half of the road. In addition, a black driving an automobile drove, of course, from the front seat unlike public transportation in the South that always assigned him or her a back seat.[86]

Blacks in the lower South not only benefited from using automobiles in the region in the 1930s, they were also conscious that they obtained advantages through an improving technology of communications. They learned that President Roosevelt and especially Mrs. Roosevelt were interested in their needs. News of the Roosevelts circulated in the black belt areas through articles from Washington correspondents, radio broadcasts, pictures and newsreels in local and regional newspapers and movie houses, and more surreptitious sources such as the Chicago *Defender* and *Crisis*.[87]

One of the most important morale builders came through newspaper and radio accounts of prize fights in the squared rings of New York or sometimes Chicago—a legacy of Joe Louis, the "Brown Bomber," a fabulously gifted fighter and heavyweight boxing champion in the middle and late 1930s. Born in a sharecropper's cabin in Alabama, always especially relevant on this account to the Cotton South, Joe Louis became a professional fighter in Chicago in 1934 and heavyweight champion of the world in 1937 at the young age of twenty-three. He systematically destroyed opposition boxers, usually whites, including his predecessor, James J. Braddock, and maintained his crown with unusual personal and boxing grace and devastating punching power through the remainder of the 1930s and beyond. Louis was not only a great fighter and champion, he was a lightning flash of confidence to American blacks everywhere; for several years of the Depression decade, he, more than any person in America, carried the fondest hopes of the race on his shoulders and it was he, again without peer, who symbolically provided African Americans with further intimations of impending success.[88] There can be no mistaking the champion's enormous appeal among blacks in the rural, lower South—that area where blacks had concealed so much frustration, half-conscious of their ability to be equal, even at times superior, but dogged by an absence of objective standards, even forced to rely on mythical figures like the powerful John Henry. Joe Louis, a genuine Titan, would move blacks several paces forward to a place where their fancied selves were, at least, dimly possible.

Farm Security Administration photographer Ben Shahn took a photograph of a middle-aged black man with only one leg sitting outside a barbershop for blacks in Biloxi, Mississippi, during the summer of 1935; the picture testified to the enormous appeal of Joe Louis to local blacks. Behind the man, who wears a faint smile, and inside the shop window, was a sign for passersby and patrons announcing a gathering to celebrate Louis's ringtime successes.[89] That same atmosphere charged with enthusiasm for Louis was found by Swedish sociologist Gunnar Myrdal. He discovered that children in a tiny, black schoolhouse in rural Georgia could not remember the name of President Roosevelt and were unable to identify leaders of the

Ben Shahn, "Black Man with One Leg in Front of Store," Natchez, MS, 1935. Photo with a sign in the shop calling for a celebration for Joe Louis underscores the heroic appeal of Louis for African Americans in the Cotton South. Reproduced from the Collections of the Library of Congress.

NAACP such as W.E.B. Du Bois or Walter White, but they could readily identify Joe Louis. Charles S. Johnson met with similar responses.[90] But it was Maya Angelou, watching the crowd in her family's country store for Louis's fight with Carnera in 1935, who best registered the depth of identification of blacks with Louis. That night in Stamps, Arkansas, she recalled:

The last inch of space was filled, yet people continued to wedge themselves along the walls of the Store. Uncle Willie had turned the radio up to its last notch. . . .

For a time Carnera seemed to be winning and enthusiasm in the crowd sagged. And then Joe Louis countered Carnera; he was mad and he began to punish his opponent with sharp blows. Carnera went down and the fight was over, with Louis as victor. Angelou records a seismic shift in group attitude in the store at that moment:

Champion of the world. A black boy. Some black mother's son. He was the strongest man in the world. People drank Coca-Cola like ambrosia and ate candy bars like Christmas. Some of the men went behind the store and poured white lightning in their soft drink bottles and a few of the bigger boys followed them. . . . It would take an hour or more before the people would leave the store and head for home

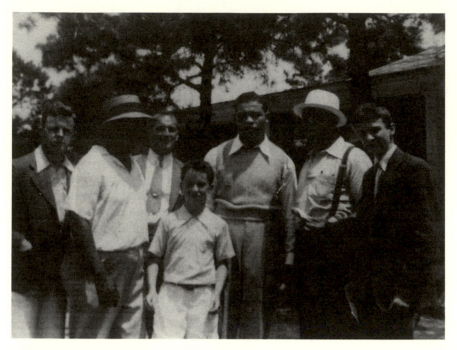

Many whites were also attracted to Joe Louis and became his fans. The author of this study, then eight years old, took a special trip with family friends to meet the ring champion in the late 1930s to an Atlantic City country club. Also present are Louis' trainers.

. . . on a night when Joe Louis had proved we were the strongest people in the world.[91]

As the example of Joe Louis illustrates, the strictures of caste came to be challenged in the 1930s as never before, by a free flow of ideas and photographs generated by a technology that originated generally outside the South—newspaper articles or photographs by Associated or United Press, and newsreels accompanying movies that more nearly reflected broader American values and ideals of democracy. These pictured African Americans in politics, entertainment, flying airplanes, in Olympic contests, and winning sporting events. Sports figures like Joe Louis made the biggest impression as Johnson discovered from his extensive interviews with youngsters growing up in the Black Belt. "This racial superiority in the field of athletics," Johnson wrote, "has contributed more to race pride than any single factor in recent years."[92] Joe Louis' many ring successes also made him popular with many white Americans. What was new about the context of this black experience in the rural South was increasing access to information about achievements by blacks nationally at a time when America was itself changing and providing them with more promising models.

Blacks in the Deep South in the 1930s also first received substantial help in their daily lives from northern-based organizations emboldened to work on their behalf. The NAACP performed yeoman labor in the 1930s to minimize the dangers of lynchings in the daily lives of rural blacks. Lynchings, often accompanied by riots, had generated such fears among local blacks earlier that they generally didn't protest these events publicly, though they sometimes stored guns to prevent the looting and burning of their homes. They were now assisted by the energetic efforts of the NAACP and its executive secretary, Walter White. A skillful conversationalist, socializer, and political activist, White could amass formidable pressures outside the South to eradicate lynching, which he considered one of the NAACP's premier goals in the 1930s. A conversation with Walter White, as Eleanor Roosevelt noted in a letter to presidential secretary Steve Early, "sooner or later turned to lynching." He communicated easily and often with Mrs. Roosevelt and was able to see the president when he felt the situation warranted his intervention.[93] White also had key friends and supporters in the Congress; twice in the 1930s, in 1935 and 1937, antilynching bills reached the floor of both houses of Congress. He was also a prime mover behind the "Art Commentary on Lynching," an exhibit held for two weeks in New York in 1935 that attracted several thousand people, including Mrs. Roosevelt, and displayed the works of such well-known artists as George Bellows, Reginald Marsh, and Jose Orozco. Clearly, the national conscience was stirring and Walter White and the NAACP were in the forefront of that agitation.[94]

These efforts conferred tangible benefits on blacks living in southern rural communities where lynchings still occurred. Blacks in and near Marianna in Florida's Jackson County were immediate beneficiaries; Marianna's vicinity was the scene of the lynching of a black, Claude Neal, on October 27, 1934, an affair so ghastly that America's foremost psychoanalyst, A. A. Brill, described it "de Sade in all his glory could not have invented a more diabolical situation."[95] Walter White, on hearing of the Neal lynching, dispatched a white liberal, Howard Kester, to the scene for a full report that was then disseminated widely to the press and civic organizations throughout the country.[96] The process encouraged local blacks, who would not otherwise have been able to express their concerns, to speak to Kester and gain a national voice; it also reassured them that a black organization with national scope stood by them to record their upset and protest the lynching of Neal. Walter White's actions helped critically in other ways; he encouraged the presence of newsmen, photographers, and filmmakers from outside the region. Their investigations reminded persons with a lynch mentality that they would be denied anonymity in the future and therefore the confidence that they could lynch with impunity. Thus, the rate and number of blacks lynched in the South declined notably after the Neal lynching.[97]

American communists also expended resources from outside the South to help a small number of southern blacks in the cotton plantation areas. Their contribution to the legal defense of the Scottsboro boys was substantial. Together with blacks, some of whom read the *Daily Worker* and possessed impressive "political sophistication," communists initiated the Alabama Sharecroppers Union (ASU) in 1931. Although membership data is sketchy and claims of 10,000 members in 1934–1935 seem excessive, the group was armed and prepared to defend itself. It called for a minimum wage for share-croppers and a ten-hour day. Members had strong racial animosities toward whites and openly discussed setting up a "Negro Republic," although it did obtain a small number of white members just before it merged in 1936 with another less radical organization.[98]

The Southern Tenant Farmers Union, founded in 1934, had a wider ter-ritorial and membership base with many whites: it may have had 25,000 members spread over Missouri (Bootheel area), Tennessee, Oklahoma, Texas, and the Mississippi Delta. The communist element here was less in-fluential; socialists, Christian socialists, and blacks active in the Garvey move-ment were its leaders. Although the movement contributed to the sense of improved possibilities for some of the South's poorest black farmers for a brief period, its momentum faltered by 1938 as a result of repression, racial rifts, and factionalism.[99]

The New Deal, of course, made unprecedented and substantial contri-butions to the welfare of African Americans in the Deep South; it inaugu-rated helpful work-relief, relief, and food programs for America's poor, including its rural poor. Although New Deal programs were often admin-istered by white officials in the South who discriminated against blacks, these still provided unusual concern for their protection and security. Surely, there can be no mistaking the immediate enthusiasm of rural blacks in cotton areas for the New Deal or President Roosevelt. Powdermaker sensed this in Cottonville even in the early years of the Roosevelt administration. She wrote,

Because of its more active part in their lives, many Negroes come more and more to direct toward the government their hopes for the future. Roosevelt has become the representative and symbol of their hopes.

She noted a poem written by a black girl in Cottonville that read, "Say, my Lord knows just how we've been fed. If it weren't for the President we'd all be dead."[100]

Other circumstances that contributed to increasing confidence and hope-fulness among blacks in the Cotton South in the 1930s derived from in-trinsic improvements in their own communities; they were better educated and strongly committed to education as a key to their future progress. Pow-dermaker, a trained observer of human behavior, was so impressed by this commitment that she titled a chapter on Cottontown's blacks "Education as Faith" to describe the phenomenon.[101] One can hardly find a stronger confirmation of the viewpoint that American society's poorest and most subjugated were still hopeful about their country and their own future in it. She wrote:

The faith of the present-day Negroes in education is much like the faith of those Americans who set up the public school system. . . . It was [is] viewed as the gateway to equal opportunity, the threshold of a new and better life.[102]

Dollard noted the same "fervor of Negro belief in education as a means of advancement" in the same community. Charles S. Johnson, whose scope was broadly rural blacks throughout the South, but principally in cotton counties, found identical information. "The results of our study indicate that the presumed values of education have become a motivating force of both parents and children to a remarkable degree, even in the plantation area," Johnson reported.[103] In Macon County, Alabama, Johnson noted this was a new spirit in the "Negro community," largely a result of improved educational influences, a "return of a small number of younger members who have been sent away to school in Tuskegee and Montgomery" and "the gradually increasing literacy of the group, beginning with the children."[104]

The material realities of the educational situation in which blacks found themselves, of course, prohibited quick results. Schools and books for rural black students were often substandard, teachers minimally qualified; economic necessity forced parents to keep their children out of school to help with the farm and children often suffered from economic and personal insecurity.[105] All the same, education had become for them and their parents a touchstone for success and achievement in American life and this, as Johnson noted, compensated for other deficiencies.[106]

There were also small signs of changes in the caste system, even in the plantation areas, that, if not encouraging to blacks, must at least have been amusing. The Depression prompted white storeowners to be more courteous to black customers. Blacks were now generally waited on more quickly and not allowed as previously to stand around and wait for a salesperson. Precedents humiliating for blacks in stores were relaxed; they were now permitted to try on clothes such as shoes, gloves, and hats in the store rather than buy first and experiment later to see if the purchased goods actually fit.[107] Upper-class whites, of course, had always shown a friendly manner with their former black servants and their families, but during the 1930s white shopkeepers tended to do the same with upper-class blacks. In "Old City," a small city of over 10,000 people and a trade center for several plantations with blacks constituting 80% of its trade-area population, clerks spoke to upper-class blacks in a friendly manner and showed "a marked increase of deference" to black patrons in general. Indeed, whites who were filling-station attendants actually tipped their hats to upper-class blacks when they supplied them with gas. One black leader in the community reported tongue-in-cheek to a large audience of blacks: "You know this depression has made the great Anglo-Saxon easier to get along with! He seems to feel more kindly to us. He smiles and is very friendly at his gas stations and stores." Symptomatic of these changes, leading stores in the community displayed art work by black students in their windows.[108]

Perhaps it was these slight changes that helped slow black migration to the North when economic conditions in both North and South were uniformly poor. Once the economy picked up in the North, many would reaffirm hopes to find a quicker path there to the "Promised Land."

For the time being, African Americans saw prospects for their fortunes improving in America with the advent of the New Deal and the beginnings of a changing and more favorable public image, thanks to the technology of communication. Through their tribulations they had retained a helpful, many-sided belief system with components in the here and hereafter as well as the present and the future. Not a little of their buoyancy derived from segregation; their common lot made for solidarity as well as good times and both were life-affirmative memberships. Religion added its own particular strengths. Besides reinforcing racial pride and personal dignity, it fostered patience and expectation of rewards for achievement as well as compensation for life's deprivations in the hereafter. This aggregate made for confidence in their ability to survive. Numbers of children were a metaphorical statement to this effect, as well as a growing attachment to education in the African-American community. Nor did they give up on government as an ally or their belief that justice would eventually be done. Indeed, the 1930s might well have been history's best time for blacks who lived in the Cotton South.

8

Seeing Tomorrow

The unmistakably positive title and tone of America's two major world's fairs in the 1930s, Chicago's Century of Progress Exhibition (1933–1934) and New York's World of Tomorrow (1939–1940), confound those who envision Americans of that decade as essentially dispirited, relatively helpless victims of the Great Depression. Nearly 85 million people attended both world's fairs at a time when the population numbered less than 130 million. Apparently few of them were shocked or reacted disbelievingly to these displays of progressive human betterment in America.[1] Some at the New York fair actually sported giveaway buttons that bumptiously declared, "I Have Seen the Future."[2] That same audacious optimism was expressed when officials of the New York World's Fair interred a time capsule not to be opened for 5,000 years; it contained objects representative of American society in the 1930s. The ceremony occurred on September 23, 1938, at twelve noon on the exact moment of the autumn equinox and news of the event was disseminated widely by radio microphones over national radio networks.[3] Spokesmen for the New York World's Fair thereby consciously assumed civilizational responsibility to instruct distant progeny on the merits of their own time and place, America in the 1930s.

Both the positive themes of the fairs—that Americans had improved their lives impressively and would continue to do so under the aegis of science and technology—and the enthusiastic response of the fair's patrons were predictable. Each was solidly rooted in axioms of American experience that a mere decade of trial could not efface. As onetime immigrants and sometime frontiersmen and women, most Americans were futurists in degree, especially so as they turned a wilderness into the world's premier industrial nation. At that time in the early years of the twentieth century, successful

American inventors and manufacturers became so emboldened by their creative achievements to predict that the nation was poised on the edge of a "second creation of the world"—the notion that those who supplied the world's goods could actually formulate a rationally organizable and beneficent system for the progressive improvement of American society.[4] It was these hopes for the future of the world through technology that prompted Henry Ford, one of its foremost practitioners, to declare confidently, "Machinery is accomplishing in the world what man has failed to do by preaching, propaganda or the written word."[5] Efficient mass production of relatively inexpensive goods had salutary effects, of course, on the morale of ordinary Americans, its consumers. As the standard of living of Americans came to exceed those of other countries, they became convinced that they were much better off in America and had good reason to believe this would continue to be so.

This unfailing resource, hopefulness, based on the historical performance of their system and their confident belief in its progressive future served Americans well in the 1930s. Robert and Helen Lynd clearly recognized this from their close familiarity with residents of Muncie, Indiana. The Lynds wrote in *Middletown in Transition* in the mid-1930s about "the reluctance of Middletown's habits of thought to accept the fact of bad times." This, because Middletown's worker's hopes for the future always outweighed their dissatisfaction with difficulties of the Depression; they accepted, according to the Lynds, the culture's formula that "tomorrow . . . always means 'progress' getting closer to whatever it is that one craves"; workers were not embittered, alienated, or radicalized, the Lynds wrote, because of "the strong, clear note of hope so conspicuous in the culture."[6]

But in their reliance on futurism to explain the hopefulness of Middletown's residents, the Lynds underestimated how much the confidence of Americans was actually inspired by their immediate successes, their own society's avant-garde accomplishments in technology, and its application to their personal lives in the 1930s. These consisted of building impressive dams in the West and the Tennessee Valley, a special decade of unprecedented height in skyscrapers, and the country's most impressive decade by far in bridge building, exceptional creativeness in invention, and applied research in diversified areas such as cars, trains, airplanes, and chemistry and in design, and the emergence of streamlining as an appealing national style. Finally, a relative democratization of possessions and comforts among Americans in the 1930s, most evident in the wider use of electricity and appliances dependent on electricity, also served to raise spirits.

The 1930s were not only a decade of exceptional creativity, its fruits were also well known by contemporary Americans from personal usage and by vicarious experience. Many used the new cars, drove on the new bridges, or turned to their new home appliances. An increasing number flew in the strikingly modern and safer commercial airlines. Others saw them pictured in magazines or read about them in local newspapers now supplied with national coverage by photographs and news information—*Life*, one of the nation's numerous picture magazines claimed 17 million readers in the late 1930s.[7] Advertising was still another way Americans of the 1930s learned how modern their country was becoming; it highlighted streamlined products and created an aura of expectations on a daily basis even for those who could not afford the goods being advertised.

In a decade characterized by outstanding achievements in public construction, none excited the public more than the great dams: the Boulder (renamed Hoover Dam in 1947), in Nevada, the Shasta in northern California, the Grand Coulee and Bonneville in the Northwest, the Fort Peck in Montana, and the numerous dams in the Tennessee Valley. Hydroelectric dams made of concrete existed earlier, but none were comparable to them or so appealed to the pride and imagination of Americans as those constructed in the 1930s.

Few New Deal programs enjoyed such public favor; the federal government had the economic and technical resources (the Bureau of Reclamation and Corps of Engineers) to undertake these vast engineering projects, and the prime purposes of the dams to prevent floods, develop hydroelectric power, and improve the standard of living of Americans through electricity were all indisputable gains. Besides, the massive size of these dams and their capacity to produce prodigious physical power generated expansive feelings among their many onlookers. Probably few beheld the grand vision of the English writer J. B. Priestly, who described the Hoover Dam in the 1930s as, "an inspiring image . . . a kind of giant symbol of the new man, a new world, a new way of life."[8] But there were unmistakable facts about this dam and others like it; they were sleek, majestic, and modern and their harnessing of power forecast a better future that man had the capacity to design for himself.

It was for these reasons that *Life* magazine, a determined advocate of the important and exciting pictorial features of the contemporary world, chose Margaret Bourke-White's photograph of the Fort Peck Dam for the cover of its first issue, November 23, 1936.[9] Bourke-White's picture, closeup yet angled to render a partial profile of the face of the dam, conveys a sense of its power and by implication the robust claims of its technicians and workers; courageous, adventurous people, the photograph attests, had worked this project and were achieving their purposes.

The Hoover Dam (1933), however, of all the dams, provided the country's prime statement of modern progressive construction. On completion, it was the first and largest of the country's dams in the 1930s, arching 727 feet above bedrock, with a base thickness of 600 feet of concrete and a width, at its gently curved crest, of nearly a quarter mile. More than any other dam it incorporated heroic elements, representing a dramatic victory over forbidding natural obstacles—jagged mountains of volcanic rock, the rapidly flowing Colorado River as it squeezed through a relatively narrow gorge, the Black Rock Canyon between Nevada and Arizona, against a backdrop of desert inhabited by creatures with stark survival needs including infestations of rattlesnakes. The Hoover Dam site was also isolated from human habitation (the model town for workers was about eight miles from the dam site) and experienced sharp cascades in temperature, 140° on the canyon floor in summer to 20° below in the winter.

There were also formidable construction problems. Waters of the Colorado had to be diverted through freshly made tunnels in nearby rocks and a temporary coffer dam while the site was cleared and the dam built. The problem of temperature stresses and possible cracks in the dam arising from the use of large volumes of concrete in relatively small areas was solved by using refrigerated water through tubes inserted in the concrete, a process that cooled the concrete and effectively sealed it only seventy-two hours after it was poured.[10]

The bravura and complexity of the project elicited both wonder and doubt among its early viewers. A writer from *Colliers* expressed amazement that engineers seemed to be on a project of "Remaking the World" while an observer from *The New York Times* titled her analysis in the newspaper's magazine section, "Taming the Untamable at Boulder Dam."[11]

Thousands of Americans paid homage to the dam even as it was under construction—many by cars over poor roads, others by a special excursion train of Union Pacific. In 1934–1935, it attracted more visitors than the Grand Canyon, with 750,000 persons in attendance. Indeed, a photograph of its vast visitor's gallery in summer defines an assemblage that looks like a crowd in a sports stadium.[12]

Those who designed roads of access to the dam wished to underscore its titanic features, and many visitors were appropriately awestruck; their first sight often came from a distant vantage on a mountain road well above the rim of the dam. There, they gazed at a smooth arch of yellow-grey concrete that stood resolutely civilized among the rugged surrounding mountains, even appearing to refine the volcanic rocks that seemed to cling to its sides. The blue water of the Colorado visible above the dam's crest often appeared deeper and darker than the sunlit sky, and this color sharply contrasted with the band of light color on the face of the dam. The river appeared tranquil at these times as it nestled behind its curved container of concrete. Joseph Stevens, the dam's historian, left vivid testimony to its overall visual impact. He wrote, "In the shadow of Hoover Dam one feels that the future is limitless, that no obstacle is insurmountable, that we have in our grasp the power to achieve anything if we can but summon the will."[13]

Hoover Dam was dedicated by President Roosevelt as Boulder Dam on May 19, 1935. The official sculptor underscored the historical significance of the moment. He commemorated the occasion by designing a special symbolism including the Great Seal of the United States and a "star map"

Downstream Face of Hoover Dam, September 11, 1936. Brown Brothers.

with accompanying chronology, placing this at the foot of a monument. He also described the exact time of the dedication ceremony. Beside that, he listed other important dates in history, including those for the construction of the pyramids and the birth of Christ.[14]

Although the Hoover Dam provided precedents for the three dams completed in the Tennessee Valley in the 1930s, the latter do not compare in size—Norris, the largest, a straight, gravity dam, was only 240 feet high. Still, the Norris Dam was designed to convey more than mere functionalism;

the dams of the Tennessee Valley Authority (TVA) were also avowedly committed to public monumentality. David Lillienthal, Chairman of the TVA in the late 1930s, once asserted that its projects would last 1,000 years.[15] Yet, if the Norris Dam does not evoke exactly the same exuberant spirit as the Hoover, it is not merely a matter of differences in height. The Norris Dam does not either win a struggle over hostile and gnarley nature, situated as it is in relatively tranquil piney hills. Nonetheless, it remained grand and powerful enough to impart character lessons to those who came to observe it: the capacity of skilled persons with appropriate equipment to deal stoutly with severe problems and solve those problems in a decisive, perhaps permanent way. Again, like the Hoover Dam, observers of the Norris Dam first confronted it in a way that exalted its image. Its architect "saw to it that [the valley dam] was approached . . . as one came around the wooded flank of a mountain side and [was] presented with a heightened sense of scale."[16]

The Tennessee Valley Authority primarily kindled hopes by improving the lives and attitudes of people under its tutelage through its programs of material assistance. The TVA Act signed into law May 18, 1933, a pet project of Senator George Norris of Nebraska and President Roosevelt, not only enjoined a government corporation to bring the Tennessee River under control, it sought also to rehabilitate the depressed rural population living in its watershed.

Improvement in living conditions in the area resulted in part from a close coordination of several dams so that they worked cooperatively and in tandem for regional development. This synchronized response allowed a handful of men who pushed buttons and turned switches to exact the river's compliance with the needs and necessities of residents of the valley: facilitating navigation, preventing floods, and eliminating such nuisances as mosquito infestation. The TVA also improved the lives of its constituency with programs for reforestation to prevent soil erosion, agricultural rehabilitation, the creation of numerous recreational lakes, fertilizer manufacture, setting up model towns, and especially the encouragement of electrification. Lillienthal believed the latter was key to the eventual viability of economic life in the valley.[17] Despite numerous squabbles with Congress and the courts over whether the government was permitted to distribute as well as generate electrical power and its increasing reliance on rural cooperatives to serve that purpose, there can be no questioning major gains from the use of electricity by valley people. The large numbers who were locally employed by the TVA and their significant gains in purchasing power also proved beneficial to the valley economy. The dams of the TVA, both operationally and symbolically, along with attendant social programs provided residents with a brighter life and better prospects for the future than previously possible.[18]

The good fortune of many rural persons in the Tennessee Valley using electricity for the first time reflected impressive advances in the use of electricity by rural Americans nationally. Although probably less than one in ten used electricity in 1930, about one in four did so by 1939, dramatic proof that the quality of rural life was improving.[19] Until 1935, farmers not only stood far behind American urbanites in electrical usage (as early as 1926, in Middletown 96% of its homes used electricity). Several European countries also had figures for the electrification of their total population, including rural, which approximated the percentage usage in Middletown.[20]

Costs of service had prohibited rural electrification in the free-market system. Rural lines cost $2,000 or more per mile, and there were usually too few dwellings for private utilities to recover investments and so they serviced urban consumers.[21] The situation might have remained static for some time, but President Roosevelt's personal determination that rural areas should be provided electricity ("Electricity is no longer a luxury, it is a definite necessity") put "Democracy on the March" for farmers. The TVA (1933) and especially the Rural Electrification Administration (REA) established in 1935 set new forces in motion. Although the TVA authorized the government not merely to generate electrical power but even to transmit it to farmers and small villages, the REA became its practical instrument as a loan agency and formed cooperatives where farmers agreed to terms of government loans.[22] Stressing the motto "If you put a light in every farm, you put a light in every heart," the REA also provided technical assistance to install the necessary equipment for electrification.[23] Despite occasional mean-spirited responses by utilities that would snake a private line into some rural areas to thwart the development of cooperatives and often parsimonious allocations by the federal government for its work, by 1939 the REA had empowered 268,000 farm households through cooperatives.[24]

There was good reason for a minister in Tennessee to recognize the great blessings electricity conferred on his life and that of his congregation, and he acknowledged that fact publicly. At the Sunday meeting, he expressed his appreciation, "Brothers and sisters, I want to tell you this. The greatest thing on earth is to have the love of God in your heart, and next greatest thing is to have electricity in your house."[25] The farmer and his family could with the aid of electricity work longer and more efficiently. A "modern clothes washer" and iron meant the end of hard manual labor for women on wash day—no more hand-carrying water long distances and making numerous trips from well to stove, or using separate pots for washing, rinsing, and bluing or the heavy slabs of metal, those "sad irons."[26] One farm woman wrote a poem to express her relief. "Blue Monday got its name from the way the women folks felt at the end of the washday. . . . Now things are different since the high line went in. There is just as much to do on the farm as ever, but it is a lot easier to do it."[27] Refrigerators also meant the end of food spoilage and improved diets.[28] Even though only 16.3% of Iowa farmhouses had refrigerators in 1940, farm wives who had electricity could not suppress their pleasure. One called electricity a "good fairy" and another wrote "farm women of yesterday envied the city women. . . . But now, with our modern homes, the city women may now envy her farm sister."[29] Electricity also improved the appearance of the farmhouse. The sundry structures that cluttered its immediate area began to disappear—the rain barrels, cisterns, smokehouses, and outdoor privys and also the cast-iron tubs just outside the house and the buckets to carry the water.[30]

With all the gratifications electricity brought farm people, it would be hard to imagine that the 15% or so who first enjoyed its advantages in the 1930s were discouraged and defeated by the Depression. They had experienced the benefits of democracy in a providential way, and other farmers who were not yet living in electrified houses recognized this as a genuine possibility in their lives as well. By 1942, 40% of farms would be using electricity and by 1946 about half.[31]

In building bridges and skyscrapers, Americans of the 1930s also enjoyed remarkable and unprecedented successes, again illustrating masterful accomplishments over the material world. Bridges erected during the Depression decade were unique for their size and number, their modern design features particularly in the middle and later years of the decade, and also the enthusiasm and pride with which the public identified with them. Special funding and personnel from New Deal agencies helped account for the phenomenon, but state funds in New York, New Jersey, California, and Louisiana contributed decisively. Most of the bridges spanned rivers or bays on the peripheries of major cities: the George Washington (1931), Bronx-Whitestone (1939), and Triborough (1939) in New York; the San Francisco–Oakland Bay Bridge (1937), the Golden Gate Bridge (1937) over San Francisco Bay; and the Huey Long Bridge over the Mississippi in New Orleans (1936)—all were over 3,000 feet in length.[32]

The George Washington Bridge, built jointly by the states of New York and New Jersey over the Hudson River between Washington Heights and the Palisades in New Jersey, was such a breathtaking accomplishment that a contemporary historian of the bridge declared enthusiastically that it "marked a great epoch in bridge engineering for it almost doubled at a single stroke the maximum length of span previously attained."[33] It was a suspension bridge typical of those completed in the 1930s. The George Washington's imposing length, 3,500 feet with two towers 635 feet above the river at their top, displayed the bridge's graceful catenary curves and bared steel trusses communicated its power. In 1933, 6 million vehicles crossed, though it was originally built to service 25 million cars a year with an estimated peak-hour capacity of 1,400. Constructed early in the 1930s, the George Washington Bridge was not entirely streamlined in the sense that the bridge's trusses in the towers are conspicuous by themselves, an effect that later bridges in the 1930s avoid with their smooth unitary flow. It is doubtful, however, if millions of motorists who used the span found this a grievous fault. Indeed, in those early years of the bridge's existence it was so attractive that 20,000 pedestrians crossed the bridge on its small walkways on a single Sunday, largely for the view and perhaps the prestige of saying they were there. In fact, the "bridge-walk" became a recreational feature of Sundays in New York for many residents in the 1930s.

The San Francisco–Oakland Bridge opened for traffic in November 1936 and was touted as "the greatest bridge in the world" because of its extravagant cost, $77 million, and total length of over eight miles, with about four miles over water and its tunnel on Yerba Buena Island, then the largest bore of any tunnel. When the twin spans were completed they were together the world's greatest bridge, but the spans of each bridge were exceeded by the George Washington and San Francisco Golden Gate Bridge. The latter had all the elements that combined to make a great bridge in the 1930s. At 4,200 feet, it was the world's longest span and represented a triumph over difficult natural conditions. The Golden Gate Bridge was imposed on the treacherous waters of San Francisco Bay closest to the Pacific Ocean, and it was astride a geological fault line, necessitating special grounding depth for its towers. Workers were buffeted by high winds and often hampered by fog. Its towers, which rose 746 feet above the bay, accommodated the passage of some of the world's largest oceangoing vessels below and helped the bridge profile to appear modern and sleek. To complete its commanding appearance, the bridge was painted "international orange" to distinguish it from the water it dominated and the land it served. Richard Guy Wilson summarized his picture of the bridge aptly. He declared:

As an experience it is overwhelming and moving. . . . The approach from either side is through natural landscape. . . . On the bridge the land masses recede. . . . The sky is high overhead and the water, with its ships like toys, miniature models, far below. The tires of the passing automobiles sing, the cables glisten as they swing down to the roadway and for a brief instant nature and machine merge.[34]

Skyscrapers like dams and bridges were also cultural as well as economic and technical statements representing human's powers over nature. By the 1920s, their presence was already perceived as a measure of a city's or even the nation's vitality and progress.[35] Powerful businessmen enjoyed the prospect of stamping their names or that of their corporations on the urban skyline. Some even courted the idea of winning tall-building wars because for them being at the top was all that mattered in advertising and personal advantages. But for all this, the top of New York's skyline had not changed in the 1920s—the Woolworth (1913) remained New York's tallest building at 792 feet.

In the 1930s, New York established its reputation as America's city of tall buildings and helped America to become known as the land of the skyscraper. The Chrysler Building touched off the building boom in 1930—with seventy-seven stories and a height of 1,048 feet. This was closely followed by the Bank of Manhattan with seventy-one stories and 925 feet and

Empire State Building, March 1931. Avery Architectural and Fine Arts Library, Columbia University in the City of New York.

the City Service Building at sixty-six stories. The Empire State Building became the city's showpiece in 1931 with its 102 stories and height of 1,472 feet, nearly a fifth of a vertical mile. The Rockefeller Center completed the ensemble of skyscrapers, though it was in fact a complex of skyscrapers, with the seventy-story RCA Building its most distinctive feature. John D. Rockefeller, Jr., in the teeth of the most severe period of the Depression, commanded resources to build the distinctive entertainment complex amid a unique architectural setting. The last rivet in Rockefeller Center was driven by Mr. Rockefeller himself, signifying completion of the project on November 1, 1939, one that virtually spanned the entire Depression decade.[36]

Skyscrapers and optimism are virtually inseparable, especially so in the 1930s. Their costs and engineering tour de force tested not merely skills and resolve on the part of builders and developers, but their faith in a benign future. The Empire State Building, a purely speculative venture, necessitated large loans just after the stock market crash, but its corporate developers headed by three-time governor of New York and presidential candidate Al Smith maintained unflagging confidence in the building's economic utility and appeal as the main attraction of New York to the country and the world. Although the Empire State Building had probably only one-fourth of its office space rented when it opened May 1, 1931, Smith exuded optimism in an official speech and called attention to its positive impact on the public. He declared:

Probably no building in history has brought such universal interest in its progress. . . . Interest in this building is not confined to our state or country; it is universal. . . . The Empire State Building stands today as the greatest monument to ingenuity, to skill, to brain power, to muscle power, the tallest thing in the world today produced by the hand of man.[37]

The New York Times in an editorial, "Building in Excelsis," affirmed Smith's view that the building had raised public morale:

Such a union of beauty and strength in a great building makes of it a valuable possession for the whole community. All must feel also that the Empire State Building is a monumental proof of hopefulness. Those who planned and erected it and found the funds for it must have been firm in the belief that the future of New York is assured, and that its fundamental interests and activities are certain to go on from year to year conquering and to conquer. Thus, today's celebrations are to be thought of as having a significance which extends far beyond the corner of Fifth Avenue and Thirty-fourth Street, and catches up the whole city, with all its diverse elements, yet with common hopes, into its inspiring sweep.[38]

The Empire State Building in New York, "first to greet the morning sun . . . and at sunset . . . wear its gold for a crown," rapidly became visible and well known across the nation through photographs and advertisements, and so its effects on public attitudes were national in scope.[39] Photographer Lewis W. Hine's personal daring in snapping pictures of the daredevil "sky boys" who built the edifice in record time left viewers as breathless as if they, too, were seventy to one hundred stories in the air. One holds a rope while standing on an exposed girder and points down almost derisively to the top of the Chrysler Building. Another sits at a dizzying height with legs dangling over an exposed beam, his back against a slightly raised girder, taking a break and smoking a cigarette. Two others at the top of the building's frame are snapped pointing at some object in the city from a position where their only visible exit is a sky hook. Hine's pictures obtained circu-

Lewis Hine, "Man on Girders, Mooring Mast, Empire State Building," 1931. Courtesy George Eastman House.

lation in his book, *Men at Work* (1932), in newspapers, and drew favorable comment in national magazines. The Empire State Building also attracted the national attention of moviegoers in 1933 as the suitable pinnacle for King Kong to defend himself against U.S. Army combat planes. In addition, it quickly became a must stop for millions of people visiting New York in the 1930s. In fact, they were numerous enough to pay the bills for an otherwise failing business proposition.[40] It was not until World War II that the great building flourished with near 100% occupancy. But its psychological benefits showed earlier as still another sustaining factor in the country's confidence in the future in the midst of depression. And since the construction of the Empire State Building was identified by the public with America's greatness, it also seemed to affirm the nation's indisputably bright future; at critical junctures in its raising and completion, in one year and forty-five days, workers incorporated this message as when they often hoisted the American flag while an orchestra played the Star Spangled Banner at the official opening.[41]

Apart from these remarkable feats of construction, among the biggest and stylistically most impressive in the country's history, there were also major developments in the American economy in the 1930s that forecast a better tomorrow for Americans. Indeed, in some of its sectors, particularly the use of electrical appliances and air travel, Americans in the 1930s were already seeing the future on a daily basis.

Businesses struggled to improve sales in the early 1930s when consumers had less money and markets were already oversupplied with unsold goods. They relied heavily on research, inventions, and innovations. Patents issued to corporations surged and many new researchers, designers, draftsmen, and engineers for developing products were added to company payrolls to facilitate sales.[42] Most companies were forced to reduce prices, but many hoped to retain profits or stave off serious losses by securing cheaper substitutes for costlier components of their products. Substitutes were often found for expensive metals, woods, and jewelry and for costly delicate materials such as silk or porcelain. Chrome, recommended by Emily Post to housewives for its "comparatively small expense," replaced silver on many tables and also made cheaper but effective cocktail shakers as did plastic, a coal-derived synthetic that had the advantage of being bright and varied and could be presented in striking colors.[43] Synthetic fabrics, rayon and nylon, were also effective substitutes for natural materials. Nylon was first worn by hostesses at the Dupont exhibit of the New York World's Fair in place of silk hose; it was heralded as more durable and requiring less time to dry. Dupont also displayed a model "dressed by chemistry" from head to toe and she, of course, wore nylons. The company placed limited amounts of nylon on sale in the fall of 1939 in Wilmington, Delaware, at about the same price as silk with a maximum of three pairs to a customer. Women who had already heard about the wonders of nylon from the World's Fair rushed the stores and rapidly bought out the short supply. Nylon had a reputation for being "sheer magic" even before mass sales began in 1940.[44]

Plastics, as *Fortune* noted in 1936, were a genuine "child of the Depression," an apt judgment in numerous ways.[45] Primarily, of course, they were relatively inexpensive to buy and manufacture, and hence attractive to hard-pressed consumers. But they also appealed because they were smooth, acceptable to feel, and could easily be displayed in a burst of colors. In their finished form, plastic goods also gave the Depression buyer a sense of being avant-garde. Besides, plastics could be used for an incredible array of goods. Bakelite's manufacturers claimed they produced "a material of 1,000 uses," and they apparently were not exaggerating. Common usages of American plastics in the 1930s included costume jewelry, phonograph records, kitchen and tableware, lampshades, lighting fixtures, cases for radios, screwdriver handles, combs, and table surfaces. Synthetics not only drove down costs and fostered a more democratic distribution of goods, their high-volume usage also reduced costs even more.[46]

A prime example of the Depression fostering modernity through plastics was radio sales. The average radio priced at $133 in 1929 in its rich wooden casing dropped to $35 in 1933. The dramatic change was primarily a result of the manufacture of very small radios that sold for about $10 and also because plastic radio cabinets became available in several brands, especially the small radios, but also including the large Pilot and the Sears Silver Tone of 1936.[47]

Electrical appliances, like radio, became a growth industry in the 1930s. Unlike the automobile market, which was saturated perhaps as early as the mid-1920s, relatively few Americans had electric appliances in their homes other than radios or vacuum cleaners when the 1930s began. Astoundingly, the number of refrigerators annually produced did not surpass the number of iceboxes until 1930. A number of factors accelerated the sale of refrigerators thereafter. Electric power was more readily available in homes as the decade progressed, and it seemed likely to be the way of the future. Producers also launched a massive sales campaign. Companies like General Electric, with a large research and engineering cohort, shifted directions and found ways to reduce costs on products. Higher volume sales contributed as well. As a consequence, refrigerators became a bright new feature of American homes. Sales went from 800,000 in 1930 to 2,300,000 in 1937. Undoubtedly bargain prices explained the turnaround. The average price of a refrigerator in 1930 was $275 but by 1933 it had fallen to $170, a representative price for the rest of the decade, though refrigerators in Middletown in 1934 even sold for less than $100. Sales plummeted again during the so-called "Roosevelt recession" of 1938 when not even low prices could stimulate sales.[48]

Corporate research and engineering not only benefited American homes with a wider distribution of satisfying, once luxury goods such as radios and refrigerators, they also inspired changes in the way Americans transported themselves by cars and especially by trains and airplanes. Here, too, changes fostered a consciousness of improvement that seemed to confirm immediate progress despite the temporality of the Depression.[49]

Although there were no epochal changes in automobile technology in the 1930s, continuous improvements marked the period; automobiles then rode more comfortably and handled more easily than any previous time. By 1934, all General Motors cars adopted independent front suspension. Widespread use of the automatic choke (1934) and the introduction of a semiautomatic transmission in Oldsmobile in 1939 made driving more enjoyable as well. An important safety feature, the turret top, was introduced on General Motors models in 1935. New conveniences included placing all instruments together on the dashboard, the beginnings of air-conditioning (1938), and automobiles with radios and push-button controls (1939).[50] Few, if any, Americans would have preferred a 1930 model to one built in 1939. The difference was progress, which automobiles proved year after year. The day each year when the new models came to the local dealerships, men folk talked about them, especially in the smaller towns and smaller cities. A visit to the local distributors was then virtually a requirement for those who prided themselves on being knowledgeable about modern life, notwithstanding the fact they firmly intended, for reasons of economy, to hold onto their old car. Local newspapers meanwhile showed pictures of the new cars and provided favorable information about them resembling advertisements as a public service. In Beloit, Kansas, the local editor declared, "Along with the many others interested in changes in cars we walked over to the Chevrolet garage to see the 1934 product at that place. . . . The salesmen at Hiserote's are well pleased with the 1934 product and we can easily understand their feeling."[51]

Train transportation—caught in a squeeze between speedy planes and automobiles that could deliver its occupants in convenient family style to the exact location of choice—experienced heavy losses even before the Depression. In 1920, the railroads had carried 1,235,000 passengers, but by 1933 the total had dipped to 433,000. During the Depression, revenues fell from $877 million in 1929 to only $320 million in the early 1930s. Railway executives recognized that a major rehabilitation was required and found their remedy in "streamliners," a high-speed train with an aerodynamic look and abundant passenger comforts. Its speed was assured by major technological adaptations—lightweight locomotives and cars made from stainless steel or aluminum and low centers of gravity that allowed trains to handle curves at greater speeds. Besides, since the streamliner resembled a wingless airplane, it looked fast and that, too, was important to the public, and many of these trains, powered with Diesel engines, achieved impressive top speeds. Despite the train's demanding schedule of stops, it averaged fifty to sixty miles per hour on shorter runs and in the eighties for longer ones. Top speed was in the range of 100 to 120 miles per hour. On one occasion the Burlington *Zephyr* flashed the 1,015 miles from Denver to Chicago in just over thirteen hours at 77.6 miles per hour, and a congratulatory crowd met the train. This attainment conferred entitlement for the *Zephyr* to appear at the Century of Progress Exposition in Chicago where it was royally welcomed by excited crowds as a genuine embodiment of progress.[52]

The Burlington *Zephyr*, one of the most streamlined trains of the 1930s. Photo courtesy: The Budd Company.

Comfort for passengers was achieved by tightly coupling coaches, using frictionless ball bearings, handsomely decorated cars, air-conditioning, ul-tracomfortable seating and berths, and a club car with wide windows that offered scenic views and other social amenities. Some streamliners also pro-vided registered nurses as did airliners. They would "prepare formulas for infant feeding, amuse the children, care for the sick and help make passengers comfortable."[53] Little wonder the observer who reported this information to the *National Geographic* titled his article "Trains of Today—and Tomorrow."[54] By 1940, the streamliner's contribution to modernizing railroads was vindicated. Passenger revenues improved, especially on the streamline trains themselves, and there were seventy-three of them on the nation's rail lines—the first had not been introduced until February 12, 1934.[55]

The streamliners had also provided the public with sights of an improving and improvable world; they were so enticing that large crowds gathered just to get a glimpse of their speed runs. Aboard the *Zephyr* a passenger noted:

Out West they [crowds] again are coming down to way stations and crossroads to see the trains go by. They come by the thousands, in roadsters and afoot, some in Model T's; I counted five horse and buggy teams.[56]

The streamlined *Henry M. Flagler* attracted an estimated 75% of the population of towns as it whizzed through Florida.[57] But, in fact, the streamliners "evoked pandemonium wherever they went. Schools let out, brass bands played, mothers held up babies for a look at the future and crowds gathered at rural crossings to see exhibition runs." An estimated 15 million people witnessed one of the modern trains in the summer of 1934.[58] Many inspected and trooped through the trains as well as viewed them. At the Chicago World's Fair alone, which attracted 39 million people, over 700,000 went through the *Zephyr*. At least one commentator on the *Zephyr* believed "It indeed became a symbol of revival of hope that the depression would soon be over."[59] The modern trains also made an impression on countless persons who did not have an opportunity to visit personally. They made excellent copy in local newspapers with pictures and vital information going on the front page (one was depicted as "Tomorrow's Train," the "very essence of modernity").[60]

No business activity requiring technological innovation better represented the forward-looking quality of the American people in the 1930s than commercial aviation.[61] Its appeal was intense, as if somehow it struck a taproot of their values. Flight seemingly symbolized triumphant possibilities and was a witness to man's relationship to the world being transformed dramatically before his eyes by human ingenuity and the use of technology.

Aviation in the wake of Lindbergh's flight to Paris (1927) provided Americans with a pantheon of heroes and heroines including the exciting figures, both men and women, who entered the annual air races.[62] In the 1930s, the public was excited by the precedent-shattering, long-distance flights by commercial airliners to Asia and Europe, planes with romantic names like the *China Clipper*. Colonel Lindbergh's wife, Anne Morrow Lindbergh, herself a gifted navigator as well as author, peaked popular interest with descriptions of her flights with Lindbergh; she captivated readers with *North to the Orient* (1935) and *Listen, the Wind* (1938). Aviation was also the subject of numerous films featuring America's top stars and often provided a leading story with pictures in local newspapers as well as picture magazines. Interest in flight meanwhile spawned a frenzy of model airplane building, prompting many boys and girls to spend numerous hours working on model airplanes.[63] Understandable, because this was still a time when a young boy or girl would willingly track an airplane from its earliest visibility to the point it disappeared across the horizon.

Airlines in America in this period were strikingly successful from every standpoint: financially, in distance of flight and flight performance, and improvements in the safety and comforts of its passengers. In the area of international flight, Pan American planes were regularly on transoceanic routes as early as 1935, a feat no other national airline mastered with an airliner of "equal weight performance" until 1957.[64] Commercial aviation was a notable growth industry during the Depression years as its passenger traffic and revenue illustrated. Only 475,000 Americans flew commercially in 1932, but over 4 million in 1941; only 95 million passenger revenue miles in 1932, but this figure was expanded seven times to 677 million in 1939.[65] Pan American, the nation's major international flight service, also reported impressive passenger growth from 44,000 to 246,000 between 1930 and 1939.[66]

The business successes of the airlines reflected improvements in the airplanes they operated. Streamlining the nose and body of the plane helped, along with the use of an all-metal frame and tight construction. Engine reliability was, of course, the key improvement. Flight required engines capable of lifting heavy payloads. This included the weight of the plane, passengers, and baggage, usually reckoned at 225 pounds per passenger and large amounts of gasoline weighing six pounds per gallon, hence requiring engines "with the best power to weight ratios and the least fuel consumption."[67] The new planes were also designed with cantilevered, low slung wings to aid their flight performance. These changes produced the Douglas DC-2 (1934) and the famous durable DC-3 (1935). The latter with its powerful Wright engines and noteworthy speed and comforts dominated the American market, constituting perhaps 80% of all commercial airliners in the United States and also selling in Europe.[68] Its passengers could fly swiftly from coast to coast, fifteen hours going east and seventeen traveling west.[69] Boeing made its mark in building long-distance clippers for Pan Am with a range near 4,000 miles. These became mail and passenger carriers to both Europe and the Far East.[70] The Boeing Clippers, the largest planes in the world weighing forty tons, replaced Martin company's famous "China Clipper" that had first established contact with the Far East in the mid-1930s. By 1937, transpacific flights were complete with an aerial link to Hong Kong at a distance of 8,500 miles from the United States. This flight necessitated island hopping from Hawaii to Midway, Wake, and Guam before reaching Manila and for its transatlantic flights to Europe that com-

A DC-3 flagship in flight in the mid-1930s—a fourteen passenger plane with pull-down sleeper beds. American Airlines C.R. Smith Museum Photo Collection.

menced June 23, 1939, with flight paths requiring refueling at the Azores en route to Lisbon or Marseilles or Newfoundland for Southampton, England. By mid-December 1939, Boeing Clippers had flown the Atlantic one hundred times.

Crowds recognized that the first days of departure of these planes for distant continents were special victories for America and themselves. They gathered and cheered when the first *China Clipper* taxied out on San Francisco Bay for departure to the Orient. And on the date of Pan Am's first flight to Europe, its base, the Long Island coastal town of Port Washington, declared a holiday. The high school band played for a crowd estimated in the thousands and a local minister invoked a blessing for those who boarded the plane before its twenty-two passengers filed aboard, six of them women. When the young daughter of one of them called to her mother and asked her to write, she replied confidently that she would be back before the letter.[71]

The airliners of the 1930s, despite making substantial headway in promoting passenger safety, still had serious problems convincing Americans that flight was safe. Although most resisted flying because it was too expen-

sive, many clearly refused out of fear. They were comforted by the advances
of national airliners and enjoyed the sense of progress this signified, but they
did not relish the risk of personal martyrdom to confirm the fact. Most
commercial pilots actually flew safer planes, however, by the late 1930s.
They benefited from radiophones for landing and taking off, received
weather information from meteorologists, and obtained direction of flight
from radio signals that would bring pilots to airfields of destination in desperate weather and at night.[72] Planes, however, as the number of crashes
testify, were still vulnerable to bad weather, heavy turbulence, and pilot or
mechanical malfunction. And increased airplane usage meant augmenting
danger in the vicinity of airports.[73] A few of the crashes involved prominent
Americans and this made for more publicity and alarm than usual. Knute
Rockne, Notre Dame's beloved coach, died in a 1931 crash, Senator Bron-
son Cutting of New Mexico in 1935, and Will Rogers and the intrepid
aviator Wiley Post in 1936. There was also a string of five crashes in the
winter of 1936–1937, most of them at night.[74]

The airlines took vigorous steps to allay anxieties. They built pressurized
planes that allowed pilots to surmount immediate turbulence.[75] They also
adopted uniform safety regulations authorized by the Civil Aeronautics Administration after 1938.[76] And they also went on an advertising offensive,
illustrating calm and happy customers lamenting that they had not flown
earlier.[77] The introduction of stewardesses in the mid-1930s was in part
prompted by a desire on the part of the companies to make air travel appear
domesticated and tranquil.[78] Other amenities were intended to prompt passengers to be mindful of comforts rather than dangers. Those included
soundproofing techniques, the introduction of carefully upholstered chairs,
airline kitchens and hot meals, and even haute cuisine with wine on international flights.[79] The most convincing evidence for public confidence came,
however, from the Civil Aeronautics director who reported in March 1940
that airlines in the United States had just completed their first year without
fatality.[80]

Business continued to sputter in the early years of the Depression despite
successes in specific fields like aviation and chemistry. Most manufacturers,
having attempted price reductions and advertising, found themselves re-
thinking sales strategies, and came slowly to the realization that considerations of style (and hence product design) might also be a way to stimulate
sales. Advertising agencies and journals encouraged this awareness as did
Fortune, which at $1 an issue enjoyed almost exclusive patronage among
the affluent.[81] With its attractive format and quality articles, *Fortune* championed improvements in design as a key to sales. It also featured photographers like Margaret Bourke-White, who startled when she remarked that
she found dynamos more attractive than pearls, and distinguished artist
Charles Sheeler (1940) who celebrated the intrinsic beauty of machine design; their displays may have contributed to the idea that the consumer was

also an artist of sorts who preferred beauty in the object he or she consumed.[82] But the strongest testimony for redesign of products came from
manufacturers who had taken the advice of designers, changed their products, and then enjoyed substantial sales. As early as 1933, Sears found better
sales for a radically redesigned washer. *Forbes* underscored this achievement
for the business community in an article April 1, 1934, titled "Best Dressed
Products Sell Best." Another significant signpost was a *Fortune* cartoon in
1934. It showed a company executive instructing board members to the
effect that he was convinced the company's new biscuit would need the
advice of a prominent industrial designer.[83] When Sears followed with a
newly designed Coldspot refrigerator in 1935, and its sales rapidly surpassed
the competition, a bandwagon effect took place.[84] By 1935, manufacturers
needed to issue newly designed products to fend off the competition as well
as placate an appreciative public.

Economic conditions necessitated that business leaders engage industrial
designers to promote sales, but for the designers this approach also held
major advantages; they now had an opportunity to implement deeply held
convictions about people and art's relationship to society. The leading industrial designers came from similar backgrounds: Henry Dreyfus and Norman Bel Geddes from theater lighting and design, Walter Teague was
formerly in advertising, and Raymond Loewy, although schooled as an engineer in France, worked in America in women's fashions.

Although diverse as personalities, there was considerable unanimity
among them on professional goals and attitudes about social change. Dreyfus, perhaps the most forthcoming, revealed his modus operandi in his autobiography, *Designing for People*. He describes how designers responded
to invitations by clients. Dreyfus, a democratic person, would then meet
with employees involved in engineering, production, advertising, and sales
of the product in question and learn their ideas about it. He would also
compare the client's product with those of competitors through photographs. And then he would raise the most important issue: would the product meet needs of the buyer? Would his client's product be as useful and
safe as possible, be reasonably priced, and have good maintenance? Dreyfus
would also consider sales appeal at this juncture (does it give pleasure, is it
reliable, and is it simple and forthright?) and finally its appearance, consideration of line, proportion, and color. Then the designer would meet with
his clients, bring in sketches, explain the advantages and costs of his new
product, and await their decision.[85]

The designers were all idealists. Teague, who wished to work for human
betterment, looked wistfully to a "humanized world" and worked to achieve
a golden age.[86] Geddes foresaw sweeping human progress, including the
eradication of disease by 1941.[87] Dreyfus, who attended the Ethical Culture
School in New York, regarded working for human uplift a prime responsibility.[88] Raymond Loewy's stated goal was "to improve things people live

with from the moment they wake up till they go to bed." Loewy was so convinced of progress that he devised evolutionary charts of design showing the progress of a variety of objects, with one illustrating improvements in female dress, but predicting dubious results in this instance. Women, according to Loewy, would soon become so sleek and trim that they would become practically unrecognizable.[89]

As artists, the designers en masse had a fondness for symmetry and simplicity—especially regular curved lines (parabolas), and they objected to the clutter and coarseness of the world they inhabited. Teague referred to his world of the 1930s as a "chaotic scene" in need of "fundamental redesign." Geddes worked on a vehicle he called "the Ultimate Car."[90] Dreyfus's goal was serenity for humans, by "relieving them of absurd and excessive decorations."[91] Loewy also took pleasure in visual simplification. With their innately platonic sense, the designers treasured fundamental, unattached forms and were convinced that human happiness was predicated on contact between persons and the inherent beauty of these simplified forms. The industrial designers saw themselves within reach of their own humanistic goals when they were invited by manufacturers of machine goods to make them more sellable because they would also make them beautiful and thereby improve society.

Given their advantageous position, the leading designers were able to incorporate exciting new forms and impart new life to the world of things in America. In so doing they created the American style of streamlining. Streamlining, or an emphasis on simple lines, especially curved lines, acquired some of its early appeal from being identified with the new era of speed emerging in America in the 1930s. In its strictest meaning and early application it referred to aircraft aerodynamics; graceful parabolic curves (the teardrop look) representing the air flowing over the rounded nose and cylindrical body of an airplane in flight. For the designers it was a convenient and modish illustration of their emphasis on simple forms and forms being functional. Geddes especially advanced the teardrop silhouette. The principle was also applied to other moving objects. The new trains, designed by Loewy and Dreyfus and others, would no longer have boxed fronts—rather they were curved and hence the term "streamliners." The 1934 Chrysler, the air-flow car designed by Geddes, had a curved top and was streamlined because it was designed to achieve speed by reducing air drag on the vehicle.[92] Streamlining as a term was also applied to the curved, simplified look of nonmobile objects that were redesigned more numerously than those that moved about.[93] For this reason, however, there is justification for preferring a generic term like "Depression Modern" to describe the streamline style.[94]

Streamlining persisted as the dominant style of the late 1930s even when engineers challenged its scientific and technical premises that it would assist the locomotion of trains and cars. The designers continued to follow their inner lights despite this setback, however, as streamlining offered smooth, calm, secure well-defined objects and emotionally satisfying, hopeful feelings that the public enjoyed.[95] Besides it was indisputably modern, even "upbeat" according to Loewy. He declared it appealed because it "symbolizes simplicity, eliminates cluttering detail and answers a subconscious yearning for the polished, orderly essential."[96] This ideal also explains why Loewy and other designers used Bakelite because it assured the smooth, symmetrical forms of a single color that they sought.[97]

The marriage of convenience between manufacturers and industrial designers was fruitful and much appreciated by business because streamlining did sell goods or, at least, helped prevent losses to competitors.[98] It sometimes failed, however, because of differences in goals between the partners. Manufacturers were inclined to seek more refinements in appearances to save costs while designers preferred both functional design changes as well as changes in appearance and the designers usually lost.[99]

It is not too much to say that the leading industrial designers remade the appearance of American life or that they made it more attractive and gratifying. What they wrought reflected their own optimism about human possibilities and the role of art in humanizing society. "In the darkest days of the Depression," as Donald Bush, a major interpreter of the streamline style, noted, "they dreamed of orderly, hygienic cities and houses, environments free of drudgery and fitted with material conveniences, looking ahead to safe, fast travel on luxurious streamlined aircraft, buses, ships and automobiles."[100] They were also able to transmit that optimism in their varied projects. Bush comments, "The streamlined form came to symbolize progress and the promise of a better future. The optimism it engendered was a boon to the decade following the market crash of 1929."[101]

Although the public benefited from the design metamorphism in the appearance and quality of American life in the 1930s, the gains that accrued to business still depended on the sales of those redesigned products and, therefore, stimulated consumer interest—hence advertising. Although the advertising industry had welcomed and championed product and design changes because it believed those changes would promote consumer interest, sales remained flat in a number of areas in the early 1930s, so advertisers were forced to mount exceptionally direct and hard-hitting sales campaigns to stimulate them.[102] They did so at an opportune time when advertising could reach virtually everyone. Very few Americans in the 1930s were so very poor or isolated as to be without a radio or a newspaper, and many read the family-style popular magazines with their abundant advertisements; an estimated 50 million Americans then read the country's four top circulating magazines—*Colliers, Liberty, Saturday Evening Post,* and *Life.*[103]

Roland Marchand has perceptively analyzed the parables advertisers collectively used to educate the buying public to select in the 1920s and 1930s. These included homilies to the buyer that in a society putting a premium on first contacts, one could not afford to be a social pariah and fail the test with halitosis, dandruff, or drooping socks. Another lesson dutifully rendered was that Americans, no matter what their class, could afford many of the products that the wealthy themselves used—a kind of "Democracy of Goods" parable. A third emphasized the merit of goods or activities that naturally attracted children.[104] Marchand also underscored, as exceptional to the early 1930s, numerous ads that encouraged readers to look on the brighter side and another set revealing "the clenched fist," a call for a tough and resourceful response to the times.[105] Marchand concluded that these images were used because they resonated with the public mood. Accounting for the clenched fist tableaux he wrote, "Finding the appeal to courage and determination, as dramatized in the clenched fist, an effective rallying cry and an appealing self-image, advertisers paraded this imagery before the consuming public."[106] He chose as an example an ad for Ethyl gas in which a young boy, upset with his father's slow driving in an old car, expresses an American outrage despite the Depression. "Gee, pop, they're all passing you."[107]

The most common parable in advertising, however, especially as conditions began to improve in the mid-1930s, might be described as "airplane symbolism," carrying the implication that Americans then lived in one of history's best times and that the future, by implication, would be even better. The airplane often appeared in advertisements that celebrated speed and newness, even when the product being advertised had no relation to flight; it hovered over sundry objects and gave its unmistakable imprimatur to myriad changes improving modern life.[108] No other image appeared more repetitively or convincingly, and there was no mistaking its symbolic message. Advertising personnel, as custodians of a new consciousness of modernity, were convinced that Americans were willing to buy products associated with progress.

The joys of being a truly liberated "modern person" are also celebrated in the advertisements of nearly every urban newspaper and national magazine in the decade. A large number of the tableaux emphasized that the product being advertised was unexcelled in quality and performance. One depicted a woman wearing "the most beautiful watch in the world," another "the newest car in the world," and still another "the safest tire ever built." The ring of most of these advertisements is captured in one with large letters resembling a newspaper headline. It read, with apparent sobriety, "No Car Manufacturer Ever Did It Before."[109]

The word "modern" apparently conferred irresistible iconographic stature on products advertised. An advertisement for Oldsmobile in *Fortune* declared that it was "as modern as the Century of Progress."[110] The 1939 Dodge was as "modern as tomorrow" and the commendable feature of the Hoover vacuum was its "modern streamlining." But even the Webster Golden Wedding Cigar was heralded as "gracefully slender—typically modern—fashionably correct." And "the modern-day way to ease colds and sore throats quickly" was Bayer aspirin. A great number of products were sold by picturing modern buildings or kitchens as a backdrop.[111] And Hammermill Bond Paper demonstrated its modern quality by showing the George Washington Bridge in the background. The ad lauded the bridge as a sign of modernity, cited the use of the company's bonded paper in administration of its wonders, and closed with "Truly we live in a remarkable age."[112]

Evidence that the advertising industry was describing the 1930s as the best of times is also implicit in countless ads and picture stories in magazines that stressed the remarkable new speed of the times. The new Plymouth for 1935 promised "more power" with its efficient engine; the supporting script for the ad declared, "We're traveling faster today. The average speed on the road is 20 miles faster than it was in 1925 . . . you need speed."[113] The Lincoln Zephyr for 1939 was so smooth to drive and well powered that "you never know what it is to reel off 400, 500 or 600 miles a day."[114] *Life* magazine, a champion of modernity, was replete with stories about transportation and communication records established in the 1930s. It assured readers that the world in pictures was at their fingertips whether the subject was Lhasa in Tibet, Peking, Algiers, or Nazi Germany. As if to demonstrate its efficiency, *Life* photographed a soldier wounded in the Spanish Civil War from a bullet that struck him only a short time earlier, with the commentator noting that "*Life*'s camera gets closer to the Spanish Civil War than any camera has ever gotten before."[115]

The many advertising messages that assured enrichments of the American family through science and technology undoubtedly affected the public positively. Foods newly available in bulk, fresh and canned, offered glowing but not unreasonable nutritional rewards—California prunes, canned pineapple, freshly sealed peas, and Sunkist navel oranges—and when a mother fretfully declared in the middle of a dark night in her room, "Turn on the light, I hear the baby," Westinghouse could reply, "Electricity's eyes never close . . . its service is never asleep."[116] But this did not mean that service would not continue to improve. An agent for the Dakota Public Service Company wrote for a special edition of the Bismarck *Tribune* in the American midlands in 1939 that only fifty years earlier Bismarck did not have electricity and now it powered many vital needs, and he forecast "In the future electricity will do many more things—things which have not yet entered the imagination of man."[117]

And so the educational message of advertising contributed to the positive outlook of Americans in the 1930s. It also enlarged their sense of seeing tomorrow sublimely, an attitude the Lynds described as a defining characteristic of people who lived in Middletown. One of the major reasons Americans were not disheartened by the difficult times that came with economic depression was because they were futurists; their devotion to this fundamental of American experience could only be threatened by severe and unremitting economic adversity combined with extraordinary political in-

eptitude and the collapse of their diverse and protective social systems, and
these dangers never materialized.

The large numbers who trooped to the world's fairs, especially the one
in New York late in the decade, were prepared for what they would see and
hear at the "World of Tomorrow." Many Americans were already conditioned to believe in striking modernism and even futurism before the fair
opened.

Writing about the New York World's Fair (1939–1940), coming as it did
after a decade of depression, a later historian of the fair observed: "It strikes
a contemporary observer as utterly inconceivable that men would believe so
fervently in a better tomorrow. But they did."[118] Although Chicago's Century of Progress Exhibition (1833–1934) portrayed positively the vast progress that had come to Chicago and the nation in the hundred years since
1833, only the leaders of the New York World's Fair addressed the future
confidently, declaring that Americans in the late 1930s were on the edge of
vast human betterment.[119] Such confidence truly appeared naive; just to hold
a world's fair in 1939–1940 required unusual confidence because, in addition to the Depression, dangers of international war seemed imminent. Anne
O'Hare McCormick wrote for *The New York Times* as the fair opened that
its existence was a statement "of undying hope." Even as "a chorus of voices
has warned us that the lights of civilization are going out," Ms. McCormick
noted, "people somehow persist in believing in the future. They are sure of
tomorrow."[120]

The New York World's Fair had as an ostensible goal, a commemoration
of George Washington's inauguration in New York as the first president in
1789, but it quickly became a fair to demonstrate and celebrate a cornu-
copian future for America to be attained around 1960.[121] The New York
World's Fair's leaders adopted "Building the World of Tomorrow" as their
official title and their exhibits confidently exuded that idea. Gerald Wendt,
a distinguished chemist and Director of Science for the New York fair, served
notice that he and his associates believed, "It is evident that the tools for
building the world of tomorrow are already in our hands. The discoveries
of science, the power of American industry, the resources for better living
and the will to cooperation are all at hand and need only an adequate understanding by the people of America to be fully utilized."[122] Fittingly, fair
officials excavated and reconstructed a dump on Flushing Meadows in
Queens to establish a site for what *Time* called "the greatest show of all
time" and *The New York Times* designated as "the biggest, costliest, most
ambitious undertaking ever attempted in the history of international exhi-
bitions." But it was the predictions of officials at the fair for the rapid attainment of a benign future for Americans and the fair's place in that future
that proved them most undaunting. Theirs was a powerful message. Cumulative knowledge in science and technology had reached the pinnacle
where men could control nature for human welfare; men and women could

now live free from constant work, see and experience more with greater mobility, better understand themselves and human relationships by increased leisure, live comfortably in attractive houses and pedestrian-safe cities. The New York fair taught that a better world was within human grasp.[123]

This sobriety of resolve committed to the fair's grand purposes is best reflected in the time capsule that fair promoters interred before opening day. In so doing, they declared the extraordinary value and utility of America in 1939 and suggested to people living in "failed civilizations" in the future to look to the legacy of the New York World's Fair for help. Wendt wrote, "It [a failed civilization] can be rebuilt with the time capsule as text."[124] This august prescription was duly safeguarded. Westinghouse Corporation prepared a sheath for the capsule from an alloy of copper, chromium, and silver that was to last 5,000 years, and so it was designed to be opened in 6939 A.D. Lowered into a fifty-foot shaft on the Westinghouse exhibit site, the seven-foot capsule was protected from historical anonymity or random discovery by careful preparations. More than 3,000 copies of a book detailing its location and contents were sent to such places, seemingly impervious to time, as libraries, monasteries, convents, and temples, and if someone stumbled on the capsule inadvertently in those 5,000 years of burial this person was cautioned by an inscribed request on the capsule, "Let him not wantonly disturb it, for to do so would be to deprive the people of the era the legacy here left them." The corporate chairman of Westinghouse intoned in the solemn ceremony, "May the time capsule sleep well. When it is awakened 5,000 years from now, may its contents be a suitable gift to our far off descendants."[125]

As Westinghouse's interest in the development of the time capsule suggests, corporate business contributed importantly to the fair and its theme of confidence in the imminence of a more perfect future. Business, in conjunction with the new technology, was selling the products that would produce that future, and the large numbers of people expected to attend the fair provided a mammoth sales opportunity. Business officials also hoped to show in their exhibits how their scientific laboratories worked to benefit everyone—in effect displaying a humane role for business, an image damaged by the rigors of the early Depression.[126]

The corporations employed the designers at handsome salaries (Geddes received $200,000 from General Motors for designing Futurama) for the teaching exhibits that attracted fair visitors.[127] In many ways the New York fair was their creation. Emerging from earlier triumphs in redesigning the appearance and function of a great variety of objects in the mid- and late 1930s, each of the major designers—Dreyfus, Geddes, Loewy, and Teague—was identified with one or two exhibits, or designing the fair's theme center. Together with similarly inspired and gifted colleagues, they turned the fairgrounds into a veritable heavenly city of industrial design. A bumptious group, a successful elite in what was then an elite profession, they had proved indispensable to business corporations that attempted to stimulate a stalled economy. Indeed, Walter Teague had no problem bracing his firm resolve with a quote from Bertrand Russell, "It may be that God made the world, but this is no reason why we should not make it over."[128]

The designers employed artful techniques to communicate their faith in products to visitors to the fair: especially airplane perspective, the diorama, and the "multi-media show." Because the airplane represented the most celebrated achievement of technology in the 1930s, the designers hit on the fortunate sales technique of providing fair patrons with a safe airplane perspective in several exhibits; they looked down on a vast landscape in miniature, the diorama, usually from a moving platform. By yoking the two, designers cast exhibits with authority and unusual dramatic appeal. Again, the better exhibits set up by the elite designers often used an exciting array of additional communication techniques: raising and lowering lights and colored lights and introducing music, voice recordings, and film.[129]

The number one hit of the fair was Norman Bel Geddes's General Motors' Futurama Exhibit, where long lines invariably waited outside to be admitted to its fifteen-minute futuristic trip across America of 1960. Viewers were seated comfortably in upholstered chairs with two seats to an enclosed car, a fact that heightened the pleasure of its low-flying airplane perspective. Photographs of the travelers moving slowly above the diorama show them peering with fixed attention at sights below. The enormous size of the diorama, a full city block, lent credence to the narrator's description of the national scene that came separately via synchronized voice into each "airborn" car.[130]

Geddes, a genius of theater design as well as automobile planning, had for many years been concerned with the steady growth of car and truck ownership in America, and the ironic failure of local, state, and federal authorities to accommodate these numbers with comparable expansion of highways. America's vast spaces underscored for Geddes the country's need to improve its roads for business and also leisure, which he envisioned as a prime concern of future Americans. Although convinced that more speed was required on the highways to maximize uses of the car, Geddes recognized that speed on American roads in the 1930s was dangerous and led to questions of automobile safety. The answer for the future, Geddes was convinced, was a superhighway system to span the country.

Passengers were presented with Geddes's vision of how Americans of 1960 would solve these problems in the layout of the diorama and comments by the narrator. They looked at many recognizable features of their own times in America, but they also came to understand, as they watched some 50,000 scaled-down models of cars plying the roads at scaled speeds from fifty to one hundred miles per hour, that Geddes was predicting that America would soon be linked by a vast superhighway system. Geddes anticipated many features of the system that came to be built in the United States after 1954, and suggested other ideas still being pondered; these included grass strips separating highways for traffic in opposite directions, elevated expressways with lanes divided to accommodate different fixed speeds of vehicles, off ramps connecting with older roads at a fifty-mile-per-hour ramp speed, lighting built into the side of the road, and traffic safety assured by technicians who radioed instructions to drivers to change lanes from numerous bridges straddling the highway.

Geddes's plans for the city, which would also have to accommodate more traffic in the future, appeared extremely innovative to the viewers of the 1930s. The diorama displayed his preferences for a city with numerous feeder highways, each with numerous lanes. The core of Geddes's city is presented with carefully spaced skyscrapers separated by parks and elevated expressways every ten blocks, permitting fast moving vehicles to exit at convenient access roads at street level. The latter posed no problems for pedestrians because all sidewalks were elevated above them, each sidewalk in turn becoming a four-way bridge at each intersection. Geddes had imaginatively transformed the city to overcome automobile congestion and secure pedestrian safety, but since he foresaw that improved automobile speed would yield swift transportation out of the city, Geddes also anticipated the great development of the suburbs. At the completion of the trip, the narrator enjoined the travelers, "All eyes to the future" and each passenger was duly awarded a button that read, "I Have Seen the Future."

The New York fair proved memorable and an enjoyable experience for its numerous visitors, yet it also influenced the thinking and attitudes of those who remained at home. Few were out of touch with the fair or its heralding of a better future.

The "World of Tomorrow" was frequently seen in the news and the picture magazines, especially *Life*, which regularly devoted features and short articles to the fair.[131] President Roosevelt's appearance and speech on opening day garnered national copy. His words on the occasion established a common ground between ideals of the nation and the fair when he declared that "America's future was hitched to a star, but it is a star of good will, a star of progress for mankind." Those who closely observed Mrs. Roosevelt's dress that day recognized its motif of the Trylon and Perisphere, the fair's theme symbols that came to be widely patterned on bric-a-brac in the period 1939–1940.[132] Advertising by big business seized on interest in the fair in national magazines as well as local newspapers. Local stores in towns and cities across the country also highlighted the fair in advertising, and small-town newspapers ran special news items on residents who went to the fair or intended to do so.[133] And Westinghouse provided informational radio programs.[134] One historian concluded that virtually every American heard news about the New York World's Fair several times a week.[135]

What was the place of the New York World's Fair in American experience? When it finally closed after 355 nights covering two separate years, what effect did it have on the Americans who attended?

Some have maintained that the prime function of the New York's World Fair "offered an escape from the imperfections of the present life into an ideal future" yet such suppositions are not based on data from actual patrons.[136] Another observed that the fair's patrons "were shown the possibilities of life as a festival or a magic show, and they accepted consumer capitalism without critical reflection because of the wonders of the process unfolded for them."[137] This may be closer to the mark, but it exaggerates the naiveté of those who attended. Polls taken at the fair tell us that 85% of the visitors enjoyed the fair and only 3% disliked it, but the polls also tell us nearly 38% of those polled (approximately 1,020 persons) had college degrees at a time when only 4% nationally had them. Photographs of fair visitors show them to be well dressed: coats and ties for men and dresses or blouses and skirts for women. To assume that a clientele with this background was easily beguiled is dubious.[138] Besides, the fair sustained the expectations it fostered with solid evidence. It first introduced large numbers of Americans to television, nylon, Kodachrome, and a variety of new features for electrical appliances for the General Electric Kitchen.[139] For many Americans "The World of Tomorrow" reinforced confidence because it confirmed what they already believed: corporations were major benefactors of Americans with employment and their new and better products; American technology was unbeatable and the future, as always, would be good, now maybe even better. The choice of the words "Building the World" in the fair's motto might also have provided reassuring resonance. Throughout the 1930s, Americans had been building an extraordinary future—massive and powerful dams, the world's tallest buildings, its longest and most beautiful bridges, its swiftest and most efficient commercial airplanes, and the world's most efficient and comfortable mass-produced cars. The public had also witnessed radical changes in design and felt swept up in the new modern style. The large number who attended the fair did not react derisively to its promises; instead they accepted and enjoyed what they saw. There is no evidence either that they regarded the fair's exhibits as unrealistic. A decade of technological and design building and its wide dissemination through artifacts, products, and advertising had prepared fair goers to relish "The World of Tomorrow."

9

Americans Go to the Movies

American movies and radio had one of their most successful decades in the 1930s. Never before were so many Americans in all parts of the country entertained and informed by standardized media. Until then, it was still possible to think of America principally in terms of regions, but by virtue of the impact of national media, national brands, and national advertising, along with improved opportunities for travel, one might, by 1940, think of America as a more unitary culture. Radio and movies not only helped formulate this homogeneity, they also, of course, supplied major clues to its identity with symbolic statements about how Depression Americans felt and what they believed. The fact that the public often sought entertainment from the movies or radio as a mode of escape does not invalidate them as a measure of the national culture. What the American people wished or allowed themselves to escape to was still part of their sensibilities. What played on the dial or on the screen does, in fact, furnish important measures of what Americans held dear while in the heart of the Great Depression.

Movies were big business in the 1930s. Hollywood, virtually synonymous with the film industry in America, was producing three-fourths of the world's motion-picture footage and was widely known as the "entertainment capital" of the world.[1] Perhaps 5,000 films came out of Hollywood in that decade.[2] Great movie studios were operating then: Metro-Goldwyn Mayer, Twentieth Century-Fox, Warner Brothers, Radio-Keith Orpheum, and Paramount. And unusually gifted movie stars, perhaps the greatest ever, captivated the decade's viewers.[3] Theaters, less sumptuous than the palaces of the 1920s, were nevertheless restyled in streamline form; they were flashy and exuded optimism for patrons. Their intent was to catch the eye of the passersby by reminding "the show began on the sidewalk." At times, theater owners, pressed for cash, could only remodel the box office, poster cases, or the marquee, but they managed to spell out Hollywood's magic for the pedestrian.[4] Hollywood's power of persuasion was also buttressed by an elaborate support industry of fan magazines and gossip columns.

That there was a meaningful dialogue between Hollywood's films and their American audiences is evident from the fact that between 60 million Americans (at the low point of the Depression) and 85 million (1939) attended the movies each week, nearly one-half to two-thirds of the country's population, though many persons attended more than once a week.[5] Put another way, nearly eighty-three cents of every dollar Americans spent on recreation in the 1930s was for movies.[6] Although there were no exit polls to tell us what patrons learned or why they liked these movies, sizable attendance establishes that movies were not merely a reliable gauge of America's popular culture in the 1930s, but had an important impact on the thoughts and behavior of many Americans.[7] The emotional setting of the movies—the dark theater with its effect of privacy for patrons and with beautiful and exciting people on screen, inviting identification of the viewer, apparently had a powerful effect, for example, on the sexual attitudes and behavior of young people. The Lynds in Middletown in 1935 noted "a sense of sharp, free behavior between the sexes (patterned on the movies) and of less disguise among the young." The Lynds were quick to observe, "This shift in public morals does not, of course, represent the behavior of everybody or even most persons in Middletown. . . . That it does represent, however, a noticeable change in the total pattern of behavior cannot be doubted."[8] Hortense Powdermaker made similar observations about young people, even young marrieds, in the conservative southern community of Indianola, Mississippi. The introduction of sound in movies (1927) heightened the audience's illusion of reality, making the remarks and actions of the stars even more compelling. The squeal of tires, the staccato burst of gunfire, the clink of ice cubes at a fashionable cocktail party, where morals were questionable, made the lines and lives of movie stars even more difficult to resist.[9]

Hollywood successfully adapted to the milieu of the postwar period and 1920s. At that time, the inclusive and cooperative spirit of Progressivism (1900–1918) manifest in its relative tolerance toward immigrants, reform of working and living conditions for labor, woman's suffrage, support for black organizations like the National Association for the Advancement of Colored People (NAACP) by prominent whites, was replaced by prohibition and gangsterism, egregious racial and religious prejudice, antagonism to labor, and the emancipatory, but often tawdry behavior of the Jazz Age. Lewis Jacobs, an authority on film in this period, noted how Hollywood responded in kind by increasing its attempt "to titillate and shock." He summed up his sense of films of that period, "the main traits of these ten years [1920s] as reflected in films were indifference to social responsibility and absorption in the individual." For Jacobs, "Once marriage and the home had broken down on the screen, there was a breakdown of morals all along the line. Impropriety, promiscuity, illicit sex relations, and bad manners were generally shown as prevailing among married and unmarried alike."[10]

Since movies achieved impressive attendance figures then, there is reason to believe that Americans accepted this image of themselves on screen. Perhaps this was so because the films permitted secondary interest in social responsibility while underscoring individual freedom and self-sufficiency of characters, hence satisfying every interest at once—the prostitute with the heart of gold or the fierce individualism of the cowboy who winds up saving the lonely town from a lawless gang. It is also true that films could better afford themes of personal laissez-faire when the economy was performing well. Prosperity reduced needs for compromise and mutual dependency.

The Depression caught Hollywood unprepared and threw it into a panic. Full realization came slowly because box-office receipts held up through 1929 and 1930. By 1931, record losses were recorded at the major studios. Economy measures were adopted, and the price of movies tickets was halved to 25 cents for adults, theater personnel reduced, gimmicks and giveaways were introduced, refreshment stands expanded, and double features became common. Still studio income plummeted in 1933. Proceeds from admissions fell 40% below 1931, a poor year. One trade film journal estimated that 5,000 of the nation's 16,000 theaters had been closed and all major studios were in "desperate trouble."[11] With a mindset shaped by the 1920s, the studios returned to the reliable genre of that period and exaggerated their use. Exotic and bizarre thrillers such as *Freaks* (1932), *Frankenstein* (1932), and *King Kong* (1933) appeared, and especially movies featuring lurid sex and violent crime became staples of the movie studios. Far from being a golden age of films, the studios chose cheap and sensational subjects and themes and imposed them on the public, hoping these time-tested formulas would draw large audiences once again and offset losses from the Depression.

Gangster films had special appeal for Hollywood in the early 1930s because they were economical to produce, very exciting, and reflected an America awash with crime. Statistics compiled by the federal government showed a constant rise in the crime rate from 6.8 homicides per 100,000 people in 1920 to 9.7 in 1933, a 30% increase and a peak for homicides in the 1930s.[12] Prohibition contributed significantly to the dramatic rise in crime and homicides.[13] Since organized crime usually carried out its operations on an interstate basis, state police were powerless to act, while the federal government's authority in interstate crime enforcement was then restricted to intercepting traffic in stolen cars. American movie audiences were interested in gangsters too because they were tough and exciting and could deal with difficulties, but also, one suspects, because they feared them as people who were turning their world upside down.[14] All these considerations explained why *Little Caesar* (1930), featuring Edward G. Robinson, and *Public Enemy* (1931), with Jimmy Cagney (both stars of unusual personal magnetism) were popular and nominated for awards.[15]

Surely, neither gave comfort or hope about the human condition at a time of deepening depression. Rico Bandello (Robinson), as "Little Caesar," with an obsessive desire "to be somebody," has a terrible sense of inferiority that he compensated for by ruthless killing. He rises to the top of his gang because he is not afraid to kill, unlike mobsters who have grown soft. He also regards discretion and interest in women as signs of weakness. Rico finally shoots the police commissioner and then a member of his own gang on the steps of the church where the gangster had gone to confess his wrongdoings. Rico himself is later gunned down by the police. It is hard to credit him with more than a perverse application of Horatio Alger; he is truly a study in "social pathos."[16]

Public Enemy (Cagney) would leave many viewers with deep feelings of misanthropy, though *Time* magazine reported that the movie fascinated audiences in New York. The movie began with a disclaimer that what the audience was going to see should not be interpreted as glamorizing crime.[17] *Public Enemy* traces the criminal life of Tom Powers who graduates into bootlegging. "There are no good characters in the film"—all people turn out to be corrupt, even those who appear otherwise.[18] Powers scoffs at patriotism in the form of the medals his brother won in World War I; he displays cool brutality throughout his life from his youth when he provides skates for a girl so he can trip her ("What do you care," he says, "it's only a girl"), to pushing a grapefruit into his girlfriend Kitty's face for saying, after noticing his lack of interest, "Maybe you got somebody else you like better," to pumping bullet after bullet into the bodies of people he has killed. The critical story line in the movie occurs when Putty Nose, the piano player who introduced Tom to crime, pleads for his life as Tom, suspecting he is a double-crosser, prepares to kill him. Putty Nose screams, "Tommy, ain't you got a heart?"[19]

In this era of movie sensationalism (1930–1934), when studios desperately sought growth in box-office receipts or faced receivership, male leads like Robinson and Cagney were empowered to run roughshod over civilization. Women stars, in keeping with contemporary roles for women, usually representing civilization in film, were generally denied misanthropic roles. In order to portray them in comparable, shocking, individualized roles, women were regularly presented as wantonly sexual—as kept women or even prostitutes.

One major actress after another capable of exhibiting a variety of personal strengths on screen now found herself cast as a morally lax woman. Greta Garbo in *Susan Lenox*, Joan Crawford in *Possessed* (both in 1931), Marlene Dietrich in *Blonde Venus*, Tallulah Bankhead in *Faithless*, Jean Harlow in *Red Dust*, and Irene Dunne in *Back Street* (all 1932). This, of course, is

James Cagney (*Public Enemy*, 1931), portraying an insolent gangster, plays out his role by pushing a grapefruit in the face of his girlfriend (played by Mae Clark) who had innocently offended him. *Public Enemy* typifies the 1930–1933 era in films that applauded antisocial and iconoclastic behavior. Museum of Modern Art Stills Archive.

also the less than subtle message from Ginger Rogers in *Gold Diggers of 1933*, when she sings with her chorus that they are so attractive and appealing to men that they never fear confronting breadlines.[20]

Some of the fallen women are retrieved on repentance, though the original impulse that drove them into prostitution was often merely some mode of altruism such as defraying medical expenses for sick husbands. Others are left to languish on tropical islands cohabiting with criminal types (Dorothy MacKail in *Safe in Hell*, 1934). A few heroines succeed through wit, will, and sexual compromises—Bette Davis in *Ex-Lady* (1933) and Barbara Stanwyck in *Baby Face* (also 1933). One critic, Gilbert Seldes, speculated that these films were ploys to bring more men into the theater audience. A variation on this theme was advanced by one of their bitterest critics, Father Daniel Lord. His explanation for the spate of racy women films was that "movie producers all owned large amounts of stock in lingerie companies."[21]

It is not a coincidence that Mae West would have her best years in the movies in the era of fallen or kept women. Unlike them, however, and their dreary victimized sexuality, West's version was robust, even predatory. She fairly sizzled on the screen, thereby exemplifying the studio's emphasis on the shocking and the sensational, but in a different direction. When she meets Cary Grant in *She Done Him Wrong* (1932), she sizes him up the way that men were long accustomed to appraising women and declares, "Why don't ya come up and see me some time. I'm home every evening." Later, when he doesn't respond, she draws the noose tighter and announces, "You can be had." And in *I'm No Angel* (1933) she asserts with consummate use of the double entendre, "When I'm good, I'm very good. But when I'm bad, I'm better." She later sings "Frankie and Johnny" with the raucous voice of a saloon queen. And with barely concealed innuendoes, she declares her preference for "A Guy What Takes His Time." As one commentator noted, she could not even sing a lullaby without making it sexy. She packed them in in movie houses in small towns as well as the big cities by providing the most provocative sexual excitement of the decade.[22] She was also the epitome of Hollywood's strategy to bring out the crowds. And Hollywood moguls paid her tribute for doing so.[23]

The Marx Brothers, however, were the most shocking exponents of sensationalism and antisocial behavior in the movie-making of the early 1930s; their great popularity in films also occurred at that time. No other person or group quite embodied their spirit of irreverence. During the period 1930 to 1934, they made four films for Paramount, the last, their famous *Duck Soup*. A distinguished critic describes these films as "Anarcho-Nihilist Laff Riots."[24] *Duck Soup* went so far as to spoof patriotism and national service as absurd. Groucho is appointed by a dowager to administer the state of Fredonia as prime minister and promptly ridicules the dignity of his office. He slides down a flagpole as part of his inaugural ceremony and then asks an ambassador attending the ceremony from another country for a loan of $12. The other Marx Brothers meanwhile are busy making the government dysfunctional. Chico is appointed secretary of war, but only after he insults Groucho. Earlier Groucho advised Chico to give up his peanut stand for an "easy government job." Groucho sees to it meanwhile that the country's civil-service examination is transformed into riddles. He is also intent on solving Fredonia's economic problems by going to war with a neighboring state. When the ambassador from that state arrives, one of the Marx Brothers slaps his face and refuses to shake hands with him—hence, parodying causes for wars. The population, meanwhile, is brainwashed when it is assembled for mass sings, "We're Going to War" and "All God's Chillun Got Guns." When the war begins, one of the brothers instructs another who is prepared to fight, "While you are out there risking your life and limb . . . we'll be in here thinking what a sucker you are."[25] The public's negative reaction to *Duck Soup* was a portent of the failure of the studio's general strategy. Effective government was merely one of the many institutions Americans regarded as essential to combat the dissolvent effects of the Great Depression.

In 1934, Hollywood began to shed its preoccupation with the destructive and outlandish with the issue of the remarkable screwball comedy *It Hap-pened One Night*, starring Claudette Colbert and Clark Gable and directed by the prophetic Frank Capra. By 1935, the changeover had become vir-tually complete; the studios had come full circle and were featuring positive interpretations of American life and applauding the nation's institutions, traditions, and opportunities. Three major factors were responsible: the New Deal stabilized American society by achieving centralization of authority and projecting a caring and benevolent sense of national community; there were also increasingly negative responses by the public to the ideology of the movies. Audiences objected to their antisocial character and their criticism of institutions and traditional values. Prominent Catholic laity and clerics would spearhead this reaction, but it is a mistake to assume that concern about these issues was restricted to Catholics. The third major factor was that movie revenues began to climb. Once the new focus for films was adopted by the major studios, Hollywood found what it was desperately searching for—a formula to prosper in the Depression.

In essence, the New Deal restored a basic order to American life by per-forming important, integrative functions. This is apparent in its impact on the cinema. By sponsoring the Twenty-first Amendment to abolish prohi-bition, the New Deal dealt a lethal blow to crime and its secretive networks. It is estimated that one-third of the homicides in America in 1933 were linked to criminal vendettas by persons violating Prohibition.[26] Now with a stroke of the pen, this species of mayhem largely disappeared. This, together with expansion of the federal government's prerogatives in interstate crime and the emergence of a prestigious Federal Bureau of Investigation (FBI), took the gangsters off the streets. Criminals who held out were rigorously pursued and each victorious outcome by federal agents became a parable for a resurgent community spirit; good and effective men wore federal insignia and big-time criminals were finally paying the wages of sin.

The impact of these developments registered quickly in Hollywood's "crime movies." Their turnaround is underscored by the fact that the new heroes, now police and FBI, were the former film gangsters, Jimmy Cagney and Edward G. Robinson, while the former crime movies became law-and-order movies.[27] Jimmy Cagney in *G-Man* (1935) comes out of a shady past, keeping alive the basis of his persona in *Public Enemy*, but with a clear change in character and a strong preference for preserving community against irresponsible individualism. Although nearly dismissed from the FBI because of his former gangland connections, he vindicates the bureau's con-fidence by avenging the death of a fellow G-man. Viewers of the film are exposed in the interim to imposing displays of the FBI's power and effi-ciency—its crime labs, fingerprinting collections, tough physical training, and competent agents. Everyone was impressed. One character who supplies information to the FBI in the film concedes he did so because he didn't want to get into trouble with its agents. A theater owner in Washington,

DC, found record audiences attending *G-Man* over a July 4th weekend in 1935. Another in Lamar, Missouri, wrote about *G-Man* "We honestly believe that every theatre should play this for the reason it leaves a lot of people thinking our government is OK."[28] *G-Man* played fifty days in New York and Los Angeles, eight more than *Little Caesar* or *Public Enemy*.[29] The new surge of anticrime movies cast Edward G. Robinson as an FBI agent in *Bullets or Ballots;* he insinuates himself into a gang and destroys it, thus becoming an antithesis of Rico. Law enforcement even came to be invested with an aura of patriotism. *Special Agent* (1935) opened with a picture of the American flag followed by a speech overheard from the Senate Building lauding the FBI for taking steps to rid the country of criminal elements.[30] There is reason to believe that the public that attended these films felt more secure and hopeful because, in fact as well as film, America's basic institutions were working.

Those offended by the brash and violent depiction of American life in the early 1930s movies also had a hand in their reformation—some actively and organizationally, most in accepting and enjoying the movies in greater numbers after they were reformed. From its inception with storefront nickelodeons for the working class in New York through the 1920s when movies attempted to go respectable with the star system and sumptuous theaters, the movie industry exploited sex, bawdy humor, and violence—a fact that prompted one Polynesian visitor to the United States to declare there were only two types of American movies; kiss, kiss, and bang, bang.[31]

After a series of well-publicized sex scandals involving movie stars in the early 1920s, the producers in Hollywood, mostly Jewish, sought to refurbish the image of their industry by appointing William H. Hays, a former postmaster of the United States and a Protestant Republican from the Midwest, as spokesman for the industry. He came to be known as "Movie Czar" and worked to improve Hollywood's reputation, but had no practical power to change the quality of films. His position was vaguely defined and wholly dependent on the pleasure and salary supplied by his employees. Although seemingly opposed to the trends of the industry in the 1920s and the 1930s, he openly acknowledged that he was powerless to influence events.[32]

Negative public reactions to the movies began to take concerted form in the 1920s. A delegation of more than 200 Protestant ministers and leaders of women's clubs lobbied Congress in 1926 for federal legislation to regulate movies that they deplored for their affronts to morality.[33] Leaders of this group also played a prominent role in securing funds from the Payne Foundation, a philanthropic organization, to study the effects of movies on children. According to film historian Robert Sklar, the intent of those behind the study was "to get the goods on the movies, to nail them to the wall." A four-year study completed in 1933 by academics left equivocal conclusions. But at least some academics and one responsible journal believed that they came close to doing just that.[34] Catholics, both laymen and clerics, were also disturbed and their leaders, with the encouragement of some in the church hierarchy, decided to write a code of moral conduct for the movies. Father Daniel Lord, S.J., a professor of dramatics at St. Louis University, was its author. The code was intended as a guide for morally acceptable movies. It acknowledged that sex outside marriage and violence were facts of life and acceptable in drama, but insisted that movie audiences not be led to confuse right and wrong; the moviegoer, according to the code, should not be permitted to leave the theater with "sympathy" for those transgressing morals. Nor should movies depict pillars of the social and political order—the courts, police, or government—as corrupt, or present the home and family in debasing terms. Elements of evil on screen were, however, acceptable (murder, adultery, cynicism, corruption) according to Father Lord's theory of compensating moral value, as long as good balanced out evil and evil deeds were counteracted by retribution, remorse, or reform of the perpetrator.[35]

The code specifically prohibited nudity, homosexuality, interracial sex, abortion, incest, and the use of drugs and profanity. The fact that Lord's prescriptions would be adopted and eventually effectively regulate the basic precepts of the movie industry in 1934 represents one of the decade's most candid statements about the culture of the 1930s. At a time when their agencies of collective security (government, family, church, community) were major material and psychological assets in struggles with the Depression, Americans took an uncharacteristic position to restrain by censorship a form of popular culture that was out of step with their needs.

Will Hays was delighted when a prominent Catholic layman, Martin Quigley, brought Father Lord's code to his attention, declaring, "This was the very thing I was looking for."[36] Hays also believed that the movie producers should show greater social responsibility, and he convinced them, in the face of the stock market crash and apparent public displeasure with films, that it was in their interest to adopt the code. The movie studios agreed, probably because their leaders regarded the code, like Hays's office, to be merely another form of showcasing. At least, for the next three years, a notoriously freewheeling period for movies, their films made a mockery of the code.[37]

American Catholics thereupon became the most outspoken and best organized critics of the movies, and some began to warn Hays of their possible boycott. Indeed, Cardinal Daugherty of Philadelphia had already declared an official boycott of the movies for Catholics in his jurisdiction. Since there were 20 million Catholics in America, roughly one of every six Americans, most of them living in cities with well-organized parishes and an effective Catholic press, the danger of this threat could hardly be ignored. Meanwhile, the Federal Council of Churches, an official interdenominational organization of Protestant churches, voted to form a united front with Catholics against offensive films, and several Protestant denominations took a determined public stand denouncing immorality in films in 1934. Circumstances had played into Will Hays's hands by this time. Loss of revenues by movie studios in the early 1930s and the threat of boycott from numerous Catholics made it possible for Hays to get a promise of firm compliance from the producers and an effective regulatory agency to assure that result. Hays set up a censorship office in Hollywood in 1934, the Production Control Administration (PCA), and appointed a zealous Catholic, Joseph I. Breen, as its director. Breen would employ Lord's code, but would do so with expanded powers. No film could be shown in America after 1934 without the PCA's seal of approval. Breen's first test involved a film, *Madame du Barry*, which depicted the lady in question not merely as Louis XV's mistress, but also his pimp, with part of the action of the film to take place in a bedroom with a mirrored ceiling. Jack Warner was irate when Breen demanded changes, but relented. The stakes were high, and Breen had been delegated the authority.[38]

From mid-1934 to the end of the decade, Hollywood's films assumed a more conservative hue and won greater public acceptance. The studios acknowledged Joe Breen's authority as arbiter of morals and Breen proved a durable helmsman. His resolve to enforce the code undercut public resistance to movies, though Catholics continued to supply pressure from the Legion of Decency (1933), issuing ratings of movies through parishes and periodicals for Catholic laity. Breen, however, never approved a film that appeared on the Legion of Decency's list of condemned films.[39] And when *Life*, an enthusiastic supporter of middle-class values, ran a five-page spread on the movie code in 1938, it questioned whether Breen's office should extend censorship to subjects of international politics, such as the Spanish Civil War, but did not challenge its role in shoring up morals at home.[40] In fact, the relative ease with which the code was instituted and lack of protests from the general audience after its inception suggest, wrote one film commentator, "that the public was closely in tune with the code." He assumed there were no outcries because films after 1935 "represented the wishes" of Americans.[41]

Movie attendance rose substantially from 70 million per week in 1934 to an average of 86.5 million per week in the last four years of the decade. An improved recovery helped explain the rise, though not entirely. Even when the economy went into a tailspin in late 1937 and early 1938, the average attendance for those two years remained high and equal to figures for the good years, 1936 and 1939. Hays and Breen believed that the surge in patronage reflected the improved moral climate of the movies.

To Breen's credit, he was no Torquemada or Cromwell. In 1936, reviewers in his office witnessed nearly 1,200 scripts and rejected first drafts of only twenty-two. In 1939, 2,873 scripts were reviewed and only fifty-three early drafts were returned for revisions. Breen may, indeed, have made American films more attractive abroad by tightening guidelines for moral propriety. Audiences of 220 million worldwide saw American films in 1938. The studios could hardly complain with these returns.[42] The record-breaking attendance at movie theaters in the late 1930s is attributed to many factors, but one was the industry's production of movies that better accorded with the way Americans both lived and idealized life amid the Depression. The movies from 1935 to 1940 were sources of public confidence and hope not because they projected a mythical America, but one that had sufficient relevance to be useful at that time.

It is appropriate to describe the great period in the history of movies from 1935 to 1939 as Hollywood's "Golden Age." Its stars were smooth and often sophisticated; its dancing in the form of Ginger Rogers and Fred Astaire classic gracefulness; its film subjects and treatments generally elevating to the spirit; its directors exceptionally talented; and its popularity then at an all-time zenith.[43] Robert Sklar sees this period as one in which film producers first became fully aware of the power of their medium and consciously crafted an affirmative view of American life to buoy the jaded spirits of depressed Americans.[44] From the standpoint of social history, it would seem correct instead to credit the American people for diverting the moguls from purely market considerations to a course that acknowledged the importance of their social values and historical traditions. Hollywood's role in the late 1930s was less one of initiative and myth-making than one of reinforcing public preferences and commitments. This explains that assortment of popular films issued in Hollywood's Golden Age that celebrate small towns and their responsible political representatives, the importance of home and family, neighborliness and generosity, love's ability to conquer class interest, the special place of America in the world, and, of course, the idea that "tomorrow, after all, is another day."

It Happened One Night (1934), Frank Capra's film, was one of the first of stature to reflect a positive and hopeful spirit among Americans in the 1930s. The fact that it was nominated by the Academy for outstanding movie of the year undoubtedly established precedents for future films. It was a "screwball comedy," the first of a genre that would produce at least ten others in the late 1930s and early 1940s. The label "screwball" is closely related to a fantastic pitch thrown by the great New York Giant left-hander, Carl Hubbell, in the mid- and late 1930s. By twisting his wrist to the inside as he released his pitch, Hubbell created a reverse curve, one that broke away from right-handed hitters and toward left-handed hitters. This was totally unexpected because a lefty's curve ball was supposed to do just the opposite. Since Hubbell also continued to throw the conventional curve, he had batters all confused. The result was something different, the opposite of what a batter expected, and so in a sense "screwy." *It Happened One Night* is "odd ball, unpredictable, giddy, unconventional, wacky, a world turned upside down"; it is presented as a love affair that grows out of what seems to be insurmountable incompatibility of the lovers. Screwball was

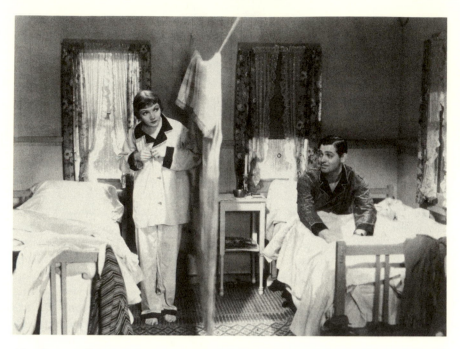

Claudette Colbert and Clark Gable in *It Happened One Night* (1934). The two, unmarried, maintain proprieties by separating themselves with a blanket (the wall of Jericho). Later, when they marry, it comes down abruptly. This film represents a shift in theme that characterizes the period of 1934–1940—an emphasis on typical American preferences and values. Museum of Modern Art Stills Archive.

compatible with the Breen office and did nothing to violate its codes, but had a merry time with sex as a game, usually as "a sex-role farce." It had a particular appeal for women because many of its female leads, Claudette Colbert, Katharine Hepburn, and Rosalind Russell are portrayed as independent by virtue of inherited wealth or professional expertise; they could engage in striking repartee and give men a challenge before settling on marriage. And for men viewers, the exciting chase was there, before mutual love triumphed.[45]

It Happened One Night stars Claudette Colbert (Ellen Andrews), a rich young woman trying to escape her father, who meets a brash reporter, Clark Gable (Peter Warne) on a bus who recognizes her through newspaper disclosures. Gable hopes to exploit his acquaintance with Colbert for newspaper articles. They both seem insufferable—she spoiled and he self-satisfied—yet in the course of their bus ride together, we learn that each has endearing qualities. He yearns for something more than the newspaper world, even if he still insists on teaching her to dunk donuts correctly; she concedes that she might act foolish at times because of her sheltered background but declares, "Would you believe it? This is the first time I've ever been alone with a man. It's a wonder I am not panic-stricken." It is their adventures together that warm their relationship. They are forced to share a room when their bus has to stop for a bridge washout, and they do so by placing a makeshift clothesline and blanket (the wall of Jericho) down the center of the room between them. This arrangement works satisfactorily and surely kindles good feelings. Colbert is no pushover, however, and when she tires of Gable's pontificating—instructing her how to hitchhike, and failing with each demonstration, she steps calmly forth, raises her skirts above her knees, and produces a squealing stop from the first car passing by. Gable learns, and so they begin to take one another seriously.

When the pair are separated and Colbert mistakenly believes Gable has forsaken her, she decides to marry again a man she does not love (the marriage the first time was not consummated because of her father's intervention), but following her own intuitions and the advice of her father she decides at the last minute to race from the altar to a waiting car. Gable had made a lasting impression on Colbert's father by asking for only $39.60 in compensation for his efforts to bring his daughter home rather than claim a large reward the father had offered. The final scene after an annulment to Colbert's first marriage takes place in a cabin after Gable and Colbert are married as a trumpet signifies the walls of Jericho have fallen. The film won numerous Academy Awards in 1934.[46]

The sizable and fond audiences that turned out to see *It Happened One Night* probably did not think the outcome naive, and most of them would have resented the idea that it was impossible. Many who attended probably believed strongly enough in democracy and open community to accept the idea that personal characteristics might be more important than status and money in determining eligibility for marriage. But if they didn't, it was still important for them to want to believe it anyhow.

In the late 1930s as the homicide rate fell and gangsters lost their premier stature, Hollywood, in keeping with the optimistic tenor of the period, turned its focus from crime to delinquency. The gangs of youngsters festering in poverty areas of inner cities now were presented as tough, but redeemable, given appropriate recreational opportunities and the good example of responsible adults. *Angels with Dirty Faces* (1938), a marvelously apt title for this type of movie, was the classic Hollywood film dealing with the subject.[47] It begins with a flashback to the youth of the protagonists, Rocky Sullivan (Jimmy Cagney) and Jerry Connally (Pat O'Brien), who are prepared to steal in order to pay for admission to a film. They are detected by police in their attempted break-in; Cagney is sent to reform school, O'Brien escapes and later becomes a priest in his old neighborhood. O'Brien's example of the priest representing benevolent authority and the power of religious people to reform the wayward and disadvantaged, a leit-motif of movies of the period, is repeated by Spencer Tracy as Father Flanagan in *Boy's Town* and William Gargan as Dolan in *You Only Live Once*. When Cagney returns to his neighborhood after release from reform school, O'Brien asks his help in reforming a group of young toughs (the Dead End Kids). He asks Cagney to teach them how to play basketball and be part of his anticrime crusade. But the priest learns that his old friend is still engaged in criminal activity and turns him in to the police. Cagney is captured and sentenced to the electric chair, but now he becomes a true hero to the Dead End Kids; they are confident he will go to his death without remorse, but O'Brien asks Cagney to show fear as he approaches "the chair" to show the boys that criminals only appear tough. He does and the boys became disillusioned with him. A simple formula indeed for ridding society of delinquency, but the film expresses a confident new faith that social problems in America are soluble; even criminals can learn social responsibilities and deter impressionable youth from crime. Religion supplies valuable resources to deal with delinquency and so, too, urban athletic programs can substitute healthy games for the anarchy and petty criminal activities of adolescent youth.

Gone with the Wind, Margaret Mitchell's Pulitzer-Prize novel in 1937 and the basis for a box-office sensation and Oscar winner as best movie in 1939, obviously made an appealing statement to Americans in the 1930s. Neither its setting—pre–Civil War, wartime, and Reconstruction South—nor its outstanding characters, the lovely Scarlett O'Hara (Vivien Leigh), attractive Melanie (Olivia deHaviland), or Rhett Butler (Clark Gable), explain entirely or mainly its unusual appeal to American audiences. That attraction came from its universality and its metaphorical relevance to Americans living in the Great Depression. This explains why American moviegoers from all sections of the country were able to locate themselves in the Old South and identify with its characters in *Gone with the Wind*.

The leitmotif of the novel is sounded when Scarlett recalls the grim days of her ancestors in Ireland and in America, and Ms. Mitchell interprets, "Malign fate had broken their necks, but never their hearts."[48] This spirit also pervades the film. Scarlett will experience great losses and threats to her survival—the destructive war, extreme poverty, the loss of those close to her (both a husband and a child)—but backed against the wall she draws on her heritage and exhibits an unswerving determination to survive and succeed. American audiences, after ten years of depression, could identify with her and probably regarded Scarlett to be a paragon and inspirational historical figure.

Scarlett did not exhibit these strengths as a young woman or even after her first marriage when she appeared to be spoiled by affluence and without vision because of her petulant egocentricity. While her cousin Melanie responds helpfully and stays in Atlanta as a nurse when Yankee troops advance, Scarlett wishes to flee the conflict to her family's plantation at Tara. But when she arrives and views the devastation brought to the plantation, Scarlett begins to find the strength to become a heroine. She vows she will live through these desperate times and never be hungry again. She becomes a spirited independent person, marries a second time, and operates a business herself. She also openly declares that she wants money more than anything else in the world. After her second husband is murdered, she exhibits her obsession for wealth by marrying Rhett Butler, a wealthy parvenu who has obtained his money under questionable circumstances. Although they have a child together and live affluently, they are rejected by Atlanta's postwar elite, which is scandalized by their display of wealth. Her family disintegrates—her child is killed and Rhett, realizing that Scarlett's needs for power and wealth are insatiable, declares, "Frankly madam, I don't give a damn" and leaves. For one who has already been so severely tested and survived, this new predicament without husband and child does not spell disaster. She thinks about Tara and her family's heritage, and her courage returns. She utters what quite possibly became a seminal statement perhaps summarizing the meaning of the Depression for Americans, "After all, tomorrow is another day."

Margaret Mitchell, steeped in southern tradition and an aficionado of its codes of gentility and lady-like refinement, admired Melanie more than Scarlett. But the movie public viewed Scarlett differently. Scarlett became selfish, and aggressive, but audiences forgave her these flaws because of her tumultuous world. The big issue was Scarlett's victory over adversity and her determination to deal with it, repeatedly if necessary. She took hold in desperate times and saved herself and her family. The audience in America in the 1930s vicariously identified with Scarlett, not Melanie. Her achievements, unlike Melanie's, were more substantial than merely preserving the niceties of a genteel culture. Melanie was really more of a victim than a survivor and that was untenable by American codes of the 1930s.

Although lacking the majestic sweep of *Gone with the Wind*, movies affirming the importance and value of American traditions typified the late years of the decade. Capra's *Mr. Deeds Goes to Town* with Gary Cooper (1936) lauds the good-natured generosity and community sense of a small town person who inherits $20 million (when he is presented with the money, he instructs the bearer to put it down on a chair and resumes his tuba lesson). Mr. Deeds goes to the city to confound shysters and promoters, who wish to manipulate him, by giving his money away—the entire 20 million—to begin a small farm project for the needy. The movie resonates with America's rural and small-town cooperative heritage and reflects the fact that nearly half of America's population still lived in that type of community. Capra's *Mr. Smith Goes to Washington* with James Stewart (1939) extended Capra's vision to politics. Jefferson Smith from rural Iowa fights a crooked machine in the Senate. The essence of Smith's goal, he explains, is "plain everyday kindness, a little looking out for the other fella, loving thy neighbor."[49] Capra's ideas about improving life through love and kindness were hardly naive from the standpoint of American political traditions. Powerful religiously based or derived values, though often transcending religious organizations, played an important role in reforming American life in the pre–Civil War and Progressive periods. And in the 1930s, the Judeo-Christian moral tradition still constituted an ethical core of responsible moral behavior for most Americans.

Film as an instrument of popular culture dramatically changed course after 1935 and became an apologist for the American way of life. It would almost seem that two such diametrically opposed spirits in film, one from 1930 to 1934, the other from 1935 to 1939, could not inhere in a single decade. In the earlier period, the movie industry panicked over declining revenues and chose for its staples violence, sexual license, and flamboyant individualism, familiar successful themes from the 1920s. Unwittingly, it imposed an unacceptable ideology for the depression decade. The displeasure of movie patrons became increasingly acute—the extreme individualism and nonconformity advanced by film jeopardized public reliance on family, religion, and community that many regarded an essential for dealing with the era's uncertainties. The movies also seemed to champion lawlessness and harpoon government that supplied indispensable services. Besides, there was fear that the movies were fostering negative views about America's ability to cope with problems such as crime and perhaps its unique ability to transcend limits that history imposed on other countries. After public protest, movies in the mid- and late 1930s made restitution. They played to banner-sized movie audiences, and they helped strengthen the social system in ways that Americans cherished. Popular culture in the term of movies then became still another instrument to help them cope with the Depression's vicissitudes.

10

Americans Listen at Home

If it is apt to describe Hollywood's successes in the mid and late 1930s as a Golden Age, radio was comparably distinguished through the entire decade both for its impact and as a source of national morale. Two national networks formed in the late 1920s, the National Broadcasting Company (NBC) and Columbia Broadcasting System (CBS), greatly helped to explain these successful outcomes. They acquired large numbers of stations and supplied them with standard programming, thereby raising the quality of radio offerings nationally, with local stations retaining a smaller segment of broadcast time. In return, the networks, now with national markets, were compensated by large advertising fees from program sponsors. With this setup and a variety of programs, a group of talented performers, radio's reputation for reliability and reasonable authority, and a major reduction in the cost of radios, radio prospered and radio sets became a household fixture.[1] Stations affiliated with networks more than doubled in the 1930s; the number of families listening to radio also nearly doubled (estimated to be 27.5 million families in 1939).[2] From 1935, when American households already owned twice as many radios as telephones, that number doubled to 44 million radio sets in 1939 when 86% of American homes had radios—some battery powered—and they listened to radio on an average of four and one-half hours a day.[3]

As a pervasive instrument of popular culture in the 1930s, radio exerted a powerful influence on American society. In 1933, a presidential commission, acknowledging radio's new outreach, highlighted its effects on society, including fostering homogeneity, diluting class and regional differences, aiding pronunciation, and providing recreation in rural areas.[4] Indeed, it seems likely that radio became at this time an essential component in the genesis and articulation of an "American Way of Life," a concept that first began to be commonly used in the 1930s.[5]

It is easy to infer that radio's power as a mass medium together with its standardizing quality threatened to impose a new, even alien culture on the American public. But such a conclusion mistakenly underestimates the claims of a tenacious national culture, the imperfect but well-developed language of good and evil of the American people already in place. This derived from broad currents in Western and American experience, especially its Judeo-Christian base, expressed in America mainly through Protestant Christianity. Radio, unlike movies, coming directly into the homes of American families was forced to confront the national culture in one of its strongholds. To appeal to its listeners and, of course, secure its proceeds, radio was obliged to present situations and settings as well as values and ideals primarily acceptable to families in their living rooms. Programming became, therefore, an unusually sensitive and reliable record of the kinds of people Americans were or wished to be in the 1930s; thus, radio accommodated the preferences of Americans for good family life, community-mindedness, and patriotism. In the process, radio achieved impressive popularity, but the American people also gained substantially. Radio's endorsement helped to reassure Americans on the merits and values of their way of life at a time when their confidence was tested by a foundering economic system; it also buttressed their voluntary safety system by portraying benefits that typified good families and good communities and the advantages of being an American. Indeed, radio's message at times became inspirational in presenting themes of family responsibility, upholding justice, helping those in need, and service to the nation.

The abundant time that networks set aside for family-oriented programs illustrated the careful attention they paid to their primary audience.[6] Many family-type programs on radio were set in small towns, including such favorites as *Ma Perkins, Just Plain Bill, David Harum*, and *Pepper Young's Family*. Others, to assure a representative sample, dealt with urban families, including *The Goldbergs*, placed in New York City, and *One Man's Family*, in San Francisco. *Fibber McGee and Molly* was also exceptional because it was a comedy and was offered at night, but it fulfilled other characteristics of family programs and portrayed family life in a positive light. The McGees lived at 79 Wistful Vista in a small town in the Midwest with well-known neighbors. *Vic and Sade*, also comic figures, lived in a "small house half way up the next block" in Illinois and gave the impression of being "friendly next-door neighbors."[7]

Families were not only the subjects of many programs; they also unfailingly portrayed upstanding family values. There were no antisocial characters starring in any of these programs. Genuine villains, when occasionally presented, were usually outwitted or transformed by the stellar example of an array of solid characters. The major networks assured this outcome because

they operated under strict self-regulatory codes. NBC pledged in all its programs that "the hero and heroine, and other sympathetic characters, must
be portrayed as intelligent and morally courageous. The theme must stress
the importance of mutual respect of one man for another, and should emphasize the desirability of fair play and honorable behavior." The moral code
operating at CBS included provisions that

the exalting, as modern heroes, of gangsters, criminals, and racketeers will not be
allowed. Disrespect for either parental or other proper authority must not be glorified
or encouraged. Cruelty, greed, and selfishness must not be presented as worthy mo-
tivations. . . . Conceit, smugness, or unwarranted sense of superiority over others less
fortunate may not be presented as laudable.[8]

This context of norms and values acceptable for home listening explained
why sex, either explicit or implied, was taboo on radio, especially after a
flare-up of animal spirits one night on the *Edgar Bergen–Charlie McCarthy
Show* in December 1937. The bawdy Mae West, in a reenactment of the
Garden of Eden scene with Don Ameche, managed to scandalize radio opinion in a skit lasting only nine minutes. Her raucous "You wanna what?" to
Ameche followed by their kiss, West's love groans, and a climactic sound of
trumpets and thunder did it. This rendition also produced loud and heated
protests, and NBC wound up banning West's name from future broadcasts.[9]
Henceforth, promising hints of sex were nipped in the bud by scriptwriters
themselves or by anxious censors employed by the networks. Twin beds were
the bill of fare for the married couples on radio and when a male actor in
one of these beds happened to be replaced by another, the public sometimes
protested the moral implications of men with different voices being in the
same bedroom with one woman. Equal disfavor befell a male actor who
played husbands in two different radio marriages.[10] On radio not only were
programs chaste in diction and tone, but hardly anyone drank, gambled, or
chased women.[11]
    There is reason to believe that the adaptable quality of programming to
the home setting also enhanced the extraordinary appeal of many radio entertainers for listeners. On the occasion of neighborly entertainer, Eddie
Cantor's, fortieth birthday, he received thousands of packages from his radio
admirers.[12] Amos and Andy were ardently admired across racial lines because
of their personal qualities as well as their humor. In the early 1930s, when
Amos and Andy had 40 million listeners, owners of motion picture theaters
found it advantageous to install radios with loudspeakers in their lobbies so
movie patrons could stay abreast of their programs. When the two comics
bemoaned the fact that they had no typewriter to help them in their business, over 1,800 typewriters were sent to them from well-wishers.[13] Touching personal tributes came repeatedly to Amos and Andy in the form of
letters from admirers; one listener wished there were more like Amos in the

world, declaring "It would [then] be a better place in which to live."[14] Others revealed that they were close to tears over their tribulations. When Amos had been caring for a stray dog that was claimed by its rightful owner, a listener from New Jersey shipped him another dog through NBC studios in New York.[15] Another ardent fan from Chicago considered extreme steps when she was prevented from hearing the program. She wrote,

You know I get so dam mad. I like to hear Amos & Andy at 10 o'clock but that dam man of mine always wants to tune on the *Tribune* at that time. I've a notion to buy another radio & put it in the cellar where I can tune it where I dam please.[16]

Fan mail for radio's daytime serial dramas for women often expressed gratitude for the moral and educational value of the programs. One young woman in Butte, Montana, wrote her local station KGIR that "listening to stories like that makes me know how other girls act and listening to the way the girl [in the program] argues, I know how to tell my boyfriend where to get off at."[17] And the *Lone Ranger* was such a stalwart, inspiring figure for listeners that he was cited in the *Congressional Record* on January 18, 1935, as a "vital factor" in sustaining the real Texas Rangers' work in maintaining law and order.[18] Indeed, radio aimed at the home audience became so upstanding that it won an abiding reputation for reliability. Little wonder a General Electric advertisement of the period shows an emotionally distraught mother standing by a radio drying her tears while her daughter tries to reassure her, "Don't cry mother. . . . it's *only* a program."[19] It was partially because radio was associated with integrity in the public mind that Orson Welles was able to stir a frenzy in his broadcast "War of the Worlds" simulating a Martian invasion of Earth October 30, 1938. He had meant it to be merely a Halloween trick.

The most popular family radio program in the 1930s was comedy, attracting about 120 million listeners a week. Its special appeal then was heightened by an unusual cluster of outstanding comedians, many from vaudeville, and, of course, by its therapeutic benefits. As Fred MacDonald remarked, "Throughout the period, letters and articles in fan magazines attest to the fact the listeners found comedy of great assistance in fighting personal despair."[20] Comedians seemingly had the ability "to cure the worst case of the blues and even make you forget the Depression."[21] Thus, a listener extolled the merits of comedian Ed Wynn for his entire family:

Dad lets the newspaper drop in his lap, Ma comes into the parlor and sits close to the radio; and Sis and I stop our schoolwork. . . . Dad, Sis, and I grin and chuckle after every joke, but Ma laughs till her sides ache. This is the one big reason why I like the Texaco Program. For fifteen minutes, Dad forgets about his job, Ma quits worrying about how she is going to pay the bills, and I am happy to see them happy. Old Man Depression is forgotten and Happiness is King.[22]

Some comedians, notably Amos and Andy, Will Rogers, and George Burns and Gracie Allen, actually alleviated the worst fears of their audiences by making wisecracks about the Depression. A sure sign that radio comedy had helped many Americans laugh off the Depression came when *Variety* reported in August 1934 that several well-known comedians had already depleted their joke repertories, which had taken them many years to assemble.[23]

Each of the comedians had a unique style or characteristic that made people laugh. Amos and Andy, white men Freeman Gosden and Charles Correll, were amusing because they impersonated blacks who had recently moved from Georgia to Chicago. Although Gosden and Correll portrayed Amos and Andy as warmhearted and humane, their humor derived from presenting them with woeful ignorance (they called the Depression, the repression) and mimicking their exaggerated dialect. Amos and Andy served national purposes, however, by poking fun at the "repression." When Andy explained that the stock market crashed to an unsophisticated lad named Lightning, he replied, "Anybody git hurt?" They also cracked jokes about prosperity being just around the corner—Andy had trouble finding the corner.[24]

Will Rogers, the Oklahoma cowboy philosopher, was, like Amos and Andy, another "radio must" for families in the early years of the Depression. He was homespun, a master of the chuckle who delivered witty monologues, usually targeting people in the headlines, especially those who took themselves too seriously. He likened the Depression to a "train that hit us." That explained, he said, "why Americans drive up to the track and we won't do anything" because "we think it might turn around and come back and hit us again," and the audience would howl.[25] On the subject of moving pictures, before reform in 1934, he said, "Compared to Hollywood, Sodom and Gomorrah were a couple of babes in the woods."[26] Parodying a session in the U.S. Senate, with himself in charge, Will Rogers instructed Huey Long to sit down and quipped, "If you can't find your place to rest, I am sure there is people in your state of Louisiana that will be glad to dig you a place to rest."[27]

The *Jack Benny Show* played at 7 o'clock, Sunday nights, for twenty-one years beginning in August 1934. Benny portrayed himself as everyone's inferior, thereby making the audience feel better and himself appear as a lovable fall guy. "I represent everything that is wrong with anybody," Benny once confided. "The minute I come on, even the most hen-pecked guy in the audience feels good." Benny allowed himself to appear as craven, hopelessly vain ("the Clark Gable of radio"), and a legendary tightwad. He steals public Christmas trees for his own use, forces friends to pay for dinners at his house, installs a pay phone in his home, and uses a meter to collect charges on a lawnmower he lends to his neighbors. Other members of the show chide Benny for his deficient traits including Rochester, his black servant. The comic effect of the ultra-penurious Benny on listeners who were forced to make fewer purchases, but who were far more liberal than Benny, made for hilarity. The program probably made many feel better about their limited purchases.[28]

Fibber McGee and Molly began slowly in the popularity ratings in the mid-1930s, but by 1939 captured 29% of the radio audience, perhaps 25 million listeners.[29] Fibber was a small-town character from the Midwest, a whopping braggart, showoff, and teller of tales. On one occasion he recounted how he swam so far from the Golden Gate Bridge in San Francisco that "I was beginning to wonder if I should ought to go on to Japan or come back to Frisco."[30] And in 1935, when G-men were in vogue, Fibber passed himself off as "Slippery McGee, the Slick Sleuth of the Secret Service."[31] At other times, he professed that he worked on a building 1,835 feet high, a Lewis Hines type of subject, but then was frightened when his car was placed on a lift in a neighborhood garage. "Touchdown McGee," the "Tuchipooka Tornado," later proved unable to play games with children.[32] Molly was the dominant figure, exposing Fibber's stories, deriding his pretensions, and replying "t'aint funny, McGee" to his corny jokes. Despite his systematic humiliations, or probably because of them, Fibber McGee was an attractive, funny fellow.

Fred Allen was radio's most gifted humorist in its Golden Age. Often described as the intellectual's comedian, he managed to bring sophisticated humor to a successful radio show. Born John J. Sullivan, near Boston, Allen brought an embittered and neglected childhood into his adult life. Herman Wouk, a distinguished novelist who was an early scriptwriter for Allen, described him as "one of those rare spirits who sees the world as it is, and who laughs in order not to weep." He satirized the contemporary scene with a caustic eye for the pompous and pretentious, especially those in positions of authority. He had a wry and kindlier humor for society's losers. One of Allen's satires concerned Caldwell Bemis, a business firm's "tenth Vice President in Charge of Licking Envelopes." Bemis disappeared one day and lay unconscious on the floor of the office washroom. He had washed his hands there three weeks earlier, but his hands became so slippery he could not open the washroom door. The problem—no paper towels. Why? Instructions in the wash room read, "Use paper towels only," and there were none: the Vice President in Charge of Paper Towels had let Bemis down completely. "Radio Uncles" might also be cuffed around by Allen. What would these sweet avuncular fellows say if they could only speak their own minds on their radio programs for children? "Hello, you punks. . . . Boy, have I got a hangover, my mouth tastes like the heel of a jitterbug's stockin" and other such amenities.[33]

Although laughter coming from these programs helped public morale by reducing anxieties, the comedians also conferred an important second bonus; they did not laugh cynically at the values or institutions that served the confidence or hopefulness of Americans—rather they endorsed them. Radio comedies in the 1930s illustrated how modern media could help stabilize society and consolidate public trust during a severe Depression.

Amos 'n' Andy, "the consummate Depression comedy," used its immense popularity to instruct audiences about the Depression, President Roosevelt's policies, and the importance of charity at times of mass poverty. They asked a national radio audience of perhaps 40 million to welcome President Roosevelt as a great leader who would do his best for the country. And Amos told his friends that before he went to bed, on the eve of the Roosevelt inaugural, he would pray for the new president.[34] On another program, Amos and Andy explained the "Bank Holiday" as a sign that President Roosevelt meant business.[35] At that time, Amos and Andy owned the "Fresh Air Taxi Company," consisting of one broken-down car without a roof, but they were confident that business would soon recover after Roosevelt began his presidency. They cautioned their audience, however, that they would have to learn to save up for a rainy day because depressions came along every few years. Amos particularly illustrated the work ethic ("If you wanna make money, you better go to work"), as well as an interest in politics.[36] Amos and Andy also demonstrated a neighborly and ecumenical spirit on their programs. At Thanksgiving, Amos called on his listeners to reflect "on the little things for which we should all be grateful." At Christmas, Amos and Andy had a special program with gifts and kind thoughts and wished everyone in their large audience a Merry Christmas.[37]

Will Rogers's popularity coincided with the best years for Amos and Andy. Although a satirist, Will Rogers personified a code of personal integrity, enterprise, and neighborliness.[38] One of his major radio programs focused on self-made Americans including Ford, Lindbergh, and Hoover, but "with little jokes to keep it from getting too serious." He satirized and admired them at the same time. Again, although he was a partisan of Franklin Roosevelt, Rogers described him as "a Houdini from Hyde Park."[39] Like Amos and Andy, he predicted an early end to the Depression after Roosevelt became president, but reminded Americans that their dilemmas were also attributable to their complacency. He once asserted: "The trouble with us in America is we are just muscle bound from holding a steering wheel, the only place we are callused is the bottom of our driving toe."[40] Will Rogers also set examples for generosity. He donated his entire check, $77,000, for a radio series, to charities, and he also counseled that America needed a more equitable distribution of wealth.[41]

Situation comedies, especially those centered on family life like *Vic and Sade* (1932) and *The Aldrich Family* (1939), consistently portrayed marriage and the family in positive, if at times, hectic terms.[42] A genial warmth also underlay the husband-and-wife banter of Fibber McGee and Molly while their neighbors were invariably welcomed at their home enthusiastically. And even Fred Allen appeared to draw the line at satirizing marriage as an institution. Allen was critical, however, of easy divorce. He quipped that laws facilitating divorce would lead to a situation where divorce would be granted by a "vending machine with a marriage certificate and your correct weight for five cents."[43]

In its daytime serials, a second major genre of programs with broad implications for popular culture, radio also managed, in extraordinary degree, to provide morale-bolstering services. At a time when the vast majority of women did not work, radio developed an exclusive daytime broadcast schedule for them at home and supplied them with a sustaining message, at once informative and a source of self-esteem.

The Depression actually served as a catalyst for a number of these programs. Many married women then felt a need to be informed about the Depression's effects on families and how other women were responding to its problems. The radio networks recognized that they could supply that information and also make their programs more lucrative.

Earlier programming for women consisted of talk shows, and special topics, but the networks quickly recognized the commercial possibilities of daytime serial dramas. Audience response was so favorable for the three "soaps" operating in 1931, that their number shot up dramatically throughout the 1930s, reaching sixty-one in 1939.[44] Among the popular daytime dramas for women in the 1930s were *One Man's Family, Ma Perkins, The O'Neills, Pepper Young's Family, Mary Martin, Just Plain Bill, The Guiding Light, Stella Dallas, Our Gal Sunday*, and *The Romance of Helen Trent*. It is estimated that they commanded an audience of about 20 million listeners each week, each program with an average of about 600,000, though *Ma Perkins* often doubled that figure. And according to one survey, members of the audience averaged 6.6 hours listening to them each weekday.

The day programs commended themselves to women who worked in the home for many reasons. One was adult companionship—a circle of new friends from radio—and another was new ideas. Clearly, radio actors and actresses became more than entertainers to their radio audiences in the home. When a researcher surveyed 100 women about the significance of the serials in their lives, she discovered that "the listeners did not experience the sketches as fiction or imaginary. They took them as "reality," a basis for "how to think and how to act."[45] How comforting Ma Perkin's example must have been for countless listeners in 1933. A reviewer described her in that year as "a resourceful, courageous widow fighting the problem of hard times with the same indomitable spirit as you and you and you are showing in like circumstances."[46]

The serial dramas also enhanced the self-worth of listeners by underscoring the moral strengths of women in family and society. Loving mothers abound in these stories, and they usually receive commensurate rewards. Molly Goldberg in *The Goldbergs*, Ma Perkins and Stella Dallas in programs with the same names, are obvious illustrations. These mothers were central to the happiness of their families. As Vic confides to Rush, his adopted son, in *Vic and Sade*, he should stop teasing his mom, Sade, because:

Excuse the wishy-washy phrase, but a lad doesn't *have* a mother *forever* . . . when she's gone, he's apt to start kickin' himself all over the place.[47]

Ma Perkins was a particularly good example of a kindhearted woman, the mainstay of her family, and one who steered others benevolently through her strong moral principles. She professed what appeared to be a strong, religiously based ethical heritage on a program in 1938 when she addressed the issue of forgiveness and contrition. Ma declared, "Anyone of this earth who's done wrong and then goes so far as to try and right that wrong, I can tell you they're well on the way to erasing the harm they did in the eyes of anyone decent."[48]

The serials also encouraged women to cherish a deeply coveted view of most married women in the 1930s, that a happy family was the most important achievement in life; it not only produced positive results in the lives of all its immediate members, but also for future generations, and even determined the future of the country as well. Here again came that refrain from out of the sensibilities of the 1930s of responsibilities to others— family, community, and nation. Despite the problems of characters in the serial dramas, and despite their disappointments, these programs claimed for women a critical role in creating some of life's greatest joys—love, children, tenderness, kindness, and a sense of life's fulfillment through the family.[49] This view was pointedly stated in an episode of *One Man's Family* in 1938 when hints of a world crisis were impinging on the Barbour's secure family in San Francisco. Father Barbour, in responding to a question from his son "What one thing is foremost in your thoughts?," replied:

Why Paul, I think "family" . . . It's my opinion that the family is the source from whence comes the moral strength of the nation. And disintegration of any nation begins with the disintegration of the family. The family is the smallest unit in society. Millions and millions of these little units make a nation. . . . A well-disciplined, morally upright family is bound to turn out good citizens! Good citizens make a good nation.[50]

Women were unquestionably dominant in most of the soaps. As one radio actress noted, radio actors often complained about "playing the wishy-washy husband who comes home and is told how to live and what to do and how to do it. . . . It was always the woman who was the strong character."[51] Yet many women listeners regarded themselves as more astute than men on many issues, especially romance and the raising and marrying of children, as well as the endless round of domestic events that consumed a substantial amount of time on the programs, and they found the soaps appealing and realistic. Anyone who dined with Ma Perkins and family as they celebrated the Fourth of July 1938 picnicking in the country gains a healthy respect for Ma's preparation for that enterprise.[52] Women listeners were probably strengthened by this candid acknowledgment of skills by radio.

The daytime serials for women also satisfied listeners' information about life outside their families and thereby supplied a sense of adventure as well. Women, as initiators of contacts with doctors in most families, were interested in the lives of doctors—hence, the series *Young Doctor Malone* and *Big Sister*. The question of how a woman fares when she marries up in class was portrayed in *Our Gal Sunday*, of marrying an actor in *Back Stage Wife*. Married women were, of course, curious about the lives of adult women who were employed and those who did not marry, hence *Joyce Jordan, M.D.*, *Portia Faces Life* (Portia was a lawyer), and the divorced dress designer, Helen Trent, in *The Romance of Helen Trent*. That program set as its central problem whether a woman could find romance after thirty-five. She must have convinced some listeners because the same woman played the part for thirty-seven years, leaving behind a long trail of rejected suitors.[53]

Given the limited employment opportunities for women in America in the 1930s and especially the premium value that Americans, including women themselves, placed on the family, radio daytime programming probably endowed many women with improved purpose and meaning in their lives and thereby enhanced the morale of the nation.

Either as an example of family drama or as a species of adolescent adventure story, one of radio's features in the 1930s was *Jack Armstrong, the All-American Boy*. Jack, though born and raised in Hudson Falls, was, nevertheless, a cosmic tour de force. He never told a lie, was captain of his football team, caught the winning pass in decisive games, won all his fights (he used the secrets of modern wrestling), was able to crack international spy rings, and could even find criminals planning mischief in "lost worlds." He also imbibed and subscribed to great truths of world religion. A lama from Tibet instructed him in 1939:

Tell the boys and girls of the United States . . . as they are, so shall the world become. If they have hearts of gold, a glorious new golden age awaits us all. . . . If they are honest, all riches will be theirs. If they are kind to one another, they shall save the whole world from the malice and the meanness and the war that is tearing its heart.

Jack promised to do so and to work the rest of his life trying to embody that message. Jack was a convincing advocate of the value of community in doing important things to help mankind. He also prompted a lot of other young boys and girls to believe that they could do the same. Although many who tuned in would outgrow the program in time, none who listened in their youth could mistake Jack's message that youth was responsible for improving the world. Especially not after the announcer introducing the program called the name "Jack Armstrong" four times—each time with more emphasis—and a chorus followed:

> Wave the flag for Hudson high, boys
> Show them where we stand!
> Ever shall our team be champions
> Known through all the land![54]

Besides, it didn't seem so difficult to stay in step with Jack because the announcer assured: "If you have your mind made up to get fresh air, sleep, and exercise, use soap and water, eat a Breakfast of Champions (Wheaties), that's a mighty strong recommendation to train the Jack Armstrong way." It would be interesting to know how many Americans who fought bravely in America's citizen military in World War II carried with them a fragment of inspiration from Jack Armstrong.

The third type of radio programs that reflected and helped to shape popular culture in America during the Depression was concerned with adventure. *The Lone Ranger* program was the most exciting, believable, and educationally effective of this genre.[55] Like *The Shadow*, who assumed the role of "protecting the weak" and *Superman*, a champion of the "oppressed" who swore "to devote his existence on earth to those in need," the Lone Ranger embodied responsibility for the well-being of the community. He did not, however, require the paraphernalia that accrued from being born on Krypton or engage in interplanetary travel, or have superordinate powers to make himself disappear; the Lone Ranger actually operated in a historical frame of reference. He engaged in an important historical process—that of bringing order and civilization to the American West in a period when that area was primitive and famous for its lawlessness. And while he was strong and resourceful, he was also vulnerable and mortal—hence believable. He once was wounded and about to die, had it not been for the devotion of his faithful Indian friend, Tonto. In a later program, the Lone Ranger remarks to Tonto, "I couldn't carry on without you; as long as we ride, we ride together." Tonto replied, "Kemo sabe (an Indian phrase meaning "faithful friend"), long as you live, long as me live, me ride with you."[56] It was this spirit of comradeship and admirable mutual loyalty that characterized their relationship throughout their programs together.[57]

The Lone Ranger was originally conceived by George W. Trendle, who owned radio station WXYZ in Detroit; Trendle envisioned his creation as "a man with a righteous purpose, a man who would serve as an example of good living and clean speech."[58] But more, Trendle regarded his fictive hero as a paragon for young people, someone to whom they might relate and hope to imitate in their adult lives. He wished, he declared, to create for his young listeners a "guardian angel," a man so virtuous he might be considered an "embodiment of granted prayer."[59]

The Lone Ranger actually became so attractive to American audiences that the program became family entertainment. A survey of 363 homes with families listening to the program in 1943 found that over half were composed of men, women, and children, another 20% were men and women, and only one of eight homes were children listening by themselves.[60] This result may have reflected the fact that the program was scheduled on the Blue network on Mondays, Wednesdays, and Fridays at 7:30 EST, convenient for family listening together, but it probably also demonstrates that children were so attracted by the program that they asked their parents to enjoy it with them.

Remarkable events of the "Masked Man's" early life foretold his advent as the consummate western hero. Originally a Texas Ranger, attempting to bring law and justice to that state, he served under the command of his brother, Captain Dan Reid. On a mission to locate Butch Cavendish, "the most dangerous and unscrupulous outlaw in the West," the Rangers, a group of six, were set up for an ambush in Bryant's Gap as the Cavendish gang fired down upon them from the hills above. All were struck down and left for dead and the outlaws rode off.

Later, the younger Reid recovered consciousness and discovered he was in a cave in the company of a tall Indian named Tonto. The Indian told him what had happened since the gunfight with the Cavendish gang. He had found Reid badly wounded and brought him to the cave. He had also buried the other Texas Rangers, leaving six graves to fool the gang should they return to the site of the gun battle. Reid decided that he would exploit Tonto's ruse and, henceforth, be known as the Lone Ranger, wear a mask to conceal his identity, and avenge the death of his brother and the other Rangers. He would find and smash the Cavendish gang and then work to restore law to the West.[61] The "Masked Rider" and Tonto would eventually disrupt the Cavendish gang and put them in jail along with a host of other outlaws. In the process, the Lone Ranger found his inimitable horse, Silver, located in the Wild Horse Valley where a great white stallion was a legendary horse. Just when it seemed that the powerful horse would never allow himself to be ridden, he accepted a saddle from the Lone Ranger. "There never was a horse like that!" the Lone Ranger commented, and so the Lone Ranger's own noble aims were matched with the brave heart and thundering hooves of his great horse.[62] Silver was the appropriate name for the champion horse because of his color, but also because the Reid brothers had jointly owned a silver mine, now operated by a retired Ranger, from which the Lone Ranger obtained money for supplies as well as the famous silver bullets that he frequently left as a sign of his presence to deter criminals rather than shoot them down. All through the 1930s, these two good men rode together through a swath of seven Western states to bring about a more decent and civilized society.

The *Lone Ranger* program broadcast as its essential message that men committed to moral values with appropriate courage could ameliorate society, and it did so with a stirring introduction, exciting music, and sound effects. The introduction in the first decade of the Lone Ranger's tenure on radio began with a series of shots, followed by the Lone Ranger's calm, deep voice, "Hi-yo, Silver." The announcer would then follow with, "A cloud of dust, a galloping horse with the speed of light, a hearty Hi-yo Silver!—the Lone Ranger," the rousing William Tell overture filled the background and played about thirty seconds, providing both the dignity and excitement to the moment preceding the program. The announcer would then return and invite the audience "Back to those days when the West was young. Hear the thundering hooves of the great white stallion, Silver. The Lone Ranger rides again!"[63]

The program suggests rich symbolic meanings. It appears to parody an epochal battle in the nation at large. The Lone Ranger first became a radio program in 1933 when public morale was at a low point, criminals occupied the spotlight in films and American institutions of government, and law appeared to be in disarray. Although hope and confidence in the future had surely not dissipated, it would be mistaken to overlook the powerful undercurrent of fear gripping the land. The "early West" with its tenuous civilization was a perfect symbolic battleground to test the outcome of the conflict. Americans not only found themselves cheering the principled ethical behavior and courage of the Lone Ranger and Tonto as they overcame people like Butch Cavendish, but probably their own triumphs over the tough times.

The Lone Ranger pledge, solemnly incumbent on all young listeners of his program, clearly stated the Lone Ranger's intent that his program would buttress the nation's ethical and moral ideals. The Lone Ranger enjoined prospective deputies: "I want each boy and girl who wants to be a deputy to raise their right hand and repeat after me a pledge of allegiance:

> I do solemnly pledge to place God and country before all else,
> To honor my father, mother, or guardian,
> To be honest and truthful,
> To pledge my hand to the weak,
> To pledge my heart to the helpless,
> To pledge my life to my fellow man."[64]

Because the Lone Ranger occupied such a lofty place in the nation's popular culture in the 1930s, the "Masked Man" was the subject of an editorial in the *New York Times*. When Earl H. Graser, long the voice of the Lone

Ranger, died in an automobile accident in April 1941, the *Times* editorialist asserted, "but he [Graser] didn't take the Lone Ranger with him. The Lone Ranger doesn't die." He noted that "the famous Masked Man had been alive for many centuries. He was Ulysses, William Tell, Robin Hood, Richard the Lion Hearted, but also the Black Prince, Kit Carson, Daniel Boone. . . . He was honest, truthful, brave, and so he remains. . . . He was as real as the policeman on the corner. Virtue never lacks for its rewards. Listen— there is a beating of hooves—Hi-yo, Silver!"[65] Ten thousand people attended Mr. Graser's funeral.

Radio and movies, the country's two major media of popular culture, served the American public well during the Depression. Both were required to make their products marketable for a public that insisted on a positive portrayal of the nation's traditional social and value systems. This served public purposes in important ways: Americans experienced confidence from this continuity despite disruption in the economy; endorsement from the media underscored the importance of preserving cooperative personal relationships critically important at a time when government assistance or individual income were at times insufficient to sustain the population. It is also likely that the media's depiction of Americans winning out as essentially good and kind and neighborly people, or, if otherwise, salvageable by influential characters like Jefferson Smith or the Lone Ranger, helped brace their confidence in a better tomorrow.

11

American Workers

After a decade of severe national Depression, one might expect that American workers, with unemployment hovering close to 20%, would be in the forefront of those disgruntled, but evidence contradicts this assumption; workers generally remained enthusiastic about the promise of American life. Less than one-fourth of non-agrarian workers joined unions and most of those who did were neither leftist radical nor militantly unionist—except sporadically. This noteworthy affirmation of the prevailing system by American workers in the 1930s tells us much about the sanguine character of American society.

When Franklin Roosevelt became president, American workers were facing discouraging prospects from a combination of antilabor hostility in the 1920s when union membership was virtually halved, as well as the personal effects of the Great Depression.[1] Perhaps 30% of the labor force was unemployed in March 1933, up sharply from 9% in 1930. Wages then were at rock bottom, and many full-time workers were forced into marginal work at menial wages while millions of transients, unable to find any jobs, were on the road.[2]

There were many good reasons for workers to join unions at that time. The threat of unemployment for those with jobs in a shaky economy was one.[3] Technological displacement of labor, with management increasingly relying on machinery to expedite work, also prompted workers to consider unions as protection for their jobs.[4] Again, they were often bothered by speedups on the job and unfair practices of employers and shop foremen.[5] Besides, the social and cultural worlds of workers were changing rapidly in the 1920s and the 1930s in ways potentially favorable to union membership; some workers with ethnic backgrounds, especially in big cities like Chicago, were becoming more comfortable joining the Congress of Industrial Organizations (CIO) that emerged in the mid-1930s because it emphasized worker solidarity and welcomed African Americans and ethnic groups as equals. The CIO's emphasis on "common ground" was palatable for second-generation American workers because of their shared commonalties of culture through movies and radio, standard brands now purchasable through chain stores, and the worker's increasingly similar urban experiences.[6] Their brief exposure to welfare capitalism in the 1920s, with programs severely retrenched or abandoned in the Depression, also prompted some workers to look to unions to replace them.[7]

Considering the deplorable reemployment opportunities in the 1930s along with the poor quality of work for some of those employed and the New Deal's favorable legislation for labor—its endorsement of labor organization and effective labor bargaining—organized labor's growth in the 1930s was, however, hardly remarkable. From a low tide of less than 3 million union members in 1930, largely in the American Federation of Labor (AFL), that number doubled by 1939 with 6.5 million members— roughly 4 million in the AFL and 2 million in its offshoot, the CIO. At that time, however, nearly 46 million Americans held jobs and so less than 16% were in unions.[8]

Apart from the cost of dues for union membership, there were substantial ideological and pragmatic reasons why workers did not join. This was particularly true for many workers from old-stock, American heritage. For example, Middletown (Muncie, Indiana), America's model small American city for Robert and Helen Lynd, with only a few immigrants, was especially resistant to unions. The Lynds explained this abstention primarily on the grounds of individualism. Middletown's industrial workers, coming from farm backgrounds, apparently did not believe in worker organizations. Walking from work in the mid-1930s, they could be overheard talking about "steaks, ball games and drives to nearby recreational areas."[9] Resentment of industrial discipline also prompted Americans, with several generations' heritage in the workforce, to oppose unions while working in Detroit, where older American workers were often "aloof and hostile" toward initial efforts to develop a union in the automobile industry.[10] But older American types were not the only ones dubious about unions. Italian immigrant workers in New Haven, Connecticut, were also cautious, perhaps because they feared reprisals from management, but also because they prized their independence. Most industrial workers in America in the 1930s were probably either immigrants or the sons of immigrants, but labor organizers often found first-generation Americans resistant to union membership, though the second generation would eventually supply the core of their unions.[11]

With the temper of the country decidedly opposed to revolution, and labor just beginning to recoup earlier membership, leaders of labor organizations, who recruited these new members, wished to avoid being labeled left-wing radicals and were generally successful in so doing. There may have been "revolutionary potential" among articulate shop leaders in the early 1930s, but there is little evidence that their zeal was convincingly transmitted to the rank and file.[12] Students of the labor movement are virtually unanimous that American labor was patriotic, not revolutionary, and that communism did not appeal to the typical worker whose basic concerns were mostly realistic—job security, better wages, and improvements in handling grievance procedures.[13]

This is not to say that communists were not active or resourceful in the union movement, but they did not control it or have a decisive voice in its overall policies. Despite their small numbers nationally (24,000 in 1934) and exceptionally large turnover in membership, communists provided, especially for the CIO, union discipline and experience in organizing and they worked effectively to build up the unions where they were members. They were strong in two major unions, the United Automobile Workers and the Maritime Unions, and they played an important role in several major strikes by other unions.[14] Communists won easy acceptance in unions in which workers such as the seamen felt rootless in their work; the Communist Party could provide them with community and camaraderie. During the San Francisco maritime strike in 1934, when the unions were accused of harboring "Red bastards," one union member protective of their interests disdainfully replied, "If they're Red bastards, they're our Red bastards."[15]

Communists were invited to join CIO unions mainly because of their utility in advancing the goals and membership of the new union. It was John L. Lewis, leader of the CIO, who purportedly divulged the rationale for the CIO-communist entente; he declared his intent to exploit the strengths of the Communist Party for the union's benefit when he realistically queried, "Who gets the bird, the hunter or the dog?" Once in the unions, however, Lewis acknowledged their ongoing capacity for "mischief," and Lewis himself actually contributed to a common public image of the CIO as being communist influenced by appointing two communists to important posts in the CIO in 1937—Lee Pressman as general counsel of the union and Len DeCaux as publicity director.[16]

Labor, having improved its position through Roosevelt's election, appeared to be making significant progress in the period from 1934 to Roosevelt's reelection in 1936. Union membership grew by more than 40% between 1933 and 1936, and the AFL, along with independent unions, won tough strikes, mostly for the right to organize in Akron, San Francisco, and Minneapolis, wringing concessions from management that had heretofore stood against them.[17] The unions also benefited from an uptake in the economy after the summer of 1935, a favorable time to enroll new members. Many union leaders as well as workers were also jubilant over the package of New Deal social programs during Roosevelt's first term. Workers, especially in the unions for mass production sponsored by the CIO first operating in 1935, began to look to the Democratic Party as an expression of their class interests. They enthused over Social Security and welcomed New Deal programs that protected home ownership and bank savings, and they cherished opportunities for themselves or their children to earn income, if unemployed, through the WPA, PWA, CWA, CCC, and NYA.[18]

The New Deal also proved an indispensable ally to assist the growth of unions. It opened the door to labor bargaining with employers under official government auspices through the National Recovery Act, Section 7A, beginning in June 1933. John L. Lewis, president of the United Mine Workers, described its import for human rights as second only to the Emancipation Proclamation; he vigorously recruited new members for his union (UMW) under the guise that joining the union was being patriotic—since the president had signed and authorized legislation sanctioning unions and their right to bargain with management. Although the NRA's potential to help labor organizations was undercut by its own administrators who allowed company-dominated unions and even multiple union affiliations in a single plant, NRA legislation was the driving force behind labor's renewed efforts to organize workers in the first two years of Roosevelt's first term.[19]

After the NRA was declared unconstitutional by the Supreme Court in May 1935, Democratic Senator Robert Wagner, without Roosevelt's support at first, secured an improved substitute in the National Labor Relations Act (Wagner Act) passed by Congress July 5, 1935. It guaranteed the rights of workers to form their own unions and choose their own representatives for collective bargaining; it also outlawed company-dominated unions and the dismissal of workers for being members of unions as unfair labor practices. Finally, the National Labor Relations Act strengthened the government's role in labor–management relations; it established a National Labor Relations Board to monitor worker elections, with its rulings reinforced through appeals to a circuit court of appeals. Labor had its charter to reorganize without obstructions from management; it could organize laborers freely and represent them in collective bargaining once a majority of workers decided to empower them to do so. The Wagner Act, as one astute labor historian noted, "carried the potential to transform radically the American social and economic order."[20]

Another factor, also keyed to the New Deal, served as a powerful stimulus for union growth: the emergence and power of the CIO. John L. Lewis, in his typical dauntless style, concluded in 1935 that the fields for union organization in mass-production industries, especially steel, automobiles, rubber, and packing were ripe to be harvested. Although the AFL had done some recruiting in mass-production industry, mostly to preserve skilled craft unions affected by them, AFL leadership counseled caution on an enterprise of this magnitude. Lewis foresaw less peril in the project not merely through his reading of worker enthusiasm for unions in the giant industries. He was also encouraged because he anticipated the likely support of President Roosevelt as an offset for the power and antilabor tenacity of industries like General Motors and U.S. Steel. Noting that business opposition to Roosevelt had stiffened, Lewis reasoned that the president would be forced to move left to consolidate his position—hence the possibility of a New Deal–labor entente.[21]

Lewis assembled a small, but powerful group of like-minded labor leaders and established an organization that, while remaining temporarily in the AFL, embarked on a distinct and different course from the AFL at large; they would, beginning in late 1935, organize unions in industries of mass production under the rubric Committee for Industrial Organization (CIO). And he immediately began to seek leverage with Roosevelt by offering speeches, political action, and lavish financial aid for the president's reelection campaign.[22] An ambitious determination to organize had joined a golden opportunity to do so provided by the Wagner Act.

The CIO formally abjured from the AFL in 1938 when it held a convention and declared itself the Congress of Industrial Organization (still abbreviated CIO). During the interim, it distinguished itself from the AFL by its organizing emphasis as well as its aggressive operational strategy. It was prepared to exercise grievance procedures on the shop floor and call for work stoppages. The CIO was also characterized by its zealous courtship of the New Deal and the tenacity and theatrics of its leader, John L. Lewis. For the time being it would steal the show from the AFL.[23] Labor's appearance of augmenting strength and momentum was actually somewhat deceptive, however, as was America's apparent swing left in the mid-1930s. As one commentator observed, "It was a big swing considering its starting point, but its starting point was Harding-Coolidge-Hoover Republicanism."[24] Nonetheless, Roosevelt's election victory in 1936 by a sweeping margin, buttressed by labor's electoral and financial support, would prompt the CIO to expect reciprocity from the Roosevelt administration.

Roosevelt gave ample evidence that he intended to settle his debts to the CIO almost immediately after the election. On December 30, 1936, workers at two large Fisher Body Plants of General Motors in Flint, Michigan, launched "the strike of the century." They took over factories, closed assembly lines, and engaged in the first major sit-down strike in American history; the issue was joined between one of the world's most powerful industrial organizations and one of America's most militant unions, the United Auto Workers (UAW), now a CIO union. One day after the strike began, Lewis announced via radio his sympathy for the strikers ("The time has passed in America when the workers can either be clubbed, gassed or shot down with impunity"), and he put the issue to the president forthrightly, "Labor will . . . expect the protection of the Federal Government in the pursuit of its lawful objectives."[25]

The strike was a newspaper reporter's front-page delight. The stay-in strikers could not be ousted by police (workers turned fire hoses on them) or the National Guard, which would have discredited General Motors. The "sit-down" was a brilliant tactic, as its historian Sidney Fine noted, because it allowed a small number of strikers to hold their ground, thus avoiding the overwhelming force that would have been massed against them in an outside strike.[26] When the strikers refused to leave the plant despite a judge's injunction, plant officials attempted but failed to force them out by turning off the heat and trying to interfere with food deliveries, usually by wives standing on ladders. And slowly, but effectively, the sit-down paralyzed production throughout the GM plants. Management agreed to negotiate at this point, and so, after forty-four days, the strikers emerged, an American flag at their head, singing "Solidarity" to the cheers of a sympathetic throng. General Motors agreed to bargain with the UAW.

Undoubtedly, an economic recovery that year strengthened the hand of union organizers, but Roosevelt played a discrete though effective role assisting the CIO's strike for recognition. He refused to declare sit-downs illegal despite their obvious repudiation of property rights. He also encouraged Frank Murphy, Democratic governor of Michigan, to work for a negotiated settlement that would include recognition of the UAW.[27]

Three weeks later another industrial giant surrendered to surging CIO power; U.S. Steel recognized the CIO as labor's agent for collective bargaining and did so without a fight. Myron Taylor, its chief executive officer, apparently foresaw a long drawn out strike that would interfere with U.S. Steel's economic recovery and, of course, he was impressed by the new political environment that had redounded to labor's advantage at Flint.[28] Chrysler Corporation and Firestone Tire followed suit in April 1937 and union power was augmenting swiftly.[29]

These victories, of course, opened the doors for union membership. Many fence-sitters began to see the benefit of joining up. Unions enlisted more than 3 million new members overall, nearly doubling their numbers, with the CIO making the most dramatic gains, but the AFL also showing impressive growth. Although the AFL had lost over a million members with the CIO walkout and expulsion in 1936–1937, it garnered three-quarters of a million new members in the same period. In 1937, organized labor claimed nearly 23% of the country's nonagricultural laborers.

Along with improvements in membership totals, wages, and working conditions, union power also produced significant social and psychological dividends. Individual workers and their families often felt better about their own chances to survive the Depression as they witnessed the successes and growing strength in numbers of their unions. Increasing use of insignia of union belonging among workers on the job, for example, fostered security; labor buttons were flaunted by union members on the shop floor and were often visible all over the workplace as proclamations of group power and reliability. Certain taverns near the plants became union hangouts where workers also experienced solidarity after working hours.[30] Indeed, in Johnstown, Pennsylvania, steelworkers of central European heritage took such special comfort in their union identity that they reminded those who opposed their strike in 1937 that after the union's victory, "You are not going to call us Hunky no more."[31]

But the unions also provided members with opportunities to socialize and to feel that they belonged to a type of extended family. The CIO applied this goal to its organizing activities as well. Special national conferences were called by the CIO to make unequivocally clear that black workers would have the same opportunities as whites to obtain equal pay for equal jobs, and black labor organizers frequently recruited both black and white workers. A gifted student of this phenomenon and of the union's policies on race contends that the CIO "went further in promoting racial harmony than any other institution in existence at the time."[32] In the interests of morale, the CIO and AFL sponsored an array of social and cultural activities to foster a spirit of mutuality among union members: these included theater and labor education and social affairs such as dances, picnics, fishing trips, women's clubs, and talent nights plus a wide variety of athletic activities for men, including teams playing in the "Greater Industrial League" and also activities for children.[33] In Chicago, the CIO showed its tolerance and inclusiveness with special events for ethnics—ethnic dances, fiestas, and "sings" attuned to tastes of the city's different ethnic groups. There were also ethnic days on the picket lines when demonstrators sported traditional European or Mexican costumes. This same sense of workers united for union goals, despite differences in background, prompted union members to serve as pickets for strikes in plants other than their own and union organizers to visit workers' houses in plants that had no unions. For women workers, the CIO established a commitment to equal pay for equal work. It also encouraged family socials among union members and organized wives of union members as volunteers to advocate union membership on a door-by-door basis in working-class neighborhoods. Thus, union activities often strengthened ties between family members as well as workers.

Political loyalty to President Roosevelt and his programs also united an overwhelming majority of workers, and their allegiance was strong enough to develop partisan feelings of "we-ness" against "they-ness" of those who opposed him. It was the working-class residential areas or the factories themselves in which Roosevelt received the largest ovations on his campaign trip in 1936, when the union motorcades rolled repeatedly on his behalf and the bars and barbershops displayed his picture in central locations visible to all patrons. People living in these neighborhoods wrote appreciative, even devotional, letters to their president, undeterred by misspellings and grammatical errors, and often with a terse prose that suggested that they and their neighbors had never done such things before. Many of them had heard over the radio his scathing denunciation of "economic royalists" and some were at Franklin Field later in the 1936 campaign when the crowd "went wild" at his promise to lead America to its "rendezvous with destiny." He may indeed have become a father surrogate, for those once more palpable fathers in peasant villages in Europe or replaced substitute figures only recently less effective in ethnic neighborhoods in America—local politicians, small store owners, or managers of mutual aid societies. The working class and their families tapped into the enormous confidence and hope he generated, and most felt that he and the Democratic Party represented them personally; they found in him and his policies their clearest vision of a realizable American Dream—an equitable and just society, bountiful in human and material riches.[34] On these accounts, President Roosevelt received an estimated 82% of votes cast by unskilled and semiskilled workers in the election of 1936.[35]

The joys and perils workers shared in the turbulent years of union struggles also reinforced bonding and mutuality. There was, of course, close fraternity among those who manned the picket lines or joined the numerous sit-ins. One occupant of a General Motors plant in Flint underscored how the sense of danger among strikers transformed them into a band of brothers; "It was like we were soldiers holding the fort. It was like war. These guys with me became my buddies."[36] At another strike in Akron, with nearly 4,000 workers occupying the Goodyear plant, "Groups of men went from one department to another, clapping their hands and singing marching songs." Friends or loved ones of the strikers later passed sandwiches to them through open windows.[37] Thousands of sympathizers gathered close to the site of another Akron strike, some seeing themselves as a reserve force for the strikers, carrying bowling pins or sawed-off cue sticks; others wore football helmets and caps padded with heavy lining.[38]

The exhilaration of winning strikes produced, of course, special expressions of fellowship. In the aftermath of the CIO's victory at Flint, when it won concessions from GM to represent the workers in collective bargaining, a celebration ensued that included a parade of 800 persons down Flint's streets and spontaneous mirth that marchers said reminded them of "Mardi Gras, Armistice Day, or a victory by Detroit in the World Series." "These people," according to one observer, "sang and joked and laughed and cried, deleriously joyful—victory meant a freedom they had never known before."[39] But defeats tightened relations between union members even more conclusively. When police fired buckshot point-blank into a crowd of sympathizers supporting truck drivers of the International Brotherhood of Teamsters (AFL) in Minneapolis in 1934, sixty-five people were wounded, most of them shot in the back, and two were killed—one a World War I veteran and father of four children. A gigantic crowd participated in a funeral procession for the deceased workers. Strikers directed traffic for the event, a sign that workers then felt obliged to be their own best friends. Similar incidents with loss of life by workers occurred in San Francisco, Cleveland,

Youngstown, Massilon, and the worst was in Chicago on Memorial Day 1937.[40]

Labor's crest came in the early months of 1937. The AFL, the older craft-based union, perhaps goaded by the impressive gains in membership of its new rival, the CIO, was already compensating for the losses incurred by the latter's independence. But all eyes were on the spectacular successes of the pace-making CIO. It had made rapid advances, was gaining momentum, and appeared on the threshold of invincibility. It had unveiled an unexcelled ploy to advance its interests in the sit-down strike and had just won the rights to bargain for the employees of several industrial giants. After its victory over General Motors, CIO members wrought a record number of work stoppages using the sit-down strike, and in one year the UAW's membership had skyrocketed from 24,000 to 175,000.[41] Unquestionably the CIO "had replaced the AFL as heart of the labor movement."[42] On this account Edward Levinson, a partisan of the CIO, penned a book in 1937 that proclaimed, *Labor on the March*.[43]

Yet, in a series of stunning reversals, beginning in May 1937, the strike against Little Steel, through the elections of 1938, the CIO suffered one grievous setback after another. Membership declined rapidly in steel, the union's vital mass-production industry, where membership plummeted 75% between April 1937 and December 1939.[44] Dues payments to the CIO declined correspondingly. The union was also rebuffed in its political aspirations at the municipal level.[45]

The most threatening external circumstance for labor's future, however, came from an unexpected quarter. The New Deal, in part because of its favorable labor policies, suffered a significant loss of public approval in the early months of 1937, and so the CIO found itself deprived of effective public backing from an indispensable ally. As we have noted earlier, the New Deal's popularity in Roosevelt's second term was tarnished; his advocacy of changes in the Supreme Court coming at virtually the same time as his support for militant labor prompted wide mistrust and candid disapproval of him in Congress, by the press, and among the public. Labor's strategy of dependence on Roosevelt had faltered; self-preservation would now force the president to distance himself from the CIO.

Roosevelt's labor policy was, in fact, always compounded with a high degree of timely political bed-fellowship. He was fundamentally committed to politics as a concert of interests in measure because he savored sweeping personal popularity. This guaranteed labor's interest as integral to the common good and, of course, as a beneficiary of national recovery along with other interest groups. As his diversified economic recovery programs establish, however, the president was no exclusive spokesman or policy-maker for labor. When his ideal "all-America team" was endangered by criticism and abstention from business, Roosevelt entered a closer relationship with labor out of necessity. He never doubted even then that his primary goal was to restore America's free-enterprise system, and he made no comment, for example, in 1934 on the violent and repressive measures taken by management in collusion with southern governors to quell strikes by textile workers in the South.[46]

Roosevelt's new, cautious attitudes toward labor were graphically demonstrated during the Little Steel strikes that began in late May and ended in mid-July 1937. The CIO's victory against U.S. Steel Corporation without battle virtually obliged the union to test its metal against Little Steel, which comprised other major manufacturing centers for steel outside Pittsburgh, including Cleveland, Canton, Youngstown and Massillon, Ohio, Bethlehem and Johnstown, Pennsylvania, Gary, Indiana, and South Chicago, Illinois, plus other centers in New York State. This amalgam of manufacturing sites was called Little Steel, not because they were small—indeed collectively they employed nearly 200,000 workers—but because they were independent of the giant U.S. Steel. For the CIO, successful strike action at Little Steel was important because the union's previous successes at Flint and Akron had relied heavily on local activists that the union had inherited; Little Steel would test its strengths exclusively.[47]

The CIO may have underestimated the strength and tenacity of its opponent because it probably overestimated help from Washington. As the strike approached, management at Little Steel skillfully exploited public opinion on such issues as the American worker's right to work independently of union mandate, threats of strikes to law and order by the union's aggressive picketing, and the New Deal's past favoritism to sit-down strikers.[48] Tom Girdler, president of Republic Steel, also used spies in the local union, stacked weapons, and placed heavily armed guards in the plant. He also devised a lockout strategy to forestall the possibility of a sit-down by the union. Strikers outside the plants were forced to fight strikebreakers and police, and even in some instances the National Guard—some skirmishings with fists, others with guns. On final count the forces siding with management that summer killed eighteen steelworkers or their sympathizers, ten in Chicago.[49] This large number in Chicago resulted from a Memorial Day march by strikers to the gates of Republic Steel. The marchers threw rocks at police and taunted them and the police responded with deadly fire. About 100 were also wounded in this incident that the CIO described as the Memorial Day Massacre.[50]

"Can it be true," John L. Lewis angrily retorted the next day, "that striking workmen may be shot down at will by the very agents of the law?" And he put the issue to President Roosevelt bluntly and publicly: "Labor will await the position of the authorities on whether our people will be protected or butchered."[51] Roosevelt replied, but nearly a month later, also publicly, at his press conference with casual evasiveness—"The majority of people are saying just one thing, a plague on both your houses."[52] And so the labor–

New Deal alliance of the middle 1930s unraveled in 1937 as Roosevelt and Lewis drifted farther apart while Republic Steel delivered the CIO its first major setback.

Roosevelt's posture of nonsupport for the CIO at Little Steel was also adopted by governors in the states affected by the strike. Particularly noteworthy were responses by Governors Martin Davey of Ohio and George Earle of Pennsylvania, both heretofore considered staunch, pro-labor Democratic governors. Davey sent the national Guard into Canton, Massillon, and Youngstown to assist local law-enforcement agencies in dealing with periodic disorder. The National Guard was also enjoined to assure safe passage for workers who continued to work in the plants and facilitate the movement of goods in and out of them.[53] Davey also ordered its units to protect all workers who wished to work, including those who had been on strike and changed their minds; some used tear gas and bayonets to clear the area in the vicinity of the plant to assist those returning to work. Davey thus assured victory for the companies in Ohio; most workers were soon back on their jobs and the strike was broken.[54] In Pennsylvania, Governor Earle pursued a similar policy of "neutrality" with identical effects.[55] These responses to labor's travail contrasted sharply with the action of Frank Murphy of Michigan only six months earlier.

Although no national poll was taken explicitly on the Little Steel strike, a Gallup poll in July while the strike was on and a *Fortune* Survey in October 1937 are illuminating about the public's reaction. The Gallup poll revealed that 50% of respondents had changed their opinions of unions "in the last six months," with 71% of this group declaring themselves less favorable. In the *Fortune* poll, even those favoring the CIO declared in slim majority their opposition to sit-down strikes.[56] Apparently, the CIO's militancy had seriously compromised the efforts of union leaders to create an acceptable public image.[57]

The CIO not only lost its first big test to organize a sizable body of steelworkers under its own banner, but the neutral and negative responses to its activities by governmental officials and the public foreshadowed future adversities for the unions. Despite an ambitious effort, the CIO failed in the same year to organize workers in the textile mills of the South where it recruited only 5% of the region's textile workers.[58] The yearlong "Roosevelt Recession" that began in May 1937 and ended in early 1938 with 2 million lost jobs, a 13% decline in national income, and a 50% drop in production of durable goods also contributed heavily to the CIO's problems. It not only undercut efforts to organize new workers, but was responsible for large layoffs of union workers in the durable goods industries in which the CIO was centered—steel, automobiles, rubber, and electrical goods—and hence led to decline in union members and funds.[59]

The decision by the CIO to field a large number of pro-labor Democrats for municipal elections in 1937 also proved a failure. Indeed, in what must have been a sobering experience, their attractive candidate for mayor of Akron, then one of America's most unionized cities, met decisive defeat.[60] Its candidate for mayor of Detroit also lost. The CIO's reliable friend, Frank Murphy, the incumbent for governor in Michigan, was also toppled in 1938 by a Republican—with Murphy's opponent basing his campaign strategy on attacking the governor for his role at Flint along with charges of communist infiltration of the UAW.[61] And in congressional elections in 1938, voters repudiated both Roosevelt and the CIO; Republicans gained eighty-one seats in the House, eight in the Senate, and thirteen governorships, while the CIO lost in congressional races where it backed Roosevelt's handpicked favorites to supplant Democratic conservatives. Since the CIO had campaigned enthusiastically on behalf of most of the president's personal choices, it also shared in Roosevelt's defeats.

For John L. Lewis, Roosevelt's changed tactics toward labor were unforgivable. Although still supporting New Deal legislation and Roosevelt in 1938, Lewis became so disaffected that he declared his support for Republican candidate for president, Wendell Willkie, in 1940 and asked labor to join him.[62] They did not because Roosevelt was still a hero to American workers. Their continuing devotion to Roosevelt was not merely a mark of appreciation for the president's programs and his winning personality, it was probably also a statement of comparative loyalties.[63]

Although the growth and achievements of labor in a society that exalted individualism were predicated on the backing of a government like the New Deal, especially Roosevelt's direct or indirect enforcement of the Wagner Act and influence with governors to refrain from using their public authority against labor, labor's successes also depended, of course, on its own militancy, but this too proved faltering. Just as reliance on Roosevelt betrayed labor's inability to promote vigorous change on its own, the careful goals chosen by its leadership and the less than militant attitudes of most of its rank and file assured only modest gains for labor.

The CIO, the militant wing of labor, regarded as central to its purposes the "continuation of the classical American economic system . . . preservation of American business institutions . . . and continuing opposition to economic philosophies which seek to destroy the present economic system in America."[64] The organization's historian observed, "It was a 'non-radical labor movement,' with its militancy directed above all else at the attainment of security, stability, and dignity on the job."[65] Others concur. An important recent interpretation of CIO workers in Chicago underscores this view. They were not anticapitalist; instead they were committed to the New Deal and the CIO to replace older benefit systems from a heritage of ethnic cooperation and corporate capitalism, both undermined by the Depression.[66]

Nor did American workers wish to lose their American identity. They lacked the angry class consciousness and righteousness to restructure a society they admired. Furthermore, since they participated in the government as voters and accepted majority decision-making as an article of faith, to overturn the system appeared a reduction to absurdity; they would be revolting against themselves—all the more so when the mood of the country was not revolutionary. Even the striking militants on the San Francisco waterfront in 1934 professed that they sought better wages and terms of work in fulfillment of their "duty" as "true Americans."[67] American flags and middle-class aspirations abound in the ranks in union marches, rallies, and victory celebrations. Union workers marching together are often dressed in coats and even ties at these times.[68] John L. Lewis, himself, was regarded as "a debonair Washingtonian." He is often pictured or described in fashionable three-piece suits; it is not surprising to find him handsomely attired on the boardwalk in Atlantic City in 1935 or enjoying his meerschaum in the garden behind his sumptuous Alexandria, Virginia, home.[69] Lewis was at one time a bank president and skillful stock investor, and he was a lifelong Republican, deviating only in 1936 when he supported Roosevelt. In 1940, he considered trying to secure the Republican nomination for Hoover and he later voted for Willkie. As his biographer observed, his position on labor questions reflected "the extent to which Lewis . . . and perhaps most workers had assimilated the values of a business civilization."[70]

Few workers adopted a militant stance or vigorously participated in strikes or, for that matter, ever went on strike. Malcolm Cowley, a leftist literary critic, wondered about the sit-down strikers whether they were "aroused by anything nobler than the hope of driving a new Buick."[71] Even in the decisive General Motors strike at Flint in 1937, most of the workers were fence-sitters and many strikers limited their militancy "to refusing to cross a picket line."[72] One observer of the group strike action at Flint wryly observed, "Those strikers have no more idea of 'revolution' than pussy cats."[73] Surprisingly few workers were involved in strikes of any kind. Less than 1% of the total number of workers employed actually engaged in strikes in July 1934, the month of major strikes in San Francisco and Minneapolis. These strikes were also of short duration and so the work time lost through strikes was minimal. And in the great strike year of 1937, a high point for the 1930s, only about 7% of those employed went on strike and they contributed to a mere loss of only 0.43% in all time worked that year.[74] This meant that 93% of American workers in the midst of the Depression were not sufficiently aggrieved by their conditions of work to strike, even when news of strikes had become typical front-page coverage in American newspapers.

The high point of militancy for American labor in the 1930s came in the aftermath of the Flint strike. At that time, in less than two months, there were over 300 strikes involving one-half million workers in automobile manufacturing, with the strikers initiating wildcats and shop-floor stoppages that convulsed General Motors and resulted in substantial victories for labor in relation to management and a great rise in UAW membership to 400,000 in August 1937. But, as a student of the phenomenon noted, "Numerical growth and collective bargaining rights did not signify that auto workers spontaneously discarded their deep-rooted caution and ambivalence toward unionization." The fighting spirit of union workers then probably arose from particular circumstances; their euphoria over union gains and their concerns that their initial contracts did not assure sufficient protection. But this militance dissipated quickly, suggesting that the union had not won permanent allegiance from pragmatic workers. Many who joined at the time of the union's sweeping victories did so with their union fees waived as an additional inducement, but they refused to maintain membership once dues were required. And so the UAW lost over half its new members. Solidarity also dissolved when production losses from wildcats caused workers in other departments to lose work time or when new changes in work rules benefited some workers but jeopardized others. Shop-floor fights and racial animosities erupted. With the recession beginning in the summer of 1937, and workers concerned about losing their jobs, wildcats virtually ceased and workers' disillusionment with the union was common because it could not protect them. Fewer than one in five workers who were laid off bothered to take "out-of-work" receipts that assured their good standing in the union even while unemployed. When the economy improved in 1938, there was no proportionate increase in union members. The UAW would not recover until the improved economic year 1940 and the especially bountiful years during World War II.[75]

One important explanation for the workers' reluctance to join unions, their subsequent passivity as members, and even their quick withdrawal lay in the large numbers who came from agrarian backgrounds in Eastern and Southern Europe. Job security and wages were their primary concerns, not crusading or ideology. Many of them, in smaller industrial cities, where ethnic traditions were relatively unchanged across generations, maintained a primary loyalty to their family of origin that depended on contributions from several family members.[76] It is likely that many of those who joined unions in the big expansion year for unions in 1937 did so to protect these contributions rather than as class-conscious unionists. As one UAW union leader remembers, they were "loyal but passive members." Such members were not apt to storm barricades for union causes or spend their time at union-sponsored socials.[77]

In Steelton, Pennsylvania (pop. 13,000), which employed 5,000 workers in its Bethlehem Steel plant, largely second-generation Slavic and Italian Americans, there was little opportunity for the newcomers to enter the mainstream of American life. They were thwarted even in the 1930s by an absence of job and residential mobility, conditions that became continuous liabilities because few completed high school. An overwhelming majority of males in these groups performed the same kinds of jobs as their fathers before them and they married almost exclusively women from their own ethnic group. They also socialized within the ethnic group as did their parents and were generally unwilling to move any distance from their parents' homes. In 1939, these groups, along with Steelton's black workers, came together and signed a charter to establish a steelworker's union that was finally recognized by the company in 1941. Although economic needs impelled divergent groups in the mixed population to surmount differences and unionize, the context of their separate community lives and intense loyalty to their ethnic families probably still assured their pragmatic outlook on union activities.[78]

In Johnstown, Pennsylvania (pop. 37,000 in the 1930s), conditions resembled those at Steelton. There, too, a large number of first- and second-generation American workers, mostly Slavic and Magyar, in Bethlehem's steel mills were from peasant heartlands in Europe. Again, their economic survival was predicated on "family collectivism" and their social association transpired almost wholly in their ethnic neighborhoods in the 1930s. Despite hardships, however, they were not dispirited; their lives in America were better than their recollections of life in peasant villages in Europe. Like a refrain, they often declared: "There we had nothing to hope for; here there was at least something for ourselves and our children." When the Depression struck, all members of these families tried to work at something, including those who moved away to other communities to get jobs—even New York—sending money home regularly. They also managed on credit, small loans from friends and relatives, and government-sponsored relief and jobs. They socialized at home or in places like the "Polish Hall."[79] A strike at Bethlehem Steel in 1937, part of the Little Steel strike, failed to win recognition for the union, though it did come in 1941. Here again, the union appeared to function as security for the primary though tenuous family system. Union workers in Johnstown still honored the maxim that loyalty began at home.[80]

Ethnic Americans diluted union militancy for other reasons. Most of them were Catholics and though some priests and an occasional bishop were outspokenly pro-labor, and there were a few activist priests for labor as well, large numbers of priests opposed the unions, especially the CIO, which they saw as communist influenced. "The big reason women didn't join the CIO at the Armour plant in Chicago" according to one woman, "is that they are ruled by the priests . . . and lots of them say the CIO is against religion and the church." Union leaders found first- and second-generation Catholics so difficult to organize on this account that they sought pro-labor priests to address workers.[81] Thus, religious considerations not only kept some workers out of unions, they sometimes made for tepid commitments after joining. Although steelworkers in neither Johnstown nor Steelton became union members en masse in the 1930s, their ambivalent loyalties probably characterized many who did. On the other side of the coin, as unions once experienced gains in membership of second-generation ethnics in 1937, the effect served to water down the message of an activist leadership. One labor historian concluded, from recollections of a union activist who witnessed the phenomenon, that expansion produced a "two-edged sword." Unions obtained membership among a broad mass of workers, but they also became vulnerable to the subcultures of their recent recruits.[82]

Unions also suffered a loss of momentum in the late 1930s because they were rent by factionalism, a product of their heterogeneous, organizational mix and especially the bitter internecine conflicts between the AFL and the CIO. In the UAW, a severe battle developed between supporters of its president, Homer Martin, who appealed to Appalachian migrants to the automobile plants, often fundamentalist Protestant and left-wing elements, exemplified by the Reuther brothers. Martin, who became president of the UAW in 1936, used spies against his enemies and banished some leaders of the left bloc from Detroit to the provinces. They and their supporters replied in kind by calling wildcat strikes, breaking up union meetings, and working to unseat Martin. He struck back by suspending five top officers of the union, allegedly in order to forestall a communist takeover of the UAW. His endeavor to centralize authority produced a reaction among many union members, and John L. Lewis intervened to restore the cashiered union leaders. Shortly thereafter, Martin resigned his position in the CIO and led a dissident faction into an automobile union in the AFL, but not until factionalism had demoralized the UAW and reduced its appeal for new members. The struggle also had negative effects on active union members because some companies witnessing the dispute refused to recognize either faction and hence jeopardized all work and security provisions between themselves and the UAW. Stability in the UAW did not return until 1939–1940.[83]

A simmering racial antagonism in the UAW during the Martin era was uncharacteristic of CIO unions.[84] In Chicago, where the CIO's race record was exemplary, blacks rallied enthusiastically to the union and rapidly became leaders in the Packing House Organizing Committee. In the racially sundered meatpacking plants, blacks witnessed remarkable improvements in race relations once their plants bargained with the CIO. One credited the CIO for "gettin' everybody who works in the yards together, and breakin' up the hate and bad feelings that used to be held against the Negro."[85] Indeed, the policy of nondiscrimination that typified the early CIO unions, especially those representing coal miners and garment workers, became the benchmark of the CIO. The record of the AFL on race was spotty, though it evolved in a more liberal direction during the 1930s. This came mainly in response to the prodding of A. Philip Randolph, the articulate black leader of the Brotherhood of Sleeping Car Porters. Although the AFL denied Randolph a charter to form an international AFL union repeatedly in the 1920s and the early 1930s, it did so in 1938. He also forced the AFL, by threat of public embarrassment, to undertake a gradual redress of discriminatory practices against African Americans in its unions.[86]

The resurgence of the AFL in the late 1930s, when it clearly outdistanced the CIO in new members each year, is attributable to several considerations. Long the major union, the AFL felt upstaged by the successes of the young and dynamic CIO for which it was an unwilling parent; pride and territoriality fueled a counteroffensive. Besides, there were important differences between the leaders of the two unions, and AFL leadership in the late 1930s saw an opportunity to exploit the differences. AFL union leaders usually had fathers who were skilled workers, but CIO leaders tended to be younger and to come from families where fathers were unskilled or semiskilled. AFL leaders also made more conservative choices in politics, club membership, public activity, and on the issue of ethnic intermarriage.[87] There were enough differences, at least, to justify a feud. In addition, large numbers of Catholics in the AFL—Americans of several generations—were especially susceptible to allegations that communists were influential in deliberations of CIO leaders. The AFL had grounds here to exploit a union red scare, and it couched its appeal as an American version of unionism.

The AFL was also abetted by the fact that its treasuries were ample since craft workers did not suffer unemployment to the same extent as the CIO's mass industrial workers in the recession of 1937–1938, so it took on the CIO toe-to-toe. It initiated new industrial labor organizations and pulled CIO members from textiles and the manufacture of automobiles (Homer Martin's faction) into its own ranks. It also blunted the CIO's growth by signing no-strike agreements with management.[88] And politically, it successfully opposed CIO-sponsored candidates, the "Labor Slate," in Detroit's mayoral and city council elections in 1937.[89]

The AFL enjoyed phenomenal growth from 1937 to 1939, particularly when compared to the setbacks experienced by the CIO. Its membership grew by 700,000 or 20% over 1937. The CIO declined by nearly 7%, and in the same period the UAW, sometimes seen as the CIO's most dynamic union, also suffered a net loss in members.[90] By 1939, the zeitgeist had turned against militant labor; as Americans became increasingly confident that their basic traditions would survive the Depression, political and social constraints forced labor into a more conservative mold. The revival of the AFL at the expense of the CIO was a definitive sign of that fact.

Karl Marx met his match in America in the 1930s. Theoretically, the times were ripe for leftist persuasions and loud and strident direct action tactics by labor, but neither happened. The Communist Party remained small and suffered serious problems of membership turnover. It remained functional in the broad American scene by adopting Popular Front tactics, allying itself with labor, student, and peace organizations, but by subordinating to the discipline of its larger and more effective mainstream cohort. The socialists, with a venerable and impressive national political history dating from the progressive era, virtually became extinct in the 1930s. And organized American labor, though doubling in members, remained singularly lacking in "hard-knuckles" militancy. Marx's predictions fell victim, not as he forecast to bourgeois repression, but to the power of responsive democratic government and the many promises of the American Dream.

Franklin Roosevelt preempted potential radical fervor among American workers with constructive programs and caring attitudes as champion of the "forgotten man." Roosevelt's programs reassured most workers and helped them to maintain faith in the benign quality of American democracy. Then again, though Americans historically have prided themselves in individualism, they have also quietly maintained a healthy regard for the benefits of cooperation in their daily lives, from their religious heritage, ethnic, racial, and rural groupings, voluntary associations, needs for corporate efficiency, and the Progressive–Populist tradition. This legacy and the cooperative behavior it inspired, together with Roosevelt's programs and leadership, protected countless persons from unwarranted failure and undue suffering during the Depression, but from unreasonable radicalism as well.

Radicalism in the labor movement also ran aground on the actual standards of living of American workers and their confidence of betterment in the future. Most steelworker families, according to a government survey taken in 1941, enjoyed an automobile, and their residences typically had plumbing and more rooms than family members.[91] This, in a society where one-third of house dwellings still lacked running water or inside toilets.[92] Many American workers were aware of their comparative advantages over the quality of life in other countries through their ethnic heritage. For that large component of organized labor that knew or could be reminded by elders what conditions were like in central or eastern Europe, America's opportunities were unquestionably better than what they or their forebears had known abroad, hardly a basis for stirring protest against American institutions. Labor leaders detected "no deep seated sense of outrage or injustice" in American labor, and polls establish that a large majority of American workers in the 1930s still believed in America as a land of opportunity and progress.[93]

Labor wrought major gains following the passage of the Wagner Act of 1935 through May 1937: rapid growth in membership, successful initiatives for collective bargaining with several of America's industrial giants, and the emergence of the CIO with its verve and skillful organizing and strike strategies. The bonding of workers in union membership was a mainspring of their confidence and that of their families during these uncertain times. It is inconceivable, however, that labor could have achieved these gains without yeoman support from the New Deal and governors allied with the New Deal. It is not a coincidence that once this favorable milieu changed, the movement lost ground.

Although there is a litany of what-ifs that might have affected the outcome for labor marginally in the 1930s, unyielding contextual considerations explain its less than spectacular growth and its relatively moderate stance. Labor militancy confronted powerful cross currents of individualism in American culture and from the subcultures of many of its union workers still oriented primarily to their families of origin. These had the general effect of reducing labor's appeal to workers and weakening the effectiveness of the unions when they joined. The enduring admiration of American workers for the long-term achievements of their country's economic and technological systems also diminished enthusiasm for unions. The New Deal's myriad programs for workers were appreciated by both unionized and nonunion labor, reassuring them that the American Way now worked both in good and bad times, and this awareness reduced dependency on unions. And because collectivist actions by unions quickly appeared extremist and even "un-American" to the public, it was clear that social tolerance and hence, ultimately, political support for unions were always marginal in America in the 1930s.

12

Urban Support Systems

America's population in 1930 had more foreign born than any time in its history; nearly 14 million, more than 10% of the country's population and together with native-born Americans who had one or two parents born abroad, their total was one-third of all Americans in 1940.[1] This large group was concentrated in the cities, constituting more than half the population in twenty of America's large cities. Immigrants and their children made up an estimated 73% of New York's population.[2] Sections of cities were still named Little Italy, Little Hungary, Little Bohemia, or for other nationalities.[3] Polish weddings, Italian festa, German beer gardens, Jewish delicatessens or synagogue centers proclaimed one enclave or another in these cities. And foreign-language newspapers, estimated to be more than 200 in New York alone, testified to the enduring vitality of Old World culture to New World inhabitants. This scene also typified Cleveland, where two-thirds of the population could be classified as ethnic, or Chicago, the city with the largest number of Scandinavians, Poles, Czechs, Serbo-Croatians, and Lithuanians.[4] In Boston, a guidebook to the city stated that a five-minute walk from the statehouse would bring a visitor to sections where English was merely a second language.[5] Altogether, 22 million people, largely with European backgrounds, informed census takers in 1930 that they used a language other than English in their homes.[6]

The foreign born and their children who came into their majority beginning in the 1920s were especially hard hit by the Depression that struck relentlessly at manufacturing and construction, two of their prime areas of employment. Rates of unemployment in the great cities in the early years of the Depression were staggering, approaching or exceeding 50%, and the toll was bitterly exacting on very recent Americans, most of whom were unskilled and poorly educated. The Depression also had a devastating impact on their mutual aid societies, banks, and building and loan societies, ethnic institutions that were mainstays for dealing with emergency situations; many collapsed when they were caught in a double bind with members unable to meet monthly payments while requests for help from those out of work simultaneously increased.[7] Reports from Harry Hopkins's special representatives dispatched to gauge the nation's morale in 1933–1934 found many newcomers to America barely scraping by. Desperate persons in those straits might pray as a family, night after night, that their father would find work the following day. Mario Puzo, raised in Hell's Kitchen in New York in the 1930s, whose father was a railroad laborer with a wife and seven children, tells an amusing yet pathetic story describing the plight of many in these marginal families. Puzo and his schoolmates were asked to contribute something to the poor. They donated to the fund en masse but only because "Every kid in that public school, out of the goodness of his heart, went out and stole a can of food from a local grocery store."[8]

That American cities remained stable, free from serious turbulence may be attributed in part to the attitudes and reactions of the foreign born and their children. New Deal programs and Franklin Roosevelt's winning personality inspiring confidence among ethnics were significant factors explaining this outcome as were effective union organizations. At the same time, the emotional, occupational, and realistic day-by-day assistance that members of ethnic groups gave one another provided support for a significant number in America's working class and helped them to weather the storm. Our presentation will deal with three important yet disparate ethnic groups arriving in the cities, roughly as contemporaries—Italians from Southern Italy, Jews from Eastern Europe, and African Americans from the American South.

Immigrants entering the United States from Southern Italy in the late nineteenth and early twentieth century found security by adhering to traditional values and practices as they adjusted to their new environment, at once foreign, hostile, and discriminatory toward them. Italian males, as principal wage earners for their families, found at first only the most menial employment; their families were obliged to live in overcrowded, often squalid neighborhoods—tenements with minimum conveniences in which they experienced high rates of infant mortality and susceptibility to contagious diseases.[9] Poor living conditions and problems of adjustment were so severe that an estimated 60% of Italians who came to America between 1908 and 1923 gave up and returned home.[10] Those who remained relied heavily on their Italian heritage and deliberately set out to form Italian neighborhoods to protect their traditions. Little Italys typified American cities. East Harlem, South Philadelphia, the North End of Boston, the Hill in Southwest St. Louis, and so on were all solidly Italian.

The family system, the backbone of socioeconomic life and values in the old country, became the institution they scrupulously attempted to preserve in these enclaves. Thus, Italian families in America expected work and income from all family members from the beginning: fathers, the main source of family income, children when they reached working age, and wives (though mainly employed at home with boarders or doing piecework). The principle governing claims on monies earned by employed family members was one of strict reciprocity; each contributed complete earnings to the family exchecquer, often deposited in china pitchers in the cupboard, as late as the 1930s. In return, the family as a whole provided for the essential needs of each of its members—their room, board, clothing, and extras.[11] Although the family's economic goals could easily submerge the interests of grown children in marriage or education and force their delay or denial, parents sought to fulfill their role in the family wage economy by purchasing homes or at least making tenements as attractive as possible for each member of the family. Italian Americans generally exceeded ethnic groups of the same American vintage in home ownership. In 1930, 69% of Italians owned their own homes in Philadelphia, 50% in St. Louis (Hill district), 42% in Cleveland, and 41% in Chicago—rates that surpassed Jewish or Greek immigrants.[12]

Italian-American families, with their emphasis on family loyalty and cooperation, produced impressive results in other ways as well. Into the 1930s, they had one of the largest, if not the largest, birth rate of all sizable ethnic groups from Europe and exceeded by far the birth rates among old American stock in American cities. As a group they also registered extremely low divorce and illegitimacy rates and very high percentages of intermarriage with fellow Italians.[13] In effect, they formed strong and stable family units in which large numbers of blood-related persons were directed to pull together and work for one another—a beneficent ethic for the times.

These same principles of family cooperation and reciprocity extended from individual families into neighborhoods. Family members lived close to one another, even after children married, for purposes of security and emotional support. Those with good jobs often found them for kin. By doing so, families fashioned safety nets for their own futures, given expectations of reciprocity.

Relations with paesani, persons from the same community or area in Italy, were also often mutually rewarding. This represented a wider sphere of personalizing the community.[14] Ideally, first-generation Italian-American families from the south of Italy sought to arrange marriages through personal linkages with families of the intended spouse. Extended family and paesani assured a broad basis of contacts for selection, preempting the American mode of choice through dating. Italian-American weddings were not merely elaborate affairs with Mass, sumptuous feasts, and dancing, they also served the purpose of extending cooperative networks; nonblood relatives were expected to become part of the family's "security or insurance system."[15]

Neighborhoods interlaced with communal relationships, like those inhabited by Italian Americans, prompted cooperative modes in the community at large. These were accentuated by defensive feelings about status and image in America, fostering in degrees a sense of kinship among all Italian ethnics, not merely family, kin, and paesani. All shared, too, the sights and sounds of community and rich smells of tomatoes, spices, and sausages and freshly baked bread, and so in some respects a community haven reinforced the haven primarily sponsored by family. These enclaves, collectively speaking, were also powerful corporate statements announcing indissoluble strength regardless of immediate problems; they were not merely terra cognita, places for familiar discussions at special markets, with barbers, shopkeepers, and bocce players in the Italian language or, at least for the second generation, in the Italian manner, they were also, because of their size and numbers, guarantors of an unfailing future.

The Italian family system and neighborhoods in America were not free from tensions, of course, and were subject to modifications among the second generation—young people having grown up in America to become adults in the 1920s and 1930s. The older generation accused some of them of being derelict in their responsibilities to the elderly. Dating and going to dances with Italian-American peers became more common, and so did greater personal choice in marriage. The gang phenomenon in Little Italys so amply described by William F. Whyte in *Street Corner Society* illustrated that young men in Boston's North End were living, socially at least, on the streets, and they increasingly deferred to the authority of their peers, though gang members displayed typical patterns of loyalty to leaders and obeyed strict reciprocity in their relations with one another.[16] Again, the massive old Italian enclaves began to dissolve in the 1920s with the desire of successful Italian Americans to find locations that more nearly reflected their achievements and status, but they often moved to locations with other Italian Americans as their neighbors.[17]

Yet, even with modifications and occasional significant departures (intimations of a crisis between generations), the family system that southern Italians brought to America remained a significant safety net in the 1930s. Many of its essential characteristics went unchanged, and it continued to exercise stabilizing emotional and material functions. The great majority of Italians still married Italians, parents generally retained some say over marital partners for their sons and daughters, families in Italian-American neighborhoods were unusually large, and divorces negligible. In fact, one historian in a careful, quantitative study that included Italian Americans in Providence, Rhode Island, presents information that suggests the Depression strengthened their family wage economy and tightened parents' control over sons and daughters who wished to marry.[18] They were now more inclined to stay home with their parents longer, or to marry and live with their parents, seeking protection while also assisting parents with their financial problems. In 1940, 60% of Italian families with married children in Providence had a married child living at home, and another 18% of these families had another married child living within two blocks.[19] Clearly, Italian family traditions reinforced and abetted extended family relationships common during the Depression.

The powerful, cooperative relationships that Italians transported to America were eminently practical. They encompassed tangible benefits and conferred a sense of corporate and community strength. But, even so, immigrants and their children could only assure themselves so much. Since most Italian Americans were also genuinely religious (though not necessarily weekly churchgoing, at least not for males), they also turned to God and the saints as a balance wheel for their human imperfections. What is particularly impressive about their devotions was how comfortably those interplayed with familiar axioms of home and street. Relationships between first and second-generation Italian Americans in East Harlem and the divine were often suffused with the same principles of respect and reciprocity that produced tangible results in Italian-American families and neighborhoods.[20]

Although there are many noteworthy facets of Italian-American religious life in the 1930s, one that enlisted more fervor and, for brief periods, more participants than any other, was a religiously inspired street festival or festa for the Madonna. This was conducted in the church and in the immediate vicinity of Our Lady of Mount Carmel, then amidst America's most densely populated Italian community on 115th Street in East Harlem on the East River in New York. By the time of that event each summer, the community had already been made ready, family members and relatives gathered, including those who had moved from the area, special Italian foods prepared including good bread and pastries, and beers and wines made ready for the select group invited to each household.[21]

The festa began with a formal Mass and widespread communions by the faithful. Some penitents attending Mass foreshadowed the unusual religious significance of the event by crawling up the steps of the church on hands and knees. After Mass, religious devotion would take to the streets of East Harlem—with bands playing, thousands chanting hymns in Italian, and a statue of our Lady of Mount Carmel carried solemnly in procession. People watching on the sidewalks often joined the marchers, many removing their shoes to convey a desire to please the Madonna by a penitential act. Others would throw themselves at her feet, and publicly relate their personal trials; those bearing the Madonna would stop and receive the penitent respectfully. After the procession and her formal coronation, hundreds—perhaps thousands—of people lined up in the church of Our Lady to present their petitions, and the atmosphere became quiet as the faithful reached the altar.

This deeply felt experience was followed by hearty meals, joyful dancing in the streets, and firecrackers. Thereafter, family get-togethers dominated activities. Perhaps the festa would last a week, but there was no definite time to end them.[22]

How was the spirit embodied in the statue of Our Lady of Mount Carmel able to command the fervent allegiance of so many Italian Americans year after year?[23] The answer is, of course, complex, but many of its facets reflect issues of human power as well as human finitude. Devotions to Mary characterized peasant life in south Italy—to transfer that allegiance to East Harlem stated a need among immigrants for her reassuring comfort and familiarity. The festa at 115th Street also asserted ethnic pride in the face of outsiders who belittled them for their poverty, crime, and foreign ways. The message of the festa was that they, too, could be triumphal. God loved them, regardless of their class or background.[24] But the festa was also a statement of human frailty and dependence on a Supreme Being. Petitions to Our Lady of Mount Carmel, amply recorded and printed up in church bulletins in the late 1920s and 1930s, stress particularly the votary's concern with family problems—a sickly daughter, a husband out of work, a son who deserted his heritage and went American, a daughter-in-law or neighbors who interfered with good family life.[25] It is clear that those petitioning for help, feeling powerless to handle a difficult problem in family life, believed they could become empowered through the intercession of those close to God. Petitioners asked Mary for help, and it is clear they felt she responded and would continue to do so if they conferred the proper respect in their petition and then would promise to reciprocate her favors by practicing special devotions or acts of penitence or good deeds. She would then respond according to the ethic of reciprocity, the keystone of ethnic Italian family and community life. As the gifted student of religion and historian of the festa on 115th Street, Robert Orsi observed, the believers who participated in the festa found a way to cope with the many hurts and disappointments of their lives and to carry on.[26]

The festa also served to extend the personalized sense of community demonstrated by Italian families in their relations with kin, paesani, and friends to the entire Italian community. It was this spirit that several of Orsi's informants declared epitomized relationships between people in East Harlem even during the Depression.[27] It also represented the sense of East Harlem described by a young soldier writing in 1943. He declared, "All my life I have lived on 104th Street and a better group of people who help one another I've yet to meet."[28]

And, of course, the festa not only conferred substantial hope on its petitioners, it also reaffirmed the basic commitments of the social system: families should and could be maintained effectively; cooperative personal relations with kin and friends were important for all those concerned; life was difficult, but with the right attitudes in one's daily life, good family networks and reliance on supernatural aid, good things were possible. As such, the phenomenon of the Festival at 115th Street also clearly demonstrates the hopefulness of Italian Americans during the 1930s.

Over 2 million East European Jews from the Russian Pale, coming to America essentially at the same time as immigrants from southern Italy (1880–1914) also transported fundamental characteristics of their traditional European family and community life. Typical of preindustrial societies in Europe, they, like the Italians, first relied for security principally on a cohesive response—a family wage economy and expectations of close kin relationships. The Jews, however, would also transplant a distinctive cultural and commercial heritage that, given opportunities in America, would provide special opportunities for social mobility and protection against ravages of the Depression.[29]

Jews from Eastern Europe brought to America a special emphasis on education and learning, especially in mastering Jewish religious lore. In the secular world of America this drive could easily transfer into a quest for rational and worldly accomplishment. A young man growing up in the intensely Jewish neighborhood of Brownsville, New York, in the 1920s and 1930s illustrated this change by underscoring the success ethic that families expected. He declared, "Our parents' job was to feed us . . . and our responsibility was not to disgrace them and to accomplish something."[30] This often took the form of rational and academic excellence. Little wonder that City College of New York (CCNY), "an overwhelmingly Jewish institution" of this time, was a place of intense intellectuality. One participant recalls the rugged debates that characterized discussions in the cafeteria's alcoves, "You caught your opponent in a fallacy, preferably a logical one, but a historical one would do. You smiled. Let him get out of *that* one. Then the bell would ring, new period, changing of the guard in the alcoves." About the worst accusation that could be made at CCNY was a thundering denunciation made by a professor to a student: "The trouble with you is that you can't think."[31] This quest for education and successful exercise of intellect would help spark a rapid expansion of a Jewish business and professional class in America in the 1920s and 1930s.

The other major difference between Jewish immigrants (1880–1920) and ethnic groups of the same vintage in America was their "nonpeasant experience"; alone, among immigrant groups of this period, their backgrounds in Europe were generally in trades, business, or small industries. Although Russian laws were often severely discriminatory—denying them ownership of land, restricting business opportunities, even impoverishing many, Jews from Eastern Europe were generally business-minded, and they therefore became swiftly upwardly mobile in America; they could invest, accept risk, delay immediate gratification, and anticipate future success.[32] They were also prepared, given a cushion of security in America, to invest in the education of their male children, making sacrifices to assist their future success. And they could also guarantee a proper respect for education among their children. Alfred Kazin noted from his own experience growing up in Brownsville in the 1920s that in the minds of Jewish schoolchildren, "All teachers were to be respected like gods."[33]

These attitudes and resulting skills quickly produced impressive gains and prompted Eastern European Jews and their American-born children to leave their original settlements for more attractive residential areas in their cities. They still relied on family and kin as primary backups, but by the 1920s and 1930s large numbers of Jews in business and the professions might also rely on friendships with middle-class Jewish associates and investors or on Jewish consumers in their large selective neighborhoods. Although Italian Americans were inclined to preserve and refine the support system they brought with them, Jews were better able to implement a complex defense system by hedging their bets and finding solidarity in a variety of ways. Their strategies were not mutually exclusive, but instead diverse and inclusive.

The Old World patterns among Jewish Americans from Eastern Europe were, of course, most sharply outlined in places of their original settlement in America: The Lower East Side of New York (where half of America's Jews lived), South Philadelphia, the area around Maxwell Street in Chicago, and the West End in Boston. European ways also tended to be maintained in places where rapid resettlement of Jews occurred, such as Brownsville in New York, an area of Brooklyn that was inhabited by Jews from their original settlement in Manhattan as early as 1900. Brownsville became a miniature "East Side," long identified as "the Jerusalem of America." All these locations were invariably crowded with Yiddish-speaking people living in tenements and often feeling alien from America. Alfred Kazin, the distinguished literary critic, recalls the Brownsville of his raising in the 1920s, though equally applicable in the 1930s:

We were the children of the immigrants who had camped at the city's back door in New York's rawest, remotest, cheapest ghetto. . . . They were New York, the Gentiles, America; We were Brownsville—*Brunzvil*, as the old folks said—the dust of the earth.[34]

Old World norms and expectations shielded immigrant anxieties in these areas—hence the family wage economy. In Providence, Rhode Island, where a detailed quantitative study of Jewish family organization from 1900 to 1940 provides authoritative information on the subject, fathers and sons, fifteen to sixteen year olds, were expected to provide the family's basic income. Jewish wives (mothers) took in boarders, worked in family shops, or took in work that could be completed in their homes. Daughters who were sixteen or older also worked, though usually in family shops or in stores or industries in which their older brothers or sisters were already employed. Parents generally exerted authority over choices and timing of marriage, work or education of children, all variables that affected the family's solvency.[35] Kin who lived in the same house or within a block or two from the family and landsmanshaftn, persons from the same place in Europe, along with mutual aid societies provided additional networks of support outside the family. Home was a place for relatives and friends, and this setting cemented relationships. Jewish families in Brownsville remained extended into the 1920s and 1930s as they did in Providence. Young men raised in them "remember being surrounded by relatives in the neighborhood, a significant minority by relatives in their building or even in their apartments."[36]

The Lower East Side and places like Brownsville also persisted as strongholds of orthodoxy; they were Jewish worlds. Synagogues were common (in Brownsville there were eighty-three in two square miles) as well as observance of the Sabbath, the Bar Mitzvah, and dietary sanctions. Alfred Kazin recalls that when he returned to his apartment from school one Friday afternoon, he fondly witnessed preparations for the Sabbath: "The warm odor of a coffee cake baking in the oven and the sight of my mother on her hands and knees scrubbing the linoleum on the dining room floor filled me with such tenderness that I could feel my senses reaching out to embrace every single object in our household."

"I waited for the streets to go dark on Friday evenings" (in readiness for the Sabbath), Kazin remembered, "as other children waited for the Christmas lights." He then narrated with loving recollection:

By sundown the streets were empty, the curtains had been drawn, the world put to rights. Even the kitchen walls had been scrubbed and now gleamed in the Sabbath candles. On the long white tablecloth were the "company" dishes, filled for some with gefilte fish on lettuce leaves, ringed by red horseradish, sour and half-sour pickles, tomato salad with a light vinegar dressing; for others, with chopped liver in a bed of lettuce leaves and white radishes; [and] the long white khalleh, the Sabbath loaf.

Observance continued until Saturday twilight. He would then race to the nearest delicatessen "panting for hot dogs." When the delicatessen's electric sign came on, it displayed an appropriate title for Brownsville. Kazin had entered the JEWISH NATIONAL DELICATESSEN.[37]

It was in these first communities for Eastern European Jews that parents were most likely to speak nostalgically about "heym" in Lithuania, Poland, or the Ukraine or to take tea in Russian style through lumps of sugar between their teeth.[38] Divorce among these Jews was negligible and, still another salient feature of traditional Jewish culture, philanthropic organizations for fellow Jews and mutual aid societies flourished.[39]

Parents in these first communities might have wished that their children preserve with them identical ways and values, but their historic legacy would be better defined as preserving the basic Jewishness of the second generation.[40] Except for the Bar Mitzvah and attendance on certain holy days, synagogue services would steadily lose their appeal. Theodore White, raised in the enveloping Jewish world of Boston's Blue Hill Avenue in the 1920s, explained this seeming discrepancy with Old World practice, reasoning that Eastern European Jews waited on God for deliverance, but in America Jews learned they might save themselves. He wrote:

The confusion that resulted was overwhelming; and you could see the confusion in the street school of Boston, where I learned so much. In Hebrew school, I learned about the God of the Jews. In the street school, other Jews were learning the American "hustle"; and I was part of both.[41]

There were many other threats to Jewish traditions unleashed by America's economy and culture. Saturday was an active day in American life; Jews often dined outside their homes and neighborhoods in American restaurants that served non-Kosher food; young women in America were relatively well educated, the near equals of young men in years of schooling, and this appealed to young Jewish women who could not find sufficient employment in family shops and businesses. They needed an education to find employment in the business world, and many would attend high school or college at night in New York.[42] These same young women would meet attractive men (not always Jewish) at work or in schools, and it was inevitable that they would eventually express their personal preferences for dating and marriage and seating for women along with men in synagogue services. Meanwhile, jazz, basketball, and baseball would fascinate young Jewish males. Artie Shaw, born on the Lower East Side, battled his parents to be a musician and Hank Greenberg would have to explain to his parents how he could hit home runs and still be Jewish.[43] When Hank was growing up in the Bronx, the neighbors in his Jewish neighborhood would say to his mother, "Mrs. Greenberg, you have such nice children. Too bad one of them has to be a bum." The bum was the baseball-playing Hank. Education, meanwhile, became a major mode of personal advancement for the second generation, thereby downgrading the importance of the family wage economy, while parents with foreign accents sometimes became an embarrassment for children attempting to find avenues to succeed in an American as well as a Jewish world.

Despite tensions and quarrels with their parents, young Jews born in America of Eastern European background retained their basic Jewish loyalties. Part of the explanation lay in the warmth and nurture supplied by their "friendly ghetto" of origins, a world suffused with Jewishness. (In Brownsville, the population was estimated to be 95% Jewish in 1925.) The streets were filled with Jewish playmates, strollers in parks pushed by Jewish mothers, schools overwhelmingly composed of Jewish students, businesses almost exclusively operated by Jews. All the major institutions were also

Jewish—synagogues, Yiddish and Hebrew schools, and philanthropic agencies. And the parents, while no longer weekly members of the synagogue congregation, remained active in "some important expression of Jewish religious observance."[44]

At issue for Jewish Americans of Eastern European origins in the 1920s was a prime dilemma of all immigrant groups in America. They prospered through hard work and improving educational qualifications and the growth of the national economy during World War I and the 1920s, and wished to move away from early settlements associated with foreign origins and to live like middle-class Americans.[45] Yet they faced a dilemma, particularly stressful for a people with thousands of years of unique religious heritage and near continuous persecution; they might in so doing lose their identity and become simply Americans.[46] To do so might also jeopardize the protection they gave one another through family and kin, the landsmanshaftn, and the protective boundaries of corporate Jewish life in the first settlements. The second generation would find a compromise that served needs for survival as well as status considerations.

They left South Philadelphia, the Lower East Side of Manhattan, the West End in Boston, and similar places and chose single or two-house dwellings or attractive apartments and streets such as the Grand Concourse in the Bronx, and even the Upper West Side in Manhattan; they also chose attractive areas such as Strawberry Mansion in Philadelphia which became emphatically Jewish in the 1920s, and Logan or Wynnefield, also in Philadelphia.[47] A desire to live in an American style powered this migration. It was facilitated by friends and relatives who were also moving or perhaps were already residents of the new Jewish neighborhoods. Effective public transportation was also a key factor as were ads in the Jewish press by Jewish builders or real estate developers.

Those moving still feared America's power to absorb them, but, as one participant observer noted, "We of the second generation were frightened of America—but we hungered for it more than we feared it."[48]

Indeed, the new Jewish residents of "ritzy" communities such as the Grand Concourse apparently made a conscious effort to live like Americans.[49] But whatever their hunger or even their conscious intents, Jews of the second generation preserved their Jewish identity. "They remained Jews," a historian of the phenomenon declared, "and brought up their children as Jews. Only a few chose to intermarry (with non-Jews) and disassociate from the group."[50] By becoming more like Americans in life style, they reduced objections to their alien ways, but by forming new self-segregated Jewish areas, Jews also assured their protection as well as an effective consciousness of Jewish religion and culture in their communities.[51]

American Jews with Eastern European origins increasingly resembled other middle-class Americans in the late 1920s and 1930s. They lived in attractive places and often drove shiny new cars and wore fashionable styles of clothing. Their daughters worked outside their homes and family shops and many attended night colleges, and women participated with men in services at Conservative (modern) synagogues. The synagogues themselves also increasingly resembled social centers especially for young people—one on the Grand Concourse included a school and a gymnasium and swimming pool as well as a formal synagogue.[52] Jews also participated in politics at all levels. Inspired by favorable attitudes toward them from liberal New York Democratic Governors Al Smith and Franklin Roosevelt, and Mayor La Guardia who appointed Jews to official posts, they also responded enthusiastically, of course, to Herbert H. Lehman, a descendant of German Jews who was four-time governor of New York after Roosevelt during the Depression years. The devotion of descendants of New York's Eastern European Jews to the Democratic Party then began to assume qualities of ethnic group loyalty.[53]

But second-generation Jews, who lived residentially separate from non-Jews, also became encapsulated in their own separate world, and, in so doing, replicated the example of their elders, though their choice was entirely voluntary, not forced on them by impoverished circumstances of immigration. Indeed, they created more clear-cut Jewish neighborhoods than their elders.[54] In the second generation, shops, drugstores, meat markets, shoestores, bake shops, delicatessens, professional people, individuals on the street, and socializing was virtually entirely Jewish. So too, its primary institutions, synagogues, and even public schools were Jewish in the sense that Jews dominated their numbers in Jewish neighborhoods. By 1940, they also supplied nearly three-fifths of all new teachers for New York's schools.[55] Even non-observing Jews felt Jewish in this milieu. As one commentator observed in the late 1920s, the separate world of Jews assured that "four-fifths of all Jews [in New York] . . . practically have no contacts with Gentiles."[56] For the same reasons, a major Jewish newspaper in New York described its Jewish neighborhoods as America's fourth city, ranking in numbers behind only New York, Chicago, and Philadelphia. The *Forward* also observed that each Jewish neighborhood was "in most of its requirements a self-contained and practically self-sustaining unit."[57] In Philadelphia, the insularity of Jews was similar and, like New York, occurred in both old and new neighborhoods.[58]

The new Jewish middle-class neighborhoods of the second generation proved a remarkable boon, both psychologically and economically, to urban Jews during the Depression. Seeing other Jews and socializing and doing business with them were normalizing experiences in uncertain times. Ethnic conflicts resulting from weakness did not add to their travails in the 1930s and homogeneity of neighborhood brought comfort and solace. When problems emerged, primarily as backwash from international tension with parading German-American Bundists or with Catholics over the Spanish Civil War or over anti-Semitic speeches of the Rev. Charles Coughlin, Jews, feeling the strength of their numbers and their support in politics, were able to reply to their critics. And European anti-Semitism centering in Nazi Germany merely strengthened Jewish ethnic identification and resulted in larger fund-giving to Zionist organizations and the Allied Jewish Appeal.[59]

The new neighborhoods also helped Jewish contractors, lenders, real estate developers, and craft workers who were key figures in developing them and provided unusual economic security for Jewish businesses, professionals, and workers who lived in virtually closed markets.[60] These opportunities helped middle-class Jews offset discrimination that Jews themselves experienced in jobs, housing, and admission to elite universities and professional schools.[61] In addition, close association between middle-class Jews in their new neighborhoods nurtured the friendships, advice, and financial assistance helpful to a business community. Possibilities for investments at these times may have been enhanced by the fact that second-generation Jewish Americans were predisposed to retain loose capital for investment; they were less inclined than Italian Americans, for example, to buy houses and remain in fixed neighborhoods, preferring renting and moving to other Jewish neighborhoods, further increasing their options for mutually helpful secondary associations.[62]

Those who became friends often visited the same resorts, sometimes together. Boston's Jews preferred Cape Cod, New York's the Catskills, and those from Philadelphia went to Atlantic City and its residential neighborhoods, Ventnor and Margate, New Jersey.[63] Advantageous advice, friendships, and business deals were all consummated amid summer breezes at the shore.

American Jews developed helpful strategies to deal with the Depression. Their enthusiasm for higher education resulted in participation in a number of middle-class occupations resistant to problems of unemployment, especially public school teaching, pharmacy, and social work.[64] Their closed neighborhoods fostered association kinship as well as genuine opportunities to provide for a relatively secure neighborhood market. Older family-style support systems also survived and provided additional economic and psychological benefits. One person, who lived in the new Jewish neighborhood of Strawberry Mansion, Philadelphia, reported that thirty-five of his forty cousins lived in the same neighborhood.[65] In smaller, less prosperous cities such as Providence, Jews retained the family income and kin residence systems more nearly intact, but the landsmanshaftn declined among the mosaic of defenses employed by the second generation.[66] American Jews from Eastern Europe not only preserved their identity in the 1930s, they were adroit in devising strategies to protect themselves against the storms of that decade.

African Americans in the great cities also employed specific strategies for survival and achievement to cope with hard times. Like Italian Americans from southern Italy and Jewish Americans from Eastern Europe, most of them also moved from a rural background—the American South after 1900.

And there is reason to believe that even those blacks who already lived in northern cities in 1900 also came in large numbers from the agrarian South. In Providence, Rhode Island, for example, excellent data reveal that this was true of over 50% of the city's black population.[67] Thus, America's new work and social environment made by industry and commerce after the 1890s would challenge many African-American migrants as well as European immigrants. Italians and Jews felt obliged to rely on traditional safeguards in their new surroundings, especially family relationships including kin. Similarly, African-American families subscribed to a family wage economy, with their wives even more inclined to work than wives in contemporary immigrant families, and they were often generous with kin by doubling up and helping one another in critical periods such as the Depression, though there appear to be fewer organizations among African Americans comparable to the paesani or landsmanshaftn. African Americans would find their additional protection in the mutual-help, broad family formula of racial solidarity.

They came north for freedom and opportunity—two million between 1910 and 1940; they relished the prospect of good jobs and improved wages (in cash) and became enthusiastic consumers of the northern cities' wealth of goods and activities. They also prized their new opportunity to vote, the prospects of an improved education for their children, and increased personal freedom. To live eventually where they chose also seemed a possibility, though in the beginning African Americans, like the Italians and the Jews, preferred close association with those in their own group. Besides, there would be no alternative as they would quickly discover; their hoped-for gains—in effect, their exercise of the basic rights of other Americans—would produce great fear and hostility among whites. And so the "land of hope" soon assumed dimensions of oppression.[68]

Particularly disturbing circumstances about their lives in northern cities would force African Americans, both residents and migrants, to adopt and implement a mutual-help philosophy for their own protection. One of these was the establishment for blacks of large, required ghettoes (1915–1930), a treatment unlike those for European immigrants who also clustered, but who lived together on a voluntary basis. They were also frustrated by the apparent restrictions placed by whites on their vertical mobility; African Americans were essentially segregated occupationally, prevented from competing for desirable jobs in a lucrative urban economy. The Depression (1929–1940) was a third, extremely irritating and anxiety-producing situation; it threatened the equanimity, even the survival, of countless persons in the "Black Metropolis."

Evidence of economic segregation and discrimination fill histories devoted to black experience in the cities in the period 1900 to 1940. In New York, African Americans were virtually excluded from managerial or clerical posts in businesses operated by whites, a reflection in part on the poor educational qualifications of great numbers, though by no means all employable blacks.[69] In Detroit, where African Americans constituted 7.6% of the city's population, they held less than 1% of public jobs. Detroit's street railway labor force, exceeding 4,500, employed only fifty-nine blacks while its two major public hospitals with over 1,400 employees had jobs for only five.[70] In Chicago, where a pair of black sociologists studied the issue, their report stated that "it is definitely not the policy in industry to place Negroes in positions where they give orders to white persons, hire and fire them, recommend them for promotion or function as technicians." Clerical work for black women outside Chicago's black belt was virtually nonexistent, and jobs for black men inside City Hall were largely janitorial.[71] Few African Americans taught in Chicago's high schools and only one school in Chicago had a black principal, appointed in 1928.[72] School administration remained in the hands of whites, even when the student body was overwhelmingly black. Likewise, it was unlikely, if not impossible, for African-American physicians to intern, let alone practice medicine in major public hospitals.[73]

These public policies together with the weak economies in black neighborhoods, the sparing controls blacks exerted over those economies, and the high rents exacted from a trapped population contributed to widespread poverty among blacks. Data by the Bureau of Labor Statistics for Chicago (1935–1936) reveal that two-thirds of African-American families had incomes of less than $1,000 a year, while only one-third of "all families" in Chicago were equally disadvantaged.[74] African Americans in New York and Chicago did not operate a single bank during the Depression, and only four black-owned insurance companies would survive the Depression—only one in New York.[75] Although blacks owned less than 20% of all businesses in Harlem, one-third of these were merely small enterprises offering personal services, such as barber shops, beauty parlors, and dry cleaners. And less than one-fifth of Harlem's grocery stores; meat markets, bakeries, restaurants, furniture and clothing stores were owned by blacks.[76] Their only monopoly was apparently the pool-room business. In Chicago's black belt in the 1930s, most of the stores were owned by whites, especially the large stores where blacks were even refused employment.[77] Chain stores owned by whites undercut prices in stores operated by African Americans, and black shoppers generally chose white businesses if their prices were lower. Black businesses also hurt their own cause since they were undercapitalized and their owners relatively inexperienced. The authors of *Black Metropolis* estimated that black businesses received less than 10% of all monies spent within the Chicago black ghetto.[78]

One of the most interesting and symptomatic facets of black enterprise in the 1930s was its singular success in the illegal numbers game, dignified by a formal title, "Policy."[79] The game, which served as a commentary on the poverty of ghetto life, also underscored the difficulties for blacks to pursue legitimate businesses in competition with whites. Policy operated on a basis of simple chance, guessing three numbers that would appear on steel balls when selected from a large drum that contained numerous balls and numbers. It required only a small investment to play, usually a dime, and the returns could be substantial—fifteen or twenty dollars. The only requirement of Policy was a substantial kickback from Policy managers to City Hall to justify its illegality. "Numbers" was the buzz word of the black ghettoes. Bets could be placed at many legitimate businesses and otherwise unkept, uninhabited places. Crowds lined up for the public drawings; people had great faith in dream books to instruct believers in the appropriate numbers, and the blacks who operated the drawings and paid off winners were considered "race heroes" because they afforded each and every member of the race an opportunity to advance. Policy managers won further esteem when they invested profits in new businesses that benefited the black community. Policy was a successful black business in Chicago; it made money, employed numerous "race people," and tapped into the hopefulness and entertainment needs of the impoverished. It also provided a hopeful metaphor for black business and even for the ghetto itself—the odds might be long, but some kind of payoff was certain.

As we noted in Chapter 1, the Depression threatened to crush Harlem's fragile economy like the proverbial house of cards. The reliable Milbank Foundation reported a 43% decline in income in Harlem from 1930 through 1933; African Americans were among the first to lose their jobs, and they also found reemployment difficult in a tight and discriminatory labor market. In 1937, for example, they constituted 15% of New York's unemployed but only 5% of the city's population.[80] In the mid-1930s, the Urban League estimated that 60% of Harlem's heads of households were unemployed. Over half of all blacks in Harlem would receive some form of relief during the decade, not a few of whom might have otherwise starved.[81]

Many African Americans who survived the Depression only did so by pluck and imagination. Women, unable to find work even though their family's welfare depended on their employment, took themselves to heavily trafficked street corners in the Bronx where they made themselves known to passersby as available for a day's work for paltry sums, perhaps even "a few cents per day." A WPA worker who found them in 1938 on Girard Avenue and 167th Street reported, "There, seated on crates and boxes were a dejected gathering of Negro women . . . youths of seventeen and elderly women of maybe seventy. These women were scantily attired—some still wearing summer clothing—and as the November wind swept and whistled through them, they ducked their heads and tried to huddle within themselves." The investigator who observed their resolute yet pitiful bargaining with prospective employers described the setting as "the Bronx slave market."[82] The Harlem Rent Party was a more whimsical approach to desperation. With the rent due and money unavailable, imaginative Harlemites improvised a rendezvous for lonely people from the street who wished to meet partners and have a good time, and simultaneously to pay their own rent. A bright light in an apartment window on a Saturday night would be the signal for a festive time. Admission was usually twenty-five cents, and each partygoer also paid for food and drinks. One couple even devised a printed card to announce their good times:

> There'll be plenty of pig feet
> An lots of gin
> Just ring the bell
> An come on in.[83]

The rent parties often supplied a couple of musicians, a setting for some fast dancing, and a fabulous home brew, known in the early years of the Depression as King Kong. Naturally, some rent parties became so successful they outgrew their original purpose and became small, lucrative businesses.

No description of the increased determination of African Americans to champion racial solidarity for mutual support could be complete without mentioning the personal influence of Marcus Aurelius Garvey and his followers. Garvey, the charismatic leader of the United Negro Improvement Association (UNIA) in the 1920s, directed the most exciting black organization of that decade. Although the membership size of the UNIA is uncertain, with estimates ranging from 300,000 to 6 million, no one can dispute Garvey's emotional appeal to African Americans in northern cities in that period. Garvey called his followers blacks, forbade advertisement of skin whiteners and hair straighteners in his newspaper, intoned the glories of African civilization, and called on his followers to rely on one another and other blacks for improvements rather than the good will of whites or the implications of democratic humanism. "Up you mighty race" was an appealing pitch for recent southern migrants who seemed powerless during the frightening wave of race riots in American cities (1917–1923) and subsequently reinforced segregation. Garvey made members of his audience proud to be black, and he set an example for their self-improvement materially by founding black businesses. Although Garvey was not on the scene in America in the 1930s, he abided in its activist causes through organizations infused with former UNIA members and their ideas—the Black Muslims, Father Divine's Peace Mission, the Peace Movement of Ethiopia—and by the consciousness he stirred in the earlier decade.[84]

As the Garvey movement signifies, solidarity as a mode of black's coping with racial adversities was not an invention of the 1930s; it had existed in muted form in the South, but in the late 1920s and 1930s, racial solidarity assumed for them a special immediacy of importance.[85] Two black sociologists who studied the black community in Chicago underscore its intensity: "In the period between the first and second World Wars," Cayton and Drake wrote in *Black Metropolis* in 1945, "this emphasis upon race pride became a mass phenomenon among the Negroes in large urban communities. Race consciousness was transformed into a positive and aggressive defensive racialism."[86] Charles Gosnell, a keen student of black politics in Chicago in the 1930s underscored "the strong racial solidarity they (African Americans) have developed." He detected, "No matter how they may be divided among themselves on issues, they are united in facing the white world when it presents a hostile front."[87] Richard Wright captured the same sensibility in the 1930s when he portrayed the murderer, Bigger Thomas, as a type of race hero in *Native Son*. Wright explained Bigger's behavior in the introduction to his novel. "He [Bigger] was attracted and repelled by the America scene. He was an American because he was a native son; but he was also a Negro nationalist. . . . because he was not allowed to live as an American."[88] Racial solidarity among African Americans was so pervasive it encompassed more than politics, social movements, and literature. The victories of Joe Louis, Jessie Owens, and Marian Anderson were also vicarious achievements of the race. Joe Louis's victory over James J. Braddock to become heavyweight champion of the world in 1938 produced "the greatest celebration of pride our generation has ever known" wrote Malcolm X, then growing up in Lansing, Michigan. Another young man in the black belt of Chicago remembered as the main consequence of the event, "The South Side has gone totally berserk, with black people running up and down streets, shouting, crying, laughing and singing as if the millennium has come."[89] Race solidarity would even extend beyond the nation's borders in the form of vigorous support for Haile Selassie and Ethiopia when Mussolini invaded the sole independent black country on the African continent in 1935.[90]

Solidarity varied in degree of intensity among African Americans, and it varied according to circumstances. Surely it was not an obsessive commitment. It did not prevent those living in Bronzeville (Chicago's black belt) from enjoying its social and economic center at Chicago's 47th Street and South Parkway. Race relations, Cayton and Drake wrote, were only one axis of their lives.[91] They were also interested in "getting ahead," "having a good time," and "serving the Lord," and, despite frequent disappointments, they enjoyed modest gains for blacks in Chicago and remained optimistic about the outcome of their struggle to participate as equals in the life of Chicago.[92] And, "as harsh as life in Detroit could be," Thomas writes, "blacks still preferred the Motor City over the South."[93] Furthermore, there were lapses in brotherly feelings between African Americans from different classes toward one another, and distinct preferences among middle- and upper-class men in Bronzeville for light-skinned over dark-skinned women.[94] Nonetheless, African Americans still looked to racial solidarity as "their ultimate hope in presenting some kind of united front against the world." To be admired as a "race man" was Bronzeville's highest compliment, and many regarded "getting ahead as a *racial* duty as well as a personal gain."[95]

Special attachment to the solidarity cause characterized three influential groups in the black community: business leaders, church leaders, and publishers of newspapers. Businessmen eyeing the large dense market of potential buyers in black neighborhoods found themselves struggling to remain competitive against better funded stores and chains owned by whites. They had to rely on appeals to race unity and brotherhood over price and would readily argue that money spent by blacks in a black store amounted to a double-duty dollar—a term widely used in Bronzeville.[96] It helped the store owner and the black community because the money remained at home. Black businessmen were forced to rely on their friends, participation in clubs, leadership in community events, and backing from influential persons like ministers or the local black newspapers to make their case, and they often benefited from this type of community support.[97]

The church remained the core institution in the black metropolis; it reached larger numbers and had more influence than any other association. Over half of Detroit's African Americans, 44,000, were church members—at least 70,000 in New York and an estimated 65,000 in Chicago attended church regularly.[98] These churches, mostly Baptist, were busy places with activities nearly every day and night of the week in addition to Sunday. Almost all (90%) functioned independently of white churches and their supervision, though there were notable exceptions with a few old-line Protestant and Catholic churches—the latter highly regarded for their parochial schools. A few of these churches were mammoth—the Abyssinian Baptist Church in Harlem with 15,000 members and at least five churches in Chicago with over 2,000 seats in the church itself. Pentecostal and Holiness places of worship outnumbered the bigger, traditional-style churches, appealing especially to recent migrants from the South. Apart from religious fervor and speaking in tongues, they were distinguished by solacing personal ties between ministers and their small congregations and personal warmth between members.[99] They frequently had only twenty-five to fifty members, met in vacant buildings dubbed storefront churches, and were often intensely otherworldly in their priorities.

In teaching and preaching solidarity, the black churches addressed the dominant ethical concern of their flocks—the need for justice in their lives. Black ministers readily taught that blacks could best advance their goals by brotherhood and cooperation. Besides, solidarity with its implications of loyalty to group and economic growth could only result in a rising tide that would benefit all institutions in the black community, including churches still in debt from elaborate building programs. Clearly, black church members themselves expected their churches to transcend partisan denominational lines and "to play a prominent part in advancing the race" as a whole. They assumed their ministers would address local political, social, and economic questions affecting the race and valued highly those ministers considered good "race men."[100]

In the early years of the Depression before the New Deal's programs began, the major black churches along with large Pentecostal churches demonstrated solidarity with remarkable social service and welfare programs for needy blacks. The Abyssinian Baptist Church, after Rev. Adam Clayton Powell, Sr.'s "Hungry God" sermon, led the way; it became a major private center for relief in Harlem. The elder Powell was convinced that society had a responsibility for its poor in hard times; "If the Bible didn't mean this, it didn't mean anything."[101] His church dispensed large quantities of food and clothing to the needy on a daily basis—an estimated 2,000 people were fed each day.[102] Other major churches in Harlem including large Pentecostal churches did the same. Nonchurch organizations such as the Urban League in Harlem also made major contributions to relief. An historian summing up the significance of these private operations between 1929 and 1933 wrote, "For four years, until their resources were almost completely depleted, Harlem organizations kept thousands from starvation and complete destitution."[103]

Such social welfare initiatives essentially represented defensive measures on behalf of black solidarity. But with the New Deal assuming this type of responsibility across the nation, beginning in late 1933, leaders in the black churches attempted in the remainder of the 1930s to tackle the root problems of black poverty in the cities—to find new jobs for blacks in positions from which they had long been excluded. They marched against and picketed offenders, winning real and important symbolic victories and attracting the attention of local politicians ever mindful of groups that could demonstrate effectively. A white journalist quickly understood this change in emphasis when he came on a sign in front of a black church in Chicago. It read, "What Must We Do To Be Saved?" and the answer below in smaller letters read, "Beset with Rent Hogs, Overcrowded in Hovels, Come to the Housing Meeting, Thursday Noon."[104] Although numerous ministers in every major black neighborhood worked in consort to promote these attitudes, the activist Adam Clayton Powell, Jr., who succeeded his father as pastor of Abyssinian Baptist in the early 1930s, best embodied the new vigorous and practical theology, espousing a more militant mode of racial solidarity.

Powell had long-range objectives that spelled economic improvements for urban blacks. He set up night classes for thousands of students in shorthand, typing, sewing, and dressmaking as well as a civil-service review course, and he initiated the "Buy Black Campaign" aimed at patronizing black businesses by blacks and boycotting white stores that did not employ blacks. He also marched on behalf of five black doctors dismissed from a Harlem hospital and was able to bring public pressure to rescind their discharge. The same tactics, usually accompanied by threats or actual boycotts, secured new jobs for blacks in "5 & 10" stores, department stores, Consolidated Edison, telephone companies, and even the World's Fair. Powell publicly condemned high rents and explained away Harlem's riot in 1935 with "People have no reason or self-discipline when their bellies are rubbing up against their backbones."[105]

Among the many African-American newspapers published in northern cities, none was more influential or better illustrated devotion to the leveraging principle of racial solidarity than the Chicago *Defender*, published by Robert S. Abbott.[106] A weekly, costing ten cents, usually about forty pages with an estimated circulation of 40,000, the *Defender* was probably read by at least 100,000 blacks each week. The newspaper was race-angled in all its dimensions, Abbott setting example in working for the improvement of the race and its community in Chicago by initiating a number of worthy causes. One was to sponsor an election for the mayor of Bronzeville every two years. The mock election stimulated a genuine political atmosphere, vigorous campaigning, and finally a victory celebration and ball presided over by a well-known black American such as Bill Robinson, the dancer, or Duke Ellington. Although the office was purely symbolic, it conveyed a sense of community and was a source of enthusiastic pride among black Chicagoans. The *Defender*'s Billikins Club provided numerous activities for black youth, including entertainment at the Royal Theatre at critical times in the year—Thanksgiving, Christmas, Easter, and during the summer; again, often with black celebrities.[107]

The *Defender* looked everywhere for achievements of African Americans and declared them not only exemplary, but within the reach of many of its readers: a local girl who was a whiz at chemistry ("a high genius") was also described as liking Swing; a recipient of a master's degree deserved a lavish article and maybe a picture, as did the first black appointed as assistant coach for a Big 10 football team; black fliers with their flight regalia were often pictured and praised. In 1936, Lieutenant Benjamin O. Davis, Jr., the "first race graduate" of West Point in several decades, received special attention together with a photograph in uniform with his fiancée. These achievers became race heroes, and the *Defender* exalted them further with "an annual achievement tea."[108] Joe Louis was the ultimate race hero, with eighty pictures of the Brown Bomber in its pages between 1933 and 1938.[109] Any failure by one of these heroes seemingly alarmed the *Defender*'s staff. A renowned black track star's defeat by a white runner was attributed to his poor condition. The newspaper staff also seriously entertained the possibility that Joe Louis had been doped when defeated in his first fight with Schmeling ("Was Joe doped? If so by whom?"). This was understandable because of the dismaying reality announced in the *Defender*'s headline on the same page—"Race Hobbling on Only 1 Leg When Joe Falls."[10] Although Abbott's paper exalted success by blacks, its praise was often subtly accompanied with caveats to the reader—the achievers had no magic formula; the price required was self-discipline and perseverance.

The *Defender* also advanced racial solidarity by going on the offensive against prejudice, paltry wages for blacks, racial slurs, and vestigial Jim Crow practices. And Abbott demanded strict legislative support from politicians whom he supported. He cautioned:

Regardless of party affiliation, we should and must vote for the man who commits himself definitely and positively to a policy of social justice, economic security for the members of Race. In so doing we will be using our votes intelligently, to our best interest and we will have wrought, in the meanwhile, a powerful weapon with which to enforce our legitimate demands.[111]

The *Defender*'s boosterism for solidarity and achievement by blacks might also be inferred by its near abstention from news of whites except where they impinged on the interests of blacks. Indeed, the newspaper closed its case on the worthiness of blacks with gentle spoofing of the foibles of whites, often displayed in cartoons. One cartoon depicts a middle-aged white couple at a floor show in a "black and tan" cabaret. A black waiter taps the husband on the back and whispers, "Jeanne [a black dancer] says 'Thank You' for the sports roadster" as his wife strains to overhear the message. In another, an attractive African American woman explains to a friend, "Honest, girl, I'm not using a stronger bleach. Two weeks in bed [ill] would make anyone this pale."[112]

Racial solidarity, manifesting itself in the nation's first decade of sustained black activism, the 1930s, produced noteworthy results. Emphatically a movement among urban blacks in the North in response to their frustrations, the movement was rooted in positive features of their lives as well. Opportunities to vote and the competitive nature of the two-party system provided protection against the anvil; small victories begot confidence and spurred further determination and genuine changes began to appear in what once seemed to be a permanent system of segregation and subordination.

They initiated mass action campaigns, marching with signs and setting up pickets where blacks were refused employment or their employment was marginalized; African Americans challenged major corporations, public utilities, City Hall, the organizations that operated the world fairs in New York City and Chicago, as well as the department stores in Harlem that were white-owned, but employed no blacks; and they often won their case, though hardly ever in the numbers they wished.[113] The Harlem riots of March 1935, resulting in property damage and injuries to scores of people, reflected their ongoing frustration and probably helped galvanize a favorable public response that took the form of new white-collar jobs for blacks in offices and public utilities and civil-service.[114]

New opportunities also developed in industrial plants and shops with CIO affiliation. The CIO, as part of its ambitious plans to supplant the AFL as the nation's premier union, sought blacks to increase its numbers and also its influence in key industries as automobiles, steel, meatpacking, and among garment workers. Union membership among blacks in Manhattan grew from 2,700 in 1932 to 39,574 in 1936, with many in the garment industry.[115]

Perceptive and sympathetic big city mayors, Fiorello La Guardia in New York and Edward Kelly in Chicago, provided African Americans with new options. A number of new jobs were placed under civil service by La Guardia who also appointed blacks to such city posts as tax commissioner, magistrate, and judge, for whom he nominated Jane Bolin.[116] Ed Kelly seemed to have genuine affection for blacks, who returned the feeling—many of them calling him admiringly "Big Red." Kelly gave a free hand to the Policy kings at the South Side and the Kelly machine secured city jobs for African Americans in "unprecedented numbers." He also appointed them to important city committees, including Robert S. Abbott.[117] Kelly sponsored the first African American to enter Congress as a Democrat from Chicago, Arthur Mitchell, and he often interceded on their behalf in ward politics. Little wonder that Kelly consistently received more votes than Roosevelt in Bronzeville.[118] Without favorable responses like these from leaders of urban government, it is unlikely that protests by local blacks would have generated the same positive results.

The most conspicuous evidence of race solidarity among big city African Americans came in their change in political allegiance from the party of Lincoln to the party of Roosevelt.[119] By 1936, that switch was decisive in every northern city except Chicago, which had, however, posted a 48.8% vote among blacks for Roosevelt, up from 21% in 1932. Since New Deal work and home-relief programs were offered on a basis of need and since African Americans were more likely to be poor and unemployed than whites, they were entitled to benefits in larger percentages than whites, but, given their new political orientation, they also stood to incur favor from democratic mayors and city bosses who knew their futures depended on distributing favors and appointments to the groups that sponsored them. At any rate, African Americans received impressive shares of material aid in several federal programs of great interest to urban blacks. In northern industrial states with large urban populations—New York, Ohio, Illinois, and Michigan—nonwhites constituted in April 1941 from 18% (New York) to 22.7% (Illinois) of all WPA workers, though they represented merely 4.1 to 5% of the states' population.[120] One-third of those employed by the WPA in Chicago in 1939 were black.[121] This data is even more impressive because recompense from WPA programs nearly equaled income these blacks would otherwise have received on the open labor market.[122] One qualified historian summed up the significance of New Deal programs for blacks in New York: "Outside aid became available to the city in its black community in unprecedented scale. Public Works and home relief agencies made millions of dollars and thousands of jobs available to the needy."[123] Again, of course, without a national government receptive to the poor and, ostensibly at least,

opposed to racial discrimination, coordinated efforts by African Americans
to develop mutual help campaigns would probably have been affected neg-
atively.

Urban enclaves in America's great cities contained large numbers of people whose historical traditions and experience empowered them to deal with
the nation's decade of discontents. They either transplanted a corpus of
wisdom that they had already developed before coming to America and its
cities to cope with hard times (Italians and Jewish Americans) or they ac-
tivated attitudes implicit, though forcibly muted, in their earlier racial relationships in the South that were aggravated by their urban experiences
and the Depression (African Americans). None of these groups were self-
sufficient on this account, but each benefited psychologically and materially
from its distinctive principles of social organization and each group was
better able to deal with problems of the Depression because of its collective
and corporate identity. Indeed, Roi Ottley, exclusively citing examples of
progress by black Americans in the 1930s, would conclude, "Throughout
his long American history, the Negro's faith has been in the ultimate
triumph of democracy. At no time has this goal been as visible as today."[124]

13

Appeal of the Great Cities

There were other unique strengths of urban life in the 1930s, which gave reassurance to their inhabitants, especially those in the great metropolitan cities (New York and Chicago, then nearly 10% of America's population): they provided valuable psychological capital for their residents, a sense they were an elite population, gifted as a community and hence also as individuals to live in incomparable places of vitality, excitement, and personal fulfillment.[1] This supposition was not merely comfortably maintained by New Yorkers and those who lived in other mammoth cities in America, it was impressively endorsed by their countrymen in the outlands who added to their rising populations or who visited ritualistically to pay them homage. Our presentation will be primarily concerned with New York, with passing references to Chicago to illustrate parallel developments in the great cities.

Although seemingly incomprehensible to later generations of Americans, the great cities of the 1930s were then considered enviable places to work and live; they enjoyed higher standards of living (they were more likely to have conveniences such as electricity, bathtubs, and hot water, and higher per-capita wealth), and were relatively safe; one could walk New York's streets at night in the most diverse locations without "the slightest sense of danger."[2] But the main appeal of the great cities for numerous Americans was their avant-garde character. They were more interesting, more stimulating, more sophisticated than other places; they provided bright lights, personal freedom, and an everyday ambient world of theater, but also the best museums, the finest entertainment, and recreation, including first-class sports and all the serious culture one wished and could afford. For these reasons, many persons living there embodied a unique and indissoluble urban pride; they were advantaged leaders in the "American good life," and they, therefore, approached the Depression with unusual verve.

The exceptional opportunities for living in the great cities—recreational, cultural, and for entertainment—explained why people living there were able to cope successfully with setbacks from the Depression. These reduced boredom and diminished chances for personal depression because they displaced public attention, given reduced prices and free public benefits from negative considerations to interesting activities in the exciting world around them; the pulsating activities of everyday urban life in New York served as an anodyne for the unsettling events of the Depression.

New Yorkers in the 1930s knew from their personal experiences that they lived in America's first city or, as they simply called it, *The City*. They may have seen the comparative figures on population that established that their city was America's biggest with a population of 7.5 million (with metro areas perhaps 10 million), more than twice the size of Chicago, its nearest competitor, but, of course, they also sensed this from the crush of subway rush hours and the simultaneous inching along of traffic over the city's lattice of roadways, tunnels, and bridges. They realized, too, that the Empire State Building was the tallest in America and in the world, that New York's skyline had no match anywhere, and they clearly recognized the Empire State Building as a tangible statement of New York's great wealth and power. New Yorkers bragged about the building's appeal for tourists who often sent home postcards to testify that they had seen one of New York's great wonders. And, at least one New Yorker, a writer for the *Journal American* who went to the top and took in the view, confided, "There stirred within me a long-dormant pride, almost a boastful pride, of *The City*."[3] Although the typical New York resident may not have known precisely that New York was by far the largest manufacturer among American cities or that its port was the busiest in the world, handling more than one-half of the nation's foreign trade, and an even larger percentage of its overseas passenger commerce, the merchant ships and great liners, accompanied by tugs and shrill whistle blasts on the East River, were daily changing sights and sounds that conveyed an understanding of the port's pivotal role in world trade and transportation.

The city's grand lighting display at night was a prime symbol of New York's avant-garde technology; its glitter and sparkle explained the city's numerous after-dark tours as well as the fact that the observation deck of the Empire State Building remained open until 1:00 A.M.[4] It also explained the spell cast on tourists and locals by the spectacular flashing colored lighting in the vicinity of Times Square (Broadway and 42nd Street) and why children often thrilled there as they walked hand-in-hand with parents into its fairyland excitement. The *Times* Building in the Square produced another of New York's flattering effects on the crowd; it spelled out "up-to-the-minute news" on its large moving electric board—also creating a surreal

New York on the night of December 9,
1939, as viewed from the 60th floor of a
Fifth Avenue building looking south toward
the Empire State Building. Visitors went to
the observation deck of the Empire State
Building, which was open until 1:00 A.M., to
enjoy New York's electric landscape. Grant
Smith/CORBIS.

effect as if that area of New York represented the heartbeat of the nation's
news information.

But in nearly every direction New York was the triumphant modern
American city. It had more legitimate theaters than any American city, its
two largest movie theaters (Radio City Music Hall and the Roxy) each provided close to 6,000 seats, it had a large number of daily newspapers, two
impressive and gigantic railroad stations (Pennsylvania Station and Grand
Central Station, the former allowing the boarding of a train directly to more
points than any other station in the country), it was the site in 1939 on
Long Island of America's Pan-Am clippers that performed regular trans-
Atlantic flights to Europe, it was a place of premier museums for the fine
arts (the Metropolitan Museum, the Whitney, and the unrivaled Museum
of Modern Art), and for music, with the "Met" and Carnegie Hall. New
York was also host to the World's Fair of 1939–1940, the twentieth century's largest international exhibition with forty-five nations attending,
served as the sports capital of America for boxing, hosting the nation's major
fights including the memorable Louis–Schmeling bouts, and provided three
of the nation's sixteen major league baseball teams.[5] One commentator
noted in a national magazine in 1939 that New York "has more telephones
than all of France, twice the total of South America or, if you like, nearly
as many as all of Asia."[6] Even its mayor, Fiorello La Guardia, a pint-sized
man, cast a gigantic image in his city and the nation. He was a major player
in New Deal politics and a friend of President Franklin Roosevelt who ben-

efited from special treatment from Washington. His image in New York was likened to that of the vigorous Theodore Roosevelt. One contemporary writer observed:

> If there is a collision on the el, the evening papers will have a picture of Mayor La Guardia churning up a ladder to inspect the accident and quiz the train crews. If there is a life-endangering fire anywhere in the Greater City, he will race to it in his telephone-and-radio equipped automobile. . . . He puts on a sand hog's helmet and slicker to "inspect" new tunnels. When the baseball season opens, he doesn't just toss out the first ball; he puts on a baseball cap, steps into the pitcher's box. . . . [7]

Oh, and yes, he did read the comics to the kids of New York on Sunday mornings when the newspapers were on strike. Truly, La Guardia reflected his city's strengths: ability, versatility, hurried energy, and showmanship. And, as if the city were somehow deficient in its theater in life, New Yorkers also put on deliberate spectacles as a community—welcoming the New Year, having a celebrated Easter Parade, and marching on St. Patrick's Day down Fifth Avenue to crowds of hundreds of thousands.

Apart from personal awareness of the city's magnitudes and riches of opportunity, New Yorkers' feelings about the superiority of their city were reinforced by bounteous tributes from other Americans. These came in many forms, sometimes as isolated comments from college girls who won contests to visit New York. Yet one senses that even the *Times* or at least its readers enjoyed hearing from one of them:

> New York provided the greatest thrills. It was exciting riding on a ferry boat and hanging on to the straps in a crowded independent subway train. It was a lovely big crowd, Miss Powell said. Every place we went, people were milling about in the streets and I never saw so many autos in my life, she continued. The New York women we saw on the streets and in the subway we thought very pretty, and all so well dressed. [8]

Each year thousands of young people, many of them college graduates, came to the city attracted by both its economic and cultural opportunities. They often served lengthy apprenticeships in a variety of jobs in department stores, newspaper and publishing houses, as dress designers and stenographers, living frugally in shared apartments and learning to enjoy Italian and Chinese cooking as well as Horn and Hardart's automat; they kept up their appearance with good clothes from sales and took in good but cheap entertainment ($1 or $1.50 for back seats at the Metropolitan Opera), and indulged in nightspots with no cover charge. They generally liked New York and hoped to make enough money—or find suitable marital prospects—to stay. And, of course, there were the more than one million tourists who annually visited the city during the Depression for various lengths of time. Their postcards sent home of the Empire State Building, Central Park, the

Lower Manhattan from under the Brooklyn Bridge, n.d. This dramatic photograph captures Manhattan below 25th Street and, as such, does not include the Chrysler Building or the Empire State Building. Its exact date is unknown, but the buildings shown here were part of New York's skyline in the 1930s. F.S. Lincoln Collection, Historical Collections and Labor Archives, Penn State.

Yankee Stadium, the view of New York's Skyline from the Brooklyn Bridge, Times Square, and so on not only certified visits to the great city, but also underlined its quality for stay-at-homes. The strongest endorsement for New York's way of life so gratifying to locals probably came, however, from its newsworthy image in the national media: newspaper stories and photographs, song lyrics, as settings for movies and radio skits, and in radio presentation of events in the city, such as programs from the Metropolitan Opera, championship fights, and the World Series, and information about the World's Fair. Hardly a late evening passed, for example, when a radio listener did not hear from a famous band playing at a New York or Chicago hotel. These diversified contacts often prompted visitors, especially from smaller urban places, to develop positive attitudes toward the great cities and even to pay them their sincerest compliment through attempted imitation.[9]

New York's lavish nightlife centering on and about Broadway near Times Square primarily illustrated the city's appeal for tourists, not an activity New Yorkers regularly themselves shared. Although locals attended café society (in the more select nightclubs), particularly young people from wealthy families and young businessmen and their wives from Central Park West or the Upper East Side, the relatively costly entertainment district was out of reach of most New Yorkers. Since New York was a premier tourist attraction in the country in the 1930s, however, and since businessmen still had expense accounts, though often reduced from the high-rolling 1920s, visitors sustained the entertainment district and helped New York's economy in the process. Tourists reveled in the sleek and streamlined settings of the nightclubs (most built or remodeled after 1934), their "miracle stages," terraced seating, and sensual atmosphere, with an element of the forbidden, mostly created by voluptuous, scantily clad dancers. The clubs were often places where tourists met other tourists.[10] Moderately priced good hotels, clustered about the entertainment district, were convenient for the outsiders to enjoy the nightlife; the New Yorker at 34th Street and Eighth Avenue advertised, for example, 2,500 rooms from $3.00 a day.[11]

Broadway's nightlife, which had suffered from a sleazy interlude during Prohibition, revived and became a central feature of New York's appeal to tourists during the mid-1930s. The repeal of Prohibition provided the clubs with an opportunity to make money and recover respectability corrupted by gangster connections in the 1920s and early 1930s; the Depression also had a salutary influence on the success of the new nightclubs because it prompted shrewd owners to be mindful of offering good returns in food and entertainment for scarce dollars. This same sensitivity encouraged management to provide entertainment extras—dancing, dining, and a floor show, all for a modest cover charge. Indeed, many clubs accentuated volume, but with small profits per customer. In the same vein, movie theaters in the entertainment district supplied stage shows and first-rate orchestras along with their movies. The nightlife places in New York also embellished their attraction to locals as well as tourists by consciously appealing to the self-expression of patrons, shedding formalities, providing rhythmic swing music, and establishing a liberal, permissive atmosphere; these provisions won many businessmen patrons seemingly overburdened by the rigors of rational processes and accountability. They welcomed the opportunity to express another side of their personalities in a New York setting many miles from monitors in their small towns and cities.

The hotels of New York (mostly on or near Broadway) and Chicago (in the Loop) were themselves in the forefront of the nightclub business. The swank hotels, such as the Palmer House (Empire Room) in Chicago, appealed to elite local society by playing softer music and featuring stylish dancers or a talented singer, but the business-class hotels in the Times Square area, such as the New Yorker, promised "swing" in its Terrace Room; it also attracted a younger crowd with a modest cover charge of fifty cents and that after 10:00 P.M. The Lincoln Hotel in the same area featured

Tommy Dorsey and had no cover.[12] In Chicago, every major nightclub, except one was located in a hotel and most, like the New York hotels, had "name bands."[13]

Nightclubs competed with the hotels offering spectacular stage productions and big bands of renown, and streamlined interiors—the whole effect emphasizing speed and luxury. Their main customers were tourists who were often advised that the club scene was a wonderful way to see New York.[14] The Rockefellers opened their restaurant and nightclub, the Rainbow Room on the 65th floor of the RCA Building in 1934, and advertised its setting, "A nightclub in the clouds." The club included such features as glass walls, a revolving dance floor, every seat a ringside seat, and, of course, outstanding orchestras. The management required formal dress at first, but quickly relaxed the code to meet the preferences of its guests.[15] Broadway's French Casino was more glitzy, but no less spectacular: according to one observer, it provided "flashy entertainment plus food and liquors, with two dance bands for what is normally the price of a theater admission."[16]

Movie houses in the entertainment district were big and offered, in addition to quality movies, spectacular stage shows and outstanding orchestras with vocalists who could compete with the performances at the hotels or nightclubs. Glen Gray and his Casa Loma band and Benny Goodman among others played at the Paramount and Ethel Merman sang there.[17] The Paramount offered the additional spectacle of raising its orchestra pit to the stage level, making it appear enlarged. Audiences for movie-stage show theaters were largely made up of locals who enjoyed many of the same benefits of nightclubs with less cost. One young New Yorker remembers skipping high school to go to the Paramount "and thrilling as the bandstand moved from below eye level to the stage above" as his favorite vocalists rendered "I Can't Get Started with You" and "The Prisoner's Song." He was present later when movie patrons, himself included, danced in the aisles to Benny Goodman's rendition of "One O'Clock Jump."[18] Radio City Music Hall in Rockefeller Center was another celebrated movie showplace for both visitors and locals, in large part because of its acclaimed Rockettes, a long, leggy chorus line that furnished a picture of beauty, rhythm, and precision dancing.

Broadway's theater restaurants offered still another variation in gratification, one that appealed heavily to tourists. Billy Rose, the owner of its two most successful showplaces featuring first-class meals, dancing, and stage spectaculars, the Casa Manana and the nationally famous Diamond Horseshoe, was a master of quality offerings for large audiences and for his bevy of beautiful chorus girls. In fact, *Fortune* magazine entitled an analysis of his business acumen, "Girls, Girls, Girls, Girls." "For a $2.50 minimum," Rose provided at the Diamond Horseshoe, "a high-speed stage show full of girls . . . you have your chance to dance as much as you like between the

The Rockettes. Radio City Music Hall (1930s). Brown Brothers.

shows, and you get a six course dinner." The check for this package with repeated drinks often came to $10 per couple, though the average was around $3.50 per person.[19]

The tiered quality of nightlife that Lewis Erenberg perceived in Chicago—with hotels like the Drake, Palmer House, Sherman, and Morrison at the top, and the Bismarck Hotel and Blackhawk Restaurant ranked second, then dance halls and neighborhood taverns with singers and small bands—also applied in New York.[20] The dance halls in New York, Roseland and the Savoy, however, were probably better known—the latter in Harlem for the famous song, "Stompin' at the Savoy," if not, by common report, for its jitterbugging and the Lindy Hop.[21] Roseland was a national monument to romance and though often worthy of notice by tourists because of its reputation and location on 52nd Street between Broadway and Eighth Avenue, the famous ballroom was mostly a place of beautiful evenings for those from New York's working class. Countless couples who danced there fell in love and were married.[22] They once were among the thousands who packed the ballroom night after night where 2,000 could dance, and the building's capacity was over 3,000. Roseland was known for its outstanding acoustics and its excellent bands, including Fletcher Henderson. The ballroom also had its own specie of diversity. Food was served and couples often came as dates, but Roseland also furnished hostesses (taxi dancers); they encouraged men who came alone and who chose them as paid partners to spend liberally on dances and drinks.[23]

New York's entertainment district offered not only memorable and exciting evenings for large numbers of New Yorkers, it had important national repercussions. The city's reputation and example for numerous visitors from all over the country spawned nightclub life as a nationwide industry in the United States in the 1930s, culminating not merely in little Broadways in other sizable cities but even in such small and conservative cities as Middletown (Muncie, Indiana). This trend to nightlife districts was one more sign of optimism in the nation, and represented a continuous development of legitimate pleasure districts in America since at least since the turn of the century, once again establishing that the 1930s were not a down-spirited time. The nightclub phenomenon, coinciding with America's changing and positive discovery of new features of life to promote happiness, also demonstrated that the 1930s were continuous in that respect with the decades that preceded and followed.[24]

At a time when baseball was distinctly America's most popular sport, New Yorkers went to baseball games in greater numbers than to any other form of public commercial entertainment with the exception of the movies.[25] Baseball remained an important, even consuming pastime for them regardless of the Depression; the successes of their teams were both diverting and protective, confirmation of their sense of New York as a superior place to live. Even in 1937, a poor year for the national economy, over 2,600,000 fans attended ball games of the Giants, Yankees, and Dodgers (attendance for all sixteen teams in both leagues totaled only 9,500,000).[26]

Baseball in the 1930s had characteristics that invited identification by fans. The permanency of a team's location was virtually assured; each team became, indeed, a major symbol of community. Also, players were likely to remain with their teams and hence to be there for their admirers for most or all of their careers in the major leagues, especially if they were among the team's stars. Fans also readily identified with them because the players, while heroes, retained human scale with salaries and lifestyles akin to their own. When Joe DiMaggio, a twenty-three year old, after three sparkling years with the Yankees, had the temerity to ask Jacob Ruppert, beer magnate and owner of the Yankees, for a $40,000 contract, fans sided with management that wished to pay him $25,000. Even after DiMaggio, a likable young man and superior player, conceded and returned to play on Colonel Ruppert's terms, he was roundly booed by the fans.[27] Salaries of players were still modest enough that they looked forward to winning their league's pennant in order to share in World Series proceeds, sometimes as much as $5,000, a sum that for many players was half their regular season salary. This was a time when a rookie who played poorly might be reminded by a veteran, "Don't do that, you are killing me," meaning the veteran could not accept inferior play by the rookie at the expense of his possible World Series check. This way the crowds who came to the ballgames experienced kinship with players who, like themselves, were working hard to make a living, and likely to give their best abilities to maintain their jobs. Furthermore, the fans felt closer to their heroes in an age when the teams were transported by rail. Players were visible and fans might assemble at downtown railroad stations to see them off or welcome their return at critical times in the season. In September 1933, 10,000 Giant fans did so to show their appreciation for their team that was returning to New York after a lengthy road trip while in the midst of a close pennant fight.[28]

The Depression, of course, had negative consequences on attendance at baseball games as it did for most forms of entertainment; fewer fans in the 1930s were comfortable paying for a grandstand seat, usually costing just over a dollar, though tickets were only half price for children in some ball parks and ladies and children were admitted free on special days.[29] Nonetheless, baseball attendance did not recover to the levels of 1929 until 1941. Major league clubs were forced to reduce salaries of players, some had to sell their best players to keep their franchises alive, and some experimented with night baseball under the lights. The Cincinnati Reds played seven games at night in 1935 and increased their attendance nearly ten times over an average weekday with crowds averaging nearly 20,000 per night game.[30] The Brooklyn Dodgers were second to do so; they introduced night ball at Ebbets Field (then the Dodgers' ballpark) on a memorable night, June 15, 1938, when young Johnny VanderMeer christened the event with his precedent-shattering second consecutive no-hit, no-run game.[31] One might suppose that radio broadcasting with revenues from advertising would have appealed to baseball owners under the circumstances, but few teams used the medium. The New York teams—Yankees, Giants, and Dodgers—all agreed to ban radio for fear it would serve to dilute attendance at games even further.[32] Owners also rejected pleas by black and white civil rights advocates to admit black players into the major leagues, a strategy that would have helped attendance at their games.[33]

Those who would search for political and social implications of baseball in the Depression with an eye to finding discontent or disillusionment of fans with conditions in America are ordained for disappointment. Fans were much more interested in the game and good times at the park than protesting social conditions. A far cry from revolutionary protest, indeed, was the response of the World Series crowd at Shibe Park, Philadelphia, to the unpopular President Hoover in September 1931. The fans booed him, of course, but they quickly changed their address and spontaneously began to chant "We Want Beer, We Want Beer," hardly a revolutionary bunch.[34] As for the stars, they were not leading their fans to the barricades either if the great Babe Ruth's remarks are indicative. When asked by reporters how he justified the fact that he was making more money than President Hoover in 1930, Babe allegedly replied, "Why not, I had a better year than he did."[35] And the class intensity of UAW workers in Flint, Michigan, was seemingly reflected when an observer likened their joy and enthusiasm on winning a strike to that of a similar group reacting to the news that the Detroit Tigers had just won the World Series.[36]

The New York baseball teams performed extraordinarily well in the 1930s. With their large population base and their excellent rosters, they invariably topped league attendance figures and often won the pennants of their respective leagues. The Giants and the Yankees justified the great enthusiasm of their fans by nine first-place finishes in the twenty-two pennant races between 1930 and 1941 (the other fourteen teams won the remaining thirteen titles).[37]

The Yankees playing in their vaunted Yankee Stadium in the Bronx were a powerhouse.[38] After winning in 1932 and three times finishing second between 1932 and 1935, the Yankees won four consecutive American League titles and four World Series, a first in baseball history. After missing in 1940, they repeated in 1941. Not only did they win each year of the 1930s after 1936, they virtually pulverized their opposition. They vanquished other teams by big margins, often banking their titles in early September of the baseball season, and they scored many more runs and hit many more home runs than other teams in the American League and many more of their players were collectively chosen by all the managers of American League teams to represent their league in the annual All Star game against rival National League stars. Manager Joe McCarthy of the Yankees, who was chosen to manage the American League All Stars in 1938 by virtue of the Yankees winning their leagues' pennant the previous year, was presented with seven possible Yankees for his starting nine, but he displayed modesty and started only six Yankees. As it turned out, the American League won the game 3–1, with the winning runs driven in by All Stars from the Yankees.[39]

The Yankees of the 1930s provided numerous stellar athletes for crowds at Yankee Stadium to admire, even venerate. Babe Ruth, literally and figuratively, the game's giant was still an active and very effective player in the early 1930s.[40] But the mainstays of their great pennant years were Lou Gehrig, first baseman, who would enter the Yankee lineup in June 1925 and play 2,130 consecutive games for them, and twenty-year-old Joe DiMaggio who joined the Yankees in 1936 and more than any player helped to make them champions for the rest of the decade.

Gehrig was one of New York's own, born in Yorkville and raised in Washington Heights. As a boy, he swam the Hudson near where the George Washington Bridge stands today. He played at Columbia before joining the Yankees. Although overshadowed by the play and theatrics of Ruth and later the play and mystique of DiMaggio, Gehrig was the key Yankee player for most of the 1930s. In ten different seasons, Gehrig, a line-drive hitter to all fields, hammered the ball for eighty or more extra base hits, including every year from 1930 to 1937. Ruth managed this only nine times in his long career. Gehrig also led his league in slugging percentage four times, and runs batted in five times (including the prodigious number, 181 RBIs in 1931).[41]

The measure of esteem Yankee fans held for Gehrig was demonstrated on Lou Gehrig Appreciation Day when many of the 61,000 fans who came to the stadium for a doubleheader, July 4, 1939, did so to pay their last respects to Gehrig in a Yankee uniform. The "Iron Horse" as the fans called him, or "Cap" as he was known to Yankee players as their team captain, had contracted a rare neurological disease, now popularly known as Lou Gehrig's disease. Having already lost some of his finer coordination, he had announced his retirement and was that day being given a tribute by the Yankee management and fans.

John Drebinger, the gifted *Times* sports reporter covering the event, wrote on the front page of the *Times* the following day that it was "perhaps as colorful and dramatic a pageant as ever was enacted on a baseball field."[42] All the old Yankees who had played with Gehrig were there as well as his present teammates. Everyone sensed the crumbling of a titan of the game. Gehrig was not scheduled to speak, but the crowd wanted to hear his last words in Yankee uniform. They began a chant, "We Want Gehrig! We Want Gehrig!" He approached the microphone and a giant hush fell over the stadium. Gehrig, barely in control, uttered his famous lines about his life spent as a Yankee; "I am the luckiest man on the face of the earth."[43] Drebinger resumed:

And for the final fadeout, there stood the still burly and hearty Babe Ruth alongside of Gehrig, their arms about each other's shoulders, facing a battery of camera men.

All through the long exercises Gehrig had tried in vain to smile, but with the irrepressible Bambino beside him he finally made it. The Babe whispered something to him and Lou chuckled. They both chuckled and the crowd roared and roared.

Lou Gehrig died on June 2, 1941, a few weeks before his thirty-eighth birthday, and less than two years after Appreciation Day.

Joe DiMaggio was voted "Rookie of the Year" in 1936. The son of an Italian fisherman's family with nine children in San Francisco, DiMaggio won quick recognition and acclaim among fans and rapidly became a team leader by virtue of his prowess on the field and the dignity with which he conducted himself as player and in his private life. He brought crowds to Yankee Stadium even in his first years in the major leagues, especially Italian Americans, but he appealed to children of immigrants across the board with his tremendous talent and work ethic, demonstrated not only in his hitting, but his superb and seemingly effortless talents patrolling the vast center field of Yankee Stadium.[44]

A Yankee teammate explained why DiMaggio meant so much to his team and Yankee fans. He noted how the great center fielder responded to a

Joe DiMaggio of the New York Yankees, 1941. The incomparable broad stance and graceful swing of DiMaggio. From 1936, his rookie year, through 1939, he averaged 139 runs batted in per season while the Yankees won four successive pennants and world championships. UPI/CORBIS-BETTMANN.

towering hit by Detroit slugger, Hank Greenberg: "DiMaggio . . . took off with the crack of the bat. . . . I don't think he ever looked back; he just seemed to have it in his head where the ball was going to come down. Right at the fence at the 460 foot mark, he just flicked out his glove and caught the ball." But what was almost as important, the player observed, "We were way behind in the game at the time and nothing was at stake."[45] Joe DiMaggio belonged, with President Roosevelt and Joe Louis, in a charmed circle of men who could do their stuff in the late 1930s.

The New York Giants, one of New York's two teams in the National League, were hardly slouches either. They won pennants in 1933, 1936, and 1937, playing the Yankees in the World Series in the latter two years. Their stadium, the Polo Grounds, just north of 155th Street in Washington Heights, was slightly more central to the city than Yankee Stadium, located in the West Bronx, and the Giants may have been more central to the hearts of many New Yorkers than the Yankees who appealed heavily to New York's tourists. Jimmy Cannon, the sports columnist raised in the cold-water tenements along the docks on the West Side of Greenwich Village, insisted that "the Giants were the New Yorkers' team" and that "the men in my neighborhood (in the 1930s) spent as many afternoons as they could watching the baseball Giants."[46] Carl Hubbell, the Giant ace left-hander, joined the team in 1930 and was so critical to Giant fortunes, often defeating the best rival pitcher on other teams in low-scoring games, that he was christened "the Meal Ticket." He was also called "King Carl," again apt because he was, season after season, a twenty-game winner for the Giants and victorious in twenty-four consecutive games in the 1936 and 1937 seasons. His most impressive pitching performance came in the All Star game of 1934 when he struck out in order the fiercest hitters in the American League—Babe Ruth, Lou Gehrig, Jimmy Foxx, Al Simmons, and Joe Cronin, mostly with his famous screwball or reverse curve ball breaking left into a left-hand batter and away from a right-hand batter, thus demoralizing the batters' expectations for a left-hand pitcher. Hubbell packed them in at the Polo Grounds and wherever he pitched while on the circuit. Giant fans virtually worshipped his prowess, especially when he defeated the Yankees 6–1 in the opening game of the 1936 World Series. The *Times* headline then read, "Screwball Ace Baffles Losers, Fanning 8 in World Series Opener."[47]

Hubbell's roommate on the road, Mel Ott, a talented right fielder who would eventually hit 511 home runs for the Giants, was only slightly less famous than Hubbell.[48] Ott had broken in as a sixteen-year-old phenomenon in 1925. He was in his prime in the 1930s. Since Ott was unusually short in stature for a ball player, he found extra leverage for his powerful hits by raising his right foot before the pitcher delivered the ball, coming down forcefully on the elevated leg as he met the pitch with his bat. Hubbell and Ott were both very popular first-class players who helped develop fierce allegiances for the Giants as they battled the Chicago Cubs, the National League team from America's other great city, for first place year after year in the 1930s. The Cubs won the pennant in 1932, 1935, and in 1938 when they took on the Yankees in the World Series.

The Brooklyn Dodgers, according to Jimmy Cannon, were not a genuine New York team and they were not pennant contenders before the early 1940s, but they were spoilers for the Giants because they played off an adrenaline high whenever the two teams met in one of baseball's fiercest rivalries.[49] The standing of the Dodgers did not undermine the near fanatical devotion of their fans or reduce the intense satisfaction the team gave their fans during the Depression years. Theirs was a tribal baseball devotion, the Giants their rich Manhattan enemy. Although Dodger Stadium held only 31,000 fans in the late 1930s, Drebinger expressed the opinion that "the majority of them would gladly have laid down their lives" to assist a Dodger victory over the Giants in their home park.[50] With the same life-and-death devotion, Pete Hamill's father reminded young Pete "in a grave voice, the Dodgers are the greatest thing on earth." Pete repeated this sage advice to other boys at his Catholic parochial school in Brooklyn the next day and as he recalled, "They all agreed with this, of course, and so did Sister, who had us pray for the Dodgers as they moved on to the World Series (1941) against the Yankees."[51]

Although baseball dominated sports activity in the great cities of the 1930s, football, especially professional football but also college football, were also major enthusiasms of New Yorkers during Depression years. Professional football's rise to popularity was a major sports trend of the 1930s as noted in an Associated Press sportswriters poll in 1938. In 1937, it drew over a million fans and reached a new high in 1938 of 1,100,000 in attendance. New York won its league football championship with the football Giants in 1938, packing in 48,000 fans in the Polo Grounds for the contest.[52] Fordham's collegiate teams were also competitive with the nation's best and one of their players, their renowned center Alex Wojciechowicz, ranked All-American standing.[53] New York's Yankee Stadium was also the playing field for the annual Army–Notre Dame game that attracted as many as 80,000 fans, the largest crowd in eastern football in 1937, and the annual Giant-College All Star game was another feature of the fall season in New York.[54] Chicago also had impressive resources for football fans—Chicago University produced Jay Berwanger, the first Heisman trophy winner in 1935, while the Bears invariably fielded strong professional football teams with George Halas as coach and Red Grange and Bronco Nagurski in their backfield. The latter was a fullback on offense and a linebacker on defense; he was a Minnesota farm boy, a football natural, who ran over defenders. Red Grange once described the effects of trying to tackle him, "When you hit him it was almost like getting an electric shock. If you hit him above the ankles, you were likely to get killed."[55] No wonder fans in Chicago idolized him.

From the standpoint of sheer diversity of quality events, New York sustained its description as "The City" with Madison Square Garden (then at Eighth Avenue and 50th Street) as the hub of a variety of popular events: the circus, basketball, track's annual Millrose games, professional hockey, skating revues, bike races, and, of course, boxing, although the great fights with special crowd appeal were held on summer nights in Yankee Stadium where the second Louis–Schmeling fight in 1938 drew 70,000 fans and grossed over a million dollars.[56]

But there was another side to New York, it was not merely white lights and exciting athletic feats. This spoke to esthetic and psychological concerns of the human spirit and buttressed the claims of New Yorkers that they were living in a true megalopolis, a universal locale with an inspiring variety of riches.

Both New York and Chicago had impressive parks and museums to give respite to hurried urbanites. New York's famous Central Park, a significant part of Manhattan from West 59th Street to West 110th Street and from Fifth Avenue to Eighth Avenue, included the New York Zoo attended by 6 million persons in its first seventeen months of operation (1934–1936), and the city's renowned Metropolitan Museum of Art. Central Park provided an amazing repertoire of activities for all age groups: a conservatory pond with a fleet of small boats in the summer and skating in the winter; a middle of the park with three baseball diamonds, each with sodden infields; twelve horseshoe courts; and two croquet courts. Similar but more numerous facilities were west of the Central Park reservoir, including playgrounds for children, though these were more common as marginal playgrounds for young children near pedestrian entrances to the park. In addition, there were areas for tennis courts, roller skating, bicycle riding (reserved for Saturday mornings), thirty-two miles of footpaths, and four miles of bridle paths for horseback riding. Children rode Shetland ponies at the zoo. And major areas of the park were reserved for sitting under the trees, relaxing, quiet conversation, and enjoying six acres of tranquil gardens of flowers. Provision was also made for young people to meet and romance with crowd chaperonage. A newspaper reporter, among an estimated crowd of 8,000, noted:

Under the elm trees that skirt the open space at the north end of the Mall in Central Park, thousands danced last night, while stars twinkled overhead. There was no charge for anything, and the band played everything that the dancers' hearts desired, for the asking.[57]

Along with all these resuscitations of spirit, Central Park, summer after summer, offered once-a-week musical performances of high quality to huge audiences.[58] Chicago provided nearly identical amenities in its parks, many of which had the additional advantage of being on the city's beautiful lakefront for Lake Michigan.

The quality of New York's museums (like Chicago's) was also world famous in the 1930s. The Cloisters, silhouetted against the Palisades, was unique in America as a museum of medieval European art and architecture, presented as a complex of buildings, chapels, rooms, and passageways. It was set as a replica of medieval monastic life, its garden opening on the Hudson. Louis Mumford contrasted its effects with New York overall as "The difference between faith and credit finance, between holy dying and profane living."[59] The Metropolitan Museum of New York, while an impressive repository, was seen as notably weak in modern art, especially modern American art. These gaps were repaired with the inception of two new art museums in New York: the Whitney, founded in 1931 by Gloria Vanderbilt Whitney, mainly devoted to modern painters of the realist tradition, and the momentous Museum of Modern Art (MOMA) founded in 1929 and heavily influenced by the Bauhaus movement in Europe. MOMA concerned itself with art in the broadest sense, including, along with painting, architecture, photography, cinema, and industrial design and art; the museum would coordinate this medley of modern arts in an effort to record and give meaning to the contemporary world.[60] MOMA promptly opened its doors with an exhibition, "Art in Our Time." Among its many exhibits, it would also show, in the 1930s, photography from the Farm Security Administration with its covey of outstanding photographers, directed by Roy Stryker.[61]

The Hayden Planetarium of the Museum of Natural History was still another famous site for tourists and locals and especially for New York schoolchildren and their teachers for its guided tours through space. The Hayden was visited by more than 2,500,000 people between its opening in 1935 and mid-1939. It also provided radio programs that probably reached 100 million listeners.[62]

Those with a taste for concerts and opera could not wish for a better location than New York during the Depression years. Classical music and opera were performed in a variety of select locations, graphically illustrated by the fact that the *Times* on January 2, 1938, devoted nearly a half-page with unusually small print to the city's weekly musical and operatic performances. These were relatively inexpensive in the back rows or balconies of the best places. Repertoires chosen were impressive, and they were invariably performed and directed by persons of rare talent. The Metropolitan Opera announced its Christmas Program for 1938 beginning with *Tannhaeuser* on December 22 and including *Tosca, Tristan and Isolde, Lucia di Lammermoor, Falstaff, Siegfried,* and *Aida.* In addition, a special performance of *Hansel and Gretel* was given for children and their parents. The talent included Flagstad, Melchior, Nissen, Pons, and Tibbett and the admission price was from $1.00 to $5.00. Opera was also available at the Hippodrome near Times Square for $0.25 to $0.75.[63] In the summer and early fall, opera was performed at various other venues. Carnegie Hall simultaneously presented a rich assortment of classical music with the New York Philharmonic, visiting orchestras from Boston and Philadelphia (Eugene Ormandy conducting), instrumental song recitals, and ensembles. Carnegie Hall also frequently hosted accomplished groups or impresarios from abroad as well as special concerts such as *The Messiah* by the Oratorio Society with 350 voices, and the smooth Duke Ellington with his swing band. Its performers were all first rank and included such exceptionally gifted musicians in its 1938 season as Fritz Kreisler, Yehudi Menuhin, and Arthur Rubenstein.[64]

New York's musical programs shifted out of doors in summer to Lewisohn Stadium at Amsterdam Avenue and 133rd Street for diversified weekly programs. (Chicago did likewise to Dyche Stadium in Evanston.) These attracted large audiences; one of its concerts there in memory of George Gershwin had an audience of 18,000. Conductors at Lewisohn included Fritz Reiner, Andre Kostalanetz, Walter Damrosch, and Effran Zimbalist, and the admission prices, $0.25 to $1.00, helped make the concerts appealing to the public. Other organizations on behalf of the arts also provided quality programs. The Brooklyn Institute of Arts offered a fall series in 1939 including an opera, a symphony, and a ballet program by the Ballet Russe de Monte Carlo.[65] And free concerts by the WPA Symphony Orchestra and its ensemble and singers were held in its Symphony Hall and in various locations in the city such as libraries, YMCAs, and music centers.

The quantity of legitimate theater may have been diluted in 1939 by stage shows such as "George White's Scandals," and the smashing success, "Hellz

A Poppin," billed as "The Laugh Sensation of This Generation," but the quality of theater devoted to traditional drama remained impeccable. *Victoria Regina* starring Helen Hayes was the leading play of the 1936 season,[66] and in 1939 the serious choices included Robert Sherwood's Pulitzer-Prize play *Abe Lincoln in Illinois*, Katherine Cornell and, originally, Lawrence Olivier in *No Time for Comedy*, Tallulah Bankhead in Lillian Hellman's *The Little Foxes*, Katharine Hepburn and Joseph Cotten in *The Philadelphia Story*, and James Barton in *Tobacco Road*, most with minimum balcony prices from $0.55 to $1.10.[67] The quality and number of theaters in New York by a wide margin outdistanced those in all other American cities.

Considerations of the ecumenism of New Yorkers invite attention to the importance of religion in their lives. The city had hundreds of churches and synagogues that serviced devotional and social needs of a huge throng of the city's residents. One participant sensed a quickening of religious faith during the Depression. She wrote about the 1930s that it was "The period of widespread daily mass on the part of ordinary Catholics," noting that "noon masses in such churches as St. Agnes's on 42nd Street were filled with working men and women from nearby offices. The same was true of churches on Wall Street and 34th Street."[68] That faith was demonstrated as well during significant times during the religious calendar year. The *Times* noted that in the Christmas season, 1938, carolers sang Christmas songs in the five boroughs of New York, particularly in well-traversed public places. The Paulist Choir also sang in numerous churches and on the radio during Christmas season. Christmas was also marked by the Salvation Army passing out thousands of food baskets, including a chicken, from nine distribution points in the city, with tons of food being set aside for 7,500 homeless men in the city, the distribution of 100,000 reconditioned toys by policemen and firemen, and a large number of baskets distributed by the city's 30,000 Boy Scouts.[69] And while many in the five boroughs celebrated the New Year with parties, and huge numbers watched the "dropping of the ball" in Times Square to signify the birth of the New Year, thousands also attended services in Protestant and Catholic Churches, with more than 3,500 reported at Saint Patrick's Cathedral. Large numbers also attended services to mark Good Friday.[70] And when Francis Joseph Spellman was installed as archbishop in the same church in May 1939, the *Times* reported the church filled to capacity with parishioners (nearly 5,000) with 50,000 standing outside for the three-hour service, lending solemnity to the occasion.[71] Similarly, in a city where Jews composed 26% of the population, there were sections of New York that became quiet and still on the Holy Sabbath, and the numerous synagogues in areas like Brownsville gave the neighborhood a decidedly Jewish character.[72]

Some New Yorkers in the Great Depression were, of course, more equal than others; not all of them experienced the same glow of pride living in the great city nor derived identical benefits from its diverting opportunities. Poverty afflicted significant numbers in the five boroughs throughout the decade. In 1933, about 37% of New York's population lived in families without employment. In 1934, the Russell Sage Foundation estimated that 2.5 million persons in New York needed assistance—again, about 37% of the city's population. At that time, however, only 350,000 persons received relief—hence 1.5 million New Yorkers received help, assuming a family of four for each relief beneficiary, but at least one million more needed help and were either unwilling or unable to secure it. In 1938, conditions had improved, but not sweepingly; numbers on work relief were reduced almost a third, but those on home relief, for reasons of economy, had increased by approximately one-eighth, leaving cumulative totals about the same.[73] But, as the decade progressed, poverty was less likely to be the wrenching kind of the early 1930s. The breadlines were gone, but an FSA photographer witnessed large numbers of men now reading new employment opportunities in front of an employment agency and, as Dorothea Lange observed in 1936, "The apple sellers had disappeared but many men were hawking hand-made ties—three for a dollar—near the garment district."[74] Nonetheless, New York City as a locale still encouraged positive outlets and a vision of hopeful opportunities for all but the most destitute. Nearly 10% of New York's youngsters attended charity or organizational camps in the summer without charge or at minimal cost. The Boys Athletic League and Girls Vacation Fund, both sponsored by charitable organizations, sent thousands of boys and girls to camps in the mountains of New York State during Depression years.[75] The Boys Athletic League also operated an indoor playground for children from Hell's Kitchen on Tenth Avenue near 49th Street.[76] Teenage boys, when they couldn't play in parks or reach community centers, played stickball and kick-the-can on the streets or improvised touch football games with empty cereal boxes as footballs. Competition was exciting and the games were fiercely contested. A survey of 22,000 children, ages six to sixteen, conducted by the Boys Athletic League, found them far from discouraged by their lives' chances—over three-fourths of those boys and girls declared that they expected to go to college.[77]

New York's subways, while often dirty and almost always crowded, were the choice in transportation about the city by most New Yorkers, and a great facilitator to exploit the city's wealth of options. For many, this was the preferred mode to go to jobs or to look for them; for others, to attend the city's night schools or colleges or simply gain access to New York's interesting streets. And for still others, to ballparks, beaches, movies, or contacts with relatives—all for five cents each way. For one young college student the subway system meant he could have a sumptuous outing downtown, once a week, for less than a dollar—thirty-five cents for a delicious lunch at Schraffts (a series of restaurants that also sold chocolates and baked goods), fifty cents for a ticket to over fifty possible plays, two subway fares, and he could still pocket a nickel.[78] If you were destined to remain downtown and wanted a great lunch or dinner in clean, comfortable surroundings, one of the Horn and Hardarts' automats would serve all those needs and inexpensively.

For dating it was possible to enjoy exotic and exciting New York without spending more than two dimes by walking in Greenwich Village or surveying Rockefeller Center. A young couple could also take the subway to Coney Island, New York's great beachside amusement area where an estimated one million city residents went bathing on July 4th, 1938.[79] Realist painter Reginald Marsh depicted the fun New Yorkers had on its boardwalks, fun palaces, and beaches. Marsh's "The Bowl" describes a group of amusement seekers sliding off a whirlaway as they try to hold their positions on top despite the machine's gathering speed. The fun was not merely trying to hold on, but the inevitable result of sliding into the arms or lap of someone else also whirling off the top while those watching in the crowd roared. One could take the subway to Coney Island wearing a bathing suit under one's clothes and avoid paying the ten-cent bathhouse fee—hence, on the return trip, the origin of the term "the Coney Island Dripper."[80] The Rockaways, with a five-mile boardwalk, amusements, and lunch counters, were never far behind Coney Island and entertained 600,000 bathers on July 4th, 1938.[81]

For a small investment, a couple could attend a movie opening (a big event in the 1930s), and have a soda near Times Square. If you went upscale to a cozy Italian restaurant in the Village, where you might find a rose on every table, chances were good that you would enjoy delightful food and pay subway costs—all for less than $2.[82] Then there were the famous dance halls, Roseland and the Savoy, that employed the best bands and kept down prices for early comers—the Savoy charged only thirty cents for dancers arriving before 6:00 P.M.[83] And, of course, there was always that occasional weekday when a man could take his girlfriend to an outstanding baseball game free on ladies day. That afternoon the cost in the bleachers and subway might be less than a dollar.

Ed Pessen leaves us with vivid recollections of the appeal of New York for a poor boy from Brooklyn in the Depression years, his father a garment worker who was "unemployed as often as not." The Pessen family moved frequently in order, Pessen later reasoned, to avoid paying their rent. Indeed, his sister chided young Pessen for spending an extra three cents to buy individual pictures of Giant players before the start of the World Series of 1936.[84] Yet Ed Pessen, who would later become a distinguished professor, remembers that epoch as "Those Marvelous Depression Years." He enjoyed sports in New York, especially the Rangers in hockey and the Giants and Dodgers, the city's extraordinary romance with music, its great entertainment centers, and general ambience of sophistication. Although his local Dodgers were appealing, he was particularly fond of Mel Ott and Carl Hubbell, the latter "as lean and dignified as Abraham Lincoln, and pitching with a skill and character that matched Honest Abe's."[85] He recalls breadlines in the early 1930s, but fondly remembers how the schoolchildren on his bus were singing "Night and Day" as they passed them.[86] Pessen, who was fond of popular music in the 1930s, exults over his pleasure in listening to and singing songs like "Someone to Watch Over Me," "I Can't Give You Anything but Love," "Am I Blue," and "More Than You Know." He remembers with great pride that New York City was "the capitol of the new [swing] music in the late thirties" hastening to add, "and what other city had jazz bands like New York's during the heart of the Depression?"[87] He marveled at the fact that, at one time, "Benny Goodman was playing the Waldorf, Artie Shaw the Lincoln, Count Basie's band had come east from Kansas City to play the Apollo theater and the Savoy Ballroom, and Duke Ellington, Tommy Dorsey and Jimmy Dorsey played at various places in the city."[88] Ed Pessen also records his great thrill in attending foreign-language film-houses such as the Apollo on 42nd Street, a legacy from his new girlfriend who already knew their value.[89] He also relished the opportunity "to hear Beethoven, Mozart, and Tschaikovsky under the stars" at the Lewisohn concert program held one summer at the athletic field of City College. Admittedly, it required a lengthy walk to the subway after the concert and then a long subway ride home. "But with a girl next to you and the melodies lingering on for the whole trip, the [subway] ride was painless."[90] And there was the exquisite pleasure of riding New York's double-decker buses one day when everyone on the bus was singing, "I've Got You Under My Skin."[91] Regardless of the hard times and Hitler, Pessen summed up the meaning of growing up poor in New York in Depression years, "It was grand to be alive, and heaven to be young in that marvelous city."[92]

How many young African Americans living in Harlem (blacks constituted 5% of New York's population) were that enthusiastic? Even at a time when African Americans were three times more likely to be unemployed than whites in New York, the great city, and especially Harlem, also nurtured positive attachments for them. African Americans who read the Amsterdam *News* were aware that in Harlem they lived in a distinctive place, a type of capital of the black world. Harlem in the 1930s was still a mecca for American intellectuals and leaders of African American descent. Thoughtful black Americans, while disabused of the notion that New York might become a Promised Land, recognized that their lives in the city allowed them to become more sophisticated, interesting, and free than their rural cousins in the South. Many in Harlem, which had over 2,000 social, political, and mutual aid societies, enjoyed a valuable social and cultural life on their own turf.[93] Few wished to abandon those advantages or to move somewhere else, least of all back to the South. Many also experienced an augmenting pride in the positive reception of white New Yorkers to their bands, entertainers, and athletes. They delighted in the achievements of Joe Louis, Bill Robin-

Joe Louis and his wife,
Marva, stroll Harlem's
streets, September 25, 1935.
New York Times Pictures.

son, Cab Calloway, Duke Ellington, and others—their successes became successes for the race as a whole. One needs merely to note the expressions on the faces of blacks on Harlem's streets as they follow champion Joe Louis and his wife down a block to know that the fight scene in New York, the crowds in Yankee Stadium, and the plaudits of whites for Louis in the press and newsreels had given them at least a conditional sense of being a first-class New Yorker.[94] The Savoy in Harlem was also their ballroom and one to which whites paid tribute by their presence and spending. It was even true in the leveling world of entertainment that a nightspot, Café Society Downtown, opened by whites in the late 1930s, not only welcomed black entertainers, but patrons as well.[95] Change was slow, but its signs were there in augmenting rivulets. In the meantime, Harlem, with all its limitations, was still for many blacks who lived there, "sweet Harlem, chocolate Harlem."

The entertainment, sporting life, and culture of New York establish that most persons living there and, by implication, those living in other large cities, found resources to deal with the misfortunes that cruelly buffeted them during the Depression. No less than those living in rural America, people in the great cities could turn the specifics of their pattern of living to advantage during the Depression. The latter saw themselves as especially endowed by virtue of their size, vitality, and success to cope with the challenges of the 1930s. And, in fact, they did enjoy remarkable resources in the rich diversity and diversions of their lives to buoy their spirits and counteract Depression-induced pessimism and despair.

14

Conclusion

This book has been dedicated to the proposition that Americans who lived in difficult times during the Great Depression deserve to be remembered as more than hapless victims. Whatever the explanation—whether the heavy impress of documentary photography or the power of romantic literature and cinema of that period, or more recently from oral history interviews, though distantly remembered and often random anecdotes in collections specifically designed to underscore the miseries and deprivations of Depression-era Americans—we have not paid them the attention they deserve. We have overlooked their diverse strengths, poise, creative adaptability, and, above all, their triumphant retention of positive values and commitments despite the beleaguering and enervating powers of the Depression. Although the United States, of all the Western democracies, experienced the most severe and protracted effects of worldwide depression in the late 1920s and 1930s with unemployment rates that exceeded those in Europe and were of longer duration, the American public remained remarkably steadfast and confident of America's institutions and future while European countries were often convulsed with revolution or torn apart by political and social factionalism. To some influential Europeans the solution appeared to be authoritarian regimes with their enforced calm, but as the punch line in the old political gag declared, the best America could come up with in these momentous times was Huey Long. Not only was America free from effective threats by extremist leaders, the society, considering the times, was surprisingly tranquil; the Communist Party declined in America and socialists virtually disappeared from the scene, unions made advances yet were seriously circumscribed if they were considered radical or communist influenced. Indeed, after 1935, even homicides declined—their number was substantially less than for corresponding years in the 1920s. Alone in its class, the American ship of state and its crew moved in the main with a kind of classic calm through the Depression's dangerous shoals and turbulent waters.

The explanation for this fortunate outcome is, of course, partially found in the remarkable personality and political skills of President Roosevelt. His unusually deep personal strengths—his courage, confidence in himself and in the future, and his caring attitudes toward the unfortunate—uniquely qualified him to serve the public interest in difficult times. He would do so with zest and special facility to communicate, in part because he worked tirelessly to achieve a concert of interest groups among the electorate, perhaps replicating childhood patterns of extraordinary efforts to please others, especially his mother, in order to receive special recognition and affection in return. Because of his ability to mediate special needs and encourage confidence, Roosevelt won great popular acclaim and was considered "the Champion" in his first term when his contributions were most needed. Indeed, his appearance was so timely it seemed to more than a few to be almost providential. Letters to the president in this period often reflect respectful, almost reverential attitudes in the population. Although Roosevelt's programs would suffer in his second term from the president's unusual political mistakes and a revival of conservative attitudes nationally, his personal popularity remained high, and hence was a stabilizing influence through the entire decade.

Apart from the president's personal contribution in calming events, the social programs of the New Deal were also critically important to this end. For the first time in the history of the Republic, the federal government between 1933 and 1936 developed, when most needed, sustained programs of relief and work relief, mandated and encouraged labor unions, provided funding to keep young people in schools and colleges, abolished child labor, protected homeowners with low-cost mortgages and offered security for the elderly. These programs explain why a commentator described Roosevelt as "at once God and their intimate friend" to persons in North and South Carolina, or why the cleanest object in the ramshackle house of Charles Zosky, a coal miner in western Pennsylvania, was a lithograph of Franklin D. Roosevelt, or why union workers in Chicago were his ardent advocates; for them the New Deal restored faith in effective and benign authority that had been diluted by their diminished confidence in local ethnic leaders and welfare capitalism. New Deal policies also explained the large voter turnout of ethnics in 1936 and the Democrats' sweep of nearly all cities and states in that year.

Although Roosevelt established himself as a liberal, putting across a significant benefits package for "ordinary citizens," his merits in this regard have more to do with the New Deal's impressive, unprecedented inclusion of this broad group as beneficiaries, rather than its creation of a comprehensive social democratic program on their behalf. A middle of the roader by background and by virtue of his commitment to a strategy of a concert of interests, Roosevelt, though unusually helpful from the standpoint of American political traditions, did not end the Depression for the poor and struggling in the 1930s or significantly reduce the number of unemployed. (The average for unemployment in the 1930s after 1933 remained 17%, down only 7% from the peak unemployment year, 1933.) Nor did the New Deal provide the unemployed with relief or work-relief income that exceeded the barest minimum for survival. Yearly relief benefits for the FERA in 1934–1935 averaged only about $350 per unemployed person. The CWA (1933–1934) was a more attractive program, with income averaging $15 a week, but it was quickly phased out in the early months of 1934, with Roosevelt telling Hopkins that "Nobody is going to starve during the warm weather." Yet, in 1936, when reliable figures are available, nearly 40% of America's families had an income of less than $1,000 a year—a time when $1,200 was considered minimum subsistence income. At the same time, a great many who were unemployed received no relief; in 1933, the worst year of the Depression, the New Deal's principal relief agencies provided income for only 8 million households when the unemployed numbered 13 million.

Roosevelt also refused to initiate adequate legislation to tax the American middle class to provide revenues for underfunded federal relief and work-relief programs. Indeed, excise taxes produced the bulk of federal revenues during the New Deal period—mainly taxes on tobacco, alcohol, radios, and cosmetics—all most likely to be paid by lower income groups who thereby paid for a large share of their own relief benefits. One of the prime examples of underfunded New Deal relief programs and its effects was the Works Progress Administration (WPA), albeit the largest federal relief program in the 1930s. The government spent (6.7 billion on the WPA beginning in 1935, a sum twice that for the FERA and PWA, and more than three times the amount spent on the CCC, though those three programs began two years earlier in 1933. President Roosevelt intended the WPA to provide work relief for all employable persons who could not find work; after its inception, all direct or home relief was to be allocated by states but only to unemployable persons—the elderly, blind, and handicapped, and so on (roughly 4 million recipients). Yet, with so much resting on the WPA and a residue of at least 8 to 10 million able-bodied unemployed eligible for work from 1935 through 1939, the WPA seldom provided more than 3 million jobs a year and at times only 2 million. Although states would pick up small numbers of able-bodied as "unemployables," the effect was to leave large numbers of unemployed (Edith Abbott estimated 1 million in 1938) ready and willing to work, without jobs, and without relief. For many Americans the years after 1935 were as difficult as the early years of the decade. We hear once again about fruit scavenged from garbage cans and scraps being sought from restaurants allegedly to feed pets, and we see numerous

FSA photographs of people with teeth missing, tent houses, homeless families on the road, and even shack towns. This, in the late 1930s after more
than ten years of Depression and nearly two terms of President Roosevelt.

Meanwhile, those fortunate enough to hold a WPA job averaged only
$55 a month, or about $700 a year, assuming continuous work, again barely
enough to subsist. Although a major problem attending the WPA's under-
funding stemmed from a negative reaction to the New Deal in the country
and in Congress in the late 1930s, as well as Roosevelt's deep cut back in
WPA funds in 1937, in effect, many Americans were still scrambling precariously at the end of the decade. The Roosevelt administration would give
further evidence of its halting liberalism by attuning to this shift in public
attitudes and withdrawing its open-handed support for labor in the wake of
the Memorial Day Massacre in Chicago in 1937.

Despite the continuing severity of the Depression, with two of five Americans living below minimum standards for income and consistent shortfalls
in New Deal relief programs, the American people, as a whole, gave no sign
of being flattened by their difficult times. A collection of diagnostic sources
for the nation at large, many of them precisely gathered to gauge the effects
of the Depression on Americans, reveal that they retained a basic confidence
in themselves and their primary institutions and remained hopeful about the
quality of life in America in the future. These sources attest to the importance of social and cultural considerations having a supplementary effect to
New Deal programs in keeping Americans on an even keel during the 1930s.

Harry Hopkins's alert, peripatetic team of sixteen investigators for the
FERA compiled over 100 reports on the state of the nation in 1933 and 1934.
They often discovered people in trying, even desperate situations, but often to
their surprise the spirits of those observed and interviewed were much better
than their circumstances. Few Americans complained or declared their situation unbearable or were prepared to raise a radical banner. The fact finders repeatedly make mention of upbeat attitudes even among the most
impoverished in the worst years of the Depression ("Morale is good" one investigator reported in a steel town with vast unemployment, "with patience
and hopefulness in the ascendancy"). Indeed, they were startled that down-
and-out Americans had not even lost their faith in individualism.

Other thorough indexes of national opinion corroborate those responses.
Americans in the 1930s were scrutinized as in no previous decade. National
polls asked them key questions about their lives and attitudes. Over 60,000
finished FSA photographs with many more negatives taken in all sections of
the country give us an unparalleled tactile sense not only for how they
looked, but how they felt. More than 1,000 post office murals commissioned by the Treasury Department help clarify their attitudes about the
communities in which they lived—past, present, and future. And abundant
statistical records for the 1930s inform us about their lives in profuse detail.

The most impressive conclusion of these surveys in which Americans were questioned, polled, painted, and configured involved identical findings: despite troublesome times, they remained even-tempered and confident about themselves, their institutions and their future.

Americans who were subjects of FSA photography often had the same worn faces and vulnerable looks that Harry Hopkins's fact finders encountered, but they also maintained the same dignity and indomitable spirit. Even "Migrant Mother," Dorothea Lange's seemingly abject photograph of Florence Thompson with three anxious-looking children in Nippomo, California, in 1936, sends a message of real courage, the characteristic Lange underscores as outstanding about her subjects when she worked for the FSA. Walker Evans's photographs of the Burroughs family for LET US NOW PRAISE FAMOUS MEN documents the primitive barrenness of their house and the up-against-it quality of their lives, but also their pride, dignity, and dogged endurance. They asked Evans to take a family picture of them before he left, and they stand in their best clothes, looking happy and with their arms around one another. Countless photographs of poor people in the FSA, collection display their pleasures and hopes—migrants playing guitars and fiddles, mothers smiling with newborns, boys with dogs and girls with favorite dolls, and groups standing attentively as "Old Glory" passes in parade on the Fourth of July. Russell Lee, the FSA's most prolific photographer, summed up his sense of all the people he pictured; he and his wife recalled "a tremendous pride and tremendous courage among Americans."

The post office murals, awarded by the Treasury Department to painters who best incorporated the views of locals about themes of their community experience, were also intimate and important symbolic statements how Americans viewed themselves in the 1930s. The most striking fact about them is their optimism; when locals were asked to view themselves symbolically in a public mural, one they would be reminded of day after day in their local post office, they chose instructive episodes in their town's history, evidences of the success of their forebears or descriptive of the constructive role of technology, steamboats, bridges, and airplanes in their lives. None of the murals presented a pessimistic picture of defeated or victimized people; Americans in community unequivocally chose to see themselves as achievers with great and ongoing potentialities.

National statistics especially after 1935 also confirmed a hopeful picture of American life. Americans lived on average more than six years longer in 1939 than in 1929; they enjoyed gains in infant mortality, and improved nutrition, especially milk, citrus foods and juice, and fresh and canned vegetables. Numbers of students exceeded counterparts in the 1920s at all levels of education. After 1935, they were also using their cars and attending movies (with cut-rate prices) more than people in the supposedly prosperous 1920s, and even spending more on vacations.

Although statistics on unemployment remained grim, the unanimous testimony of these diverse sources illustrate that depressed economics do not necessarily ensure hopeless people. Often discouraged, the American people were not beaten. President Roosevelt's caring, compassionate attitudes helped to sustain confidence, especially in his first term, and gradual improvement in several standards of living helped after 1935. But an important explanation for this disjunction between hard times and hopeful people centered in the long-term confidence of Americans rooted in their history, institutions, and values. For them, these commitments were such that the Depression was merely an unfortunate aberration.

Americans not only extricated themselves from disturbing daily realities by finding assurance in the sterling successes of their country in the past—both as a hallmark of freedom and opportunity and a place where economic improvement surpassed those of any other nation—but also as a country whose continuous progress presaged an incomparable future. From this standpoint, past and future together looked bright enough to temporize with immediate dissatisfactions. The Lynds clearly understood this issue when they attempted to explain why Muncie's workers were not more upset over the Depression's effects on their lives. They accepted, according to Robert and Helen Lynd, the culture's mandate that "tomorrow . . . always means 'progress,' getting closer to whatever it is one craves." This explained "the strong, clear note of hope so conspicuous in the culture."[1]

What the Lynds underestimated about the optimism Americans showed in the 1930s, however, was how much the extraordinary achievements of their own decade also buoyed confidence. These consisted of building masterful dams in the West and the Tennessee Valley, the world's tallest skyscrapers, and many of its longest, most impressive bridges, exceptional applied research to use plastics and improve the quality of cars and trains and especially airplanes. Significantly, as well, the 1930s were marked by a democratizing usage of electricity and appliances dependent on electricity—surely an additional source of positive attitudes for its widening circle of beneficiaries. Many Americans used these new appliances and saw progress firsthand; they rode in the improved cars and trains and a growing number flew in the modern airplane that epitomized progress and was the subject of voluminous magazine copy and advertising devoted to its importance. Advertising devoted its considerable resources, especially through *Life* magazine (17 million readers in the late 1930s) to apotheosize modern living. It created an air of expectations for inevitable progress, even among those who could not afford the goods advertised; they too became witnesses to progress all the same. Part of the appeal of new goods was their radical new design—streamlining that beautified and virtually made a cult of modern things. Americans in the 1930s were so conditioned to the promising expectations of the modern world that nearly 50 million would attend the 1939–1940 New York's World Fair titled "Building the World of

Tomorrow." They were enthusiastic about the fair and readily accepted its presentation of a cornucopia of America's future improvements as persuasive and realizable.

The impressive size of rural America's population and its abiding conservatism were also major factors in explaining what was basically an unruffled, accepting response of most Americans to buffeting from the Depression. Although there were short-term relatively small movements of protest in farm areas, the Farmer's Holiday Association in the Midwest and Southern Tenant Farmers' Union in the South, the overwhelming majority of those 45% of Americans living in rural territory in 1930 managed hard times through conventional political channels and with relative equanimity. They did so because of the enduring strength of rural culture that emphasized hard work, family responsibility for its own well-being, cooperation within the family, with farmers and rural villagers or townsmen who served the farmers, and a psychology of moderate expectations for personal gains. Although this sensibility was being undermined by modern urban culture, as well as farmers' increasing reliance on machinery and some New Deal programs, farms were still family farms in the 1930s, and farm parents continued to teach their children traditional rural values while rural areas remained resistant to the influence of peer groups and a culture of entertainment. The notions that children in farm areas should be raised to contribute to the welfare of the family group and pull their share in the family economy continued unchanged; members of solvent farm families pitched in and continued to do what had to be done. Economic pressures of the Depression were not only mitigated by close family cooperation but by expectations of cooperation with other farm families for shared tasks and with persons in the neighboring community with whom farm families were mutually dependent.

Rural Americans were also inclined to join churches and practice their religion, embracing still another institution that generally stabilized their lives. Data on church membership in the 1930s show remarkable increases in Baptist and Pentecostal churches, and religion's importance in the lives of rural people is a major theme in the Federal Writers' Project interviews, especially its Southern History Collection. But Christianity in rural America was more than a formula for coping; it deeply touched the lives of individuals in small-town communities, and it helped to establish conservative norms there that became atmospheric. Editors of newspapers in these towns would highlight activities of the churches, admonish readers to attend services, and even profess their ardent faith in editorials. Even news coverage was also suffused with a religious tone; the deaths of prominent persons, for example, were often described as that person being "summoned" or "called."

The third major institution that shaped personality and character in rural America, adding to family and church, was community; together this aggregate made for a culture that provided stabilizing collective strengths to diminish effects of the Depression when individuals by themselves could be especially susceptible to danger. Community between farmers and country/town residents was based on mutual needs and facilitated by the farmer's increased access to town by use of cars. And it was strongly enhanced by local newspapers that endorsed and defined community for both sets of their readers. Editors of those papers taught that "community" represented the willingness of individuals to work and accept responsibility for others. Progress in the community and ultimately in the nation depended on people in rural communities "rearing children in habits of useful work and right living and supplying examples that elevate the moral and intellectual level of their communities—these are the men and women of real influence and power."[2] Outstanding citizens lauded by the local press were those who embodied neighborliness, kindness, or public service and patriotism—those who brought people together and made communities work. Editors praised people who persevered with these attitudes through the Depression as "the hope of the nation." A spirit of community was, indeed, widely practiced in small rural towns by a variety of local groups, and this, together with reliance on family, church, and confidence in the virtues of their country and its future, insulated rural people from radicalism or severe anxieties.

Urban Americans, who especially benefited from New Deal relief and work-relief programs, also found residual strengths in their own city environments, organizations, and inherent social support systems. An active union movement, both the CIO (after 1935) and the AFL, responded to the uncertain employment of urban workers as well as their dissatisfaction with low wages and "speedup" engineered by management. The CIO especially exploited the commonalities of the urban worker's culture—to offset ethnic and racial divisions, which had hampered the labor movement earlier, to recruit within the multiethnic, multiracial mix of the city's industrial workers. The CIO would also play a key role in supporting President Roosevelt and would enjoy reciprocal favors. The New Deal not only guaranteed the rights of workers to form their own unions and engage in collective bargaining with their own representatives (National Labor Relations Act, 1935), the president and loyal Democrat governors provided direct and indirect support to unions as they successfully challenged industrial giants and unionized their workforces for the first time in the mid-1930s. As a consequence, union workers consolidated tangible gains in wages and working conditions; these gains in turn spurred union membership that increased from 3 million in the early 1930s to over 6 million in the middle of that decade. Workers were also helped substantially by social and psychological benefits of their organizational bonding. Members of unions often felt a corporate strength that reassured them and their families about their chances to weather the Depression. Both major unions also sponsored a wide variety of social activities for members—hence they became a variety of extended family. The joys and perils of organizing and striking also, of course, fostered an intense esprit de corps.

Although the growth of unions and the bonding of their workers served as bulwarks of confidence to many laborers and their families, surely deterring as well their defection to radical causes, union growth in the 1930s was far from spectacular. At the end of the decade only 16% of Americans who had jobs were in unions. This small percentage of workers in unions and the moderate temper of the two major unions tell us much about the sanguine spirit of the times in America in the 1930s. Relatively few American workers regarded the situation to be so threatening to warrant union membership. And on closer inspection, only 7% of union workers saw fit to "go out" in the great strike year of 1937. Roosevelt's programs were sufficient to diminish labor radicalism, and he may have actually stymied the union movement in the late 1930s when he registered public disapproval of seeming union radicalism in connection with the Little Steel strike in the summer of 1937.

Apart from membership in unions, Americans living in cities enjoyed other advantages that made the Depression bearable. Most American cities contained large numbers of immigrants and migrants and their children who brought with them culturally based strategies for coping with life's problems. Italians from Southern Italy and East European Jews mostly came to America from 1880 to 1915 and were in the 1930s representative of other first- and second-generation ethnic Americans. Each group came from a preindustrial ethos in Europe, and each emphasized close family relationships as a primary mode of problem-solving. Immediate family members all contributed to the family exchequer when of age, and relatives were expected to be loyal to one another and to assume reciprocal responsibilities. When their family systems were transplanted to America, a new dimension of "family" was added, the Italian paesani and the Jewish landsmanshaftn, those from the same communities or areas in the old country who now came together for mutual help.

Although those family systems were modified by their American environment, especially in the American-raised second generation, each ethnic group preserved impressive residues in the 1930s. Italian-American families were unusually stable—high birth rates and intermarriage rates with Italians and low divorce rates and a strong sense of family loyalty and kinship ties. The latter meant useful social relationships and practical help for one another. Since Italian Americans from Southern Italy also lived together in large ethnic neighborhoods, they enjoyed as well the psychological advantages of familiar association and a sense of their numerical strength. This confraternity made possible community-sponsored festa, including the impressive demonstration of faith for the Madonna of 115th Street in East Harlem. The latter illustrated still another powerful resource of an Italian-

American community in the Great Depression: a wholehearted belief in the power of God and saints that would be liberally dispensed to deserving believers to help with life's problems.

American Jews from Eastern Europe also professed essential features of Europe's traditional preindustrial family system in the 1930s—and hence had many of the same advantages as Italians from Southern Italy—but they also expanded their options in the direction of a new kind of associational family. Utilizing their considerable backgrounds in business and enthusiasm for education and exploiting the freedom and opportunity of their new American setting, they achieved precocious mobility and rapidly became middle class. They thereby developed close business and professional linkages with fellow Jews. This associational "broad family" strategy supplemented natural family ties as a reliable basis for survival and success. Both resources were reinforced by the institution by second-generation Jews of large, nearly exclusive, Jewish middle class neighborhoods for economic, religious, as well as psychological benefits.

By the 1930s, a majority of African Americans living as migrants in the big northern cities also had origins in a preindustrial matrix—the rural South. They too relied on a family wage economy, with wives in their families being even more inclined to work outside their homes than those in the first two American generations of immigrant families. And they would often double up their families with relatives and offer generous support to them during the Depression. African Americans would find, however, their most powerful leveraging principle to defend themselves and improve their opportunities during the Depression in the mutual-help, broad family position of racial solidarity.

Racial solidarity among blacks has its origins in the racial imbalances and repression in the Old South. It was not often announced then or politicized out of fear. The hopeful prospects of the North as a "Promised Land" may have also temporarily diluted the position, but the impact of Marcus Aurelius Garvey in the 1920s especially on recent African-American migrants to northern cities reveals the depth of those sentiments when urban life could no longer be idealized. The Depression would represent a final blow to these hopeful prospects because African Americans were then confronted with deep and pervasive signs of injustice and at the same time exposed to real threats to survival. The Depression became their crucible of creativity, a provocation launching demonstrations, picketing, aggressive use of politics, and even a riot with important consequences in jobs, political victories, and a growing conviction that in racial unity they could find a principle and organizational direction to continue to improve their lot.

The great cities of America were also stable places in the 1930s because they counteracted the Depression with a rich palette of activities for their residents. The valuable theater of their streets and their distinctive entertainment, superior sports, and culture provided abundant resources to deal with the demoralizing effects of the Depression. Residents of New York and Chicago were convinced that they lived in superior places and would manifest a dauntless urban pride despite troubling economic circumstances, and they were tempted to find so many diverse ways to enjoy themselves that there was little time for them to become revolutionary or hostile to American society. The name bands were there, along with a romance for music, and the great baseball teams—Cubs, Giants, and Yankees and their fabulous stars. The outstanding musical artists and the great museums, cheap public transportation, good inexpensive restaurants, and reduced and back seat prices for shows, movies, and concerts; also the energy and bustle and, if you were young, a surge of excitement over a wealth of relatively cheap options for dating and fun. Although there were large numbers of poor people in the great cities, only the most destitute were deprived of all these gratifications or opportunities for identification.

As this study attempts to demonstrate, there are numerous reasons why a great variety of Americans responded confidently and hopefully to the trials of the Depression decade and how this stabilized America. Indeed, scrutiny of the two seemingly most disadvantaged groups in America at that time— Okie migrants to California and African Americans, largely tenants and sharecroppers in the Cotton South—reveals that they, too, generally looked to the future positively.

The Okies were more resourceful and successful than the images portrayed by Dorothea Lange's "Migrant Mother" (Migrant Madonna) or the novel or cinematic version of *The Grapes of Wrath*. Their strengths derived mainly from their rural heritage. Like farm people in other areas of America, they were optimistic about their choices, given hard work and a determination to succeed, yet not overly expectant, accepting of difficult circumstances as well as merely modest gains. They were especially committed to their families working together, an important basis of their confidence and self-reliance, and yet, like farm people everywhere, they also valued mutual help relationships with neighbors and townspeople. When they could not work out problems by this combination of determination and effort, family loyalty, and cooperation with those around them, the Okies, as a religious people, could also maintain positive attitudes about their lives by recourse to faith.

This heritage produced significant successes for the Okies beginning in the 1930s after only a few years in California. The rewards were not material in the sense that Okie farm laborers rapidly amassed wealth or power—their net worth in 1938 represented only a small improvement over 1935—but almost all Okies did manage in those years to settle in a single town, rather than work as farm migrants throughout California's vast farmlands, thus stabilizing family life and providing steady educational and health facilities for members of their families. In addition, large numbers built their own houses, modest to be sure, but gradually improved in time as each family member helped with construction. Owning houses gave roots and pride to Okies in California.

Numerous persons in close contact with the Okie population in the San Joaquin Valley described them in the late 1930s as having excellent morale, hopefulness, and resistant to hardship. Theirs was a self-fulfilling prophecy. Because of bedrock convictions and unusual determination to succeed, they effectively managed a difficult uprooting in perilous times and established a new permanent location in one of America's most affluent states.

African Americans in the Cotton South appeared in the 1930s as even more abject than the Okies, who were, at least, white and free from rigid caste regulations. On the surface it would seem they were an alienated and hopeless people—poor and held in check by a pervasive racial system with its ever-present threat of lynching. Yet, there is abundant evidence that this was not so and even that they found reason to feel better about themselves in the 1930s.

African Americans living in the Cotton South discovered many ways to compensate for their problems, even to maintain their pride and hopes for the future. They found strength in solidarity, hence the pleasures of their own company and their compensatory fun-poking at the foibles of whites served to dilute the pretensions of whites to superiority. Race pride also manifest itself in a variety of other ways—singing the black anthem, twisting the caste system to their own advantage, and seeing themselves as true Christians. Religion thereby fostered race pride and personal dignity and explained away life's sizable deprivations with the promise of future rewards. Together, these and other advantages made life for them tolerable, an attitude that expressed itself in a fondness for large families and children.

In the 1930s, a number of changing developments improved their lives. Several sociologists in the Cotton South noted a quickening faith among blacks in education "as a gateway to equal opportunity." Blacks also noted improved courtesies when shopping that they attributed to the insecurity of the white owners during the Depression. In the long run, however, most new advantages for these African Americans were initiated outside the South: the NAACP's vigor in pushing the antilynching cause in the South and the noteworthy diminution of lynchings in America by the mid-1930s; they also benefited from the New Deal's programs for the poor, the emergence of the great black sports heroes, especially Joe Louis, and the beginning of a changing and more positive image of blacks nationally through an improving and increasingly diverse technology of communications.

Popular culture, in the form of movies and radio, provided still other resources to buttress public confidence in the 1930s. This was especially true for movies after 1934 when the public reacted to a spate of films, supposed moneymakers, that endorsed violence and flamboyant nonconformity. Filmmakers were forced to adjust to public preferences for positive

portrayals of family, religion, community, and government—staples in supplying protective and helpful services during the Depression's storms. Films
in the later 1930s played to record audiences and reaffirmed positive and
hopeful public attitudes. Radio also enjoyed a landmark decade in the 1930s
with 44 million radio sets in American homes. This setting, given public
preferences, guaranteed a positive interpretation of America's social and
value systems that, in turn, assured radio's popularity. Radio, even in its
numerous comedy programs, did not poke fun at American institutions or
mores, then promoting sanguine responses among Americans. The tone and
message of Ma Perkins, Jack Armstrong, the Lone Ranger, and a host of
other, less well-known programs endorsed stabilizing features of American
life and played a part in confirming what Americans already believed.

By employing diverse facets of America's social and political experience in
the 1930s to illustrate that American society was stable and that the American people remained typically confident and hopeful, this study attempts to
restore a reasonable symmetry to the historical architecture of the early decades of twentieth-century America. From a historical perspective, the 1930s
deserve to be seen in conjunction with the times that preceded and immediately followed, not merely as a decade somehow wrenched free by the
force of the Great Depression.

When Americans faced a massive challenge of protracted unemployment
and contraction in the standard of living in the 1930s, they did so with
insights from the precepts and attitudes of previous times. Urban America
had made steady progress in numbers and impact in earlier decades of the
twentieth century and with it a zeitgeist of basic confidence in American
democratic institutions, efficiency, technology, and an improved future. The
large number of immigrants who entered America then (comprising in 1930
nearly one-third of Americans either born abroad or having one parent born
abroad) found nothing objectionable in this script, having, in fact, immi-
grated for most of these reasons. Rural America, though declining in numbers and influence, nevertheless, kept alive its own corpus of positive values
of optimism, confidence in family self-help, reciprocal mutual aid, religion,
and patriotism. This aggregate would not only exercise powerful suasion in
the 1930s, it would also encourage Americans of the 1940s, in protection
of their lives and values, to take on heavy responsibilities against totalitarian
systems from the right and left.

The power of these values, sustained by a variety of historical and sociological props in the experience of the American people helped explain their
positive responses during the Great Depression. Were there limits to their
commitments? Of course. A more severe and longer-lasting Depression
combined with bungling political ineptitude or a dissolution of numerous
voluntary and protective mutual-help systems would have tested these convictions severely. In the 1930s, however, responsive and innovative govern-

ment under Roosevelt, together with protective social institutions of a voluntary nature, public confidence in the virtues of America, the promise of American technology and the American Dream sufficed to produce a remarkably stable and productive society in difficult times.

Notes

CHAPTER 1

1. Frances Perkins, *The Roosevelt I Knew* (New York: Harper and Row, 1946), 139; "The Meaning of Barter Exchanges," *The New Republic* (January 4, 1933), 203.

2. *The New York Times*, March 5, 1933.

3. Samuel Rosenman, *The Public Papers and Addresses of Franklin D. Roosevelt* (New York, 1938–1950), ii, 11–15; hereafter cited as Rosenman, *The Public Papers.*

4. Herbert Feis, *1933: Characters in Crisis* (Boston: Little Brown, 1966), 96–97. *The New York Times*, March 5, 1933, reported 100,000 people at the Inaugural giving frequent applause.

5. Rita Kleeman, *Gracious Lady* (New York: Appleton Century, 1938), 300.

6. James T. Patterson, *The New Deal and the States: Federalism in Transition* (Princeton, NJ: Princeton University Press, 1969), 26–49.

7. Josephine C. Brown, *Public Relief, 1929–1939* (New York: Holt, 1940), 126.

8. William O. Douglas, *Go East, Young Man: The Autobiography of William O. Douglas* (New York: Random House, 1974), 353.

9. Louise V. Armstrong, *We Too Are People* (New York: Little, Brown, 1972), 50.

10. Edmund Wilson, *American Earthquake* (Garden City: Doubleday, 1958), 464.

11. There was no data collected year by year during the decade of the 1930s. All estimates are interpolations based on a variety of sources: *Historical Statistics of the United States, Colonial Times to 1951* (Washington, DC: Government Printing Office, 1960), 70; hereafter cited as *Historical Statistics.*

12. Robert R. Nathan, "Estimates of Unemployment in the United States, 1929–1935," *International Labor Review* 63 (January 1936), 49–73.

13. Irving Bernstein, *A Caring Society: The New Deal, the Worker, and the Great Depression* (Boston: Houghton Mifflin, 1985), 18.

14. Sidney E. Goldstein, U.S. Congress, Senate sub-committee on Manufacturers, *Hearings, Federal Cooperation on Unemployment Relief*, 72nd Congress (1933), 146; hereafter referred to as *Unemployment Relief* or *Federal Aid for Unemployment Relief*.

15. Maurice Levin, Harold G. Moulton, and Clark Warburton, *America's Capacity to Consume* (Washington, DC: The Brookings Institution, 1934), 54, 56.

16. James T. Patterson, *America's Struggle Against Poverty, 1900–1980* (Cambridge, MA: Harvard University Press, 1981), 42.

17. Russell Baker, *Growing Up* (New York: Signet, 1982), 88–89.

18. "No One Has Starved," *Fortune* 6 (September 1932), 21.

19. Karl de Schweinetz, *Hearings, Federal Aid for Unemployment Relief* (1933), 120.

20. *The New York Times*, February 2, 1932.

21. Dorothy Kahn, *Hearings, Unemployment Relief* (1932), 74–75.

22. Lester Chandler, *America's Greatest Depression* (New York: Harper and Row, 1970), 63–65.

23. William Hodson, Executive Director of the Welfare Council of New York, *Hearings, Unemployment Relief* (1931), 13.

24. Lorena Hickok to Harry Hopkins, October 2–12, 1933, Franklin D. Roosevelt Library, Hopkins Papers; hereafter referred to as (HP).

25. John F. Bauman, *The City, the Depression and Relief: The Philadelphia Experience* (Ann Arbor: Microfilm Corporation, 1969), 134.

26. Helen Hale, *Hearings, Federal Aid for Unemployment Relief* (1933), 389.

27. Federal Writers' Project, Southern Historical Collection, Tennessee, "I'd Rather Die," interviewer Aswell, n.d., Chapel Hill, NC.

28. Gayle Kaprowski-Krout "The Depression's Effects on a Milwaukee Family," *Milwaukee History* 40 (Winter 1980), 84–90.

29. Nan E. Woodruff, *The Great Southern Drought of 1930–1932: A Study in Rural Relief* (Ann Arbor: Microfilm Corporation, 1977), 122–123.

30. Mary Breckenridge, "The Corn Bread Line," *Survey* 64 (August 15, 1930), 422–423.

31. Bill O'Neil, "The Personal Side of the Great Depression," *East Texas Historical Journal* 18 (Winter 1980), 4.

32. George Huddleston, *Hearings, Unemployment Relief* (1932), 245.

33. Paul E. Mertz, *New Deal Policy and Southern Rural Poverty* (Baton Rouge: Louisiana State University Press, 1978), 1.

34. Charles W. Morton, *It Has Its Charms* (Philadelphia: Lippincott, 1966), 181–182.

35. Hugo Jorgenson, "Bread Line," *The Atlantic Monthly* 158 (August 1936), 164.

36. Joan M. Crouse, *The Homeless Transient in the Great Depression: New York State, 1929–1941* (Albany: State University of New York, 1986), 96–103.

37. Lorena Hickok to Harry Hopkins, April 13, 1934, Box 11 (HP).

38. Ruth L. Porterfield, "Women Available," *American Mercury* 34 (April 1935), 473–478.

39. A good summary of the transient's way of life is found in Joan M. Crouse, op. cit., 95–123.

40. Harvey Sletten, "Having the Time of My Life: Letters from a Wanderer, 1930–1932," *North Dakota History* 40 (1979), 15.

41. Thomas Minehan, *Boy and Girl Tramps of America* (New York: Farrar and Rinehart, 1934), 24, 37, 42, 48, 53. Many of the 466 boys and girls he interrogated underscored how hard times impelled them to leave home. Some believed that they were thereby helping at home.

42. Crouse, op. cit., 112–117.

43. Jacob Billikopf, *Hearings, Federal Aid for Unemployment Relief* (1933), 14–15.

44. Mertz, op. cit., 58.

45. Hortense Powdermaker, *After Freedom, A Cultural Study of the Deep South* (New York: Russell and Russell, 1968); John Dollard, *Caste and Class in a Southern Town* (Garden City, NY: Doubleday Anchor, 1957); Charles S. Johnson, *Shadows of the Plantation* (Chicago: University of Chicago Press, 1934); Arthur F. Raper, *Preface to Peasantry* (Chapel Hill: University of North Carolina Press, 1936).

46. Dollard, op. cit., 97–187, 331. On lynchings in the South, see James R. McGovern, *Anatomy of a Lynching: The Killing of Claude Neal* (Baton Rouge: Louisiana State University, 1982).

47. Hortense Powdermaker, who spent a year studying Indianola, Mississippi, in the early 1930s, believed that only about one-quarter of the planters were honest with their black sharecroppers. Powdermaker, op. cit., 86.

48. Richard Sterner, *The Negro's Share: A Study of Income, Consumption, Housing and Public Assistance* (New York: Harper & Brothers, 1943), 18, 220–233. Mertz, op. cit., 15, 23–29. An excellent account of blacks and the AAA is Raymond Wolters, *Negroes and the Great Depression: The Problem of Economic Recovery* (Westport, CT: Greenwood Press, 1970), Chapters 1 and 2.

49. Mertz, op. cit., 89–90, notes disparities in black and white clients' loans under the FERA in seven southeastern states as of June 1935: whites averaged $205 and blacks only $122 after acceptance into government programs.

50. Cheryl Lynn Greenberg, *Or Does It Explode? Black Harlem in the Great Depression* (New York: Oxford University Press, 1991), 28–29, 75–80.

51. Ibid., 29.

52. In Chicago, 30% of white males were unemployed and 43% of black males. In Detroit, 60% of black males and only 32% of white males. For black females, 58% were unemployed to 19% of whites and in Detroit, 75% of black females were without jobs compared to 17% of white women. Estimates for unemployment for blacks in Harlem in 1937 hold that while constituting only 5% of New York's population they were 15% of the unemployed. Ibid., 44, 66.

53. Sterner, op. cit., 227–228; Greenberg, op. cit., 66.

54. Patterson, op. cit., 59; Edward Webster to Harry Hopkins, December 8, 1934, Franklin D. Roosevelt Library, Box 67 (HP).

55. *Duncan McHolthausen, The Volume of Consumer Installment Credit, 1929–1938* (Washington, DC: National Bureau of Economic Research, 1940), 107.

56. These may be found in the Harry Hopkins Papers (HP), Boxes 65–68, in the Franklin D. Roosevelt Library, Hyde Park, NY. Small numbers may also be found in the Eleanor Roosevelt Papers in the same library and also in the National Archives.

57. Edward Webster to Harry Hopkins, December 8, 1934, Box 67 (HP).

58. Julian Claff to Harry Hopkins, December 2, 1934, Box 65 (HP).

59. Thomas Steep to Harry Hopkins, November 4, 1934, Box 66 (HP).

60. Ernestine Ball to Kathryn Godwin, October 29, 1934, Box 65 (HP).

61. Henry S. Francis to Harry Hopkins, November 10, 1934, November 3, 1934, Box 66 (HP).

62. Helen Reavis to Harry Hopkins, November 18, 1934, Box 66 (HP).

63. Wayne Parrish to Harry Hopkins, November 11, 1934, December 13, 1934, Box 66 (HP); David Maynard to Harry Hopkins, November 12–17, 1934, Box 66 (HP).

64. Edward Webster to Harry Hopkins, November 2, 1934, Box 67, (HP).

65. Martha Bruere to Harry Hopkins, November 27, 1934, Box 65 (HP).

66. Martha Gellhorn to Harry Hopkins, December 19, 1934, Box 66 (HP).

67. Wayne Parrish to Harry Hopkins, November 11, 1934, Box 66 (HP).

68. Bruce McLure to Harry Hopkins, November 1934, Box 66 (HP).

69. Lorena Hickok to Eleanor Roosevelt, October 31, 1933, Box 12, Lorena Hickok Papers, Franklin D. Roosevelt Library, Hyde Park.

70. Hazel Reavis to Harry Hopkins, November 12, 1934, Box 66 (HP).

71. Thomas Steep to Harry Hopkins, November 10, 1934, Box 66 (HP).

72. Henry W. Francis to Harry Hopkins, November 10, 1934, Box 66 (HP).

73. Lorena Hickok, "The Unsung Heroes of the Depression," in Richard Lowitt and Maurine Beasley, ed., *One Third of a Nation: Lorena Hickok Reports on the Great Depression* (Urbana: University of Illinois Press, 1981), xii.

74. E. Wight Bakke, *Citizens Without Work: A Study of the Effects of Unemployment upon the Worker's Relations and Practices* (New Haven: Yale University Press, 1940), 200.

75. Louise Armstrong, *We Too Are People* (New York: Arno Press, 1971), 31–32.

76. "No One Has Starved," *Fortune* 6 (September 1932), 19.

77. Catherine McNicol Stock, *Main Street in Crisis: The Great Depression and the Middle Class on the Northern Plains* (Chapel Hill: University of North Carolina Press, 1992), 17–30.

78. Martha Gellhorn to Harry Hopkins, November 11, 1934, Box 66 (HP).

79. Henry W. Francis to Harry Hopkins, November 10, 1934, Box 66 (HP).

CHAPTER 2

1. Dixon Wecter, *The Hero in America: A Chronicle of Hero-Worship* (Ann Arbor: University of Michigan Press, 1963), 429, 470.

2. *The New York Times*, March 5, 13, 1933.

3. Marquis Childs, *I Write from Washington* (New York: Harper and Brothers, 1941), 15.

4. Quoted in Arthur Schlesinger, *The Age of Roosevelt, The Coming of the New Deal* (Cambridge: Houghton Mifflin, 1958), 13.

5. E. Francis Brown, "Roosevelt Takes Control," *Current History* 38 (April 1933), 87.

6. Donald Day, ed., *The Autobiography of Will Rogers* (Boston: Houghton Mifflin, 1949), 301.

7. Ira Smith, *Dear Mr. President: The Story of Fifty Years in the White House Mail Room* (New York: Julian Messner, 1949), 12, 196.

8. Dr. C. G. Bergmann, to President Roosevelt, March 13, 1933, President's Personal File (hereafter PPF), 200B.

9. O. Boetticher to President Roosevelt, March 20, 1933, PPF, 200B.

10. G. J. Hansen to President Roosevelt, March 13, 1933, PPF, 200B.

11. I.R.H. and friends to Senator Robert F. Wagner, March 31, 1933, Robert F. Wagner Papers, Georgetown University Library, Washington, DC, Drawer Q-2 as seen in Robert McElvaine, *Down and Out in the Great Depression* (Chapel Hill: University of North Carolina Press, 1983), 217–218.

12. *The New York Times*, March 5, 1933.

13. Useful discussions of charisma are found in Ann Ruth Willner, *The Spellbinders: Charismatic Political Leadership* (New Haven: Yale University Press, 1984); Jay A. Conger, *The Charismatic Leader: Behind the Mystique of Exceptional Leadership* (San Francisco: Jossey-Bass, 1989); Arthur Scheweitzer, *The Age of Charisma* (Chicago: Nelson-Hall, 1984), 245–252. On Roosevelt, see also Jerold M. Post, "Narcissism and the Charismatic Leader–Follower Relationship," *Political Psychology 7*, No. 4 (1986), 675–688.

14. Eleanor Roosevelt, *This I Remember* (New York: Harper, 1949), 146–147.

15. Ibid.

16. Wechter, op. cit., 457.

17. Arthur M. Schlesinger, Jr., *The Age of Roosevelt: The Politics of Upheaval* (Boston: Houghton Mifflin, 1966), 585.

18. Leila Sussman, *Dear FDR: A Study of Political Letter Writing* (Totowa, NJ: Bedminister Press, 1963), 113.

19. Mrs. Lorraine Hill to President Roosevelt, March 13, 1933, PPF, 200B.

20. Syd Hutch to President Roosevelt, March 13, 1933, PPF, 200B.

21. Joe Frego to President Roosevelt, June 29, 1936, PPF, 200B.

22. Mrs. Jean Dupont to President Roosevelt, June 27, 1936, PPF, 200B.

23. Mrs. J. F. Eastwood to President Roosevelt, June 29, 1936, PPF, 200B.

24. Miss Shirley to President Roosevelt, June 28, 1936, PPF, 200B.

25. Frank W. Street, to President Roosevelt, June 28, 1936, PPF, 200B.

26. Dan V. Stephens to President Roosevelt, June 29, 1936, PPF, 200B.

27. Ruth K. Cummings to President Roosevelt, January 3, 1938, PPF, 200B.

28. J. Bleiman to President Roosevelt, January 3, 1938, PPF, 200B.

29. Lillian Rogers Parks, *My Thirty Years Backstairs at the White House* (New York: Fleet Publishing, 1961), 261.

30. Martha Gellhorn to Harry Hopkins, November 11, 1934, Box 66 (HP).

31. There are two substantial attempts to identify Roosevelt's personality as insightful biography: Hugh Gregory Gallagher, *FDR's Splendid Deception* (New York: Dodd, Mead and Company, 1985), and Richard Thayer Goldberg, *The Making of Franklin D. Roosevelt: Triumph over Disability* (Cambridge, MA: Aft Books, 1981). Both emphasize the impact of polio on his personality and life goals. Gallagher's study is the more perceptive because it better relates the impact of polio to his personality, which was already well formed by the time of his affliction when he was thirty-nine years old. Among the scholars on whom we rely for the major biographies of the president, Kenneth S. Davis in *FDR: The Beckoning of Destiny, 1882–1928: A History* (New York: G. P. Putnam's Sons, 1972), and Geoffrey C. Ward, *Before the Trumpet* (New York: Harper & Row, 1985), are most forthcoming with useful information from his early life. John Gunther's *Roosevelt in Retrospect: A Profile in*

History (New York: Harper & Row, 1947) provides keen observations based on extensive personal investigation, yet Gunther throws up his hands over "the mysteries and paradoxes" of Roosevelt (p. 30). William Leuchtenburg in *Franklin D. Roosevelt and the New Deal* (New York: Harper and Row, 1963), offers essentially a political history with helpful descriptions, but relies on the "inscrutability" theme. James McGregor Burns wrote, "No biographer of Roosevelt, I think feels he really understands the man." *The New York Times Book Review*, October 18, 1959, 10. Frank Freidel's several volumes on Roosevelt; while excellent and discerning on his life and achievements, offer little on his emotional makeup.

32. Ward, op. cit., 253.

33. Ray Moley, *After Seven Years* (New York: Harper and Bros., 1939), 342, 350.

34. Eleanor Roosevelt, op. cit., 3; James Roosevelt, *Affectionately, F.D.R.: A Son's Story of a Lonely Man* (New York: Harcourt Brace and Company, 1959), 315.

35. Mme. Sanchez, a French-speaking Swiss governess for Franklin, described Sara Roosevelt as "très formidable." Kenneth S. Davis, *FDR: The Beckoning of Destiny, 1882–1928*, 152; Eleanor Roosevelt, op. cit., 11.

36. Eleanor Roosevelt, op. cit., 67.

37. Davis, op. cit., 70.

38. Ibid., 68.

39. Ward, op. cit., 159–160; Davis, op. cit., 72.

40. Ibid., 53; James Roosevelt, *Affectionately, F.D.R.*, 17.

41. Ward, op. cit., 128; Davis, op. cit., 69.

42. Ward, op. cit., 177.

43. Ward, op. cit., 245.

44. Sara D. Roosevelt to Franklin Roosevelt, Roosevelt Family Papers, Donated by Children, Roosevelt Library, June 16, 1934; Eleanor Roosevelt, op. cit., 16.

45. Ward, op. cit., 116.

46. Sara Delano Roosevelt to Franklin D. Roosevelt and Eleanor Roosevelt, Donated by Children, Roosevelt Family Papers, July 8, 1921; August 10, 1922, Box 9.

47. Ward, op. cit., 184–186.

48. Davis, op. cit., 84–85; Eleanor Roosevelt, op. cit., 11.

49. Davis, op. cit., 660; Eleanor Roosevelt, op. cit., 68.

50. Gunther, op. cit., 62. Gunther quotes Anne O'Hare McCormick.

51. *The New York Times*, July 3, 1932.

52. Moley, op. cit., 139.

53. Samuel Rosenman, *The Public Papers* II, March 12, 1933, 65.

54. Ibid., July 24, 1933, 302.

55. E. Francis Brown, "Roosevelt Takes Control," *Current History* 38 (April 1933), 77.

56. Edith Hensey to President Roosevelt, March 14, 1933, PPF, 200B. Ms. Hensey was a school nurse in Ottumwa, Iowa.

57. E. J. Huyge to President Roosevelt, March 13, 1933, PPF, 200B.

58. Wilbert P. Brunner to President Roosevelt, March 13, 1933, PPF, 200B.

59. J. W. Horner to President Roosevelt, March 14, 1933, PPF, 200B.

60. A. G. to Federal Emergency Relief Administration, December 12, 1934, in Charles McElvaine, op. cit., 60.

61. Anonymous to President Theo. [*sic*] D. Roosevelt, August 22, 1935, in McElvaine, op. cit., 116.

62. Anonymous [children in Warren, Ohio] to President Roosevelt, December 22, 1935, in McElvaine, op. cit., 116.

63. Harry Lewis to President Roosevelt, May 4, 1939, PPF, 200B.

64. *The New York Times*, December 25, 1934.

65. Mrs. M.H.A. to Mrs. F. D. Roosevelt, June 14, 1934, in McElvaine, op. cit., 54–55.

66. Ward, op. cit., 113.

67. Davis, op. cit., 67.

68. Ward, op. cit., 149.

69. Sara Delano Roosevelt to Franklin D. Roosevelt, Roosevelt Family Papers, Donated by Children, n.d. Fall 1896, #7.

70. Sara Delano Roosevelt to Franklin D. Roosevelt, Ibid., October 4, 1896, #10.

71. Sara Delano Roosevelt to Franklin D. Roosevelt, Ibid., January 9, 1903, #8.

72. Sara Delano Roosevelt to Franklin D. Roosevelt, Ibid., April 28, 1903, #8.

73. Arthur M. Schlesinger, Jr., *The Age of Roosevelt: The Crisis of the Old Order, 1919–1933* (Boston: Houghton Mifflin, 1957), 377. Kenneth S. Davis, *FDR: The Beckoning of Destiny*, 125. B. H. Winfield, "Franklin D. Roosevelt's Efforts to Influence News During His First Term Press Conferences," *Presidential Studies Quarterly* II (Spring 1981), 192. Winfield described Roosevelt's press conferences as "the greatest regular show in Washington." John Gunther, op. cit., 62. Abel Green and Joe Laurie, Jr., *Show Biz from Vaude to Video* (New York: Henry Holt and Co., 1961), 405. Gallagher, op. cit., xxii–xiv, 114–116, 190; Ira R. T. Smith, op. cit., 156.

74. Elliot Roosevelt, *An Untold Story* (New York: Putnam and Sons, 1973), 308.

75. James Roosevelt, *Affectionately, FDR*.

76. John A. Boettinger, *A Love in Shadow* (New York: Norton, 1978), 32.

77. Gallagher, op. cit., 135.

78. Gallagher, op. cit., 68–69, for Roosevelt's plans for rehabilitation and recovery in the late 1920s.

79. James Roosevelt, op. cit., 317, Gallagher, op. cit., 136–141. Gallagher states, "It seems almost certain that FDR was not sexually intimate with Missy." Ibid., 138.

80. James Roosevelt, *My Parents: A Differing View* (Chicago: Playboy Press Book, 1976), 17.

81. Gallagher, op. cit., 24–25. Gallagher emphasizes Roosevelt's use of denial in connection with polio.

82. James Roosevelt, *My Parents: A Differing View*, 163.

83. Moley, op. cit., 10, 52. James P. Warburg, an economic advisor of President Roosevelt in 1933, cited the president's desire to be admired as a prime characteristic of his personality. James P. Warburg, *Hell Bent for Election* (Garden City, NY: Doubleday Doran, 1935), 64.

84. Gunther, op. cit., 24–25; Gallagher, op. cit., 115–116.

85. Kenneth S. Davis, *FDR, The New Deal Years, 1933–1937: A History* (New York: Random House, 1986), 202–203, 206; Gallagher, op. cit., 124–129.

86. Daniel J. Boorstin, "Selling the President to the People," *Commentary* 20 (November 1955), 421–427. Newspapers had an average daily circulation of over 44

million in 1930. Radio sets had expanded from 8.5 million in 1928 to 18 million in 1932 and 36 million in 1936.

87. Boettinger, op. cit., 73.

88. Betty H. Winfield, "Franklin D. Roosevelt's Efforts to Influence the News During His First Term Press Conferences," 189–190.

89. Winfield, *FDR and the News Media* (Urbana: University of Illinois Press, 1980), 43.

90. Winfield, "Franklin D. Roosevelt's Efforts to Influence the News During His First Term Press Conferences," 192.

91. Winfield, *FDR and the News Media*, 65.

92. Ibid., 57.

93. *The New York Times*, May 25, 1934.

94. Ibid., September 12, 1935.

95. Ibid., April 14, 1935.

96. Winfield, *FDR and the News Media*, 61.

97. The relations between President Roosevelt and the newspaper media are ably discussed in Richard W. Steele, *Propaganda in an Open Society: The Roosevelt Administration and the Media, 1933–1941* (Westport, CT: Greenwood Press, 1985), 33–65 and Winfield, *FDR and the News Media*, 26–43.

98. Steele, op. cit., 39.

99. A. Merriam Smith, *Thank You Mr. President: A White House Notebook* (New York: Harper and Bros., 1946), 23; Winfield, *FDR and the News Media*, 60, 63–66.

100. Steele, op. cit., 51.

101. Perkins, op. cit., 72.

102. Mrs. Walter F. Hodges, March 13, 1933, PPF 200B.

103. Louis Hofacker, Jr., March 13, 1933, PPF 200B.

104. Ben E. Harris, March 13, 1933, PPF 200B.

CHAPTER 3

1. Walter Lippman, *Interpretations, 1933–1935* (New York: Macmillan, 1936), 249.

2. *Historical Statistics of the United States*, I, 228.

3. Ibid., 319.

4. Ibid., 241.

5. Ibid., 319; ibid., II, 718.

6. Ibid., I, 522.

7. Ibid., 400.

8. Ibid., II, 992–993; Frank Freidel, "The New Deal Laying the Foundation for Modern America," in Wilbur Cohen, ed., *The Roosevelt New Deal: A Program Assessment after Fifty Years* (Austin, TX: Lyndon B. Johnson School of Public Affairs, 1986), 14–15. See also Bradford Lee, "The New Deal Reconsidered," *Wilson Quarterly* 6 (Spring 1982), 64.

9. *Statistical Abstract of the United States, 1939* (Washington, DC, 1939), 315; *Statistical Abstract of the United States, 1943* (Washington, DC, 1943), 398–399.

10. A complete breakdown on unemployment figures for 1932 through 1940 reveals:

Year	Civilian Labor Force	Employed	Unemployed	% Unemployed (in millions)
1932	51,000	38,940	12,060	23.6
1933	51,590	38,760	12,830	24.9
1934	52,230	40,890	11,340	21.7
1935	52,870	42,260	10,610	20.1
1936	53,440	44,410	9,030	16.9
1937	54,000	46,300	7,700	14.3
1938	54,610	44,220	10,390	19.0
1939	55,230	45,750	9,480	17.2
1940	55,640	47,520	8,120	14.6

Historical Statistics of the United States I, 126, 135.

11. Ibid., 299. Accurate figures are available only for 1935–1936 when 38% received less than $1,000 per year. This information came from *Consumer Incomes in the United States: Their Distribution in 1935–1936* (Washington, DC, 1938); The figure for minimum subsistence is cited in James T. Patterson, *America's Struggle Against Poverty*, 59.

12. Esther Fano. "A Wastage of Men: Technological Progress and Unemployment in the United States," *Technology and Culture* 32 (1991), 264–292.

13. Ibid., 277.

14. See a very perceptive article by Richard J. Jensen, "The Causes and Cures of Unemployment: The Great Depression," *The Journal of Interdisciplinary History* 19 (Spring 1989), 553–584. Note Edward Webster to Harry Hopkins, December 8, 1934, Box 67 (HP).

15. Perkins, op. cit., 328.

16. Frank Freidel, *The New Deal in Historical Perspective* (Washington, DC: Service Center for Teachers of History, 1965), in Barton Bernstein and Allen Matusow, eds. *Twentieth Century America: Recent Interpretations* (New York: Harcourt Brace, 1969), 251.

17. Grace Tully, *F.D.R. My Boss* (New York: Scribners, 1949), 112.

18. Rosenman, *The Public Papers* 1, 754–755.

19. Ibid., V, 233.

20. Ibid., V, 488, IV, 341.

21. For the view of Roosevelt as a conservative though rhetorical liberal, see Barton Bernstein, "The New Deal: The Conservative Achievements of Liberal Reform," in Barton Bernstein, ed., *Towards a New Past, Dissenting Essays in American History* (New York: Pantheon Books, 1968), 263–288.

22. Rosenman, *The Public Papers*, V, 389–390.

23. Rosenman, *The Public Papers*, 1, 649.

24. James MacGregor Burns, *The Lion and the Fox* (New York: Harcourt Brace, 1956), 183–208, develops the position that Roosevelt's policies in 1933 and 1934 resembled that of a "master broker" among interest groups. Professor Ellis W. Hawley believes that a major goal among architects of the New Deal especially before 1935 was to develop an effective business–government partnership, "an organizational commonwealth," to benefit society, and hence a larger perspective than interest-group politics. Its essence remained, however, cooperative attitudes and actions between business, government, and society. Ellis W. Hawley "The Corporate

Ideal and Liberal Philosophy in the New Deal," in Wilbur Cohen (ed.), *The Roosevelt New Deal* (1986), 85–103. Hawley more than Burns notes the persistence of the "associative vision" in the New Deal after 1934.

25. Albert U. Romasco, *The Politics of Recovery: Roosevelt's New Deal* (New York: Oxford University Press, 1983), 243–245. On New Deal expenditures in different parts of the country, see Leonard J. Arrington, "The Sagebrush Resurrection: New Deal Expenditures in Western States, 1933–1939," in *Pacific Historical Review* 52, No. 1 (1983), 6–7.

26. Burns, op. cit., 184.

27. William E. Leuchtenburg, *Franklin D. Roosevelt and the New Deal* (New York: Harper and Row, 1963), 146–147, 163.

28. Burns, op. cit., 197–205.

29. Moley, op. cit., 159.

30. Romasco, op. cit., 48.

31. Burns, op. cit., 183.

32. On the New Deal's agricultural programs and their effects, see Richard S. Kirkendall, "The New Deal and Agriculture," in John Braemen, Robert Bremner, and David Brody, eds., *The New Deal: The National Level* (Columbus: Ohio State University Press, 1975), 83–108; Paul L. Mertz, *New Deal Policy and Southern Rural Poverty* (Baton Rouge: Louisiana State University Press, 1978) *passim*; and Pete Daniel, *Breaking the Land: The Transformation of Cotton, Tobacco, and Rice Cultures Since 1880* (Urbana and Chicago: University of Illinois Press, 1985), 90–109. For Roosevelt's statement to Norman Thomas, see Freidel, *Franklin D. Roosevelt: A Rendezvous with Destiny* (Boston: Little Brown, 1990), 145.

33. Kirkendall, "The New Deal and Agriculture," 98–100.

34. Ellis W. Hawley, *The New Deal and the Problem of Monopoly* (Princeton, NJ: Princeton University Press, 1966), 35–36. See also Kim McQuaid, *Big Business and Presidential Power, From FDR to Reagan* (New York: William Morrow and Co., 1982), 18–61.

35. Leuchtenburg, op. cit., 57–58, 63–71.

36. Romasco, op. cit., 191.

37. Ibid., 214.

38. James A. Hodges, *New Deal Labor Policy and the Southern Textile Industry* (Knoxville: University of Tennessee, 1986), 28–29, 139–140.

39. Leuchtenburg, op. cit., 69; Romasco, op. cit., 214.

40. Patterson, *America's Struggle Against Poverty*, 57.

41. Ibid., 76.

42. Ibid., 58–59.

43. Ibid.

44. Freidel, *Franklin D. Roosevelt* op. cit., 135; Bonnie Fox Schwartz, *The Civil Works Administration, 1933–1934; The Business of Emergency Employment in the New Deal* (Princeton, NJ: Princeton University Press, 1984), 213–220.

45. Romasco, op. cit., 52–64.

46. James S. Olson, *Saving Capitalism, The Reconstruction Finance Corporation and the New Deal, 1933–1940* (Princeton, NJ: Princeton University Press, 1988), 127.

47. Arrington, "The Sagebrush Resurrection: New Deal Expenditures in the Western States, 1933–1939," 6.

48. On Roosevelt's popularity in 1934, see Bruce Bliven, "What of Roosevelt Now?" *Current History* 40 (April 1934), 1–2.

49. Arthur M. Schlesinger, Jr., *The Age of Roosevelt: The Coming of the New Deal* (Boston: Houghton Mifflin, 1958), 499–500.

50. Romasco, op. cit., 216–222.

51. The classic study on the subject is George Wolfskill and John A. Hudson, *All But the People, Franklin D. Roosevelt and His Critics* (London: The Macmillan Company, 1969).

52. William O. Douglas, *Go East, Young Man, The Early Years: The Autobiography of William O. Douglas* (New York: Random House, 1974), 363.

53. Freidel, op. cit., 145.

54. Burns, op cit., 223.

55. Leuchtenburg, op. cit., 146; Frank Freidel declares Roosevelt "never ceased to hope for business cooperation with the New Deal." Freidel, op. cit., 257.

56. Alan Brinkley, *Voices of Protest: Huey Long, Father Coughlin and the Great Depression* (New York: Knopf, 1982), 72.

57. William I. Hair, *The Kingfish and His Realm: The Life and Times of Huey P. Long* (Baton Rouge: Louisiana State University Press, 1992), 285–288.

58. David M. Kennedy, *Freedom From Fear: The American People in Depression and War* (New York: Oxford University Press, 1999), 218–248; Romasco, op. cit., 204.

59. Rosenman, *The Public Papers*, IV, 15, 21–22. Roosevelt told an emissary of publisher William Randolph Hearst in May 1935, "I am fighting communism, Huey Longism, Coughlinism, Townsendism." And he added, "I want to save our system, the capitalistic system; to save it is to give some heed to world thought of today. I want to equalize the distribution of wealth." Arthur Schlesinger, Jr., *The Age of Roosevelt: The Politics of Upheaval, 1935–1936* (Boston: Houghton Mifflin 1966), 325.

60. Freidel, op. cit., 168.

61. Ibid., 169.

62. James T. Patterson, *Congressional Conservatism and the New Deal* (Lexington: University of Kentucky Press, 1967), 52.

63. Walter Lippman, *Interpretations, 1933–1935* (New York: Macmillian, 1936), as quoted by Freidel, op. cit., 169.

64. J. Joseph Huthmacher, *Senator Robert Wagner and the Rise of Liberalism* (New York: Atheneum, 1968), 194.

65. Irving Bernstein, *A Caring Society: The New Deal, the Worker, and the Great Depression* (Boston: Houghton Mifflin, 1985), 50.

66. Arthur M. Schlesinger, Jr., *The Coming of the New Deal* (Boston: Houghton Mifflin, 1958), 301–315; Frances Fox Piven and Richard A. Cloward, *Regulating the Poor: The Function of Public Welfare* (New York: Vintage Books, 1971), 91–94.

67. James T. Patterson, "Comparative Welfare History: Britain and the United States, 1930–1945," in Wilbur Cohen, ed., op. cit., 125–143.

68. Mark H. Leff, *The Limits of Symbolic Reform: The New Deal and Taxation, 1933–1939* (New York: Cambridge University Press, 1984), 1–19.

69. Rosenman, *Public Papers*, IV, 271–275; Leff, op. cit., 152.

70. Leff, op. cit., 11–47; see especially Table 1 on page 12.

71. Patterson, *Congressional Conservatism and the New Deal*, 69.

72. Rosenman, *Public Papers*, V, 40.

73. Arrington, op. cit., 6.

74. Patterson, *America's Struggle Against Poverty*, 63.

75. Bernstein, *A Caring Society*, 151; William R. Brock, *Welfare, Democracy and the New Deal* (New York: Cambridge University Press, 1988), 280.

76. Patterson, *America's Struggle Against Poverty*, 63–64; Piven and Cloward, op. cit., 98; Irving Bernstein, op. cit., 151.

77. Patterson, op. cit., 61–62; Piven and Cloward, op. cit., 112.

78. Patterson, op. cit., 62; Piven and Cloward, op. cit., 284–290.

79. Brock, op. cit., 281.

80. Patterson, op. cit., 64.

81. Bernstein, *A Caring Society*, 154.

82. Brock, op. cit., 326–327.

83. Patterson, op. cit., 62.

84. D. Jerome Tweton, *The New Deal at the Grass Roots: Programs for the People in Otter Tail County, Minnesota* (St. Paul: Minnesota Historical Society, 1988), 52.

85. Ellery F. Reed, "What Turning Relief Back to Local Community Meant in Cincinnati," *The Social Science Review* 12 (1939), 1–20; Brock, op. cit., 327–328.

86. Piven and Cloward, op. cit., 109.

87. Ben Shahn (October 1935), 6036-M2, 6069-M1, 6106-M5, 6032-M1; photographs taken by photographers of the Farm Security Administration may be found in Prints and Photography Division of the Library of Congress; hereafter cited as (LC).

88. Russell Lee (June 1939), 33672-D, 12267-M3 (LC).

89. Russell Lee (April 1939), 32793-D; John Vachon (1939), 61913D(LC).

90. Dorothea Lange (February 1939), 19075-E(LC).

91. Russell Lee (August–November 1937), 30442-D, 30732-A, 30453-D(LC).

92. Arthur Rothstein (January 1939), 26821-D, 26811-D(LC).

93. Russell Lee (July 1939), 33871-D, 33945-D, 33845-D(LC).

94. Burns, op. cit., 289; Leuchtenburg, op. cit., 231–251; Freidel, op. cit., 240–257.

95. Rosenman, *Public Papers*, VI, 387.

96. James T. Patterson, *Congressional Conservatism and the New Deal*, 327.

97. Patterson, ibid., 325–337; Freidel, op. cit., 240–242.

98. Patterson, ibid., 334–335.

99. An anti-lynching bill, which Roosevelt supported, was filibustered into extinction in February 1938; Freidel, op. cit., 247.

100. Patterson, op. cit., 334–337. The Fair Labor Standards Act provided for a 40-cent minimum wage and 40 hour maximum worktime for workers, beginning in 1940, but permitted numerous exemptions and exceptions. Nevertheless, the bill raised wages for workers in many industries, including southern textiles and shoes, and effectively prohibited child labor.

101. Ibid., 288–324.

102. Leuchtenburg, op. cit., 231–251; Kennedy, op. cit., 325–338.

103. Freidel, op. cit., 255–256; Alan Brinkley, *The End of Reform: New Deal Liberalism in Recession and War* (New York: Alfred A. Knopf, 1995), 99.

104. George Gallup, *The Gallup Poll: Public Opinion, 1935–1971* (New York: Random House, 1972), 183.

105. *The New York Times*, March 5, 1935; *The Washington Post*, March 5, 1935; New York *Herald Tribune*, March 5, 1935.

106. Irving Bernstein, *A History of the American Worker, 1920–1933: The Lean Years* (Boston: Houghton Mifflin, 1960), 416–455. Ronald Lawson, ed., with the assistance of Mark Naison, *The Tenement Movement in New York City* (New Brunswick, NJ: Rutgers University Press, 1986), 99–118.

107. Arthur M. Schlesinger, Jr., *The Crisis of the Old Order, 1919–1933*, 255–256, 263–264.

108. Stock, op. cit., 39.

CHAPTER 4

1. Hope's role in the positive behavioral results of individuals is extensively explained in psychological literature, especially in cognitive psychology. A good introduction to this research is in C. R. Snyder and Donelson Forsyth, *Handbook of Social and Clinical Psychology* (New York: Pergamon Press, 1990), 287–303; C. Rick Snyder, "Hope for the Journey," a paper by Snyder given at the University of Kansas, June 5–6, 1991, sponsored by the Beach Center on Families and Disabilities at the University of Kansas (courtesy of the author), a dissertation by one of Snyder's students, John R. Anderson, "The Role of Hope, Goal Setting, Expectancy About Future Success, and Coping" (University of Kansas, 1988), which reviews literature in the field. See also Jerome D. Frank, "The Role of Hope in Psychotherapy," *International Journal of Psychiatry* 5 (1968), 363–397; C. R. Snyder et al., "The Will and the Ways," *Journal of Personality and Social Psychology* 60 (1991), 570–585; Michael F. Schier and Charles J. Carver, "Optimism, Coping and Health: Assessment and Implications of Generalized Outcome Expectancies," *Health Psychology* 4 (1985), 219–247. On self-efficacy, the classic article is Albert Bandura, "Self-Efficacy: Towards a Unifying Theory of Behavioral Change," *Psychological Review* 84 (1977), 191–215.

2. "What I want you to do," Harry Hopkins told Lorena Hickok, an FERA reporter in July 1933, "is to go out around the country and look this thing over. I don't want statistics from you. I don't want the social worker angle. I just want your own reaction, as an ordinary citizen." Richard Lowitt and Maurine Beasley, *One Third of a Nation: Lorena Hickok Reports on the Great Depression* (Urbana: University of Illinois Press 1981), ix. Another massive effort that led to national self-discovery through federal auspices came later, after 1935, through thousands of life histories (interviews) of the Federal Writer's Project with ordinary Americans. Despite weaknesses in the methods of interviews, untrained interviewers, some rewriting of interviews for literary purposes, and the determination of William Couch, director of the FWP life history project in the South, to focus the attention of his interviewers on sturdy southern folk to compensate for the distorted image of the South portrayed by writers like Erskine Caldwell, the life histories, overall, provide useful qualitative information for the historian. I have chosen to use material from this vast source, not as part of the "American Scene," but rather in a discussion of rural America, "Small Worlds Sustained" (Chapter 5).

3. Erskine Caldwell and Margaret Bourke-White, *Say, Is This the U.S.A.* (New York: Duell, Sloan and Pearce, 1941), 10–11.

4. Harry W. Francis to Harry Hopkins, December 7, 1934, Box 65 (HP).

5. Lowitt and Beasley, op. cit., 85.

6. David P. Peeler, "Unlonesome Highway: The Quest for Fact and Fellowship in Depression America," *Journal of American Studies* 18 (1984), 200–201, 203. There were, of course, desperate people described by the travelers. One might note Theodore Dreiser's description of an unemployed worker who committed suicide in *Tragic America* (New York: Horace Liverwright, 1932), 16–17, and a similar description in Erskine Caldwell, *Some American People* (New York: Robert M. McBride and Company, 1935), 118–123.

7. Lowitt and Beasley, op. cit., 44–51.

8. Ibid., 72.

9. Ibid., 83–84.

10. Ibid., 90, 117.

11. Ibid., 190.

12. Ibid., 338, 340.

13. Ibid., 335, 341.

14. Ibid., 112, 119.

15. Henry W. Francis to Harry Hopkins, November 25, 1934, Box 66 (HP).

16. Henry W. Francis to Harry Hopkins, December 7, 1934, Box 66 (HP).

17. Henry W. Francis to Harry Hopkins, November 10, 1934, Box 66 (HP).

18. David Maynard to Harry Hopkins, November 15, 1934, Box 66 (HP).

19. Hazel Reavis to Harry Hopkins, November 12, 1934, Box 66 (HP).

20. Hazel Reavis to Harry Hopkins, November 18, 1934, Box 66 (HP).

21. Thomas Steep to Harry Hopkins, November 17, 1934, Box 66 (HP).

22. Martha Gellhorn to Harry Hopkins, November 11, 1934, Box 66 (HP).

23. James Rorty, *Where Life Is Better: An Unsentimental American Journey* (New York: Reynolds & Hitchcock, 1936), 55.

24. Sherwood Anderson, *Puzzled America* (Mamaroneck, NY: P. P. Appel, 1970), 166.

25. Lowitt and Beasley, op. cit., 223.

26. Ibid., 36, 37.

27. Ibid., 126–127, 335.

28. Ibid., 204–205.

29. Ibid., 206.

30. Wayne Parrish to Harry Hopkins, November 11, 1934, Box 66 (HP).

31. Lisa Wilson to Harry Hopkins, December 6, 1934, Box 67 (HP).

32. Wayne Parrish to Harry Hopkins, November 24, 1934, Box 66 (HP).

33. Thomas Steep to Harry Hopkins, November 4, 1934, Box 66 (HP).

34. Thomas Steep to Harry Hopkins, November 4, 1934, Box 66 (HP).

35. Lowitt and Beasley, op. cit., 275.

36. Wayne Parrish to Harry Hopkins, November 11, 1934, Box 66 (HP).

37. The polls conducted in March and December 1939 were announced by the Roper Center in Williamstown, Massachusetts, and were summarized in "The People of the U.S.A.," *Fortune* 21 (February 1940), 14, 20, 28, 133, 134, 136. A valuable interpretation of their contents may be found in Sidney Verba and Kay Lehman Schlozman, "Unemployment, Class Consciousness, and Radical Politics: What Didn't Happen in the Thirties," *The Journal of Politics* 39 (May 1977), 291–323. As Verba and Schlozman attest, the value of the Roper polls would be enhanced if more un-

employed workers had been surveyed. They constituted in poll percentage less than half their number in society. Ibid., 298.

38. Ibid., 302.

39. Ibid., 305–306, 309.

40. Ibid., 319–321.

41. The FSA photographs numbering in excess of 60,000 along with more than 180,000 negatives are in the Prints and Photographs Division of the Library of Congress in the FSA-OWI collection. This includes pictures by photographers of the Resettlement Administration from 1935 to 1937 when that organization was replaced by the FSA. Percentages of photographs in the FSA collections other than the South were 22% for the West, 23% for the North Central, and 12.9% for the Northeast. See Nicholas Natanson, *The Black Image in the New Deal: The Politics of FSA Photography* (Knoxville: University of Tennessee Press, 1992), 69.

42. Paul Hendrickson, *Looking for the Light: The Hidden Life and Art of Marion Post Wolcott* (New York: Knopf, 1992), 53.

43. Dorothea Lange to Roy Stryker, December 13, 1939, Roy E. Stryker Papers, microfilm, University of Louisville.

44. Roy E. Stryker and Nancy Wood, *In This Proud Land: America 1935–1943 as Seen in the FSA Photographs* (Greenwich, CT: New York Graphic Society, 1973), 14.

45. Werner J. Severin, "Cameras with a Purpose: The Photojournalists of F.S.A," *Journalism Quarterly* 41 (1964), 194. Severin estimates that about 175 newspapers and magazines used FSA pictures between 1938 and 1940. On additional FSA picture distribution information, see Moren Stange, *Symbols of Ideal Life: Social Documentary Photography in America, 1900–1950* (New York: Cambridge University Press, 1989), 108.

46. David P. Peeler, *Hope Among Us Yet: Social Criticism and Social Solace in Depression America* (Athens: University of Georgia, 1987), 81; James Curtis, *Mind's Eye, Mind's Truth: FSA Photography Reconsidered* (Philadelphia: Temple University Press, 1989), 49–50.

47. Ibid., 23–44, for a sharp criticism of Evans whom Curtis regards as too artistic to be objective or reliable with the camera. For identical criticism, see James C. Curtis and Sheila Grannen, "Let Us Now Approve Famous Photographs," *Winterthur Portfolio* 15 (Spring 1980), 1–25.

48. Natanson, op. cit., 11.

49. Curtis, op. cit., 32. For the essential quality of Walker Evans's photographs of the Burroughs and their house, see Michael Brix and Birgit Mayer, *Walker Evans America* (New York: Rizzoli 1991), photographs, 78–96.

50. Curtis, op. cit., 52–55.

51. Ibid., 101–103.

52. Dorothea Lange, "Former Nebraska Farmer, Now a Migrant Farm Worker in Oregon," August 1939, Prints and Photographs Division, Library of Congress, 20908-D; hereafter cited as (LC).

53. James Agee and Walker Evans, *Let Us Now Praise Famous Men* (Boston: Houghton Mifflin, 1942); William Stott, *Documentary Expression and Thirties America* (Chicago: University of Chicago, 1986), 286–287; Lawrence W. Levine, "The Historian and the Icon," in Carl Fleischauer and Beverly Brannon, *Documenting America* (Berkeley: University of California Press, 1988), 21–22.

54. R. Lee, June 1939, 33418-D (LC).

55. R. Lee, August 1937, 11256-M2 (LC).

56. R. Lee, September 1937, 11319-M4; R. Lee, May 1938, 11448-M2 (LC).

57. John Vachon, July 1940, 1991-M3 (LC).

58. R. Lee, February 1940, 35086-D; another typical example is R. Lee, May 1938, 31161-D (LC).

59. Dorothea Lange, October 1939, 21381-D (LC).

60. R. Lee, September 1937, 11319-M5 (LC).

61. John Vachon, July 1940, 1973-M3 (LC).

62. R. Lee, June 1938, 33597-D (LC).

63. R. Lee, May 1938, 61044-D, 31188-D (LC).

64. John Vachon, September 1939, 1502-M1 (LC).

65. Peeler, *Hope Among Us Yet*, 65, 103.

66. John Szarkowski, *Photography Until Now* (New York: Museum of Modern Art, 1989), 216.

67. Stryker and Wood, op. cit., 7, 14.

68. The murals by the Treasury Section of Fine Arts (called the Treasury Section of Painting and Sculpture until 1937) decorating public buildings as well as post offices are less numerous than those provided by the Federal Arts Project. The section's murals are, however, much more useful for a student of popular culture because historical records on the evolution of the murals, including reactions of persons in the community for which the mural was designed, are complete. Not so for the Federal Arts Program murals. Karal Ann Marling, *Wall-to-Wall America: A Cultural History of Post Offices in the Great Depression* (Minneapolis: University of Minnesota Press, 1982), viii–ix.

69. Karal Ann Marling, "A Note on New Deal Iconography; Futurology and the Historical Myth," in Jack Solzman ed., *Prospects: An Annual of American Cultural Studies* IV, (1979), 425–426. This is an especially valuable article.

70. Sue Bridwell Beckham, *Depression Post Office Murals and Southern Culture* (Baton Rouge and London: Louisiana State University, 1989), 151–244, 292–293; Marling, *Wall-to-Wall America*, 248–249.

71. Beckham, op. cit., 102–107.

72. Ibid., 50–55.

73. Marling, *Wall-to-Wall America*, 213–219.

74. Ibid., 174–175.

75. Ibid., 62–71.

76. Ibid., 136–141, 143–145, 149, 152–155; Marling, "A Note on New Deal Iconography," 433–437.

77. Marling, "A Note on New Deal Iconography," 438.

78. John J. Griffin, Public Reaction, March 4, 1933, PPF 200B; Tom Coffey to President Roosevelt, Public Reaction, March 4, 1933, PPF 200B.

79. Mrs. Joseph Goodman to President Roosevelt, Public Reaction, March 4, 1933, PPF 200B, Mr. Louis Issaccson to President Roosevelt, Public Reaction, March 4, 1933, PPF 200B.

80. Mrs. E. L. Asnis to President Roosevelt, Public Reaction, January 4, 1935, PPF 200B.

81. Edwin C. Hill to President Roosevelt, Public Reaction, March 4, 1933, PPF 200B.

82. Walton Sims to President Roosevelt, Public Reaction, June 28, 1934, PPF 200B.

83. O. A. Seideman to President Roosevelt, Public Reaction, April 28, 1935, PPF 200B.

84. Elias Brailas to President Roosevelt, Public Reaction, June 27, 1936, PPF 200B.

85. Dr. Werner Boer to President Roosevelt, Public Reaction, June 27, 1936, PPF 200B.

86. John Vachon, Cincinnati, Ohio, October 1938, 1210-M2, 1214-M3 (LC).

87. John Vachon, Omaha, Nebraska, November 1938, 1306-M5, 1300-M1 (LC).

88. Russell Lee, Donaldsonville, Louisiana, November 1938, 11784-M1 (LC).

89. Ben Shahn, Ashville, Ohio, July 4, 1938, 6444-M2 (LC).

90. Russell Lee, Posey, Indiana, February 1937, 10398-E (LC); St. Augustine, Texas, April 1939, 33006-D (LC).

91. Russell Lee, The Scarborough Family, Laurel, Mississippi, 1939, in Patti Carr Black, *Documentary Photographs of Mississippi: The Thirties* (Jackson: University Press of Mississippi, 1982), 72.

92. Ibid., 114.

93. Russell Lee, New Madrid County, Missouri, May 1938, 31195-D (LC); Russell Lee, Warner, Oklahoma, June 1939, 33472-D (LC).

94. *Historical Statistics of the United States*, I, 55.

95. *Statistical Abstract of the United States, 1943*, 78–79.

96. *Historical Statistics*, I, 74.

97. Faith M. Williams, "Changes in Family Expenditures in the Post-war Period," *Monthly Labor Review* (November 1938), 973.

98. *Historical Statistics*, I, 330.

99. *Historical Statistics*, I, 379, 386; *Statistical Abstract, 1942*, 139.

100. *Historical Statistics*, II, 783, 808–809.

101. Examples of this are Walker Evans's street scene in Vicksburg, Mississippi, March 1936, in Patti Carr Black, op. cit., 36, and Ben Shahn's picture of Plain City, Ohio, August 1938, 6646-M2 (LC).

102. Duncan McHolthousen, op. cit., 112.

103. Lowitt and Beasley, op. cit., 335.

104. *Statistical Abstract, 1942*, 465; *Historical Statistics*, I, 711, 716, 718. On auto operating expenses, see Julius Weinberger, "Economic Aspects of Recreation," *Harvard Business Review* 15 (Summer 1937), 462. On filling stations, see *Statistical Abstract, 1942*, 965.

105. Marion Post Wolcott, 30436-M2, 30439-M2, 30439-M3 (LC). On the Hialeah racetrack see, for example, 30461-M4, 30473-M4 (LC).

106. *Historical Statistics*, I, 401.

107. *The New York Times*, August 15, 1934.

108. James Rorty, op. cit., 273–274.

CHAPTER 5

1. The best study of radicalism among farmers in the Midwest, centering on the Farmer's Holiday Association, is John Shover, *Cornbelt Rebellion: The Farmer's Hol-*

iday Association (Urbana: University of Illinois Press, 1965). For the South, see Donald H. Grubbs, *Cry from Cotton: The Southern Tenant Farmer's Union and the New Deal* (Chapel Hill: University of North Carolina Press, 1971), and Jack Temple Kirby, *Rural Worlds Lost: The American South, 1920–1960* (Baton Rouge and London: Louisiana State University Press, 1987), 259–271. Both the Farmer's Holiday Association and the Southern Tenant Farmers' Union had small memberships and limited geographic outreach and both dissolved as effective organizations during the 1930s.

  2. There have been a number of excellent studies of rural life describing its economic and social transformation in the twentieth century. For one that stresses the pivotal influence of the 1920s, see Don S. Kirschner, *City and Country: Rural Responses to Urbanization in the 1920's* (Westport, CT: Greenwood, 1940). Kirschner describes changes "transforming the nation from a basically rural to an increasingly urban society" (12). He also observed that urban "bright lights" were gradually seducing ruralities from their "simple living." David B. Danborn, *The Resisted Revolution: Urban America and the Industrialization of Agriculture, 1900–1930* (Ames: University of Iowa Press, 1979), notes sweeping changes in rural life by 1930. Some very exceptional recent books have dealt with the same subject: Catherine McNicol Stock, *Main Street in Crisis: The Great Depression and the Old Middle Class on the Northern Plains* (Chapel Hill: University of North Carolina Press, 1992); Pete Daniel, *Breaking the Land: The Transformation of Cotton, Tobacco, and Rice Cultures Since 1880* (Urbana: University of Illinois Press, 1985); and Jack Temple Kirby, *Rural Worlds Lost; the American South 1920–1960* (Baton Rouge: Louisiana State University Press, 1987). The thrust of each of these studies is primarily economic, though Stock notes that the ideals of "Dakotans" survived the New Deal and that they remained, in keeping with tradition, opposed to big government and welfare policies after the 1930s. Daniel emphasizes the triumph of big agriculture in the 1930s, resulting in an "enclosure movement" that displaced the croppers, depopulated rural areas, and diminished the sense of community that had existed in the rural South. Since Daniel's emphasis is economic transformation, he makes little mention of the older rural South that survived, such as family life, churches, rural newspapers, and small-town sanctions. Jack T. Kirby better noted the gradual character of transformation in the South and how incomplete that change was by 1940. Note Kirby, op. cit., 118–154. Although Kirby recognized the impact of modernization in the South in the 1930s, he puts emphasis "on the most dramatic transformations" in the 1940s and 1950s. Ibid., 275. Kirby sees modernization a result of farmers abandoning self-sustaining farms, possible once automobiles led to cash jobs and hence migration to the cities and ultimately the triumph of the supermarket or company store as food supplier. Concurrently, rural youth were attracted to the city by better economic opportunities. Kirby also notes, however, that the older rural culture in the South was still strong in the 1930s with loafing, visiting cockfighting, traveling carnivals, moonshine, local fairs, local baseball teams, hunting, fishing, and so on. See Kirby, op. cit., 300–303, 204–214. The National Automobile Chamber of Commerce estimated in 1930, for example, that 42% of automobiles registered were on farms and in towns of less than 1,000 residents, and 47.6% were registered for persons in communities with populations less than 2,500. Michael Berger, *The Devil's Wagon in God's Country: The Automobile and Social Change in Rural America, 1893–1929* (Hamden, CT: Archon, 1979), 51.

3. Edward Moe and Carl C. Taylor, *Culture of a Contemporary Rural Community: Irwin, Iowa* (Washington, DC: U.S. Department of Agriculture, 1942), 1.

4. Henry C. Nixon, *Possum Trot: Rural Community South* (Norman: University of Oklahoma Press, 1941), 9–56.

5. Edmund de S. Brunner and H. Kolb, *Rural Social Trends* (New York: McGraw-Hill, 1933), 151–159, 217, on abandonment of weaker churches and presence of chain stores in rural areas and small towns. Dwight Sanderson, *Research Memorandum on Rural Life in the Depression* (New York: Social Science Research Council, 1937), 85–87, on rural school consolidation. See also Kirby, op. cit., 115–154; Stock, op. cit., 155–156; Moe and Taylor, op. cit., 42, 72.

6. James West (Carl Withers), *Plainville, U.S.A.* (New York: Columbia University Press, 1945), 3–4.

7. Carl H. Bell, *Culture of a Contemporary Rural Community: Sublette, Kansas* (Washington, DC: Department of Agriculture, 1942), 68–70.

8. Margaret Jarman Hagood, "The Farm Home and Family," in Carl C. Taylor, *Rural Life in the United States* (Westport, CT: Greenwood Press, 1972), 52–53.

9. Deborah Fink, *Agrarian Women: Wives and Mothers in Rural Nebraska, 1880–1940* (Chapel Hill: University of North Carolina Press, 1992), 173.

10. Moe and Taylor, op. cit., 30, 70; Stock, op. cit., 89; Bell, op. cit., 102; Kenneth MacLeish and Kimball Young, *Culture of a Contemporary Rural Community: Landaff, New Hampshire* (Washington, DC: U.S. Department of Agriculture, 1942), 67, 89.

11. Bell, op. cit., 102; Mary Neth, "Leisure and Generational Change: Farm Youth in the Midwest, 1910–1940," *Agricultural History* 67 (Spring 1993), 172; Fink, op. cit., 117.

12. Pete Daniel, op. cit., 168–183; Jack T. Kirby, op. cit., 77–78; William Graeber, "A Farm Family Enters the Modern World," *The Palimpsest* 68 (Summer 1987), 89–90.

13. The Brattleboro *Reformer*, June 7, 1936, July 3, 1936; see also for examples the *Beloit* (Kansas) *Call*, July 14, 1936. Russell Lee provided a picture of "swing dancing" in a roadhouse in Vacherie, Louisiana, in September 1938. Russell Lee 11661-M2 (LC).

14. Augusta (Kansas) *Daily Gazette*, July 21, 1934; DeKalb (Illinois) *Chronicle*, January 6, 1934; note as well Grand Rapids (Minn.) *Herald Review*, April 11, 1934.

15. Russell Lee, August 1937, 11291-M3; September 1938, 11805-M5, (LC).

16. Augusta (Kansas) *Daily Gazette*, July 1, 1933; Elba (Alabama) *Clipper*, January 19, 1933.

17. West, op. cit., 110.

18. Bell, op. cit., 75. Moe and Taylor, op. cit., 53. Hortense Powdermaker, *After Freedom: A Cultural Study in the Deep South* (New York: Russell and Russell, 1968), 18.

19. Jacquelyn Dowd Hall et al., *Like a Family: The Making of a Southern Cotton Mill World* (Chapel Hill: University of North Carolina Press, 1987), 258. An excellent exposition of resistance by rural youth as well as acceptance of modern culture in the 1930s is Mary Neth, "Leisure and Generational Change: Farm Youth in the Midwest 1910–1940," op. cit., 163–184.

20. John Leighly, ed., *Land and Life: A Selection from the Writings of Carl Ortwin Sauer* (Berkeley and Los Angeles: University of California Press, 1963), 41.

21. Margaret Jarman Hagood, "The Farm Home and Family," in *Rural Life in the United States*, 41–42. Hagood observes that in the 1940s approximately nine out of ten farms were still family farms.

22. Margaret Jarman Hagood, "Rural Population Characteristics," in *Rural Life in the United States*, 228; *Sixteenth Census of the United States Population*, vols. II and IV. An exception to this rule occurred among black farm families in the South where, according to FERA calculations among relief recipients in cotton areas in 1933–1934, more than 17% had one adult as head, though this included widows, widowers, and those deserted and divorced. The same investigation for whites revealed 6% in the same categories. Kirby, op. cit., 173.

23. Harry Crews, *A Childhood: The Biography of a Place* (New York: Harper and Row, 1978), 14. Most births in rural areas as late as 1942 did not occur in hospitals. Douglas Ensminger and T. Wilson Longmore, "Rural Health," in *Rural Life in the United States*, 165.

24. Fink, op. cit., 162.

25. Hagood, "The Farm Home and Family," op. cit., 39–40. Katherine Jellison, *Entitled to Power: Farm Women and Technology, 1913–1963* (Chapel Hill: University of North Carolina Press, 1993), 91, notes the widespread use of battery-powered radios in the farm households; 87.2% in North Dakota, 73.2% in Kansas and 76.7% in Nebraska. Moe and Taylor, op. cit., 55. John Modell, *Into One's Own: From Youth to Adulthood in the United States* (Berkeley: University of California Press, 1989), 89.

26. Moe and Taylor, op. cit., 41–42, 48; Bell, op. cit., 75; MacLeish and Young, op. cit., 7, 41; Stock, op. cit., 48–52.

27. James Hearst, "Farm Life When the Power Changed," *The Palimpsest*, 60, no. 5 (1979), 157–159. For a similar report on farmers in the Dakotas, see Stock, op. cit., 48–52.

28. Wynne Waller, *Culture of a Contemporary Rural Community: Harmony, Georgia* (Washington, DC: Bureau of Agricultural Economics, 1943), 49. Walter M. Kollmorgen, *Culture of a Contemporary Rural Community: The Old Order Amish in Lancaster County, Pennsylvania* (Washington, DC: Bureau of Agricultural Economics, 1942), 82–83. Jellison, op. cit., 120–121; Bell, op. cit., 74; Neth, op. cit., 53–54.

29. James Hearst, "We All Worked Together, A Memory of Drought and Depression," *The Palimpsest* 59, no. 3 (1978), 70, 76.

30. Moe and Taylor, op. cit., 55.

31. Marion Royalhouse, "Big Enough to Tell Weeds from the Beans: The Impact of Industry on Women in the Twentieth Century South," in Bruce Clayton and John A. Salmond, eds., *The South Is Another Land: Essays on the Twentieth Century South* (New York: Greenwood Press, 1987), 85; Margaret Jarman Hagood, *Mothers of the South: Portraiture of the White Tenant Farm Woman* (Chapel Hill: University of North Carolina Press, 1939), 143.

32. Fink, op. cit., 164.

33. Dorothea Lange, Pearson County Georgia, July 1934, 19910-E, 19978-E, 20175-E, 20193-E, 20187-E, (LC). Bell, op. cit., 77; Moe and Taylor, op. cit., 71; Fink, op. cit., 179–181; N.G.T., "Weary Willie," Paris, Tennessee, October 7, 1938; Bernice K. Harris, "I Ain't Lost Heart," Seabord, North Carolina, June 14, 1939; Bernice K. Harris, "The Mack Faisons," Pleasant Hill, North Carolina, December

31, 1938; Federal Writer's Project Papers, Southern Historical Collection, Chapel Hill, North Carolina.

34. See Stock, op. cit., 48–49, 73–74, 148–152; Jellison, *Entitled to Power*, op. cit., 107–129; Dorothy Schweider, "South Dakota Women and the Great Depression," *Journal of the West* 24 (October 1985), 8–18.

35. Indiana led farm states in the Midwest with 37% of its farms electrified on June 30, 1939, Wisconsin 36%, Illinois 26%, Iowa 23%, Minnesota 17%, Nebraska 13%, Kansas 11%, South Dakota 4%, and North Dakota only 2%. Electrification of farms in the South was 21% for Virginia, 19% for North Carolina, 14% for Georgia and South Carolina, 10% for Florida, 8% for Kentucky, 7% for Louisiana, and 4% for Mississippi. Robert T. Beall, "Rural Electrification," in *The Yearbook of Agriculture*, edited by Gove Hambridge (Washington, DC: Government Printing Office, 1940), 802. See Hagood, *Mothers of the South*, for revelations about emotional maturity, 75–76; for references to absences of conveniences in houses of white tenants, 92–107.

36. Jellison, *Entitled to Power*, op. cit., 108–109, 114–115.

37. Schweider, op. cit., 17; Hagood, "The Farm Home and Family," op. cit., 45–46, *Mothers of the South*, op. cit., 83–84, 89–90; Stock, op. cit., 74, 151; Mary Neth, *Preserving the Family Farm: Women, Community, and the Foundations of Agribusiness in the Midwest, 1900–1940* (Baltimore and London: Johns Hopkins University Press, 1995), 28, 45, 49, 148–150.

38. Russell Lee, 10580-D (LC); Ann Marie Low, *Dust Bowl Diary* (Lincoln: University of Nebraska Press, 1984), 68.

39. Kirby, op. cit., 170–173; Stock, op. cit., 153.

40. *White House Conference on Child Health and Protection, Adolescent* (New York, 1936), 133, 138, 160–161, 163–164, 167, 357, appendix, Tables 28 and 29.

41. Stock, op. cit., 90–91.

42. Orval Eugene Faubus, *In This Faraway Land* (Conway, AK: Riverroad Press, 1971), 11–12.

43. Kirby, op. cit., 123.

44. Lowitt and Beasley, op. cit., 27; Hagood, op. cit., 176–177.

45. MacLeish and Young, op. cit., 74; Neth, op. cit., 147–151; Wynne Waller, op. cit., 43.

46. Moe and Taylor, op. cit., 51.

47. Ibid., 51. For a similar response in Haskell County, Kansas, see Bell, op. cit., 73. See also Robert Dallek, *Lone Star Rising: Lyndon Johnson and His Times 1908–1960* (New York: Oxford University Press, 1991), 53.

48. West, op. cit., 142.

49. Arthur Raper, *Preface to Peasantry* (Chapel Hill: University of North Carolina, 1936), 354–356; Liston Pope, *Millhands and Preachers: A Study of Gastonia* (New Haven and London: Yale University Press, 1942), 44, 85, 98.

50. Bureau of the Census, *Religious Bodies: 1936*, I, 314–315, 318–319. For example, the Church of the Nazarene grew in membership from 63,000 to 136,000 between 1925 and 1935, Assemblies of God from 47,000 to 148,000, and Seventh Day Adventists from 112,000 to 181,000.

51. Verner Lee with Silas Harmon, n.d., Columbia, South Carolina (Mr. Harmon was raised in the community of Dutch Fork, South Carolina); Bernice K. Harris, "I Ain't Lost Heart," Seabord, North Carolina, June 14, 1939; Margaret Jeffries inter-

view with Fleety Dodson, January 31, 1939, Culpepper, Va., all from Federal Writer's Project Papers, Southern History Collection, Chapel Hill, NC. "From the Mountains Faring," in Tom E. Terrill and Jerold Hirsch, eds., *Such as Us: Southern Voices Out of the Thirties* (Chapel Hill: University of North Carolina Press, 1978), 127; Ibid., "In Abraham's Bosom," 84.

52. Russell Lee, Oklahoma City, July 1939, 34009-D (LC).
53. The Elba (Alabama) *Clipper*, January 5, 1933.
54. Moe and Taylor, op. cit., 60–62.
55. West, op. cit., 162.
56. The *Randolf* (W.Va.) *Review*, December 20, 1935.
57. Grand Rapids (Minn.) *Herald Review*, December 25, 1935.
58. The Augusta (Kansas) *Daily Gazette*, May 31, 1933.
59. The Bozeman (Montana) *Daily Chronicle*, April 9, 1939. Bozeman's population in 1930 was 6,855.
60. Marianna (Florida) *Daily Times Courier*, December 22, 1932, cited in McGovern, op. cit., 33. Jackson County *Floridan*, August 25, 1933, 1. Also cited in McGovern, op. cit., 33.
61. Taylor (Florida) *County News*, March 14, 1935.
62. Mandan (North Dakota) *Daily Pioneer*, May 30, 1934; Bozeman *Daily Chronicle*, April 17, 1938, December 25, 1938; Dekalb (Illinois) *Daily Chronicle*, April 10, 1935; Augusta *Daily Gazette*, December 23, 1933.
63. The Beloit *Daily Call*, February 26, 1934.
64. Dekalb *Chronicle*, January 12, 1934; Grand Rapids *Herald Review*, November 20, 1935.
65. John Vachon, May 1940, 61930-D, October 1938, 1228-M2(LC); Russell Lee, September 1940, 8991-E (LC), October 1937, 30774-D (LC), 30975-D (LC), June 1939, 33403-D (LC); Dorothea Lange, October 1939, 21228-E (LC); Ben Shahn, Summer 1939, 6460-M4 (LC).
66. Russell Lee, July 1939, 12337-M5 (LC), June 1939, 12253-M3 (LC), October 1938, 11702-M3 (LC), November 1938, 11785-M1 (LC); Dorothea Lange, July 1939, 20017-E (LC), July 1939, 20245-E (LC).
67. Kenneth P. Wilkinson, *The Community in Rural America* (Westport, CT: Greenwood Press, 1991), 60–86.
68. Ibid.; Catherine McNicol Stock rightly emphasizes the intolerance of persons in farm areas toward minorities; their support for the Klan in the 1920s, contempt for those who would not try to help themselves, and animosity toward ethnics. Stock, op. cit., 63–85.
69. Raper, op. cit., 394–395; McGovern, op. cit., 22.
70. R. Lee, August 1938, 11595-M5, 11596-MC (LC); Arthur Rothstein, September 1939, 28042 (LC).
71. The Hastings (Minn.) *Gazette*, January 12, 1935.
72. Augusta *Daily Gazette*, February 15, 1934.
73. Brattleboro *Daily Reformer*, January 6, 1933.
74. Grand Rapids *Herald Review*, July 5, 1933, June 12, 1935.
75. Bismarck *Tribune*, July 27, 1935; Beloit *Daily Call*, November 2, 1932, April 18, 1936.
76. Grand Rapids *Herald Review*, February 3, 1932; September 11, 1935; Augusta *Daily Gazette*, May 27, 1933; Bozeman *Chronicle*, February 16, 1938; Has-

tings *Gazette*, March 31, 1933; DeKalb *Daily Chronicle*, April 4, 1935; Chillicothe (Mo.) *Constitution Tribune*, December 6, 1934; Taylor County *News*, May 23, 1935.

77. Chillicothe *Constitution Tribune*, January 4, 1935.

78. Bozeman *Daily Chronicle*, October 21, 1938; Beloit *Daily Call*, August 13, 1935; *Randolf Review*, November 29, 1934; Hastings *Gazette*, March 3, 1933; Taylor County *News*, July 4, 1935; Hastings *Gazette*, January 27, 1937; Atmore (Alabama) *Advance*, December 21, 1933.

79. Brattleboro *Daily Reformer*, March 7, 1935; Taylor County *News*, February 21, 1935; Rufus Sheafe, Federal Writers Project (FWP), State Historical File, Burlington, Iowa (LC); Mrs. Everett Johnson, FWP, State Historical File, Waterloo, Iowa (LC). On athletics, James West, op. cit., 80–81; E. Bell, op. cit., 85. Note the extraordinary interest in high school teams as well as local semiprofessional baseball teams in small cities as "Baseball Grips City," in Bismarck *Tribune*, August 12, 1933. On plays, concerts, community balls, Grand Rapids *Herald Review*, February 24, 1932; Beloit *Daily Call*, October 8, 1933; Hastings *Gazette*, December 15, 1933; Bozeman *Daily Chronicle*, August 17, 1938; DeKalb *Chronicle*, January 17, 1934.

80. DeKalb *Chronicle*, January 4, 1934; Chillicothe *Constitution Tribune*, March 6, 1935; Brattleboro *Daily Reformer*, January 14, 1938; Grand Rapids *Herald Review*, February 28, 1934; Brattleboro *Daily Reformer*, January 4, 1938; Augusta *Daily Gazette*, December 21, 1933; Pendleton *East Oregonian*, April 3, 1933.

81. Stock, op. cit., 58.

82. Augusta *Daily Gazette*, September 22, 1933.

83. Bismarck *Tribune*, November 27, 1935.

84. Cairo (Illinois) *Evening Citizen and Bulletin*, November 24, 1932.

85. Grand Rapids *Herald Review*, November 28, 1932.

86. Pendleton *East Oregonian*, July 4, 1932; Beloit *Daily Call*, October 12, 1932. Parades on the Fourth of July were invariably well attended in the rural towns.

87. DeKalb *Chronicle*, January 2, 1934.

88. Brattleboro *Daily Reformer*, March 9, 1933.

89. McGovern, op. cit., 32–33.

90. Jackson County *Floridan*, April 20, 1934, as quoted in McGovern, op. cit., 33.

CHAPTER 6

1. This theme is richly developed by Charles Shindo in *Dust Bowl Migrants in the American Imagination* (Lawrence: University of Kansas Press, 1997). Shindo summarizes his assessment with "Each [Lange, Steinbeck, Ford, Guthrie] saw the migrant as a victim. . . . It is this representation of the migrant as downtrodden and forgotten that is at the center of their persistent image," 8. Shindo's study explains why their representation has mistakenly "dominated our understanding of the Okie migrant," 10.

2. Sheila Goldring Manes, *Depression Pioneers: The Confusion of an American Odyssey. Oklahoma to California, 1930–1950, a Reinterpretation* (Ann Arbor: Microfilm Corporation, 1982), 34.

3. *Sixteenth Census of the United States, 1940 Population, Interstate Migration, Color and Sex of Migrants* (Washington, DC: GPO, 1943) Table 16, 105, 112–114.

See also House Select Committee to Investigate Interstate Migration of Destitute Citizens, Pursuant to House Resolution 63. 491 (76th Congress) 1940 and House resolution 16 (77th Congress) (Washington, DC, 1941), Part 6, 2783. Hereafter cited as Tolan Committee *Hearings.*

4. James N. Gregory, *American Exodus: The Dust Bowl Migration and Okie Culture in California* (New York and London: Oxford University Press, 1989), 27–28. Stuart M. Jamison, "A Settlement of Rural Families in the Sacramento Valley," *Rural Sociology* 8 (March 1942), 53. Jamison found that a majority of migrants in a typical Okie settlement had come to California on the strength of favorable reports by family or friends already there.

5. Tolan Committee *Hearings,* Part 6, 2210–2211; ibid., Part 7, 2904–2906.

6. Ibid., Part 6, 2374; Varden Fuller and Seymore Janow, "Migrants," *Land Policy Review* (March-April 1940), 37.

7. Donald Worster, *Dustbowl: The Southern Plains in the 1930s* (New York: Oxford University Press, 1979), 50; note also Tolan Committee *Hearings,* Part 6, 2211–2212, Part 7, 2904.

8. Marvin Montgomery from Oklahoma declared before the Tolan Committee, "I knew exactly where I was going." He explained, "I had a son and daughter here [in California]." Tolan Committee *Hearings,* Part 7, 2905. In some cases, kin encouraged relatives to stay with them and helped to find them jobs. Jamison, op. cit., 53–54; Gregory, op. cit., 28.

9. Ibid., 36–52.

10. Ibid., 59. Only 2% of migrants to the San Joaquin Valley in the 1930s became farm owners, tenants, or managers by 1940.

11. Ibid., 68; Varden Fuller in Tolan Committee *Hearings,* Part 6, 2256.

12. Gregory, op. cit., 64–66; Jacqueline Gordon Sherman, *The Oklahomans in California During the Depression Decade, 1931–1941* (Ann Arbor: Microfilm Corporation, 1979), especially 195–205. Southwesterners who came to California and decided to farm on circuit as laborers in the late 1930s were still forced to undergo a challenging first year, but more numerous quality camps for transients maintained by the federal government (by 1940, thirteen fixed camps were maintained by the Farm Security Administration) made their living more comfortable. Sherman, op. cit., 205–210. It was at Weedpatch, a federal camp, that the literary Joads found sanitary toilets, Rose of Sharon took her first shower and received prenatal attention, and Ma "felt like people again."

13. John Steinbeck, *Grapes of Wrath,* 280, 291.

14. Jerry Stanley, *Children of the Dust Bowl: The True Story of the School at Weedpatch Camp* (New York: Crown Publishing, 1992), 36–37.

15. Walter Stein, *California and the Dust Bowl Migration* (Westport, CT: Greenwood Press, 1973), 46.

16. Gregory, op. cit., 83–100.

17. Jerry Stanley, op. cit., 36–39.

18. Walter Goldschmidt, *As You Sow* (New York: Harcourt Brace, 1947), 73.

19. Ibid., 161.

20. Walter Goldschmidt, an anthropologist who studied at length the relations of Okies and Californians in several communities in the San Joaquin Valley, concluded that poverty with its social ramifications prevented Okies from being fully accepted by the dominant group, though the system was open for those who could pass the

tests required by the local middle class. Stuart Jamison studying Okies in the Sacramento Valley believed differently that the Okies had become a distinct ethnic group. Both were probably correct. A few passed the social bar, with most finding gratification with their own kind. See Stuart M. Jamison, "A Study of Rural Migrant Families in the Sacramento Valley, California," *Rural Sociology* 7 (March 1942), 50, 51, 57.

21. Lillian Creisler, " 'Little Oklahomas' or the Airport Community: A Study of the Social and Economic Adjustment of Self-settled Agricultural Drought and Depression Refugees" (unpublished M.A. Thesis, University of California, Berkeley, 1940), 12, 66.

22. Ibid., 63.

23. Tolan Committee *Hearings*, Part 7, 2823.

24. U.S. Bureau of the Census, *Sixteenth Census of the United States: 1940 Population, Internal Migration 1935–1940, Color and Sex of Migrants*.

25. Ibid., 2, 5, passim.

26. Gregory, op. cit., 9–10, 39–41.

27. Although exact numbers on migration are unavailable for the period 1930 to 1935, Gregory believes an accurate enumeration might show 375,000 Southwesterners moving into California in the 1930s. Gregory, op. cit., 261, n.20. On the rural settlement of Okies in California, see Donald J. Bogue, Henry S. Shyrock, and Siegfried A. Hoermann, *Subregional Migration in the United States, 1935–1940* (Oxford, Ohio: Miami University, 1953–57), Table 1, vii–cli; Gregory, op. cit., 83.

28. Manes, op. cit., 269.

29. Ibid., 275.

30. Ibid., 264–265, 273, 280–287, 349.

31. Worster, op. cit., 58.

32. Stein, op. cit., 3–70; Worster, op. cit., 49–63; Manes, op. cit., 264–381; Gregory, op. cit., 3–35.

33. U.S. Bureau of the Census, *Sixteenth Census of the United States: 1940 Population, Internal Migration 1935–1940, Color and Sex of Migrants*.

34. Stein, op. cit., 39–40. See Tolan Committee *Hearings*, Part 6, 2210.

35. See map detailing residence of "19,786 Agricultural Families Moving to California, 1930–1939," in Seymour J. Janow and Davis McEntire, "The Migrants," *Land Policy Review* (July-August 1940), 29; Sherman, op. cit., 74.

36. Gregory, op. cit., 6–25.

37. Ibid., 27–28, 269 n.84.

38. Manes, op. cit., 26.

39. Ibid., 313.

40. Robert T. McMillian, "Migration of Population in Five Oklahoma Townships," Bulletin 3–271, *Oklahoma Agricultural Experiment Station* (October 1943), 26.

41. 1940 Census, Public Use Microdata Sample reported in Gregory, op. cit., 19, 265 n.46.

42. Paul S. Taylor and Edward J. Rowell, "Patterns of Agricultural Labor Migration within California," *Monthly Labor Review* 47 (November 1938), 980–990.

43. A study of 1,000 families in California, mostly migrants from agricultural backgrounds, by the Bureau of Agriculture in 1939 revealed that approximately two-thirds received public assistance in 1938, receiving on average about one-eighth of their

income in so doing. Tolan Committee *Hearings*, 2370. Although the Okies preferred to work than go on relief, a WPA director in Modesto reported that nearly every head of family in Okieville had at one time worked for the WPA. Gregory, op. cit., 25; Creisler, op. cit., 42. The Okies were severely critical of their members who were on relief when work was available. Walter J. Stein, "The 'Okie' as Farm Laborer," *Agricultural History* 49 (January 1975), 211–212.

44. Sherman, op. cit., 188–189; Gregory, op. cit., 68–69; Stein, op. cit., 50; Goldschmidt, op. cit., 69.

45. Stein, *California and the Dust Bowl Migration*, 50.

46. Creisler, op. cit., 11; See also Dorothea Lange, April 1939, 19475-C (LC) for Lange's appended comments from a grandmother, a fourteen-month resident of California, "the main thing is to get our families settled and quieted down."

47. Sherman, op. cit., 231, quoting a memorandum by Carey McWilliams, California's Chief of the Division of Immigration and Housing.

48. In Modesto, as of January 1938, only two Okie families rented houses and nearly two hundred owned their houses. Creisler, op. cit., 15, 26. Creisler writes, "These people wanted fiercely to resettle on property of their own."

49. Ibid., 80.

50. Gregory, op. cit., 71.

51. Creisler, op. cit., 21–26; Sherman, op. cit., 228–235.

52. Gregory, op. cit., 72. One resident of a new house informed Creisler that it could be built for $135 if you did your own work, Creisler, 26.

53. Creisler, 12, 143.

54. Goldschmidt, op. cit., 88.

55. Creisler, op. cit., 71.

56. Ibid., 70.

57. Tolan Committee *Hearings*, Part 5, 2141–2142.

58. Gerald Haslam, *The Nation* 220 (March 15, 1975), 302; Gregory, op. cit., 144–149; Creisler, op. cit., 70.

59. Jerry Stanley, op. cit., 32.

60. Gregory, op. cit., 146.

61. Ibid., 146–148.

62. *The New York Times*, March 6, 1940, 25.

63. Dan Morgan, *Rising in the West: The True Story of an "Okie" Family from the Great Depression Through the Reagan Years* (New York: Knopf, 1992), 105.

64. Tolan Committee *Hearings*, Part 6, 2619, 2405–2409.

65. Goldschmidt, op. cit., 124–147; Morgan, op. cit., 113–115, 126–133.

66. Morgan, 133.

67. Criesler, op. cit., 63.

68. McMillan, op. cit., 35–37.

69. Gregory, op. cit., 23–25, 75–77.

70. Varden Fuller and Seymour S. Janow, "The Migrants," *Land Policy Review* (March–April 1940), 37–38.

71. Tolan Committee *Hearings*, Part 6, 2578.

72. Ibid., Part 6, 2375.

73. Miss Bauer, Tolan Committee *Hearings*, Part 6, 2577; Carey McWilliams, ibid., 2545–2547.

74. "Grapes of Joy—Okies Forge Ahead," *Current History* 51 (March 1940), 48–49.
75. Creisler, op. cit., 21; see also Byron Darnton, "Migrants Dreams of Owning Land Makes Them a Conservative Lot," *The New York Times*, March 6, 1940.
76. Criesler, op. cit., 12.
77. Camille Gavin, "Depression Wasn't All Tragedy, But It Was Tough," *The Bakersfield Californian*, September 9, 1979, B-10.
78. Creisler, op. cit., 10.
79. Gregory, op. cit., 75; Gregory quotes from Kern County Health Department, *Kern County Migratory Labor Problem*, July 1, 1939, 7. See also n.116, 284.
80. Sherman, op. cit., 278. Evidence of President Roosevelt's reply to Ralph Lavin, supervisor, Third Supervisional District, Kern County, California, is found in the President's Personal File 6511 at the Roosevelt Library, Hyde Park, New York.
81. Creisler, op. cit., 78; Sherman, op. cit., 232, notes as well that the morale of the [Okie] migrants was climbing.

CHAPTER 7

1. Charles S. Johnson, *Growing Up in the Black Belt: Negro Youth in the Rural South* (Washington, DC: American Council on Education, 1941), 50–52. Outside the cotton plantation areas, percentage ownership by blacks was more profuse, with many counties showing 30% black ownership and in Virginia nearly 62%.
2. James R. McGovern, *Anatomy of a Lynching: The Killing of Claude Neal* (Baton Rouge: Louisiana State University Press, 1982), 38.
3. Jack Temple Kirby, "Black and White in the Rural South, 1915–1954," *Agricultural History* 58 (July 1984), 411–413; *Rural Worlds Lost*, 232–237; Raper, op. cit., 149. General data on various types and numbers of farmers in the South may be found in *Historical Statistics of the United States*, I, 465.
4. Charles S. Johnson, *Growing Up in the Black Belt*, 53–57, *Shadow of the Plantation* (Chicago: University of Chicago Press, 1934), 80–100.
5. A major study on this subject throughout is Paul E. Mertz, *New Deal Policy and Southern Rural Poverty* (Baton Rouge: Louisiana State University Press, 1978). See also Raper, op. cit., 153–155, 250–251, and Pete Daniel, *Breaking the Land: The Transformation of Cotton, Tobacco and Rice Cultures since 1880* (Urbana and Chicago: University of Illinois Press, 1985), 80–81, 90–109.
6. Particularly valuable studies for the social historian, all published after lengthy personal investigation in the community by the author or authors, are John Dollard, *Caste and Class in a Southern Town* (Garden City, NY: Doubleday, 3rd edition, 1957), first published by Yale in 1937; Allison Davis, Burleigh B. Gardner, and Mary Gardner, *Deep South: A Social-Anthropological Study of Caste and Class* (Chicago: University of Chicago Press, 1941); and Hortense Powdermaker, *After Freedom: A Cultural Study in the Deep South* (New York: Russell and Russell, 1939). Charles S. Johnson provides three valuable studies: *Growing Up in the Black Belt: Negro Youth in the Rural South, Shadow of the Plantation* that focus on blacks in Macon County, Alabama, a cotton-growing area, and *Patterns of Negro Segregation* (New York: Harper and Brothers, 1943).
7. Powdermaker, op. cit., 12–13.

8. Davis, op. cit., 22; Dollard, op. cit., 102–104.

9. Dollard, op. cit., 96.

10. Ibid., 48.

11. Ibid., 60–96, especially 62. See also Davis, op. cit., 25–26.

12. Ibid., 12–18, 21; Powdermaker, op. cit., 23–24, 28; Dollard, op. cit., 69, refers to whites' attribution of "animal character" to blacks.

13. Jack Kirby, *Agricultural History* 58 (July 1984), 411; Theodore Rosengarten, *All God's Dangers: The Life of Nate Shaw* (New York: Avon Books, 1974), 512.

14. Dollard, op. cit., 63–66; Powdermaker, op. cit., 23–24, refers to "white attitudes toward the Negro" as "articles of faith, constituting a creed of racial relations . . . held almost universally by whites" in Cottonville.

15. Davis, op. cit., 48–49; Dollard, op. cit., 325–333. Although there were 3,724 lynchings in America from 1889 to 1930, four-fifths of whom were blacks as victims, only one-sixth of this number were accused of rape. Arthur F. Raper, *The Tragedy of Lynching* (Chapel Hill: University of North Carolina Press, 1932), 1. Yet accusations of rape were most likely to result in the lynching of blacks.

16. McGovern, op. cit., 7–8.

17. Dollard, op. cit., especially 315–363. See Raper, *The Tragedy of Lynching*, op. cit., 28–29, for the revelation that lynchings were largely confined to the poor rural South. See also McGovern, op. cit., for chapters "Lynch Law," 1–15, and "The End of an American Tragedy," 140–148. James H. Chadbourn, *Lynching and the Law* (Chapel Hill: University of North Carolina Press, 1933), 13, 48, 58. Cumulative data on numbers of lynchings through 1968 may be found in Daniel T. Williams, comp., *Eight Negro Bibliographies* (New York: Kraus Reprint Co., 1970), 6–15.

18. McGovern, op. cit., 140–152.

19. Dollard, op. cit., 331. Note Richard Wright's remarks on frequent news of lynchings that reached blacks in the South, Richard Wright, *Black Boy: A Record of Childhood and Youth* (New York and London: Harper and Brothers, 1945), 65. Wright observed that he imagined that he had been "the victim of a thousand lynchings."

20. Dollard, op. cit., 83–91, 209–212. For assumption that solidarity among blacks was essentially passive, 71–72.

21. Powdermaker, op. cit., 331.

22. Johnson, *Patterns of Negro Segregation*, 257.

23. Ibid., 270–271.

24. Ibid., 269.

25. Maya Angelou, *I Know Why the Caged Bird Sings* (New York: Random House, 1970), 27.

26. Johnson, *Patterns of Negro Segregation*, 269.

27. Ibid., 270.

28. Johnson, *Growing Up in the Black Belt*, 294–295.

29. Powdermaker, op. cit., 284.

30. Ibid., 340.

31. Ibid., 346.

32. Dollard, op. cit., 309; Powdermaker, op. cit., 330.

33. Angelou, op. cit., 24–25, 31–32, 178–179; Albert Murray, *South to a Very Old Place* (New York: McGraw-Hill, 1971), 87.

34. Henry Louis Gates, Jr., *Colored People* (New York: Alfred Knopf, 1994), 7–9.

35. Ibid., 64–65.
36. Ibid., 16, 19, 39, 208–213.
37. Richard Wright, *Native Son* (New York: Harper and Row, 1940), viii–xi. Wright discusses "How 'Bigger' was Born."
38. Dollard, op. cit., 340.
39. Johnson, *Growing Up in the Black Belt*, 282; Davis, op. cit., 533–534.
40. Raper, op. cit., 71.
41. Dollard, op. cit., 155.
42. Ibid., 291.
43. Powdermaker, op. cit., 345–346.
44. Angelou, op. cit., 178–179.
45. Dollard, op. cit., 305–306.
46. Ibid., 390–433.
47. Ibid., 393–400; Dollard also underscores a third gain for "lower-class Negroes," greater freedom of aggression and resentment in his own group.
48. Johnson, *Patterns of Segregation*, 261.
49. Davis, op. cit., 468–469.
50. Powdermaker, op. cit., 119–120. Dollard seemed to accept the view that "Around Southerntown. . . . white people have a special tolerance for Negro vagaries, rather expect them in fact." Dollard, op. cit., 432.
51. Powdermaker, op. cit., 173.
52. Kirby, *Agricultural History* 58 (July 1984), 416–417; Kirby quotes from "When Water Was Hot." Lee Carey interviewed by Kattye Orr, n.d., "Our Lives," Project Files, Works Progress Administration in Kentucky Collection, State Archives, Frankfort, Ky.
53. Johnson, *Patterns of Segregation*, 284.
54. Dollard, op. cit., 400.
55. Ibid., 409; Powdermaker, op. cit., 372; Gates, op. cit., 184.
56. Angelou, op. cit., 133–136; Gates, op. cit., 116, 166–171.
57. Dollard, op. cit., 409; Nicholas Lemann, *The Promised Land: The Great Black Migration and How It Changed America* (New York: Alfred Knopf 1981), 279.
58. Dollard, op. cit., 226–236.
59. Powdermaker, op. cit., 236–237. There were special community events for blacks in some southern towns. Blacks near Wabash, Georgia, celebrated May 20th with "trunks of food, pies and all that cooked food from home." They played games and partied till sundown. See "Going to Live Like My Father Lived," in *When I Was Coming Up: An Oral History of Aged Blacks* (Hamden, CT: Archon Books, 1982), 129. Games, speeches, and music with prominent American flags featured a July 4th celebration by blacks in Beaufort, Georgia. See Marion Post Wolcott, Beaufort, SC, July 1939, 30418-M2, 30417-M1. Black communities sponsored "Emancipation Day" on August 8. Jacqueline Jones, *The Dispossessed: America's Underclass from the Civil War to the Present*, 164. Note mentionings of community picnics in Angelou, op. cit., 133–136, and Gates, op. cit., 66–71. On organizations in community sponsored by church members, see Raper, op. cit., 375–386.
60. Dollard, op. cit., 394–398; Powdermaker, op. cit., 68. Although "impulse freedom" was greatest among lower rural classes, middle-class blacks (servants, manual laborers, and shopkeepers) also carried on outside marriage, though more secretly

and more frequently when they were younger. Powdermaker, op. cit., 67–68; Davis, op. cit., 219–220.

61. Powdermaker, op. cit., 168–169. Note the photographs of blacks having fun at jukes by Marion Post Wolcott in November 1939 in Clarksdale, Mississippi, another "cotton-pickin" town. See Patti Carr Black, *Documentary Photographs of Mississippi: The Thirties* (Jackson: University Press of Mississippi, 1982), 83–84.

62. Angelou, op. cit., 116–117.

63. Powdermaker, op. cit., 232–236.

64. Ibid., 236, 269.

65. Dollard, op. cit., 235–236; Powdermaker, op. cit., 272.

66. Dollard, op. cit., 249.

67. Rosengarten, op. cit., 295–334, 349–352.

68. Angelou, op. cit., 29–32.

69. Powdermaker, op. cit., 271.

70. "By the Glory of God," Harrison Waters, edited by Jack Kytle, Taladega Springs, Alabama, October 21, 1938 in Federal Writers Project, Southern Historical Collection, Chapel Hill, NC.

71. Powdermaker, op. cit., 239.

72. Dollard, op. cit., 236–240.

73. Powdermaker, op. cit., 250–252; Gates, op. cit., 210.

74. Angelou, op. cit., 125.

75. Ibid., 127–128.

76. Ibid., 128.

77. Johnson, *Shadow of the Plantation*, 57–66; Powdermaker, op. cit., 148–204.

78. Powdermaker, op. cit., 200.

79. Johnson, *Shadow of the Plantation*, 57–58.

80. Powdermaker, op. cit., 201.

81. Johnson, *Shadow of the Plantation*, 64–65.

82. Ibid., 63.

83. Ibid., 64; Powdermaker, op. cit., 146, 201.

84. Raper, *Preface to Peasantry*, 174–176.

85. Ibid., 174.

86. Victory for self-expression was far from complete, however. There were still instances of whites driving in the middle of the road to prevent blacks driving behind them from passing, and of passing cars with blacks without honking their horns and, of course, there was always the danger in event of an accident between a black driver and a white driver that the black would be held automatically accountable. Johnson, *Patterns of Negro Segregation*, 250; Powdermaker, op. cit., 49–50; McGovern, op. cit., 38.

87. Dollard, op. cit., 339.

88. Chris Mead, *Champion Joe Louis: Black Hero in White America* (New York: Charles Scribners, 1985), especially 192–205.

89. Patti Carr Black, op. cit., 24.

90. Gunnar Myrdal, *An American Dilemma: The Negro Problem and Modern Democracy*, 20th anniversary edition (New York: Harper and Row, 1962), 903–904; Johnson, *Growing Up in the Black Belt*, 246.

91. Angelou, op. cit., 129–132.

92. Johnson, *Growing Up in the Black Belt*, 246.

93. Eleanor Roosevelt to Steve Early, August 8, 1935, in Eleanor Roosevelt Papers, Series 100, Franklin D. Roosevelt Library, Hyde Park, New York. In November–December 1934, when White was pressing for the passage of a federal anti-lynching bill, he communicated eleven times with Mrs. Roosevelt, National Association for the Advancement of Colored People Papers, Manuscript Division, Library of Congress I, C-78, reel 12. See also McGovern op. cit., 124–125.

94. Ibid., 115–139.

95. A. A. Brill to Walter White, November 24, 1934 in NAACP Papers, Manuscript Division of Library of Congress.

96. McGovern, op. cit., 126–130.

97. Ibid., 140–142, 151.

98. Jack T. Kirby, *Rural Worlds Lost*, 259.

99. Ibid., 260–271; Donald Grubb, *Cry from Cotton* (Chapel Hill: University of North Carolina Press, 1971) provides a detailed discussion of the Southern Tenant Farmers' Union.

100. Powdermaker, op. cit., 138–139.

101. Ibid., 299–300.

102. Ibid., 317–322.

103. Johnson, *Growing Up in the Black Belt*, 114–115.

104. Johnson, *Shadow of the Plantation*, 28.

105. See Johnson, "Youth and the School," in *Growing Up in the Black Belt*, especially 102–105, 110, 121, 125–126.

106. Ibid., 134.

107. Powdermaker, op. cit., 50.

108. Davis, op. cit., 53, 458, 463–464.

CHAPTER 8

1. Gallup polling data revealed only 3% of those who attended the New York World's Fair disliked it while at least 85% enjoyed it. *The Gallup Poll: Public Opinion, 1935–71* (New York: Random House, 1971), August 28, 1939, 175–176.

2. Helen A. Harrison, *Dawn of a New Day: The New York World's Fair, 1939–1940* (New York: New York University Press, 1980), 118.

3. Donald J. Bush, *The Streamlined Decade* (New York: George Braziller, 1975), 168; Robert Ascher, "How to Build a Time Capsule," *Journal of Popular Culture* 8 (Fall 1974), 241–253.

4. This is a theme of Thomas P. Hughes, historian of technology, in his study, *American Genesis: A Century of Invention and Technological Enthusiasm, 1870–1970* (New York: Viking, 1989), 2–3.

5. Richard Guy Wilson, Dianne H. Pilgrim, Dickran Rashjian, *Machine Age in America, 1918–1941* (New York: Harry N. Abrams, 1986), 40, quotes Henry Ford, "Machinery the New Messiah," *The Forum* 79 (March 1928), 363.

6. Robert S. Lynd and Helen M. Lynd, *Middletown in Transition: A Study in Cultural Conflicts* (New York: Harcourt Brace, 1937), 15, 454–455.

7. *Life*, March 6, 1939, 53. An excellent analysis of this subject by a renowned scholar is in Richard Guy Wilson, op. cit., 91–125. The information is handsomely illustrated.

8. Richard Guy Wilson, op. cit., 111.

9. *Life*, November 23, 1936, cover.

10. Richard Guy Wilson, "Machine Age Iconography in the American West: The Design of the Hoover Dam," *Pacific Historical Review* 59 (November 1985), 463–493; *Technological Trends and National Policy Including the Social Implications of New Inventions*, Report of the Subcommittee on Technology to the National Resources Committee (Washington, DC: GPO, 1937), 380.

11. "Remaking the World," *Colliers* 155 (March 16, 1935), 60; Mildred Adams, "Taming the Untamable at Boulder Dam," *The New York Times Magazine* (February 24, 1935), 5, 19.

12. David E. Nye, *American Technological Sublime* (Cambridge: Massachusetts Institute of Technology Press, 1994), 137–139.

13. Joseph E. Stevens, *Hoover Dam: An American Adventure* (Norman: University of Oklahoma, 1990), 267.

14. Richard Guy Wilson, "Machine Age Iconography in the American West," 491.

15. Literature on the TVA is extensive. For the purposes of this presentation, useful information was found in Marian Moffett and Lawrence Wodenhouse, *Built for the People of the United States: Fifty Years of TVA Architecture* (Knoxville: University of Tennessee Press, 1983), and especially Walter L. Creese, *TVA's Public Planning: The Vision, The Reality* (Knoxville: University of Tennessee Press, 1990), 168–182. A worthwhile essay from a contemporary is in *Architectural Forum* 71 (August 1939), 73–114. On Lillienthal's comment, see Creese, op. cit., 176.

16. Creese, op. cit., 169–174; the quote is found on 174.

17. Ibid., 67.

18. A careful analysis of conditions in the Tennessee Valley and the "People's Reaction to the TVA" is in Creese, *TVA's Public Planning*, 85–113.

19. D. Clayton Brown, *Electricity for Rural America: The Fight for the REA* (Westport, CT: Greenwood Press, 1980), 75; David E. Nye, *Electrifying America: Social Meanings of a New Technology, 1880–1940* (Cambridge: Massachusetts Institute of Technology Press, 1990), 296–297.

20. Ibid., 261, 299. In certain sections of the United States rural electrification was particularly scant, particularly the South and Southwest and the North Central cluster of Montana, Colorado, and North and South Dakota. Ibid., 299–300.

21. Brown, op. cit., 5.

22. Nye, *Electrifying America*, 317–321; Brown, op. cit., 5.

23. Brown, op. cit., 69.

24. Ibid., 75.

25. "The Next Greatest Thing," *Tennessee Magazine* (May 1985), 8, as cited by Nye, *Electrifying America*, 304.

26. Ibid., 303–304.

27. Brown, op. cit., 75.

28. Nye, *Electrifying America*, 323–324.

29. Katherine Jellison, "Let Your Cornstalks Buy a Maytag," *The Palimpsest* 69, no. 3 (1988), 138.

30. D. Clayton Brown, "Farm Life Before and After Electrification," *Proceedings of the Annual Meeting, The Association for Living Historical Farms and Agricultural*

Museums (Washington, DC: Smithsonian Institution, 1975), 3–4; Nye, *Electrifying America*, 323–324.

31. *Historical Statistics of the United States*, II, 827.

32. On bridge building in the 1920s and the early 1930s, see Wilbur Watson, *A Decade of Bridges* (Cleveland: J. H. Jansen, 1937), 40–42, 44–52, 84–85, and the informative essay by Richard Guy Wilson, "*The Machine Age in America, 1918–1941*, 103–110; Irving F. Morrow, "Beauty Marks G. G. Bridge Design," *The Architect and Engineer* 128 (March 1937), 21–24. Morrow was a consulting architect on the Golden Gate Bridge.

33. Wilbur Watson, op. cit., 44–45.

34. Wilson, *Machine Age*, 110.

35. Carol Willis, "Skyscraper Utopia: Visionary Urbanism in the 1920s," in Joseph J. Corn, ed., *Imagining Tomorrow: History, Technology and the American Future* (New York: Oxford University Press, 1983), 165, 184. Plans for both the Chrysler Building and Empire State Building were revised to assure their dominance in the skyline, *The New York Times*, May 2, 1931.

36. Paul Goldberger, *The Skyscraper* (New York: Alfred A. Knopf, 1981), 77; Raymond B. Fosdick, *John D. Rockefeller Jr., A Portrait* (New York: Harper and Brothers, 1956), 269, and David Loth, *The City within a City: The Romance of Rockefeller Center* (New York: William Morrow, 1966), 172–173. Other, lesser skyscrapers were built in New York in the 1930s, the most noteworthy being the McGraw-Hill Building. *The New York Times* recounts rivalry among builders to construct New York's tallest building, May 2, 1931.

37. Theodore James Jr., *The Empire State Building* (New York: Harper and Row, 1975), 90, 99. The Empire State was an unusually stable building, a true technological wonder. During the hurricane of 1938 with 110 to 120 mile-per-hour winds, it is said to have swayed only 4 inches for 7.5 seconds. John Tauranac, *The Empire State Building: The Making of a Landmark* (New York: St. Martin's Griffen, 1995), 245.

38. *The New York Times*, May 1, 1931, 26.

39. Ibid.

40. James, op. cit., 74–85. James speculates that over one million persons a year paid one dollar admission to "90 to the top" based on the fact that 100,000 persons paid to visit the building in its first month. Ibid., 115. The Empire State averaged 2,200 visitors a day in November 1935. Tauranac, op. cit., 236. On Lewis Hine, see *Men at Work: Photographic Studies of Men and Machines* (New York: Dover Publications, 1977). Original publication was 1932.

41. James, op. cit., 78, 85–86, 97; *The New York Times*, May 2, 1931.

42. Patents to corporations from 1931 to 1935 averaged approximately 24,000 per year compared to 18,000 per year in the late 1920s. *Historical Statistics of the United States*, II, 958.

43. Richard Guy Wilson, *Machine Age in America, 1918–1941*, 312–336.

44. Jeffrey L. Meikle, *American Plastic: A Cultural History* (New Brunswick, NJ: Rutgers University Press, 1995), 139–146. For contemporary report, see *Colliers*, "Sheer Magic" (April 13, 1940), 69–70.

45. "What Man Has Joined Together," *Fortune* 13 (March 1936), 69.

46. See also Jeffrey L. Meikle, "Plastic Material of a Thousand Uses," in Joseph J. Corn, *Imagining Tomorrow*, 77–96, and Martin Greif, *Depression Modern: Thirties*

Style America (New York: Universe Books, 1975), 37, for a more complete list of plastic goods available in the 1930s.

47. Meikle, *American Plastic*, 105–106.

48. Jeffrey L. Meikle, *Twentieth Century Limited* (Philadelphia: Temple University Press, 1979), 96–97; on the research component of General Electric's development in the 1930s, see David E. Nye, *Electrifying America*, 351; on prices of refrigerators in Middletown, ibid., 356; on sales campaign for refrigerators, see Susan Strasser, *Never Done: History of American Housework* (New York: Pantheon Books, 1982), 265.

49. As Richard Guy Wilson and colleagues Dianne H. Pilgrim and Dickvan Tashjian note, "During the 1930s this almost blind faith in the power of the machine helped hold a badly shattered nation together." *Machine Age in America*, 335.

50. Reginald Cleveland, *The Road Is Yours* (New York: Greystone Press, 1951), 292–297.

51. Beloit *Daily Call*, January 27, 1934 (front page); Grand Rapids *Herald Review*, December 21, 1932 (front page); Taylor County *News*, January 3, 1935; Chillicothe, *Constitution* January 5, 1935.

52. "The Streamliners after Six Years," *Business Week*, February 10, 1940, 47–53; Streamliners—1 South, 1 East," ibid., July 6, 1935, 10–11; ibid., "New Crack Trains," March 20, 1937, 29; "Streamlined New Light Weight Trains," *Travel* 69 (August 1937), 4.

53. Wilson, *Machine Age*, 136–142; Bush, op. cit., 64–72. See also "When the Zephyr Breezed into Colorado," Colorado *Heritage* (Winter 1984), 23–28.

54. J. R. Hildebrand, "Trains of Today and Tomorrow," *National Geographic* 70 (November 1936), 537; "The Streamliners," 47–53.

55. "The Streamliners," 47–53.

56. J. R. Hildebrand, op. cit., 542.

57. "The Streamliners," 50.

58. Meikle, *Twentieth Century Limited*, 160.

59. Henry Kisor, *Zephyr: Tracking a Dream Across America* (New York: Times Books, 1994), 16.

60. Centralia (Illinois) *Sentinel*, January 24, 1934; DeKalb *Chronicle*, January 5, 1934; Centralia *Sentinel*, January 5, 1934.

61. Richard K. Smith, "The Intercontinental Airliner, and the Essence of Airplane Performance, 1929–1939," *Technology and Culture* 24 (July 1983), 447.

62. Especially fruitful for women's aviation in the 1930s, including women's participation in the air races, is Joseph J. Corn, op. cit., 71–91.

63. Films included *Dawn Patrol* (1930), *Night Flight* (1933), *Test Pilot* (1938), and *China Clipper*, also 1938. Stars were Jimmy Cagney, Spencer Tracy, Clark Gable, and Humphrey Bogart. Note the stories about flight in small-town newspapers such as the Centralia *Sentinel*, January 9, 1934, Chillicothe *Constitution-Tribune*, April 17, 1933, and the Bozeman *Daily Chronicle*, December 3, 1933, September 11, 1938. On model airplanes and young people, see Corn, op. cit., 113–133.

64. R. K. Smith, op. cit., 448.

65. Roger E. Bilstein, *Flight in America* (Baltimore: Johns Hopkins University Press, 1988), 100, 104.

66. Carl Solberg, *Conquest of the Skies: A History of Commercial Aviation in America* (Boston: Little Brown and Co., 1979), 227.

67. R. K. Smith, op. cit., 429–430.

68. Bilstein, op. cit., 90–91.

69. Solberg, op. cit., 172.

70. Bilstein, op. cit., 92–93.

71. Ibid.; Solberg, op. cit., 241; R. K. Smith, op. cit., 447.

72. Bilstein, op. cit., 97. Yet a Gallup poll in 1939 revealed that nearly three of five Americans would not be willing to fly in a commercial airliner across the Atlantic even if someone else paid for the trip. *The Gallup Poll* (New York: Random House, 1972), 142.

73. Bilstein, op. cit., 97–99.

74. Solberg, op. cit., 195–198.

75. Ibid., 182, 189.

76. Ibid., 201–205; Bilstein, op. cit., 97–99.

77. Ibid., 104–105.

78. Ibid., 101–102.

79. Ibid., 93, 96; Solberg, op. cit., 214, 220.

80. Ibid., 205.

81. Meikle, *Twentieth Century Limited*, 73–76. See, for example, Sheeler's paintings of a generator, a dam, and an airplane in "A Portfolio by Charles Sheeler," *Fortune* 22 (December 1940), 73–83. The accompanying script by *Fortune*'s writers conveys almost a reverential tone about the machine's contribution to society and progress.

82. Margaret Bourke-White, *Portrait of Myself* (New York: Simon and Schuster, 1963), 40; Nye, *Electrifying America*, 354–355.

83. The cartoon is pictured in Wilson, *The Machine Age*, 87.

84. Meikle, op. cit., 101–106.

85. Henry Dreyfus, *Designing for People* (New York: Simon and Schuster, 1955), 45–47, 179–183.

86. Meikle, *Twentieth Century Limited*, 47, 139; Walter D. Teague, *Design This Day: The Technique of Order in the Machine Age* (New York: Harcourt Brace, 1940), introduction, 17–19.

87. Norman Bel Geddes, "Ten Years from Now," *Ladies Home Journal* 48 (January 1931), 3.

88. Henry Dreyfus, op. cit., 239–240.

89. Martin Greif, *Depression Modern: The Thirties Style in America* (New York: Universe Books, 1975), 22.

90. Teague, op. cit., 19.

91. Henry Dreyfus, op. cit., 240.

92. Meikle, *Twentieth Century Limited*, 135–152, 167–168.

93. Geddes, for example, designed display windows, radios, service stations, stores, and scales in modern style. Dreyfus used the word "clean lining" to characterize his style instead of "streamlining" but the effect was similar. He developed simplified and useful phone styles for Bell, toasters, refrigerators, vacuum cleaners, an alarm clock, and a washer. Teague designed cameras, machine tools, space heaters, storefronts, Texaco service stations, and a number of exemplary advertisements in the streamline style. Loewy designed tractors, ship interiors, women's fashions, stores, refrigerators, advertisements, and pencil sharpeners. For illustrations, see Meikle,

Twentieth Century Limited, and Donald J. Bush, *The Streamlined Decade* (New York: George Braziller, 1975).

94. Martin Greif, passim.
95. Meikle, op. cit., 151–152.
96. Ibid., 165.
97. Ibid., 80–81.
98. Ibid., 96–99.
99. Ibid., 95.
100. Bush, op. cit., 2.
101. Ibid., 3.
102. A major study of American advertising in the 1920s and 1930s is Roland Marchand, *Advertising and the American Dream* (Berkeley: University of California Press, 1985). Also useful is Otis Pease, *The Responsibilities of American Advertising: Private Control and Public Influence, 1920–1940* (New Haven: Yale University Press, 1958).
103. *Life,* March 6, 1939, 53.
104. Marchand, op. cit., 207–234.
105. Ibid., 320–324.
106. Ibid., 325.
107. Ibid., 326–327.
108. There are large numbers of advertisements on behalf of airplanes and including airplanes, and many with veiled references to them at both national and local levels of print media. Model airplanes helped sell Quaker Oats in the Grand Rapids *Herald Review* July 13, 1938. Cars tilted like airplanes go over the crest of a hill. Ibid., May 10, 1939. Note perfection of this type of ad in *The New Yorker,* April 19, 1941, before page 1. Planes gave a sense of discovery when viewed flying low over an island's boat people in South America, *Life,* August 14, 1939, 8. Airplanes carried the mail in a Tydol Flying A gasoline ad, Brattleboro *Democratic Reformer,* July 4, 1940, and lofted in a sovereign manner over a streamlined car and train in another, ibid., June 17, 1939. Airplanes sold Beechnut gum on the back cover of *Life,* August 28, 1939, and cigarettes on the back cover of *Life,* August 8, 1938. An inverted plane aloft provided the picture for an ad on Conoco Oil in Bismarck *Tribune,* July 26, 1939. An article in *Life* was probably worth a thousand advertisements. *Life*'s devotion to airplanes is impressive. Note, for example, *Life,* August 22, 1938, 45–55; July 4, 1938, 2–5; December 26, 1938, 55. Advertisements on air travel invariably show attractive trend-setting people about to board. See *Fortune* (20 July 1939), 37. Some *Times* ads impute special prowess to aviation. Note "While the World Sleeps," which shows a United Airline plane in the skies at night doing its work. *Saturday Evening Post,* July 23, 1938, 41.
109. *Saturday Evening Post,* December 17, 1932, 56; ibid., January 22, 1938, 31; ibid., July 2, 1932, 60; *Life,* August 14, 1939, 69; ibid., August 9, 1937, 59 and ibid., July 3, 1939, 1.
110. *Fortune* 7 (April 1933), 79.
111. *Life,* March 13, 1939, 65; ibid., March 6, 1939, 56; ibid., Nov. 7, 1938; 3; Grand Rapids *Herald,* February 16, 1938; ibid., April 6, 1935.
112. *Saturday Evening Post,* February 8, 1936, 79.
113. Ibid., January 13, 1935, 62.
114. Ibid., January 14, 1939.

115. *Life*, December 12, 1938, 29–30.

116. *Saturday Evening Post*, January 14, 1933, 36, 84; *Saturday Evening Post*, June 4, 1938, 83.

117. Bismarck *Tribune*, Special Edition, August 15, 1939.

118. Alice Goldfarb Marquis, *Hope and Ashes: The Birth of Modern Times* (New York: Free Press, 1986), 230.

119. The best book on the Chicago World's Fair, impressively researched, is Robert W. Rydell, *World of Fairs: Century of Progress Expositions Chicago* (Chicago: University of Chicago Press, 1993). Other fairs of lesser significance in the 1930s included the San Francisco Golden Gate International Exposition (1939) and Expositions in San Diego (1935), Dallas (1936), and Cleveland (1939). All emphasized sales and progress. Rydell, op. cit., 123, 245. n. 10, 11.

120. *The New York Times*, March 5, 1939, Magazine Section, 16, 69.

121. Useful general works on the New York World's Fair include Helen A. Harrison, ed., *Dawn of a New Day: The New York World's Fair, 1939–1940* (New York: New York University Press, 1980); Herbert Rolfes, *The World of Tomorrow, 1939: New York World's Fair* (New York: Harper and Row, 1988); David Gerlernter, *The Lost World of the Fair* (New York: Free Press, 1995); and Barbara Cohen, S. Heller, S. Chwast, *Trylon and Perisphere—The 1939 World's Fair* (New York: Harry N. Abrams, Inc. 1989). See also Warren Susman, "The People's Fair," in *Culture as History: The Transformation of American Society in the Twentieth Century* (New York: Pantheon Books, 1984), 211–229.

122. Gerald Wendt, *Science for the World of Tomorrow* (New York: Norton, 1939), 20.

123. Donald Bush, op. cit., 154–170.

124. Wendt, op. cit., 117.

125. Davis S. Youngholm, "The Time Capsule," *Science* 92 (October 4, 1940), 301–302; G. Edward Pendray, "The Story of the Time Capsule," *Annual Report of the Smithsonian Institution, 1939*, Smithsonian Institution Publication 3555, 1940, 533–544. The contents of the time capsule including *Gone with the Wind*, the Sears Roebuck Catalogue for 1938–1939, a film of a world record flight by Howard Hughes, Jesse Owens' Olympic feats in 1936, etc., are described in Helen A. Harrison, op. cit., 74.

126. Nye, *American Technological Sublime*, 199.

127. Geoffrey T. Hillman, "Profiles," *The New Yorker*, February 8, 1941, 24.

128. Marquis, op. cit., 211.

129. An excellent discussion of these techniques is in Nye, *American Technological Sublime*, 210–224.

130. Extremely useful information on Futurama can be found in the "Brochure for General Motors Pavillion, New York World's Fair," New York Public Library. Also helpful are Bush, op. cit., 154–170; Meikle, *Twentieth Century Limited*, 200–210; Nye, *American Technological Sublime*, 218–222; Marquis, op. cit., 202–205.

131. A good summary description of efforts by fair organizations to stimulate national interest is in Nye, *American Technological Sublime*, 210–211. Note Brattleboro *Reformer*, June 21, 1939, for front-page notice of New Hampshire Day at the Fair with participation by a New Hampshire high school. On *Life* and the fair, note cover picture, May 22, 1939, of "Girl Guides of the Fair," April 24, 1939; on Futurama exhibit, June 5, 1939, 79–84; and the copious coverage "*Life* Goes to the

New York World's Fair; It Turns Out to be a Wonderful Place," July 3, 1939, 54–69.

132. *The New York Times*, May 1, 1939.

133. Note mentionings in ads in the Brattleboro *Reformer*, May 5, 1939, and June 16, 1939, and in Grand Rapids *Herald Review*, June 21, 1939, July 5, 1939, and August 2, 23, 1939.

134. Bismarck *Tribune*, July 15, 1939.

135. Nye, op. cit., 210.

136. Nye, op. cit., 204–205; Helen Harrison in her introduction to *Dawn of a New Day* endorses this view when she writes the fair "was attractive to a generation that experienced a decade of depression and the news of war in Europe."

137. Warren Susman, "The People's Fair; Cultural Contradictions of a Consumer Society," in Warren I. Susman, *Culture as History, The Transformation of American Society in the Twentieth Century* (New York: Pantheon Books, 1984), 220.

138. Market Analysts, Inc. conducted interviews in August 1939 with 1,020 visitors. These are in the New York Public Library, World's Fair Collection, 1934–1940, and are titled "Attendance and Amusement Area Survey of New York's Worlds Fair 1939, Incorporated."

139. Marquis, op. cit., 199; Helen F. Brown, "The Worlds Fair and Housing," *Current History* 50 (August 1939), 56–58; and Gerlernter, op. cit., 36–37.

CHAPTER 9

1. Nick Roddick, *A New Deal in Entertainment: Warner Brothers in the 1930s* (London: British Film Institute, 1983), 3–9.

2. Robert Sklar, *Movie Made America: A Cultural History of American Movies* (New York: Vintage, 1994), 178.

3. Robert B. Ray, *A Certain Tendency of the Hollywood Cinema, 1930–1980* (Princeton: Princeton University Press, 1985), 25–26.

4. Maggie Valentine, *The Show Starts on the Sidewalk: An Architectural History of the Movie Theaters, Starring S. Charles Lee* (New Haven: Yale University, 1994); 5–20, passim; Roddick, op. cit., 8.

5. *Historical Statistics of the United States*, I, 400.

6. Ray, op. cit., 26.

7. Sklar, op. cit., 16.

8. Robert S. Lynd and Helen Merrel Lynd, *Middletown in Transition: A Study in Cultural Conflicts* (New York: Harcourt Brace, 1937), 170, 173–174.

9. Hortense Powdermaker, *After Freedom: A Cultural Study in the Deep South* (New York: Russell and Russell, 1968), 18.

10. Lewis Jacobs, *The Rise of the American Film: A Critical History* (New York: Columbia University Teacher's College Press, 1967), 397–404.

11. Andrew Bergman, *We're in the Money: Depression America and Its Films* (New York: New York University Press, 1971), xix–xxii; John Izod, *Hollywood and the Box Office, 1895–1986* (New York: Columbia University Press, 1988), 96.

12. *Historical Statistics*, I, 414.

13. Margaret A. Zann, "Homicide in the Twentieth Century United States," in James A. Inciardi and Charles E. Faupel, eds., *History and Crime: Implications for Criminal Justice Policy* (Beverly Hills: Sage Publications, 1980), 117.

14. Eugene Rosow, *Born to Lose: The Gangster Film in America* (New York: Oxford University Press, 1978), 160–161.

15. Roddick, op. cit., 264; perhaps as many as forty "gangster movies" were produced in the wake of success with *Little Caesar* (1930), with about 10% of the movies made in 1931. Carlos Clarens, *Crime Movies from Griffith to the Godfather* (New York: Norton, 1980), 81.

16. Sklar, op. cit., 181.

17. Ibid., an excellent study of both *Little Caesar* and *Public Enemy* are in Stephen L. Karpf, *The Gangster Film: Emergence, Variation, and Decay of a Genre, 1930–1940* (New York: Arno Press, 1973), 43–59, and 61–85 (*Public Enemy*). A special value of the study is the inclusion of extensive dialogue.

18. Ibid., 62.

19. Ibid., 64, 75, 78.

20. Bergman, op. cit., 62. See Arthur Hove, *Gold Diggers of 1933* (Madison: University of Wisconsin Press, 1980) for script.

21. Gregory D. Black, *Hollywood Censored: Morality Codes, Catholics, and the Movies* (New York: Cambridge University Press, 1994), 64, 81, n. 24; Sklar, op. cit., 178.

22. Black, op. cit., 72–80; Bergman, op. cit., 54–57.

23. Black, op. cit., 80.

24. Bergman, op. cit., 30.

25. Ibid., 30–38. The Marx Brothers would regain popularity with a good-natured romp in *A Night at the Opera* (1935).

26. Margaret Zahn, "Homicide in the Twentieth Century United States," 117.

27. Roddick, op. cit., 106–112, and Bergman, op. cit., 83–88.

28. Bergman, op. cit., 84–87.

29. Roddick, op. cit., 277.

30. Ibid., 110–111.

31. Pauline Kael, the distinguished movie critic, used this expression as the title of her movie reviews. Pauline Kael, *Kiss, Kiss, Bang, Bang* (New York: Bantam Books, 1969). See also her study *I Lost It at the Movies* (Boston: Little, Brown, 1985).

32. Black, op. cit., 31–32, 36, 41.

33. Ibid., 33–34.

34. Ibid., 150–154; Sklar, op. cit., 134–135.

35. Black, op. cit., 39–43. A working draft of this code, called the Lord-Quigley Code by virtue of contributions from Catholic layman Martin I. Quigley, may be found in Black, op. cit., 302–308.

36. Ibid., 40.

37. Ibid., 50–71.

38. On Protestant action siding with the Legion of Decency or denouncing "indecent motion pictures," *The New York Times*, June 23, 1934, 1; ibid., June 25, 1934, 17; ibid., June 29, 1934, 23; ibid., July 14, 1934, 15; ibid., October 6, 1934, 18; ibid., October 19, 1934, 20. I am indebted to the excellent study of Gregory D. Black, *Hollywood Censored Morality Codes, Catholics and the Movies* for the bulk of my information on the background of the Production Code Authority, and the work of Joseph I. Breen, its director. See especially, Black, op. cit., 149–192. On *Madame du Barry* film, ibid., 176–178.

39. Black, op. cit., 238. Father Lord's code, implemented by the Production Con-

trol Administration, survived to govern the production of films in America until 1966.

40. *Life*, July 18, 1938, 50–55.

41. Ralph Brauer, "When the Lights Went Out—Hollywood, the Depression and the Thirties," *Journal of Popular Film and Journalism* 8 No. 4 (1987), 24–25.

42. Black, op. cit., 238–239.

43. Attendance exceeded the 87 million Americans who went to the movies per week in 1937 only in the years 1947 to 1949 when about 90 million went to the movies. *Historical Statistics*, I, 400. Noteworthy subjects that became major movies in the period included *Mutiny on the Bounty* (1935), *Anna Karenina* (1935), *Romeo and Juliet* (1936), *A Tale of Two Cities* (1936), *The Story of Louis Pasteur* (1936), *The Life of Emile Zola* (1937), *The Good Earth* (1937), *The Adventures of Robin Hood* (1938), *Pygmalion* (1938), *Alexander Nevsky* (1938), *Wuthering Heights* (1938), and *The Hunchback of Notre Dame* (1939).

44. Sklar, op. cit., 175, 196.

45. Ed Sikos, *Screwball: Hollywood's Madcap Romantic Comedies* (New York: Crown Publishers, 1989). Molly Haskell writes the foreword to this study. I am indebted to her for observations on the nature of screwball comedy and its salient characteristics. Popular screwball comedies included *My Man Godfrey* (1936), *The Awful Truth, Nothing Sacred, Easy Living*, and *Topper* (1937), *Bringing Up Baby, Holiday*, and *Joy of Living* (1938), *Midnight* (1939). There were also several movies with screwball elements in the early 1940s including *His Girl Friday, My Favorite Wife, The Lady Eve*, and *Palm Beach Story*.

47. Bergman, op. cit., 160–162; Clarens, op. cit., 154.

48. Margaret Mitchell, *Gone with the Wind* (New York: Pocketbooks, 1973), 414. Useful for its copious pictures from the movie is Judy Cameron and Paul J. Christman, *The Art of Gone with the Wind* (New York: Prentice-Hall, 1989). See also Marion J. Morton, "My Dear, I Don't Give a Damn: Scarlett O'Hara and the Great Depression," *Frontiers* 5, No. 3 (1981), 52–56, for a very useful interpretation of the film's appeal to American audiences during the Depression period.

49. Sklar, op. cit., 210.

CHAPTER 10

1. Eric Barnouw, *The Golden Web: A History of Broadcasting in the United States, 1933–1953*, vol. II (New York: Oxford University Press, 1968), 57–58; J. Fred MacDonald, *Don't Touch That Dial: Radio Programming in American Life, 1920–1960* (Chicago: Nelson Hall, 1979), 39–44. New radio stars of the early and mid-1930s included Jack Benny, Fred Allen, Ed Wynn, George Burns, Bing Crosby, and broadcast journalists Lowell Thomas and Gabriel Heater. Popular new programs included *One Man's Family, Ma Perkins, Jack Armstrong, The Shadow, The Green Hornet*, and *The Lone Ranger*.

2. *Special Reports on American Broadcasting* (New York: Arno Press, 1974, reprint edition), 15, 113.

3. Alice G. Marquis, *Hopes and Ashes: The Birth of Modern Times, 1929–1939* (New York: Free Press, 1986), 41; radios produced grew from 3.7 million in 1930 to 10.8 million in 1939. *Historical Statistics*, I, 796.

4. *Recent Social Trends in the United States: Report to the President's Research Committee on Social Trends*, I (New York: McGraw-Hill, 1933), 152–157.

5. Warren Susman, "The Culture of the Thirties," *Culture as History* (New York: Pantheon, 1984), 157–159.

6. The Bismarck, North Dakota, station, KFYR, an affiliate, usually programmed six family shows a day in the late 1930s. Bismarck *Tribune*, July 15, 1939.

7. Arthur F. Wertheim, *Radio Comedy* (New York: Oxford University Press, 1979), 245.

8. MacDonald, op. cit., 45–46.

9. Ibid., 106–107.

10. James Thurber, *The Beast in Me and Other Animals* (New York: Harcourt Brace, 1948), 251–260.

11. There were a few exceptions. Doc Long, a major character in *I Love a Mystery*, was a woman chaser though a friend to the central figure, Jack Packard, who was abstemious in morals. Jim Harmon, *The Great Radio Heroes* (New York: Doubleday, 1967), 25–26. Phil Harris, the bandleader on the *Jack Benny Show*, was a playboy as was Rochester, Benny's black servant. Rochester also liked to gamble. Margaret T. McFadden, "America's Boyfriend Who Can't Get a Date: Gender, Race, and the Cultural Work of the Jack Benny Program," *The Journal of American History* 98 (June 1993), 127–132.

12. Wertheim, *Radio Comedy*, 89–90.

13. Marquis, op. cit., 29.

14. Melvin O. Ely, *The Adventures of Amos 'n' Andy: A Social History of an American Phenomenon* (New York: Maxwell McMillan International, 1991), 144.

15. Ibid., 146–147.

16. Arthur Wertheim, "Relieving Social Tensions: Radio Comedy and the Great Depression," *Journal of Popular Culture* 10, No. 3 (1976), 515.

17. Mary Murphy, "Messenger of a New Age Station: KGIR in Butte," *Montana* 39, No. 4 (1989), 58.

18. MacDonald, op. cit., 215.

19. William Stott, op. cit., 137–138. Radio's reputation for honest reporting of the news also contributed to its reputation for reliability; ibid., 78–79, 88–91.

20. MacDonald, op. cit., 113.

21. Ibid., 92.

22. Murphy, op. cit., 60. Note as well letters to Amos and Andy from listeners in Wertheim, *Radio Comedy*, 55–56.

23. *Variety*, August 14, 1934, 31.

24. Wertheim, *Radio Comedy*, 35–41; Wertheim, "Relieving Social Tension," 502–506.

25. Wertheim, *Radio Comedy*, 71.

26. Ibid., 70.

27. Ibid., 84.

28. Margaret T. McFadden, op. cit., 120.

29. MacDonald, op. cit., 136–137.

30. NBC Script, Fibber McGee #14, July 15, 1935 (University of Maryland).

31. NBC Script, Fibber McGee #13, July 8, 1935 (University of Maryland).

32. Wertheim, *Radio Comedy*, 218–219.

33. Allen Havig, *Fred Allen's Radio Comedy* (Philadelphia: Temple University Press, 1990), 17, 164–165, 172.

34. Wertheim, *Radio Comedy*, 39.

35. Ibid., 38–39.

36. Ely, op. cit., 83–84, 123; Wertheim, op. cit., 43.

37. Wertheim, ibid., 44–45.

38. Ibid., 76.

39. McDonald, op. cit., 126.

40. Wertheim, *Radio Comedy*, 77.

41. Ibid., 75, 77.

42. Ibid., 253; MacDonald, op. cit., 140–142.

43. Havig, op. cit., 133.

44. MacDonald, op. cit., 240–241.

45. Thurber op. cit., 152; Daniel J. Czitrom, *Media and the American Mind* (Chapel Hill: University of North Carolina Press, 1982), 85; Herta Herzog, "On Borrowed Experience: An Analysis of Listening to Daytime Sketches," *Studies in Philosophy and Social Science* 9 (1941), 65–91; Warren Susman, *Culture as History* (New York: Pantheon, 1984), 160.

46. *Variety*, December 19, 1933, 40.

47. Wertheim, *Radio Comedy*, 253.

48. MacDonald, op. cit., 244.

49. Ibid., 236–239.

50. Jim Harmon, *The Great Radio Heroes* (New York: Doubleday & Company, 1967), 193.

51. MacDonald, op. cit., 243.

52. Ma Perkins Script, "The Trailer Plot," July 4, 1938 (University of Maryland).

53. Adequate summaries of the contents of individual serials in the 1930s may be found in J. Fred MacDonald, *Don't Touch That Dial*, 231–257, and Harmon, op. cit., 171–194. James Thurber's *The Beast in Me and Other Animals* is typically witty, but finds little to justify the "Soaps." Mary Jane Higby, *Tune in Tomorrow* (New York: Cowles, 1968) brings useful background information from a participant.

54. Harmon, op. cit., 257, 244.

55. Others included *Sam Spade, Boston Blackie, Mr. Keen, Gangbusters, The Shadow, The Green Hornet, Captain Midnight, Inner Sanctum, Sergeant Preston of the Yukon, Renfrew of the Royal Mounted, Tom Mix, Don Winslow of the Navy.*

56. The Lone Ranger, "Origin of the Masked Man," a recording of Old Time Radio Co., Grand Rapids, Michigan, audited Michigan State University Voice Library.

57. Harmon, op. cit., 197–198.

58. Page Smith, *Redeeming the Time* (New York: McGraw-Hill, 1987), 920.

59. Harmon, op. cit., 202.

60. Matthew N. Chappell and C. E. Hooper, *Radio Audience Measurement* (New York: Stephen Daye, 1944), 36.

61. "Origin of the Masked Man"; this program offered on the twentieth anniversary of the Lone Ranger was Program 3,128 of the "Masked Rider of the Plains." It sums up the early history of the Lone Ranger and Tonto (Michigan State University, Voice Library).

62. Harmon, op. cit., 198.

63. Ibid., 202–203.
64. Michigan State University, Voice Library.
65. *The New York Times*, April 10, 1941, 22.

CHAPTER 11

1. Leo Wolman, *Ebb and Flow in Trade Unionism* (New York: National Bureau of Economic Research, 1936), *passim*. Senior labor historian Irving Bernstein refers to the Depression's effect on labor as an "unrelieved disaster." Irving Bernstein, *A Caring Society: The New Deal, The Worker and The Great Depression* (Boston: Houghton Mifflin, 1985), 276–277.

2. Irving Bernstein, "The Growth of American Unions," *American Economic Review* 44 (June 1954), 301–318.

3. Bernstein, *A Caring Society*, 276.

4. Esther Fano, "A Wastage of Men: Technological Progress and Unemployment in the United States," *Technology and Culture* 32 (1991), 264–292.

5. Ann Banks, *First Person America* (New York: Knopf, 1980), 54–55. Speed-ups were key issues in the mammoth strike against General Motors in 1936–1937, Sidney Fine, *Sit Down: The General Motors Strike of 1936–1937* (Ann Arbor: The University of Michigan Press, 1969), 57–58, and in strikes in Akron. See Daniel Nelson, *American Rubber Workers and Organized Labor, 1900–1941* (Princeton: Princeton University Press, 1988), 139. James McDonnell, "Treating Men Like Dirty Dogs," *New York Folklore* 10, No. 3 (1984), 65–75.

6. Lizabeth Cohen, *Making a New Deal: Industrial Workers in Chicago, 1919–1939* (Cambridge, MA: Cambridge University Press, 1990), 323–333.

7. Ibid., 172–216.

8. Leo Troy, *Trade Union Membership, 1877–1962* (New York: National Bureau of Economic Research, 1965), Appendix 1–27, and Leo Wolman, op. cit., 172–192. Both authorities use paid union dues as criteria of union membership. Wolman estimated less than 25% of workers in all nonagricultural industries were in unions in the 1930s. Walter Galenson, *The CIO Challenge to the AFL: A History of the American Labor Movement, 1935–1941* (Cambridge, MA: Harvard University Press, 1960), 592; *Historical Statistics of the United States*, I, 178.

9. Robert and Helen Lynd, *Middletown in Transition* (New York: Harcourt Brace, 1937), 26, 449, 452–53.

10. Russell Kirk, "I Must See the Things; I Must See the Men," *Imprimis* 16 Hillsdale College, Michigan (October 1987) n.p.; Peter Friedlander, *The Emergence of a UAW Local, 1936–1939: A Study of Class and Culture* (Pittsburgh: Pittsburgh University Press, 1975), 20, 45.

11. Edward Wight Bakke, *The Unemployed Worker* (New Haven: Yale University Press, 1940), 30, 40, 44; Mike Davis, "The Barren Marriage of Labor and the Democratic Party," *New Left Review* 124 (November–December 1980), 46.

12. Bert Cochran, *Labor and Communism: The Conflict That Shaped American Unions* (Princeton: Princeton University Press, 1977), 90.

13. Support for the thesis of the "revolutionary potential" of American labor is found in Staughton Lynd, "The Possibilities of Radicalism in the Early 1930s: The Case of Steel," *Radical America* 6 (November–December 1972), 51–56, but John

Bodnar finds no revolutionary spirit among labor leaders he interviewed or among workers, and Robert Zieger concludes that grass-roots militancy, while present, was not revolutionary. John Bodnar, "Immigration, Kinship and the Rise of the Working Class Realism in Industrial America," *Journal of Social History* 14 (Fall 1980), 51–58; Robert H. Zieger, "The Limits of Militancy: Organizing Paper Workers, 1933–1935," *Journal of American History* 63 (December 1976), 640–647.

14. Irving Bernstein, *Turbulent Years: A History of the American Worker 1933–1941* (Boston: Houghton Mifflin, 1969), 782–783; Cochran, op. cit., 46, 90; Robert H. Zieger, *The CIO, 1933–1955* (Chapel Hill: University of North Carolina Press, 1995), 77–78, 82, 100–101.

15. Bruce Nelson, *Workers on the Waterfront: Seamen, Longshoremen and Unionism in the 1930's* (Urbana and Chicago: University of Illinois Press, 1988), 26–27, 29.

16. Cochran, op. cit., 96–102; Melvyn Dubofsky and Warren Van Tine, *John L. Lewis: A Biography* (New York: Quadrangle, 1977), 288–291, 309, 385, 389; Robert H. Zieger, *American Workers, American Unions, 1920–1985* (Baltimore: Johns Hopkins Press, 1986), 56–57.

17. AFL affiliates grew from 2,317,000 members in 1933 to 3,218,000 in 1935. Wolman, op. cit., 172–192; Bernstein, *Turbulent Years*, 217–317. Note the rapid expansion of the AFL in Akron after passage of the NRA when rubber workers "swamped" AFL unions. See Daniel Nelson, "The CIO at Bay: Labor, Militancy and Politics in Akron, 1936–1938," *Journal of American History* 71 (December 1984), 568.

18. L. Cohen, op. cit., 270–278, 286–287.

19. Dubofsky and Van Tine, op. cit., 184, 186.

20. An excellent treatment of these issues may be found in Melvyn Dubofsky, *The State and Labor in Modern America* (Chapel Hill: University of North Carolina Press, 1994), 107–135.

21. Ibid., 131–135.

22. Zieger, *The CIO, 1933–1935*, 39.

23. Ibid., 97; Zieger, *American Workers, American Unions*, 51–55.

24. Cochran, op. cit., 46.

25. Dubofsky, *The State and Labor in Modern America*, 139.

26. Fine, op. cit., 310.

27. Dubofsky, *The State and Labor in Modern America*, 138–142; Fine, op. cit., 71–120.

28. David Brody, *Labor in Crisis: The Steel Strike of 1919* (Urbana and Chicago: University of Illinois Press, 1987), 179–183.

29. D. Nelson, "The CIO at Bay," 574; Dubofsky, *The State and Labor*, 37.

30. L. Cohen, op. cit., 336–347.

31. Eva Morawska, *For Bread with Butter: The Life Worlds of East Central Europeans in Johnston, Pennsylvania, 1890–1940* (Cambridge, NY: Cambridge University Press, 1985), 273.

32. L. Cohen, op. cit., 337; Ann Banks, op. cit., 67.

33. Elizabeth Fones-Wolf, "Industrial Unionism and Labor Movement Culture in Depression Era Philadelphia," *The Pennsylvania Magazine of History and Biography* 109 (January 1985), 3–26.

34. Lizabeth Cohen emphasizes the continuing impact of capitalist welfare pro-

grams from the 1920s on workers' goals in the 1930s. She believes workers sought moral capitalism, reminiscent of capitalist benefit programs in the 1920s, and that the New Deal together with effective unions provided substitutes for older, displaced security systems in the ethnic neighborhood and welfare capitalism, L. Cohen, op. cit., 283–289; see Friedlander, op. cit., 112–113 for Slavic workers support for Roosevelt.

35. Kornhauser, "Analysis of 'Class' Structure of Contemporary American Society," in Hartman and Newcombs, eds., *Industrial Conflict*, 234–237, quoted by L. Cohen, 288, and cited on 487–488, n. 85.

36. Dubofsky and Van Tine, op. cit., 258.

37. D. Nelson, *American Rubber Workers*, 268.

38. Ibid., 191, quoted from Akron *Beacon Journal*, February 25, 1936; D. Nelson, *American Rubber Workers*, 142.

39. Fine, op. cit., 312; for similar reaction see D. Nelson, *American Rubber Workers*, 142.

40. Bernstein, *Turbulent Years*, 241–245; Zieger, *CIO*, 62–63.

41. D. Nelson, "How the UAW Grew," *Labor History* 35 (Winter 1994), 11; *Historical Statistics of the United States*, I, 179.

42. Dubofsky, *The State and Labor in Modern America*, 137.

43. Edward Levinson, *Labor on the March* (Ithaca, NY: Cornell University Press, 1995), reprint.

44. "A Symposium in Making a Deal," *Labor History* 32 (Fall 1991), 562–598; comments by Bruce Nelson, 587.

45. Ibid., 590.

46. Dubofsky, "The New Deal and the American Labor Movement," in Wilbur Cohen, ed., *The Roosevelt New Deal: An Assessment Fifty Years Later* (Austin, TX: Lyndon Baines Johnson Library, 1986), 75.

47. Zieger, *The CIO*, 61.

48. Michael Speer, "The Little Steel Strike: Conflict for Control," *Ohio History* 78 (Autumn 1968), 274–287.

49. Zieger, *The CIO*, 62.

50. The standard account is Donald G. Sofchalk, "The Chicago Memorial Day Incident, An Episode of Mass Action," *Labor History* (Winter 1965), 3–43.

51. CIO Files of John L. Lewis, microfilm as quoted in Zieger, *The CIO*, 62.

52. *The New York Times*, June 2, 1937.

53. John F. Shiner, "The 1937 Steel Labor Dispute and the Ohio National Guard," *Ohio History* 84 (Autumn 1975), 186–190.

54. Ibid., 190–195.

55. Dubofsky and Van Tine, op. cit., 314.

56. "Survey," *Fortune* 16 (July 1937), 100; *The Gallup Poll* (New York: Random House, 1971), I, 63.

57. D. Nelson, "The CIO at Bay," 574.

58. Dubofsky and Van Tine, op. cit., 315.

59. Kenneth D. Roose, *The Economics of Recession and Revival: An Interpretation of 1937–1938* (New Haven: Yale University Press, 1954), 37, 42, 55.

60. D. Nelson, "The CIO at Bay," 572–577.

61. Samuel T. McSeveney, "The Michigan Gubernatorial Campaign of 1938," *Michigan History* 45 (June 1961), 111.

62. Dubofsky and Van Tine, op. cit., 328–329, 357–364.

63. Irving Bernstein, "John L. Lewis and the Voting Behavior of the CIO," *Public Opinion Quarterly* 5 (June 1941), 232–249.

64. Zieger, *The CIO*, 70. The quote is from David McDonald, Secretary/Treasurer of the CIO's Steel Workers Organization Committee, and is regarded by Zieger as "characteristic of the [CIO's] priorities."

65. Ibid., 71.

66. L. Cohen, op. cit., 218–246, 312–321, 324–333, 355, 365–366.

67. B. Nelson, op. cit., 180.

68. Ibid., following 126.

69. Dubofsky and Van Tine, op. cit., 154, 336–337.

70. Dubofsky, "Not So Turbulent Years: Another Look at the American 1930s," *Amerikstudien* 24 (1980), 19. This useful article is reprinted in Melvyn Dubofsky and Stephen Burwood, eds., *Labor* (New York: Garland, 1990), 286–301.

71. Malcolm Cowley, *The Dream of the Golden Mountains* (New York: Viking Press, 1980), 316.

72. Fine, op. cit., 167–169, 174, 228–229.

73. Ibid., 331.

74. Dubofsky, "Not So Turbulent Years," 12; *Historical Statistics*, I, 179.

75. I am indebted for this summary to the analysis of Ray Boryczka, "Militancy and Factionalism in the United Auto Workers Union; 1937–1941," *The Maryland Historian* 8 (1977), 13–25.

76. John Bodnar, "Immigration, Kinship and the Rise of Working Class Realism," 50–59.

77. Friedlander, op. cit., 121; Fones-Wolf, op. cit., 24; Robert H. Zieger, *Madison's Battery Workers, 1934–1952: A History of Federal Labor Union 19587* (Ithaca: New York State School of Industrial and Labor Relations, Cornell University, 1977).

78. John Bodnar, *Immigration and Industrialization: Ethnicity in an American Mill Town, 1870–1940* (Pittsburgh: University of Pittsburgh Press, 1947), 102, 127, 129, 136–137.

79. Eva Morawska, op. cit., 185, 216–218, 220.

80. Ibid., 160; Japanese Americans in the 1930s illustrate how the family system and paternalism ruled out effective unionization in their small business communities. See Edna Bonacich and John Modell, *The Economic Basis of Ethnic Solidarity: Small Business in Japanese-American Community* (Berkeley: University of California Press, 1980).

81. Betty Burke interviews Anna Novak, May 1, 1939, Folklore Life Histories, Chicago (LC). D. Nelson, *American Rubber Workers*, 304; Steve Fraser and Gary Gerstle, *The Rise and Fall of the New Deal Order, 1930–1980* (Princeton: Princeton University Press, 1989), 73; and Steve Fraser, *Labor Will Rule: Sydney Hillman and the Rise of American Labor* (New York: Free Press, 1991), 424–425. Edmond Kord, a union leader and organizer for the UAW, described most Catholic clergy in the Detroit area as showing "open hostility to the very idea of unionism and communism," Friedlander, op. cit., 4. Useful articles on Catholics and the labor movement in the 1930s are David O'Brien, "American Catholics and Organized Labor in the 1930s," *The Catholic Historical Review* 52 (October 1966), 323–349, and Neil Betten, "Charles Owen Rice, Pittsburgh Labor Priest, 1936–1940," *Pennsylvania Magazine of History and Biography* (October 1970), 518–532, and "The Great

Depression and Activities of the Catholic Worker Movement," *Labor History* 12 (Spring 1971), 243–258.

82. Friedlander, op. cit., 131. The author's full quote is "Expansion of the union was thus a two-edged sword. If in theory the Left welcomed the chance to draw in the broad mass of workers, in practice the working class was not so much influenced by the Left as the UAW was influenced by the church, the political machine, several kinds of rural Protestant conservatism, and a variety of local pre-political subcultures."

83. Roger R. Keeran, "The Communists and UAW Factionalism, 1937–1939," *Michigan History* 60 (Summer 1976), 115–136. On background for the controversy see Ray Boryczka, "Seasons of Discontent: Auto Union Factionalism and the Motor Products Strike of 1935–1936," *Michigan History* 61 (Spring 1977), 3–32 and Cochran, op. cit., especially 127–138.

84. Zieger, *The CIO*, 85.

85. Paul Street, "The Logic and Limits of 'Plant Loyalty': Black Workers, White Labor, and Corporate Racial Paternalism in Chicago's Stockyards, 1916–1940," *Journal of Social History* 29, No. 3 (1996), 659–681; L. Cohen, op. cit., 337.

86. Galenson, op. cit., 627–631. See also William H. Harris, "A. Philip Randolph as Charismatic Leader, 1925–1941," *Journal of Negro History* 64 (Fall 1979), 301–315. For the role of women and women's auxiliaries in the Brotherhood of Sleeping Car Porters (BSCP), see Paula F. Pfeffer, "The Women Behind the Union," *Labor History* 36 (Fall 1995), 576–582.

87. Walter Licht and Hal Seth Barron, "Labor's Men: A Collective Biography of Officials During the New Deal Years," *Labor History* 19 (Fall 1978), 533–538, 541–542.

88. Fraser and Gerstle, op. cit., 74; Davis, op. cit., 58.

89. Bruce Nelson, "The Uneven Development of Class and Consciousness," in "A Symposium on Making a New Deal," *Labor History* 32 (1991), 591.

90. Daniel Nelson, "How the UAW Grew," *Labor History* 35 (Winter 1994), 9, 11, 13; Christopher L. Tomlins, "AFL Unions in the 1930s: Their Performance in Historical Significance," *Journal of American History* 65 (March 1979), 1023.

91. Zieger, *The CIO*, 115.

92. Ibid., 115. In 1939, manufacturing workers averaged $1,250 a year in earnings whereas 58% of working men received less than $1,000 a year. Richard Polenberg, *One Nation Divisible* (New York: V. King, 1980), 18–19.

93. Zieger, *The CIO*, 116; Sidney Verba and Kay Lehman Schlozman, "Unemployment, Class Consciousness and Radical Politics: What Didn't Happen in the Thirties," *Journal of Politics* 39 (May 1977), 291–323.

CHAPTER 12

1. *Historical Statistics of the United States*, 118.

2. "New York City," *Fortune* 20 (July 1939), 74.

3. Ibid., 171–172, 174, 177.

4. Stephen Shaw, *The Catholic Parish as a Way Station of Ethnicity and Americanization: Chicago's Germans and Italians, 1903–1939* (Brooklyn, NY: Carlson, 1991), 179.

5. Federal Writers Project, *Massachusetts: A Guide to Its Places and People* (Boston: Houghton-Mifflin, 1937), 136.

6. Richard Polenberg, *One Nation Divisible: Class, Race and Ethnicity in the United States Since 1938* (New York: The Viking Press, 1980), 36.

7. Lizabeth Cohen, *Making a New Deal*, 227–231.

8. Mario Puzo, "Choosing a Dream," in Thomas C. Wheeler, *The Immigrant Experience: The Anguish of Becoming American* (Baltimore: Penguin Books, 1972), 41.

9. Robert A. Orsi, *The Madonna of 115th Street: Faith and Community in Italian Harlem* (New Haven and London: Yale University Press, 1995), 14–49. Virginia Yans-McLaughlin, *Family and Community: Italian Immigrants in Buffalo 1880–1930* (Ithaca, NY: Cornell University Press, 1978), 19.

10. Dino Cinel, *Conservative Adventurers: Italian Migrants in Italy and San Francisco* (Ann Arbor: Microfilm Corporation, 1979), 1; Junve Ferenczi, "A Historical Study of Migration Statistics," *International Labor Review* 20 (1929), 356–384.

11. Emphasis on the smooth transition of the Italian family from Europe to America and its cooperative quality may be found in Virginia Yans-McLaughlin, op. cit., xx, 23, 157–179; Judith Smith, *Family Connections: A History of Italian and Jewish Immigrant Lives in Providence, Rhode Island* (Albany: State University Press of New York, 1985), 84–88, 98–107; Gary Mormino, *Immigrants on the Hill: Italian Americans in St. Louis* (Urbana: University of Illinois Press, 1986), 110–111. This position is also adopted in the classic revisionist history, John Bodnar, *The Transplanted: A History of Immigrants in Urban America* (Bloomington: University of Indiana Press, 1985), 73–74. The big essay on the relationship between preindustrial cultures and an industrial one is Herbert Gutman, "Work Culture and Society in Industrializing America, 1815–1919," *American Historical Review* 78 (1973), 531–588.

12. 15th Census, Special Report on the Foreign Born, Tables 20, 21; Mormino, op. cit., 116–117; Yans-McLaughlin, op. cit., 174–177.

13. Yans-McLaughlin, op. cit., 91, 106–107, 221–259, especially 255–257; on intermarriage, Mormino, op. cit., 73–74, Ceri Peach, "Which Triple Melting Pot? A Reexamination of Ethnic Intermarriage in New Haven, 1900–1950," *Ethnic and Racial Studies* 3, No. 1 (1980), 6; Josef J. Barton, *Peasants and Strangers: Italians, Rumanians and Slovaks in an American City, 1890–1950* (Cambridge, MA: Harvard University Press, 1975), 166; Richard D. Alba, *Ethnic Identity: The Transformation of White America* (New Haven and London: Yale University Press, 1990), 13.

14. Yans-McLaughlin, op. cit., 74–81.

15. Ibid., 81.

16. William Foote Whyte, *Street Corner Society: The Social Structure of an Italian Slum* (Chicago: University of Chicago Press, 1981).

17. Humbert Nelli, *Italians in Chicago, 1880–1930* (New York: Oxford University Press, 1970), 207, 209, 239.

18. Yans-McLaughlin, op. cit., 181–257; Smith, op. cit., 121–123; For a demurral, see Robert Orsi, "The Fault of Memory," *Journal of Family History* 15, No. 2 (1990), 133–147.

19. Smith, op. cit., 107–108.

20. Robert A. Orsi, op. cit., 219–231. Orsi's study of devotions to the Madonna of 115th Street in East Harlem is a careful analysis of an important religious experience.

21. Ibid., 1–13.

22. Ibid.

23. Ibid., 168–218.

24. Ibid., 48–49.

25. Ibid., 74, 174–178.

26. Ibid., 165, 174.

27. Ibid., 187.

28. Ibid., 46.

29. Nathan Glazer emphasizes Jewish commercial and cultural traditions as keys to their mobility and success of Jews in America. Nathan Glazer, "The American Jew and the Attainment of Middle Class Rank," in *The Jews: Social Patterns of an American Group*, ed. Marshall Sklare (Glencoe, IL: Free Press, 1958), 142–144. See also Nathan Glazer, "Social Characteristics of American Jews, 1654–1954," *American Jewish Year Book* 56 (1955), 3–41. For a comparative analysis of the mobility of ethnic groups in America, see Stephen Thernstrom, *The Other Bostonians: Progress and Poverty in the American Metropolis* (Cambridge, MA: Harvard University Press, 1973).

30. Gerald Sorin, *The Nurturing Neighborhood: The Brownsville Boys Club and Jewish Community in Urban America, 1940–1960* (New York: New York University Press, 1990), 64–65.

31. Alexander Bloom, *Prodigal Sons: The New York Intellectuals and Their World* (New York: Oxford University Press, 1986), 38, 40.

32. Nathan Glazer, "Social Characteristics of American Jews, 1654–1954," passim; Joel Perlmann, *Ethnic Differences: Schooling and Social Structure Among the Irish, Italians, Jews and Blacks in an American City, 1880–1935* (Cambridge and New York: Cambridge University Press, 1988), 132–139.

33. Alfred Kazin, *A Walker in the City* (New York: Harcourt, Brace and World, 1951), 18.

34. Ibid., 12.

35. Judith E. Smith, op. cit., 73–75, 111–117; Sydney Stahl Weinberg, *The World of Our Mothers* (Chapel Hill: University of North Carolina Press, 1988), 94–95.

36. Sorin, op. cit., 15, 62–63.

37. Kazin, op. cit., 34, 52–54.

38. Ibid., 54, 58–59.

39. Sorin, op. cit., 72, 75.

40. Debra D. Moore, *At Home in America: Second Generation New York Jews* (New York: Columbia University Press, 1981), 45, 61–63, 123–145.

41. Theodore H. White, *In Search of History: A Personal Adventure* (New York, Harper and Row, 1978), 26.

42. Weinberg, op. cit., 175–177.

43. Artie Shaw, *The Trouble with Cinderella: An Outline with Identity* (New York: Farrar, Straus and Young 1952), 56–58; Ira Berkow, *Hank Greenberg: The Story of My Life* (New York: Times Books, 1989) 1–7. The best study of American Jews and sports is Peter Levine, *Ellis Island to Ebbets Field* (New York: Oxford University Press, 1992).

44. Sorin, op. cit., 14–16, 29–33, 63, 72–75.

45. Beth S. Wenger, *New York Jews and the Great Depression: Uncertain Promise*

(New Haven: Yale University Press, 1996), 15. Even in the mid-1930s, half of New York's Jewish families were considered to be white collar.

46. Jewish religious leaders at this time were profoundly concerned about the dangers of assimilation. Rabbi Mordecai M. Kaplan, a teacher at Yeshiva Seminary and a leading social thinker among Jews, pondered the problem and took solace from the example of Irish Catholics in New York City. For Kaplan, they established a precedent for Jews who wished to avoid assimilation. He believed Catholics avoided "succumbing to attrition" by parochial schools, bans on intermarriage and preserving their own charitable organizations. S. Mutterpearl, another Jewish social commentator in the 1920s, saw the principle of Jewish neighborhoods as "one of our greatest bulwarks in our struggle against absorption into the maelstrom of American civilization." Moore, op. cit., 5, 64–65.

47. Ibid., 68–69, 77–78; Robert P. Tabak, *The Transformation of Jewish Identity: The Philadelphia Experience, 1919–1945* (Ann Arbor: Microfilm Corporation, 1990), 193, 216–247.

48. Vivian Gornick, "There Is No More Community," *Interchange* (April 1977), 4, as quoted in Moore op. cit., 86.

49. Ibid., 76.

50. Ibid., 4.

51. Tabak, op. cit., 198–210; Moore, op. cit., 30.

52. Ibid., 135.

53. Ibid., 217–225; Wenger, 132–134.

54. Tabak, op. cit., 67.

55. Moore, op. cit., 96, 105. Even extracurricular activities in New York's high schools sorted out with each ethnic group, including the Jews, specializing in particular clubs and activities. Paula S. Fass, *Outside In: Minorities and the Transformation of American Education* (New York: Oxford University Press, 1989), 77–111.

56. Moore, op. cit., 85–86, 62.

57. Ibid.

58. Tabak, op. cit., 221–224; Wenger, 80–102.

59. See John F. Stack, Jr., *International Conflict in an American City: Boston's Irish, Italians, and Jews, 1935–1944* (Westport, CT: Greenwood Press, 1979), and Ronald H. Bayor, *Neighbors in Conflict: The Irish, Germans, Jews, and Italians of New York City, 1929–1941* (Baltimore and London: Johns Hopkins Press, 1978); Stack, op. cit., 94–100; Tabak, op. cit., 289–295.

60. Moore, op. cit., 48.

61. Ibid., 36, 38, 180, 192; Wenger, op. cit., 21–24, 61, 188–190.

62. Tabak, op. cit., 190–192.

63. Ibid., 77–78, 101–103.

64. Moore, op. cit., 13.

65. Tabak, op. cit., 78.

66. Smith, op. cit., 108, 121–122, 125.

67. Perlmann, op. cit., 164–165. U. S. Bureau of the Census, *Negro Population, 1790–1915*, 90, gives urbanization figure for Negroes as 15.3%.

68. The best study on this subject is James R. Grossman, *Land of Hope: Black Southerners and the Great Migration* (Chicago: University of Chicago Press, 1989) 13–207 especially. Also see 259–265 for conclusions of Professor Grossman's study;

Bureau of the Census, *Historical Statistics of the United States, Colonial Times to 1970* (Washington, DC, 1975), I, 95, on numbers migrating.

69. Larry A. Greene, *Harlem in the Great Depression, 1928–1936* (Ann Arbor: Microfilm Corporation, 1979), 99–105.

70. Thomas, op. cit., 150.

71. Horace R. Cayton and St. Clair Drake, *Black Metropolis: A Study of Negro Life in a Northern City* (New York: Harper and Row, 1962), I, 256–257, 229–235.

72. Grossman, op. cit., 254.

73. Harold F. Gosnell, *Negro Politicians: The Rise of Negro Politics in Chicago* (Chicago: University of Chicago Press, 1967), 287–294.

74. *Family Income in Chicago, 1935–36* (Bureau of Labor Statistics, Washington DC., 1939), Bulletin 642, Vol. I, Table 3, 8.

75. Greene, op. cit., 165; Cayton and Drake, op. cit., 436, 462.

76. Greene, op. cit., 159–160.

77. Cayton and Drake, op. cit., 433–437.

78. Ibid., 438.

79. Alan Erenhalt, *The Lost City: Discovering the Forgotten Virtues of Community in the Chicago of the 1950s* (New York: Basic Books, 1995), 166–168; Thomas, op. cit., 116–117; Cayton and Drake, op. cit., 490–494.

80. Greenberg, op. cit., 66; Greene, op. cit., 62–63.

81. Greenberg, op. cit., 145, 174.

82. Vivian Morris, Federal Writers' Project Life Histories, "The Bronx Slave Market," New York Files, December 6, 1938 (LC).

83. Frank Byrd, Federal Writers' Project, Life Histories, "Harlem Rent Parties," New York Files, August 23, 1938 (LC).

84. Theodore Vincent Carter, *Black Power and the Garvey Movement* (Berkeley, CA: Ramparts Press, 1975), 221–233.

85. These points are repeatedly made in various ways and degrees in the scholarly literature. Greenberg, op. cit., 176, 217; Kusmer, op. cit., 216, 234; Cayton and Drake, op. cit., 390–391, 430–432, 733; Thomas, op. cit., 175.

86. Cayton and Drake, op. cit., 391.

87. Gosnell, op. cit., 19.

88. Richard Wright, *Native Son* (New York: Harper and Row, 1940), Introduction, xxiv.

89. Malcolm X, *The Autobiography of Malcolm X* (New York: Ballantine Books, 1964), 23; Dempsey J. Travis, *An Autobiography of Black Chicago* (Chicago: Urban Research Institute, 1981), 80.

90. William R. Scott, *The Sons of Sheba's Race: African-Americans and the Italo-Ethiopian War, 1935–1941* (Bloomington: University of Indiana Press, 1993), and Joseph E. Harris, *African-American Reactions to War in Ethiopia, 1936–1941* (Baton Rouge: Louisiana State University Press, 1994).

91. Cayton and Drake, op. cit., 385–395.

92. Ibid., 276, 716.

93. Thomas, op. cit., 108.

94. Cayton and Drake, op. cit., 496–503, 720–722.

95. Ibid., 723, 389.

96. Ibid., 430–432.

97. Note speeches in ibid., 431.

98. Thomas, op. cit., 179; Greenberg, op. cit., 105; Cayton and Drake, op. cit., 416.

99. Note especially the dissertation by Sidney H. Moore, *Family and Social Networks in an Urban Black Storefront Church* (Ann Arbor: Microfilm Corporation, 1975), especially 286–292.

100. Cayton and Drake, op. cit., 412–413, 424.

101. John W. Kinney, *Adam Clayton Powell, Sr. and Adam Clayton Powell, Jr.: A Historical and Theological Analysis* (Ann Arbor: Microfilm Corporation, 1979), 140.

102. Roi Ottley, *New World A-Coming* (New York: Arno Press, 1968), 226.

103. Greenberg, op. cit., 57.

104. Ottley, op. cit., 223.

105. Kinney, op. cit., 175–176, 181–193.

106. Cayton and Drake, op. cit., 399–412.

107. On elections, see, for example, Chicago *Defender* July 4, 1936, August 26, 1936; on activities of the mayor of Bronzeville, December 26, 1936; on Billikens activities for Christmas, December 5, 1936; for Easter, March 4, 1939; on the Tuskegee-Wilberforce game and beauty pageants, October 17, 1936.

108. Ibid., August 1, 1936, March 4, 1939, June 3, 1939; on Davis, ibid., June 20, 1936.

109. Cayton and Drake, op. cit., 403.

110. Chicago *Defender*, June 27, 1936.

111. Ibid., March 20, 1939.

112. Ibid., June 3, 1939, 19; May 6, 1939, 19.

113. Cayton and Drake, op. cit., 296; Greenberg, op. cit., 115–139.

114. Ibid., 3–6, 221.

115. Cohen, op. cit., 333–337, 367; Thomas, op. cit., 283–284, 301–302; Greene, op. cit., 140–141.

116. Ibid., 115; Roi Ottley and William J. Weatherby, *The Negro in New York: An Informal Social History* (New York: New York Public Library, 1967), 292.

117. Roger Biles, "Big Red in Bronzeville," *Chicago History* 10, No. 2 (1981), 101–103.

118. Ibid., 103–106; Richard Keiser, "Explaining African-American Political Empowerment," *Urban Affairs Quarterly* 29 (September 1993), 89–95.

119. Nancy J. Weiss, *Farewell to the Party of Lincoln* (Princeton: Princeton University Press, 1983).

120. Sterner, op. cit., 239–241. On other federal programs disproportionately favorable to blacks in urban areas see ibid., 276, on old-age assistance, and ibid., 317, for federal housing.

121. L. Cohen, op. cit., 279.

122. Greenberg, op. cit., 317.

123. Ibid.

124. Ottley, op. cit., 293. *The Negro in New York* (1967) was published posthumously from Roi Ottley's "Harlem: The Negro in New York," a manuscript written by Ottley under the auspices of the Federal Writer's Project in the 1930s.

CHAPTER 13

1. *Historical Statistics of the United States*, I, 414.

2. Vermont Royster, *My Own, My Country's Time: A Journalist's Journey* (New York: Algonquin Books, 1983), 45; David Gerlernter, *1939: The Lost-World of the Fair*, 4.

3. John Tauranac, *The Empire State Building: The Making of a Landmark* (New York: St. Martin's Griffin Press, 1995), 238.

4. *The WPA Guide to New York* (New York: Random House, 1939), 35.

5. On New York's theater district in the late 1930s, see Brooks McNamara, "The Entertainment District at the End of the 1930s," in William R. Taylor, *Culture and Commerce at the Crossroads of the World* (New York: Russell Sage Foundation, 1995), 183–184. The three major league baseball teams in New York were, of course, the New York Yankees (American League), the New York Giants, and the Brooklyn Dodgers (National League).

6. "New York City," *Fortune* 20 (July 1939), 194.

7. Ibid., 93.

8. *The New York Times*, July 11, 1939, 21.

9. For very complimentary depictions of New York in the 1920s and 1930s, see Sherwood Anderson, "New York," *Vanity Fair* (July 1927), 33, 94; John Dos Passos describes New York as "the capitol now" in John Dos Passos, *The Big Money: USA*, vol. 3 (New York: Random House Modern Library, 1937), 65. Hollywood's opting for New York settings and scenes is pervasive. Note examples *42nd Street* (1938), *Gold Diggers of 1933* and *Gold Diggers of 1935*, *King Kong* (1933), *Swing Time* (1936), *My Man Godfrey* (1936), *The Women of New York* (1939), etc. Floyd M. Henderson, "The Image of New York in American Popular Music: 1890–1970," *New York Folk Quarterly* 30 (December 1974), 267–278, demonstrates that "during the depression years of the 1930s, New York City reached its peak as a subject of popular music." Examples of well-known lyrics on New York are "The Lullaby of Broadway," "Forty-Second Street," and "Stompin' at the Savoy."

10. Lewis A. Erenberg, *Steppin' Out: New York Nightlife and the Transformation of American Culture* (Chicago and London: University of Chicago Press, 1994), provides important background information for "nightlife" in New York in the 1930s. His article "From New York to Middletown: Repeal and Legitimization of Nightlife in the Great Depression," *American Quarterly* 38, No. 5 (1986), 760–778, is very useful as is his essay "Impresarios of Nightlife" in Taylor, *Inventing Times Square*, 158–177. On interest of New Yorkers in night spots, see New York, *Fortune* 20 (July 1939); ibid., especially "The Metropolitanites," 84–87, 214–217 and "Girls, Girls, Girls, Girls," 119–121. See also McNamara, "The Entertainment District." The show business newspaper-magazine *Variety* is invaluable for the nuances of nightlife in New York.

11. *The New York Times*, April 1, 1936, 28.

12. Ibid.

13. Erenberg, "From New York to Middletown," 768.

14. Erenberg, "Impresarios," 175.

15. Abel Green and Joe Laurie Jr., *Show Biz from Vaude to Video* (New York: Henry Holt, 1951), 440–441.

16. Erenberg, "Impresarios," 174.

17. *Variety*, January 5, 1936, 21; April 15, 1936, 19.

18. Edward Pessen, "Those Marvelous Depression Years: Reminiscences of the Big Apple," *New York History* 62 (April 1981), 192–194.

19. *Fortune* (July 1939), "Girls, Girls, Girls, Girls," 119–121, 178–180.

20. Erenberg, "From New York to Middletown," 765.

21. Green and Laurie, op cit., 437, for remarks on jitterbugging. Note discussion of jitterbugging in New York in the Chicago *Defender*, March 11, 1939, 18.

22. Roseland currently features a wall of pictures of couples who danced there and later married.

23. *Fortune* (July 1939), "New York," 119.

24. Erenberg, "From New York to Middletown," 765–775.

25. In a poll, April 19, 1937, one-third of those polled declared baseball to be their favorite sport, football was preferred by 23%, basketball by 8% and boxing by 3%. Hadley Cantril, (ed.), *Public Opinion, 1935–46* (Princeton: Princeton University Press, 1951), 810.

26. *World Almanac, 1938*, 866.

27. Noel Busch, "Joe DiMaggio," *Life* (May 1, 1939), 68.

28. Richard C. Crepeau, *Baseball: America's Diamond Mind, 1919–1941* (Orlando: University of Central Florida, 1980), 58.

29. Paul N. Angle, "Mr. Wrigley's Cubs," *Chicago History* 5, No. 2 (1976), 107.

30. Benjamin G. Rader, *Baseball: A History of America's Game* (Urbana and Chicago: University of Illinois Press, 1992), 135–137; Crepeau, op. cit., 191.

31. *The New York Times*, June 19, 1938, 8.

32. Crepeau, op. cit., 186.

33. Ibid., 171.

34. Rader, op. cit., 136.

35. Lawrence S. Ritter, *Babe: A Life in Pictures* (New York: Ticknor and Fields, 1988), 175.

36. Fine, op. cit., 312.

37. Rader, op. cit., 126–127.

38. Ray Robinson and Christopher Jennison, *Yankee Stadium: 75 Years of Drama, Glamour and Glory* (New York: Penguin Studio, 1998).

39. *The New York Times*, July 12, 1939, 23.

40. In 1931, Ruth led the American League in every department of the offensive game, hitting forty-six home runs and batting 373. Ritter, op. cit., 178; George Will, *Men at Work: The Craft of Baseball* (New York: Harper Perennial, 1990), 297.

41. Ray Robinson, *Iron Horse: Lou Gehrig in His Time* (New York: W. W. Norton, 1990), 33; Robert A. Murden, "Baseball's Most Complete Slugger," *Baseball Research Journal* 15 (1986), 35–38; Terrence Huge, "Measuring Prime Performance," ibid., 19–20.

42. *The New York Times*, July 5, 1939, 1.

43. See Ray Robinson, *Yankee Stadium*, op. cit., 55, for full text of Gehrig's remarks.

44. Frank Graham, *The New York Yankees: An Informal History* (New York: G. P. Putnam, 1948), 226–227; on DiMaggio's defensive skills, note Joe McCarthy's praise in Jack B. Moore, *Joe DiMaggio: A Bio-Bibliography* (New York: Greenwood, 1986), 31. Also see Crepeau, op. cit., 123–124.

45. Donald Honig, *Baseball When the Grass Was Real* (New York: Coward, McCann and Geoghegan 1975), 231–232.

46. Jack and Tom Cannon, eds., *Nobody Asked Me, But: The World of Jimmy Cannon* (New York: Holt Rinehart and Winston, 1978), 8–9.

47. *The New York Times*, October 1, 1936, 1.

48. Arthur Daley, *Inside Baseball: A Half Century of the National Pastime* (New York: Grosset and Dunlap, 1971), 115–124. The Chicago Cubs won the National League pennant in 1932, 1935, and 1938 and were tenacious competitors with the Giants.

49. The Dodgers were responsible for ending "King Carl" Hubbell's outstanding victory skein at twenty-four. Note commentary by distinguished sports scribe John Kieran, *The New York Times*, June 1, 1937, 31.

50. *The New York Times*, April 23, 1938, 10.

51. Pete Hamill, *A Drinking Life: A Memoir* (New York: Little, Brown and Company, 1994), 8.

52. *The New York Times*, December 12, 1938, 22; December 25, 1938, Sports Section, 4.

53. Ibid., November 28, 1937, 1; April 1, 1938, 24.

54. Ibid., November 16, 1937, 13; ibid., September 8, 1938, 28.

55. On Nagurski, see Kevin Britz, "Of Football and Frontiers: The Meaning of Bronco Nagurski," *Journal of Sports History* 20 (Summer 1993), 101–127. Quote from Grange is on 112. See also Richard Whittingham, *The Chicago Bears: An Illustrated History* (Chicago: Rand McNally, 1979).

56. On the Millrose games at Madison Square Garden featuring the famed Wannamaker Mile and championship miler Glen Cunningham (Galloping Glen) and his foes, note *The New York Times*, January 29, 1939, Sports Section, 5. On circus, note *Variety*, April 15, 1936, 62.

57. *The New York Times*, June 6, 1934, 1; April 12, 1936, II, 1; on the zoo, see ibid., April 16, 1936, 21. Other impressive botanical gardens were in Brooklyn and the Bronx. See *The WPA Guide to New York City*, 351–353.

58. *The New York Times*, August 20, 1939, IX, 5.

59. Robert A. M. Stern, Gregory Gilmartin, and Thomas Mellins, *New York: Architecture and Urbanism Between the Two World Wars* (New York: Rizzoli, 1987), 131. Note observations of *WPA Guide*, 303.

60. Stern, op. cit., 140–142.

61. Note Whitney exhibits on modern American artists with realist orientation reviewed in *The New York Times*, December 2, 1934, X, 9.

62. *The New York Times*, January 3, 1938, 10; May 4, 1939, 22; *The New York Times Magazine*, January 29, 1939, 4. In Chicago, the big three museums in the 1930s, all renowned nationally, were the Art Institute, the Field Museum of Natural History, and the Museum of Science and Industry. The Art Institute was known for its impressionist and postimpressionist paintings, its holdings in Chinese bronzes and jades and Japanese prints, and its American moderns. The Field Museum offered its visitors, for nominal fees, one of the world's best collections on dinosaurs, Egyptian mummies, fossils, Indian artifacts, plant and animal history, and numerous dioramas of early societies. The Museum of Science and Industry was one of Chicago's major attractions for tourists as well as locals. In the 1930s it was especially attractive for its replica of a coal mine in southern Illinois, and also for its many demonstrations

of scientific and technical processes. Victor J. Danilov, *Chicago's Museums* (Chicago: Chicago Review Press, 1987), 1–14.

63. *The New York Times*, December 22, 1938, 24.

64. Ibid., January 2, 1938, X, 6; September 4, 1938, X, 6; December 21, 1938, 29. On Creisler at Carnegie Hall, *Variety*, September 25, 1935, 75.

65. *The New York Times*, July 2, 1939, IX, 8; July 11, 1939, 22; August 13, 1939, IX, 5. On prices at Lewisohn, see ibid., July 14, 1939, 11. The dance scene in New York was enlivened by the presence of both Martha Graham and Agnes de Mille and was a regular feature in New York. Ibid., December 25, 1938, IX, 10.

66. *Variety*, January 22, 1936, 63.

67. *The New York Times*, July 14, 1939, 11.

68. Florence Henderson Davis, "Lay Movements in New York City during the Thirties and Forties," *U.S. Catholic Historian* 9, No. 4 (1990), 401. Note listings of churches in *WPA Guide to New York*, Index, 665–666.

69. *The New York Times*, December 25, 1938, 1, 12.

70. Ibid., January 1, 1938, 2; April 8, 1939, 12.

71. *The New York Times*, May 24, 1939, 1.

72. Deborah Dash Moore, *At Home in America: Second Generation New York Jews* (New York: Columbia University Press, 1981), 21, 125.

73. Greenberg, op. cit., 144–145.

74. Arthur Rothstein, December, 1937, 2680-M3, 2672-MS; Dorothea Lange, November, 1936, 11036-M1 (Library of Congress).

75. *The New York Times*, September 19, 1937, II, 8.

76. Ibid., December 8, 1937, 11.

77. Ibid., January 14, 1938, 25.

78. Clifton Hood, *722 Miles: The Building of the Subways and How They Transformed New York* (New York: Simon and Schuster, 1993), 215–219.

79. *The New York Times*, July 4, 1938, 2.

80. David Nasaw, *Going Out: The Rise and Fall of Public Amusements* (New York: Basic Books 1995), 242.

81. *The New York Times*, July 4, 1938, 2.

82. Reference to the roses on tables is in Albert Halper, *Good-bye Union Square: A Writer's Memoir of the Thirties* (Chicago: Quadrangle, 1970), 3.

83. Nasaw, op. cit., 242.

84. Pessen, op. cit., 199.

85. Ibid., 191.

86. Ibid.

87. Ibid., 193–194.

88. Ibid.

89. Ibid., 196.

90. Ibid., 198.

91. Ibid., 199.

92. Ibid.

93. Greenberg, op. cit., 195.

94. Peter Galassi and Susan Kismaric, eds., *Pictures of the Times: A Century of Photography from the New York Times* (New York: Museum of Modern Art, 1996), 83.

95. James Gavin, *Intimate Nights: The Golden Age of New York Cabarets* (New

York: Grove Weidenfeld, 1991), 33–35. Barney Josephson was owner of Café Society Downtown.

CHAPTER 14

1. Robert S. and Helen Merrell Lynd, *Middletown in Transition: A Study in Cultural Conflicts* (New York: Harcourt Brace, 1937), 15, 454–455.
2. Augusta (Kansas) *Daily Gazette*, February 15, 1934.

Selected Bibliography

The most important sources for this study are in the Roosevelt Library, Hyde Park, New York, for the Roosevelt Family Papers, the Harry Hopkins Papers and the President's Personal File and the Library of Congress for the Life Histories, Ethnic and Folklore materials of the Federal Writer's Project and thousands of photographs in the Library's Prints and Photographs Division. Access to copious materials of the Federal Writer's Project has been facilitated by the ready availability of life histories for the South via microfilm from the University of North Carolina Library, Chapel Hill. The National Archives in Washington, DC, along with its state repositories provided copies of congressional hearings. The Michigan State University Voice Archives presented valuable holdings in radio scripts. Newspapers have been indispensable, especially *The New York Times* and the Chicago *Defender*, along with a host of small-town and small-city newspapers for insights on rural America in the 1930s. These included the Elba (AL) *Clipper*, Grand Rapids (MN) *Herald Review*, Augusta (KS) *Daily Gazette*, Bozeman (MT) *Daily Chronicle*, DeKalb (IL) *Chronicle*, Chillicothe (MO) *Constitution-Tribune*, Pendleton *East Oregonian*, Brattleboro (VT) *Daily Reformer*, Beloit (KS) *Daily Call*, Taylor County (FL) *News* and Bismarck, (ND) *Tribune*. All are available on microfilm.

A large amount of source material came through published works, all referred to in the abundant end notes of this study. These included, of course, numerous books by members of President Roosevelt's family and the president's associates in the White House. Very valuable insights came from Eleanor Roosevelt and sons Eliot and James Roosevelt. Also useful were comments and observations of seasoned reporters in newspapers and magazines. Post office murals of the 1930s, pictured in studies by Karal Marling and Sue Bridwell Beckham, and accompanied by their interpretations have enriched perspectives for the theories of this book. Polls and statistics, amply available in the 1930s, also helped round out interpretations.

For rural America a series of thoughtful reports by observers from the U.S. Department of Agriculture, all living in the small communities, were helpful in developing essential themes. Similarly, sociologists and anthropologists, often residing for extended periods in cotton towns and small cities embedded in rural areas, provide important information on race relations and life in the African-American community. Autobiographical literature has served the same purpose exceptionally well. The NAACP Papers in the Library of Congress afford unusual insight into the question of lynching and the determination of its leaders, especially Walter White, to eradicate it.

A firsthand understanding of the significance of technology and engineering in the 1930s is graphically conveyed by its artifacts, still impressively standing—dams, bridges, and buildings, all of which convey the sense of a people confident that they could improve their world even in the trying times of the Depression. Surely, no less can be said for the remarkable designers of the 1930s, Henry Dreyfus, Norman Bel Geddes, Raymond Loewy, and Walter Teague, who were determined to beautify many facets of American life through streamlining, from its airplanes, cars, and trains to its toasters, alarm clocks, phones, and pencil sharpeners. Unlike the artifacts, the bumptious assertions of contemporary advertising and the special claims of the World's Fair in New York, 1939–1940, now remain visible only through printed words and photographs, but many of them also tell the story firsthand.

The following select bibliography represents a list of books especially helpful to the author.

Agee, James, and Walker Evans. *Let Us Now Praise Famous Men.* Boston: Houghton Mifflin, 1942.

Angelou, Maya. *I Know Why the Caged Bird Sings.* New York: Random House, 1970.

Beckham, Sue Bridwell. *Depression Post Office Murals and Southern Culture.* Baton Rouge and London: Louisiana State University Press, 1989.

Bergman, Andrew. *We're in the Money: Depression America and Its Films.* New York: New York University Press, 1971.

Bernstein, Irving. *Turbulent Years: A History of the American Worker, 1933–1941.* Boston: Houghton Mifflin, 1969.

Bilstein, Roger E. *Flight in America.* Baltimore: Johns Hopkins Press, 1988.

Burns, James MacGregor. *Roosevelt: The Lion and the Fox.* New York: Harcourt Brace & World, 1956.

Bush, Donald. *The Streamlined Decade.* New York: George Braziller, 1975.

Cayton, Horace R., and Drake St. Clair. *Black Metropolis: A Study of Negro Life in a Northern City*, 2 vols. New York: Harper and Row, 1962.

Cohen, Lizabeth. *Making a New Deal: Industrial Workers in Chicago, 1919–1939.* Cambridge, MA: Cambridge University Press, 1990.

Daniel, Pete. *Breaking the Land: The Transformation of Cotton, Tobacco and Rice Cultures Since 1880.* Urbana and Chicago: University of Illinois Press, 1985.

Davis, Allison, Burleigh B. Gardner, and Mary Gardner. *Deep South: A Social-Anthropological Study of Caste and Class.* Chicago: University of Chicago Press, 1941.

Dollard, John. *Caste and Class in a Southern Town.* Garden City, NY: Doubleday Anchor, 1957.

Dubofsky, Melvyn. *The State and Labor in Modern America.* Chapel Hill: University of North Carolina Press, 1994.

Erenberg, Lewis A. *Steppin' Out: New York Night Life and the Transformation of American Culture.* Chicago and London: University of Chicago Press, 1994.

Fleischauer, Carl, and Beverly Bannon. *Documenting America.* Berkeley: University of California Press, 1988.

Freidel, Frank. *Franklin D. Roosevelt: A Rendezvous with Destiny.* Boston: Little Brown, 1990.

Gallagher, Hugh Gregory. *FDR's Splendid Deception.* New York: Dodd and Mead, 1985.

Gates, Henry Louis. *Colored People.* New York: Alfred Knopf, 1994.

Greenberg, Cheryl Lynn. *Or Does It Explode? Black Harlem in the Great Depression.* New York: Oxford University Press, 1991.

Gregory, James N. *American Exodus: The Dust Bowl Migration and Okie Culture in California.* New York and London: Oxford University Press, 1989.

Grossman, James R. *Land of Hope: Black Southerners and the Great Migration.* Chicago: University of Chicago Press, 1989.

Gunther, John. *Roosevelt in Retrospect: A Profile in History.* New York: Harper and Row, 1947.

Hagood, Margaret Jarman. *Mothers of the South: Portraiture of the White Southern Farm Woman.* Chapel Hill: University of North Carolina Press, 1939.

Harmon, Jim. *The Great Radio Heros.* New York: Doubleday, 1967.

Harrison, Helen A., ed. *Dawn of a New Day: The New York World's Fair, 1939–1940.* New York: New York University Press, 1980.

Jellison, Katherine. *Entitled to Power: Farm Women and Technology, 1919–1963.* Chapel Hill: University of North Carolina Press, 1993.

Johnson, Charles S. *Growing Up in the Black Belt: Negro Youth in the Rural South.* Washington, DC: American Council on Education, 1941.

———. *Patterns of Negro Segregation.* New York: Harper and Brothers, 1943.

———. *Shadows of the Plantation.* Chicago: University of Chicago Press, 1934.

Kirby, Jack Temple. *Rural Worlds Lost: The American South, 1920–1960.* Baton Rouge: Louisiana State University Press, 1987.

Leff, Mark H. *The Limits of Symbolic Reform: The New Deal and Taxation, 1933–1939.* New York: Cambridge University Press, 1984.

Leuchtenburg, William E. *Franklin D. Roosevelt and the New Deal.* New York: Harper and Row, 1963.

Lippman, Walter. *Interpretations, 1933–1935.* New York: Macmillan, 1936.

Lowitt, Richard, and Maurine Beasley. *One Third of a Nation: Lorena Hickock Reports on the Great Depression.* Urbana: University of Illinois Press, 1981.

Lynd, Robert, and Helen M. Lynd. *Middletown in Transition: A Study in Cultural Conflicts.* New York: Harcourt Brace and Co., 1937.

MacDonald, J. Fred. *Don't Touch That Dial: Radio Programming in American Life, 1920–1960.* Chicago: Nelson Hall, 1979.

Marchand, Roland. *Advertising and the American Dream.* Berkeley: University of California Press, 1985.

Marling, Karal Ann. *Wall-to-Wall America: A Cultural History of Post Offices in the Great Depression.* Minneapolis: University of Minnesota Press, 1982.

McGovern, James R. *Anatomy of a Lynching: The Killing of Claude Neal.* Baton Rouge: Louisiana State University Press, 1982.

Meikle, Jeffrey L. *Twentieth Century Limited*. Philadelphia: Temple University Press, 1979.

Moe, Edward, and Carl C. Taylor. *Culture of a Contemporary Rural Community in Iowa*. Washington, DC: Department of Agriculture, 1942.

Moore, Debra D. *At Home in America: Second Generation New York Jews*. New York: Columbia University Press, 1981.

Neth, Mary. *Preserving the Farm Family: Women, Community and the Foundation of Agribusiness in the Mid-West*. Baltimore and London: Johns Hopkins Press, 1995.

Nye, David E. *American Technological Sublime*. Cambridge: Massachusetts Institute of Technology, 1994.

―――. *Electrifying America: Social Meanings of a New Technology, 1880–1940*. Cambridge: Massachusetts Institute of Technology, 1990.

Orsi, Robert A. *The Madonna of 115th Street: Faith and Community in Italian Harlem*. New Haven and London: Yale University Press, 1995.

Ottley, Roi. *The Negro in New York: An Informal Social History*. New York: New York Public Library, 1967.

Patterson, James T. *America's Struggle Against Poverty*. Cambridge: Harvard University Press, 1981.

―――. *Congressional Conservatism and the New Deal*. Lexington: University of Kentucky Press, 1967.

―――. *The New Deal and the States: Federalism in Transition*. Princeton, NJ: Princeton University Press, 1969.

Perkins, Francis. *The Roosevelt I Knew*. New York: Harper and Row, 1946.

Powdermaker, Hortense. *After Freedom: A Cultural Study of the Deep South*. New York: Russell and Russell, 1968.

Raper, Arthur F. *Preface to Peasantry*. Chapel Hill: University of North Carolina Press, 1936.

Romasco, Albert U. *The Politics of Recovery: Roosevelt's New Deal*. New York: Oxford University Press, 1983.

Roosevelt, Eleanor. *This I Remember*. New York: Harper, 1949.

Schlesinger, Arthur M., Jr. *The Age of Roosevelt: The Coming of the New Deal*. Boston: Houghton Mifflin Co., 1958.

Sikos, Ed. *Screwball: Hollywood's Madcap Romantic Comedies*. New York: Crown Publishers, 1989.

Sklar, Robert. *Movie Made America: A Cultural History of American Movies*. New York: Vintage, 1994.

Smith, Judith. *Family Connections: A History of Italian and Jewish Immigrant Lives in Providence, Rhode Island*. Albany: State University Press of New York, 1985.

Solberg, Carol. *Conquest of the Skies: A History of Commercial Aviation in America*. Boston: Little Brown and Co., 1979.

Sorin, Gerald. *The Nurturing Neighborhood: The Brownsville Boys Club and Jewish Community in America, 1940–1960*. New York: New York University Press.

Stern, Robert A. M., Gregory Gilmartin, and Thomas Mellins. *New York: Architecture and Urbanism Between the Two World Wars*. New York: Rizzoli, 1987.

Sterner, Richard. *The Negro's Share: A Study of Income, Consumption, Housing and Public Assistance*. New York: Harper and Bros., 1943.

Stock, Catherine McNichol. *Main Street in Crisis: The Great Depression and the Middle Class on the Northern Plains.* Chapel Hill: University of North Carolina Press, 1992.

Stott, William. *Documentary Expression and Thirties America.* Chicago: University of Chicago Press, 1986.

Taylor, Carl C. *Rural Life in the United States.* Westport, CT: Greenwood Press, 1972.

Ward, Geoffrey. *Before the Trumpet.* New York: Harper & Row, 1985.

Wenger, Beth S. *New York Jews and the Depression: Uncertain Promise.* New Haven: Yale University Press, 1996.

Wilner, Ann Ruth. *The Spellbinders: Charismatic Political Leadership.* New Haven: Yale University Press, 1984.

Wilson, Richard Guyand, Dianne H. Pilgrim, Dickran Rashjian. *Machine Age in America, 1918–1941.* New York: Harry N. Abrams, 1986.

Wright, Richard. *Native Son.* New York: Harper and Row, 1940.

Yans-McLaughlin, Virginia. *Family and Community: Italian Immigrants in Buffalo, 1880–1930.* Ithaca: Cornell University Press, 1971.

Zieger, Robert H. *American Workers, American Unions, 1920–1985.* Baltimore: Johns Hopkins Press, 1986.

———. *The CIO, 1933–1955.* Chapel Hill: University of North Carolina Press, 1995.

Index

About the Author

JAMES R. McGOVERN is Emeritus Professor of History at the University of West Florida. His study *Anatomy of a Lynching: The Killing of Claude Neal* (1982) won the Patrick Rembert Award for Outstanding Book on Florida history.

ISBN 0-275-96786-7